Get the inside scoop with Mobil's new City Guide series.

- Written for busy travelers who are always on the hunt for the best places to visit during a short jaunt to destination cities

- Anonymous inspectors rate the best hotels, restaurants and spas while top-notch local writers provide the most up-to-date coverage of a city

- Available January 2009 where books are sold

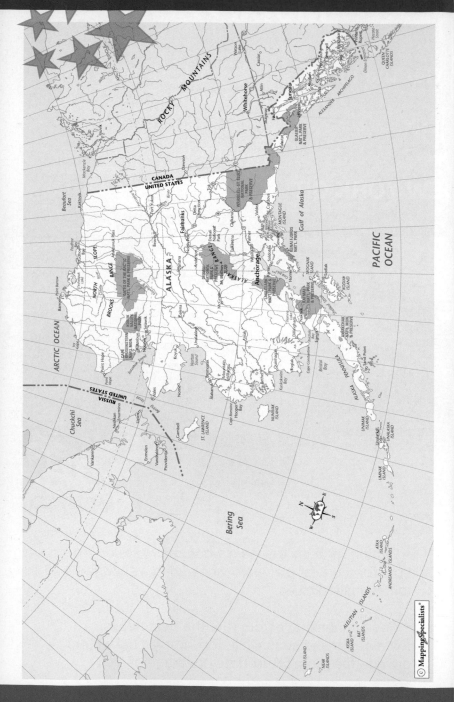

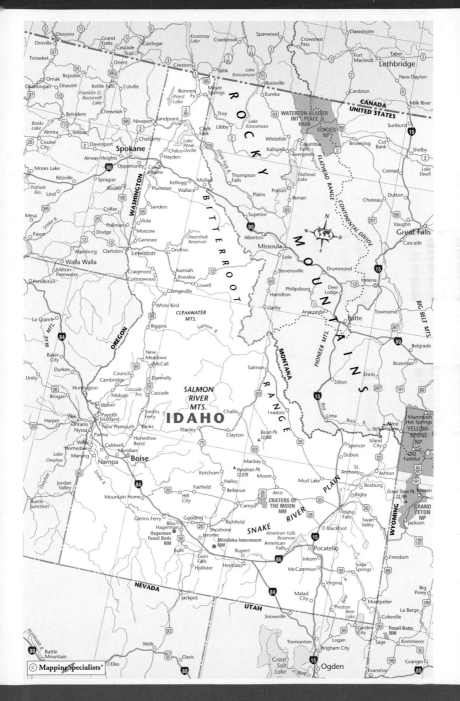

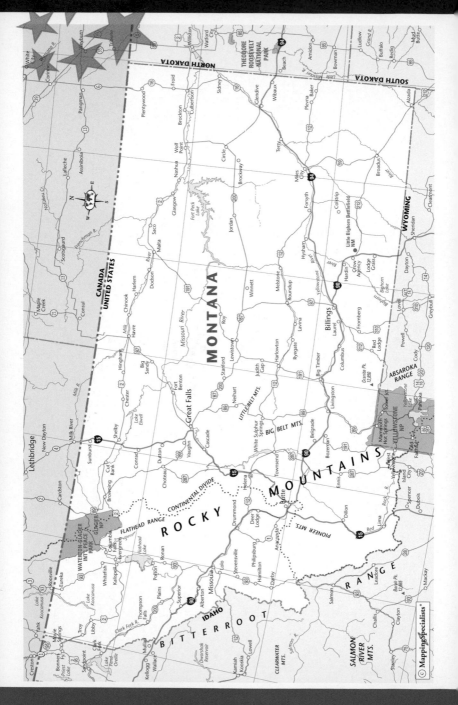

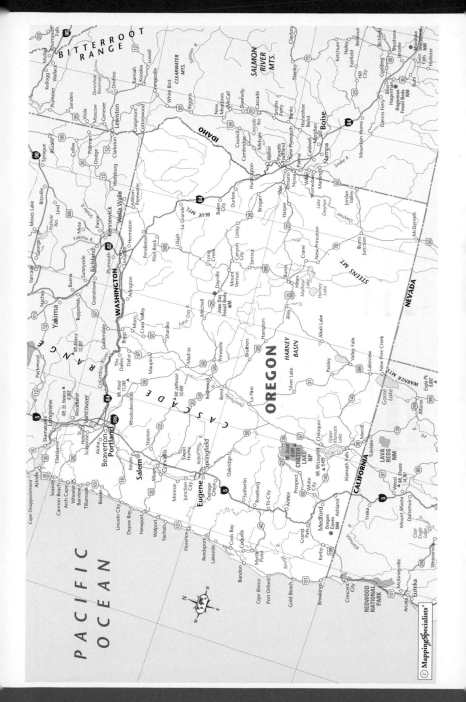

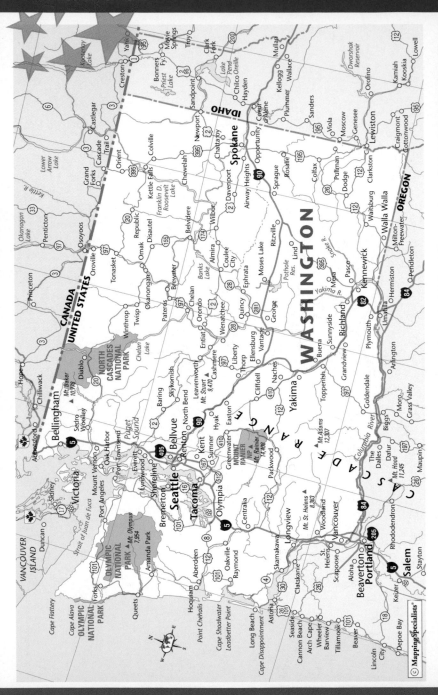

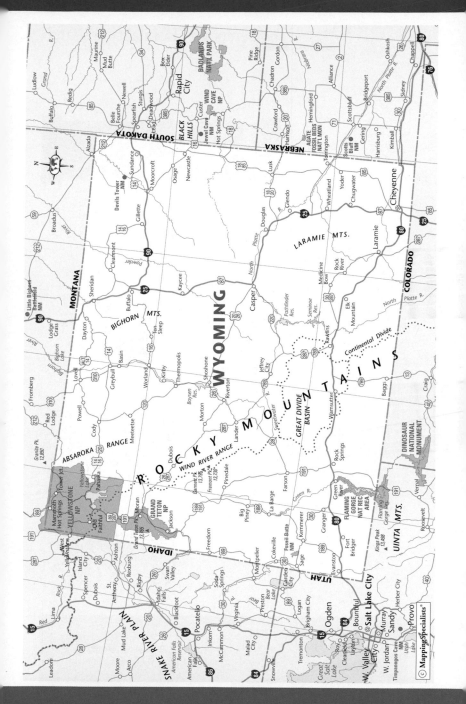

The Center for Hospitality Research
Hospitality Leadership Through Learning

The Cornell School of Hotel Administration's
world-class faculty explores new ways
to refine the practice of hospitality
management.

Our research drives better results.
Better strategy.
Better management.
Better operations.

See our work at:
www.chr.cornell.edu

537 Statler Hall • hosp_research@cornell.edu • 607.255.9780

Cornell University
School of Hotel Administration

NORTHWEST

ACKNOWLEDGMENTS

We gratefully acknowledge the help of our representatives for their efficient and perceptive inspections of the lodging and dining establishments listed, the establishments' proprietors for their cooperation in showing their facilities and providing information about them, and the many users of previous editions who have taken the time to share their experiences. Mobil Travel Guide is also grateful to all the talented writers who contributed entries to this book.

Front and back cover images: ©iStockPhoto.com

All maps: created by Mapping Specialists

ISBN: 9-780841-60865-8   Manufactured in Canada

10 9 8 7 6 5 4 3 2 1

TABLE OF CONTENTS

3

NORTHWEST

★
★★
★★★
★★

WRITTEN IN THE STARS

Because time is precious and the travel industry is ever-changing, having accurate, reliable travel information at your fingertips has never been more important. With this in mind, Mobil Travel Guide has provided invaluable insight to travelers through its Star Rating system for more than 50 years.

The Mobil Corporation (known as Exxon Mobil Corporation since a 1999 merger) began producing the Mobil Travel Guide books in 1958 following the introduction of the U.S.-interstate highway system in 1956. The first edition covered only five Southwestern states. Since then, our books have become the premier travel guides in North America, covering all 50 states and Canada, and beginning in 2008, international destinations such as Hong Kong and Beijing.

Today, the concept of a "five-star" experience is one that permeates the collective conciousness, but few people realize it's one that originated with Mobil. We created our star rating system to give travelers an easy-to-recognize quality scale for choosing where to stay, dine and spa. Based on an objective process, we make recommendations to our readers that we believe will enhance the quality and value of their travel experiences. Our trusted Mobil One- to Five-Star rating system is the oldest and most respected lodging and restaurant inspection and rating program in North America. Most hoteliers, restaurateurs and industry observers favorably regard the rigor of our inspection program and understand the prestige and benefits that come with receiving a Mobil Star rating.

The Mobil Travel Guide process of rating each establishment includes unannounced inspections, incognito evaluations and a review of unsolicted comments from the general public. We inspect more than 500 attributes at each property we visit, from cleanliness to the condition of the rooms and public spaces, to employee attitude and courtesy. It's a system that rewards those properties that strive for and achieve excellence each year. And the very best properties raise the bar for those that wish to compete with them.

Only facilities that meet Mobil Travel Guide's standards earn the privilege of being listed in the guide. Properties are continuously updated, and deteriorating, poorly managed establishments are removed. We wouldn't recommend that you visit a hotel, restaurant or spa that we wouldn't want to visit ourselves.

★★★★★The Mobil Five-Star Award indicates that a property is one of the very best in the country and consistently provides gracious and courteous service, superlative quality in its facility and a unique ambience. The lodgings and restaurants at the Mobil Five-Star level consistently continue their commitment to excellence, doing so with grace and perseverance.

★★★★The Mobil Four-Star Award honors properties for outstanding achievement in overall facility and for providing very strong service levels in all areas. These award winners provide a distinctive experience for the ever-demanding and sophisticated consumer.

★★★The Mobil Three-Star Award recognizes an excellent property that provides full services and amenities. This category ranges from exceptional hotels with limited services to elegant restaurants with a less formal atmosphere.

★★The Mobil Two-Star property is a clean and comfortable establishment that has expanded amenities or a distinctive environment. These properties are an excellent place to stay or dine.

★The Mobil One-Star property is limited in its amenities and services but provides a value experience while meeting travelers' expectations. The properties should be clean, comfortable and convenient.

We do not charge establishments for inclusion in our guides. We have no relationship with any of the businesses and attractions we list and act only as a consumer advocate. We do the investigative legwork so that you won't have to.

Restaurants and hotels—particularly small chains and stand-alone establishments—change management or even go out of business with surprising quickness. Although we make every effort to continuously update information, we recommend that you call ahead to make sure the place you've selected is still open.

STAR RATINGS

MOBIL RATED HOTELS

Whether you're looking for the ultimate in luxury or the best bang for your travel buck, we have a hotel recommendation for you. To help you pinpoint properties that meet your needs, Mobil Travel Guide classifies each lodging by type according to the following characteristics.

★★★★★The Mobil Five-Star hotel provides consistently superlative service in an exceptionally distinctive luxury environment. Attention to detail is evident throughout the hotel, resort or inn, from bed linens to staff uniforms.

★★★★The Mobil Four-Star hotel provides a luxury experience with expanded amenities in a distinctive environment. Services may include automatic turndown service, 24-hour room service and valet parking.

★★★The Mobil Three-Star hotel is well appointed, with a full-service restaurant and expanded amenities, such as a fitness center, golf course, tennis courts, 24-hour room service and optional turndown service.

★★The Mobil Two-Star hotel is considered a clean, comfortable and reliable establishment that has expanded amenities, such as a full-service restaurant.

★The Mobil One-Star lodging is a limited-service hotel, motel or inn that is considered a clean, comfortable and reliable establishment.

For every property, we also provide pricing information. The pricing categories break down as follows:

$ = Up to $150

$$ = $151-$250

$$$ = $251-$350

$$$$ = $351 and up

All prices quoted are accurate at the time of publication; however, prices cannot be guaranteed.

MOBIL RATED RESTAURANTS

Every restaurant in this book has been visited by Mobil Travel Guide's team of experts and comes highly recommended as an outstanding dining experience.

★★★★★The Mobil Five-Star restaurant offers one of few flawless dining experiences in the country. These establishments consistently provide their guests with exceptional food, superlative service, elegant décor and exquisite presentations of each detail surrounding a meal.

★★★★The Mobil Four-Star restaurant provides professional service, distinctive presentations and wonderful food.

★★★The Mobil Three-Star restaurant has good food, warm and skillful service and enjoyable décor.

★★The Mobil Two-Star restaurant serves fresh food in a clean setting with efficient service. Value is considered in this category, as is family friendliness.

★The Mobil One-Star restaurant provides a distinctive experience through culinary specialty, local flair or individual atmosphere.

Because menu prices can fluctuate, we list a pricing category rather than specific prices. The pricing categories are defined as follows, per diner, and assume that you order an appetizer or dessert, an entrée and one drink:

$ = $15 and under

$$ = $16-$35

$$$ = $36-$85

$$$$ = $86 and up

MOBIL RATED SPAS

Mobil Travel Guide's spa ratings are based on objective evaluations of hundreds of attributes. About half of these criteria assess basic expectations, such as staff courtesy, the technical proficiency and skill of the employees and whether the facility is clean and maintained properly. Several standards address issues that impact a guest's physical comfort and convenience, as well as the staff's ability to impart a sense of personalized service. Additional criteria measure the spa's ability to create a completely calming ambience.

★★★★★The Mobil Five-Star spa provides consistently superlative service in an exceptionally distinctive luxury environment with extensive amenities. The staff at a Mobil Five-Star spa provides extraordinary service beyond the traditional spa experience, allowing guests to achieve the highest level of relaxation and pampering. These spas offer an extensive array of treatments, often incorporating international themes and products. Attention to detail is evident throughout the spa, from arrival to departure.

★★★★The Mobil Four-Star spa provides a luxurious experience with expanded amenities in an elegant and serene environment. Throughout the spa facility, guests experience personalized service. Amenities might include, but are not limited to, single-sex relaxation rooms where guests wait for their treatments, plunge pools and whirlpools in both men's and women's locker rooms, and an array of treatments, including a selection of massages, body therapies, facials and a variety of salon services.

★★★The Mobil Three-Star spa is physically well appointed and has a full complement of staff.

INTRODUCTION

If you've been a reader of Mobil Travel Guides, you may have noticed a new look and style in our guidebooks. Since 1958, Mobil Travel Guide has assisted travelers in making smart decisions about where to stay and dine. Fifty-one years later, our mission has not changed: We are committed to our rigorous inspections of hotels, restaurants and, now, spas, to help you cut through all the clutter, and make easy and informed decisions on where you should spend your time and budget. Our team of anonymous inspectors are constantly on the road, sleeping in hotels, eating in restaurants and making spa appointments, evaluating hundreds of standards to determine a property's star rating.

As you read these pages, we hope you get a flavor of the places included in the guides and that you will feel even more inspired to visit and take it all in. We hope you'll experience what it's like to stay in a guest room in the hotels we've rated, taste the food in a restaurant or feel the excitement at an outdoor music venue. We understand the importance of finding the best value when you travel, and making the most of your time. That's why for more than 50 years, Mobil Travel Guide has been the most trusted name in travel.

If any aspect of your accommodation, dining, spa or sightseeing experience motivates you to comment, please contact us at Mobil Travel Guide, 200 W. Madison St., Suite 3950, Chicago, IL 60606, or send an email to info@mobiltravelguide.com Happy travels.

★
★
★
★

ALASKA

THE MIND-BLOWING BEAUTY OF MILLION-YEAR-OLD GLACIERS, A TRULY UNSPOILED landscape and plentiful wildlife make Alaska a paradise for nature lovers. Its national forests and parks are America's largest—the state has twice as many caribou as people—and the abundant coastal waters provide some of the best salmon and halibut fishing in the world. Veteran rock and ice climbers routinely assault Mount McKinley, the highest peak in North America at 20,320 feet, and the truly intrepid compete in the annual Iditarod sled dog race.

The great Yukon River cuts the Alaskan interior almost in half, carving tremendous valleys along the way as it makes its 1,265-mile journey from the state's border to the Bering Sea. The mazelike convergence of land and water in the famed Inside Passage of the panhandle was sculpted into its present form by thousands of years of glacial ice scoring its way toward the sea and eventually melting.

Meanwhile, in contrast, there is the relative bustle of Anchorage. Surprisingly cosmopolitan and comfortable, it's home to about half of the state's population and is teeming with first-class restaurants, nightclubs and entertainment.

Information: Juneau Convention & Visitors Bureau, 1 Sealaska Plaza, Juneau, 907-586-1737; www.travelalaska.com

★ **FUN FACTS**

Alaska is the northern, western and easternmost point in the U.S. (the Aleutians stretch into the Eastern Hemisphere).

Alaska is the only state to have coastlines on three different seas: the Pacific Ocean, Bering Sea and Arctic Ocean.

The state has one registered pilot for every 58 people, six times as many pilots per capita than the rest of the country.

ANCHOR POINT

Located in the southwestern corner of the Kenai Peninsula, Anchor Point's main claim to fame is its placement as the westernmost point on the U.S. highway system. But its spectacular setting is what really makes it so appealing: The town is nestled in the middle of an untamed landscape of rugged, windswept beaches, densely wooded hills and icy rivers and streams. It's a popular destination for fishermen, who have the option of freshwater fishing in the Anchor River for salmon and steelhead trout or saltwater fishing for halibut and salmon on one of the many charter boats based at the local harbor. The town also has a number of public campgrounds that provide primitive camping facilities along with easy access to the Anchor River and nearby beaches.

Information: Anchor Point Chamber of Commerce, 34175 Sterling Highway, Anchor Point, 907-235-2600; www.anchorpointchamber.org

WHAT TO SEE AND DO
ANCHOR RIVER STATE RECREATION AREA
Anchor Point, 907-262-5581; www.dnr.state.ak.us

This area got its name in the 1770s when Captain James Cook lost an anchor at the mouth of the river. Today, people venture here to catch glimpses of moose, beaver, mink and bald eagles, along with the beluga whales, harbor seals and sea otters that hang around near the shore of Cook Inlet. You also can see three volcanoes across the inlet: Mount Augustine to the south, and Mount Iliamna and Mount Redoubt to the north.

ANCHOR POINT
907-235-1236; www.clivesalaskafishing.com

Known for excellent silver and king salmon runs, the Anchor River is also a popular spot to catch steelhead and rainbow trout. Anglers heading out to Cook Inlet for halibut, salmon and rockfish can launch their own boats for a fee at the end of Anchor River Road or can join one of the fishing charters that depart on most days during the summer. Several companies offer charters to anglers, including Alaska Sport Fishing Tours (907-235-2556) and Tall Tales Charters (907-235-6271).

HOTEL
★★ANCHOR RIVER INN
34358 Old Sterling Highway, Anchor Point, 907-235-8531, 800-435-8531; www.anchorriverinn.com

20 rooms. Restaurant. Fitness center. $

ANCHORAGE

With a population of about 260,000, Anchorage is the largest city in Alaska and one of the most ethnically and culturally diverse. It also has the richest history: In 1915, three years after Alaska became an official U.S. territory, the site of present-day Anchorage was selected as a construction base for a rail line built from Seward into the Interior. With the railroad came people attracted by the lure of jobs, adventure and uncharted wilderness. The city grew steadily the first few decades after its founding, and by 1950 had surpassed Juneau as the largest city in the Territory of Alaska.

Although it is farther north than St. Petersburg, Russia, Anchorage's weather is surprisingly mild—the result of Japanese currents pushing warm air up into the Gulf of Alaska. Winter daytime highs hover around 20 degrees with an average of 69 inches of snow falling each year. Summer daytime highs average 65 degrees with more than 19 hours of daylight on the summer solstice. Geographically, the city is bounded by the Chugach Range and the waters of Knik Arm, Turnagain Arm and Cook Inlet. Downtown Anchorage sits on a bluff overlooking the Inlet, and on a clear day, you can see the Alaska Range and Mount McKinley on the horizon—a distance of nearly 150 miles.

In summer, the city comes alive with numerous festivals and exhibits, millions of flowers and seemingly endless outdoor activities, as locals make the most of long daylight hours and mild temperatures. The municipal area is crisscrossed by a network of 120 miles of paved trails, and another 180 miles of wilderness trails popular with mountain bikers, hikers and runners. Within the city limits, Delaney Park, Earthquake Park, Resolution Park and Kincaid Park provide scenic venues for outdoor entertainment and relaxation. One of the most popular attractions downtown during

ALASKA

★
★★
★
★

the summer is the huge outdoor market held every Saturday in the Third Avenue parking lot between C and E streets. The Summer Solstice Festival also attracts a lot of tourists and locals with a blend of arts and crafts exhibits, Alaskan food stalls and local dancers, singers, musicians and poets to entertain the crowds.

Another of Anchorage's main roles is that of a convenient staging area and embarkation point for wilderness exploration and adventure. As Alaska's main rail, air and road hub, the city serves as the gateway to the Kenai Peninsula to the south and Denali National Park and Fairbanks to the north, and provides access to hundreds of remote towns and villages via Anchorage International Airport, Merrill Field and the floatplane base at Lake Hood.

Information: Convention & Visitors Bureau, 524 W. Fourth Ave., 907-276-4118; www.anchorage.net

WHAT TO SEE AND DO
ALASKA AVIATION HERITAGE MUSEUM
4721 Aircraft Drive, Anchorage, 907-248-5325; www.alaskaairmuseum.org
Located on the shores of Lake Hood near Ted Stevens Anchorage International Airport, this private museum aims to preserve and document Alaska's rich aviation history. Interpretive exhibits, vintage photographs, scale models and an extensive collection of aviation memorabilia offer insight into the evolution of flying in Alaska. An onsite hangar houses an extensive collection of preserved and restored aircraft. May 15-September 15, daily 9 a.m.-5 p.m.; September 15-May 14, Wednesday-Sunday 9 a.m.-5 p.m.; closed Monday and Tuesday.

ALASKA CENTER FOR THE PERFORMING ARTS
621 W. Sixth Ave., Anchorage, 907-263-2900, 877-278-7849; www.alaskapac.org
Opened in 1988, the Alaska Center for the Performing Arts features four state-of-the-art performance spaces and is home to eight resident companies, including the Alaska Dance Theatre, the Anchorage Symphony Orchestra and the Anchorage Opera.

ALASKA NATIVE HERITAGE CENTER
8800 Heritage Center Drive, Anchorage, 907-330-8000, 800-315-6608; www.alaskanative.net
Spotlighting the native cultures of Alaska, the Center offers interpretive displays; outdoor demonstrations of traditional hunting, fishing and construction techniques; traditional villages exhibits and live performances of native songs and dances in the 95-seat Welcome House theater. May-September, daily 9 a.m.-5 p.m.

ALASKA ZOO
4731 O'Malley Road, Anchorage, 907-346-2133; www.alaskazoo.org
With annual attendance at more than 200,000 visitors, the Alaska Zoo is one of the most frequently visited places in the state. It exhibits 38 species of arctic and subarctic wildlife on 25 acres of land. Daily 10 a.m.-5 p.m.

ANCHORAGE COASTAL WILDLIFE REFUGE AT POTTER MARSH
Seward Highway, 907-267-2556; www.state.ak.us
Known locally as Potters Marsh, this 540-acre refuge at the southern edge of Anchorage is a popular spot for bird-watching. At various times of the year, the marshlands

are home to arctic terns, Canada geese, trumpeter swans, Pacific loons and a variety of other shorebirds. A 1,500-foot wooden boardwalk built out over the marsh enables visitors to venture far from the parking lot without damaging the wetlands or disturbing the wildlife in the area.

ANCHORAGE FIFTH AVENUE MALL
320 W. Fifth Ave., Anchorage, 907-258-5535; www.simon.com
One of the largest malls in Alaska, it contains 110 shops on the first three levels and a food court on the fourth. Expect to find national chain stores as well as uniquely Alaskan shops. Monday-Friday 10 a.m.-9 p.m., Saturday 10 a.m.-8 p.m., Sunday 11 a.m.-6 p.m.

ANCHORAGE MUSEUM AT RASMUSON CENTER
121 W. Seventh Ave., Anchorage, 907-343-6173; www.anchoragemuseum.org
Divided into two distinct parts, the Museum's ground floor features six art galleries displaying art of the North, including works by celebrated Alaskan artist Sydney Laurence. The upper floor focuses on Alaskan history and is packed with artifacts, displays and exhibits that depict the lives and cultures of the groups that have shaped Alaska. September 22-May 10, Tuesday-Saturday 10 a.m.-6 p.m., Sunday noon-6 p.m., closed Monday; May 11-September 21, daily 9 a.m.-6 p.m.

CHUGACH NATIONAL FOREST
3301 C St., Anchorage, 907-743-9500; www.fs.fed.us
Roughly the same size as Massachusetts and Rhode Island combined, the Chugach (pronounced CHEW-gatch) is the northernmost national forest, only 500 miles south of the Arctic Circle. One-third of the Chugach is composed of rocks and moving ice. The remainder is a diverse and majestic tapestry of land, water, plants and animals.

CYRANO'S OFF CENTER PLAYHOUSE
413 D St., Anchorage, 907-274-2599; www.cyranos.org
This small, independent downtown theater puts on a slew of plays each year, from classic dramas to contemporary comedies. The atmosphere is decidedly informal, but the productions are first rate.

EARTHQUAKE PARK
Northern Lights Blvd., Anchorage, 907-276-4118; www.anchorage.net
Located at the west end of Northern Lights Boulevard, this large, forested park was established near the site where a housing development slid into Cook Inlet during the 1964 Good Friday earthquake. The main trail from the parking lot leads to a small exhibit that explains the geological factors that caused the land beneath the subdivision to collapse. The park also serves as an access point to the Tony Knowles Coastal Trail.

EKLUTNA FLATS AND PALMER HAY FLATS
Anchorage, at the head of the Knik Arm in Cook Inlet, 907-267-2182
The Eklutna Flats and Palmer Hay Flats are a tidally influenced wetlands area at the confluence of the Knik and Matanuska rivers. It provides the broadest view of the Matanuska Valley bordered by the Chugach Mountains, a stone's throw to the east. The ancient Talkeetna Mountains rise in the distance.

13

ALASKA

★
★
★
★
★

THE LAST GREAT RACE ON EARTH

An event unlike any other, the famed Iditarod Trail Sled Dog Race shakes Alaska out of the winter doldrums, attracting thousands of spectators and volunteers to the state, along with approximately 75 mushers and their respective dog teams. The Iditarod bills itself as the Last Great Race on Earth. That's a bold claim, but it would be difficult to argue that any race demands more of its competitors. Starting in Anchorage and finishing in Nome, the race covers roughly 1,100 miles along the historic Iditarod Trail. The grueling journey tests the conditioning and resolve of the mushers and their dogs as they endure up to 17 days of subzero temperatures and howling winds, traversing an ever-changing terrain of mountain, forest, tundra and coastline.

At its core, Alaska's Iditarod is a celebration of sled dogs and their key role in the state's history and development. Sled dogs demonstrated their importance most prominently during the winter of 1925, when diphtheria afflicted the children of Nome. Medicine could not be delivered to the city, reachable only by plane and boat, as winter storms and a frozen Bering Sea made Nome inaccessible. Sled dog teams were used to transport a lifesaving serum. Musher Gunnar Kaasen took the reins for the last leg of the trip, pulled by a team of huskies led by a young pup named Balto. The sled dog team endured fierce winds, blinding snow and temperatures as low as 60 degrees below zero, but made it to Nome and delivered the serum.

In 1973, the first Anchorage-to-Nome Iditarod was held, staged to help preserve the state's mushing heritage. Plane travel had diminished the need for sled dogs. Dick Wilmarth won the 1973 Iditarod, completing the race in just under three weeks—more than twice the pace of today's winning sled teams.

The Iditarod is not the ideal spectator sport, with much of the action unfolding in remote wilderness. Nonetheless, crowds gather at the start and finish lines to cheer on the mushers and their dogs. A great way to be a part of the race is to serve as a volunteer, helping with trail communications, caring for the dogs or transporting supplies. Check-out the official Iditarod Web site (www.iditarod.com) for information about volunteer opportunities.

KEPLER-BRADLEY STATE PARK

550 W. Seventh Ave., Anchorage, 907-269-8400;
www.alaskastateparks.org

A fisherman's paradise, this popular state park comprises several trout- and grayling-filled lakes. Kepler-Bradley State Park is within easy driving distance of Anchorage. Trails from the park connect to the Mat/Su Borough Crevasse Moraine Trail System.

PORTAGE GLACIER AND BEGICH, BOGGS VISITOR CENTER

Glacier Ranger District, Girdwood, Portage, 907-783-2326; www.fs.fed.us

Located 50 miles south of Anchorage, Portage Glacier is one of Alaska's most visited tourist attractions. Although the glacier is no longer visible from the shores of Portage Lake, visitors to the area can still marvel at the massive blue icebergs floating in the water and enjoy the area's spectacular scenery. See the glacier firsthand onboard the M/V *Ptarmigan,* a sightseeing boat run by Gray Line Tours (907-277-5581 or 800-544-2206; www.graylinealaska.com), located on the shore of the lake just past the visitor center.

WRANGELL-ST. ELIAS NATIONAL PARK AND PRESERVE
Copper Center, 907-822-5234; www.nps.gov/wrst

This Preserve is worth a visit, as it boasts North America's greatest collection of mountain peaks above 16,000 feet, highlighted by 18,008-foot-high Mount St. Elias, the second-highest peak in the United States. It's the nation's largest national park, with more than 13 million acres of rugged wilderness, a landscape of towering mountains, sweeping valleys, massive glaciers and powerful rivers. Wrangell-St. Elias is one of four contiguous parks situated along the U.S.-Canada border, the other three being Glacier Bay National Park and Preserve (Alaska), Kluane National Park Reserve (Yukon Territory) and the Alsek-Tatshenshini Provincial Park (British Columbia). Together, these four parks comprise the world's largest internationally protected area. Wrangell-St. Elias headquarters can be found in Copper Center, a four-hour drive from Anchorage on the Alaska Highway. Two gravel roads provide access into the park. Nabesna Road (42 miles long) offers spectacular scenery, while McCarthy Road (60 miles long) leads to exceptional hiking, fishing and camping. The National Park Service recommends drivers on either of these two roads have a spare tire in tow, as the terrain is rough.

HOTELS

★★A LOON'S NEST BED & BREAKFAST
1455 Hillcrest Drive, Anchorage, 907-279-9884, 800-786-9884; www.aloonsnest.com
Two rooms. Complimentary continental breakfast. $

★ANCHORAGE GRAND HOTEL
505 W. Second Ave., Anchorage, 907-929-8888, 888-800-0640; www.anchoragegrandhotel.com
31 rooms. Complimentary continental breakfast. High-speed Internet access. Business center. $$

★★★ANCHORAGE MARRIOTT DOWNTOWN
820 W. Seventh Ave., Anchorage, 907-279-8000, 800-228-9290; www.marriott.com
Every guest room at this bright and cheery hotel has oversized picture windows that flood the rooms with natural light while providing excellent views of either Cook Inlet or the Chugach Mountains. Its proximity to the Delaney Park Strip and the Tony Knowles Coastal Trail also make it a great location for guests looking for a bit of outdoor recreation. 398 rooms. Restaurant, bar. Pool. Fitness center. Business Center. Wireless Internet access. $$$

★BEST VALUE INN EXECUTIVE SUITES
4360 Spenard Road, Anchorage, 907-243-6366, 800-770-6366; www.executivesuitehotel.com
102 rooms. Complimentary continental breakfast. Wireless Internet access. Pets accepted. $

★
★
★
★
☆

★★BEST WESTERN GOLDEN LION HOTEL

1000 E. 36th Ave., Anchorage, 907-561-1522, 877-935-5466;
www.bestwesterngoldenlion.com

83 rooms. Restaurant. Fitness center. Business Center. Wireless Internet access. **$$**

★CLARION SUITES HOTEL

325 W. Eighth Ave., Anchorage, 907-274-1000, 877-424-6423; www.choicehotels.com

110 rooms, all suites. Complimentary continental breakfast. Fitness center. Pool. Wireless Internet access. Business Center. **$$**

★★COAST INTERNATIONAL INN

3450 Aviation Ave., Anchorage, 907-243-2233; www.coasthotels.com

141 rooms. Restaurant. Fitness center. Wireless Internet access. Business center. **$**

★COMFORT INN

111 Ship Creek Ave., Anchorage, 907-277-6887, 877-424-6423;
www.choicehotels.com

100 rooms. Complimentary continental breakfast. Fitness center. Pool. Business Center. Pets accepted. **$$**

★★COURTYARD ANCHORAGE AIRPORT

4901 Spenard Road, Anchorage, 907-245-0322, 800-314-0782; www.courtyard.com

154 rooms. Restaurant. Fitness center. High-speed Internet access. Pool. Business Center. **$$**

★
★★
★★★
★★

★DAYS INN

321 E. Fifth Ave., Anchorage, 907-276-7226, 800-329-7466; www.daysinn.com

130 rooms. Restaurant. Business Center. High-speed Internet access. Fitness center. Pets accepted. **$$**

★★★DIMOND CENTER HOTEL

700 E. Dimond Blvd., Anchorage, 907-770-5000, 866-770-5002;
www.dimondcenterhotel.com

This contemporary boutique hotel has spacious rooms equipped with luxury beds, Egyptian cotton linens and Aveda bath products. Guests have access to the adjacent Dimond Center Athletic Club, which offers everything from kickboxing to indoor swimming. 109 rooms. Complimentary continental breakfast. High-speed Internet access. Pool. **$$**

★HAMPTON INN

4301 Credit Union Drive, Anchorage, 907-550-7000, 800-426-7866;
www.hamptoninn.com

101 rooms. Complimentary continental breakfast. Pool. Business Center. Fitness center. High-speed Internet access. **$$**

★HAWTHORN SUITES

1110 W. Eighth Ave., Anchorage, 907-222-5005, 888-469-6575; www.hawthorn.com

110 rooms, all suites. Complimentary full breakfast. High-speed Internet access. Pool. Fitness center. Business Center. Pets accepeted. **$$**

★★★HILTON ANCHORAGE

500 W. Third Ave., Anchorage, 907-272-7411, 800-455-8667; www.hilton.com

Located downtown, the towers of the Hilton hotel offer sweeping views of the Anchorage area and beyond. On exceptionally clear days, in fact, guests with north-facing rooms can see as far as Mount McKinley, more than 100 miles away. The main draw of the hotel, though, is its ability to bring a sense of grandiose style and glamour to the edge of the Alaskan frontier. 600 rooms. Restaurant. Pool. High-speed Internet access. Business Center. Fitness center. Pets accepted. **$$$**

★★HILTON GARDEN INN ANCHORAGE

4555 Union Square Drive, Anchorage, 907-729-7000; www.hiltongardeninn.com

125 rooms. High-speed Internet access. Restaurant. Fitness center. Pool. Business Center. **$$**

★★THE HISTORIC ANCHORAGE HOTEL

330 E St., Anchorage, 907-272-4553, 800-544-0988; www.historicanchoragehotel.com

26 rooms. Complimentary continental breakfast. High-speed Internet access. **$$**

★HOLIDAY INN EXPRESS

4411 Spenard Road, Anchorage, 907-248-8848, 888-465-4329; www.hiexpress.com

128 rooms. Complimentary continental breakfast. Pool. Fitness center. High-speed Internet access. **$$**

★★★THE HOTEL CAPTAIN COOK

939 W. 5th Ave., Anchorage, 907-276-6000, 800-843-1950; www.captaincook.com

One of Alaska's best independent hotels, Hotel Captain Cook offers twice-daily housekeeping service, nightly turndown and top-quality furnishings (including down comforters, plush towels and 250-threadcount sheets). Other highlights are three full-service restaurants, a selection of chic boutique shops and art galleries, an onsite athletic club and a wealth of original artworks and artifacts on display throughout the public areas. 547 rooms. Restaurant, bar. Fitness center. Pool. Wireless Internet access. **$$**

★★HOWARD JOHNSON PLAZA HOTEL ANCHORAGE

239 W. Fourth Ave., Anchorage, 907-793-5500; www.hjplazaanchorage.com

251 rooms. Restaurant, bar. Fitness center. Pool. **$$**

★★INLET TOWER HOTEL & SUITES

1200 L St., Anchorage, 907-276-0110, 800-544-0786; www.inlettower.com

180 rooms. High-speed Internet access. Restaurant. **$$**

★LAKESHORE MOTOR INN

3009 Lakeshore Drive, Anchorage, 907-248-3485, 800-770-3000;
www.lakeshoremotorinn.com

44 rooms. Complimentary continental breakfast. **$**

★LONG HOUSE ALASKAN HOTEL

4335 Wisconsin St., Anchorage, 907-243-2133, 888-243-2133; www.longhousehotel.com

54 rooms. Complimentary continental breakfast. High-speed Internet access. **$$**

ALASKA

★
★
★
★
★

★MICROTEL INN & SUITES

5205 Northwood Drive, Anchorage, 907-245-5002, 888-680-4500;
www.microtelinn.com/anchorageak

79 rooms. Complimentary continental breakfast. Pets accepted. High-speed Internet access. $

★★★MILLENNIUM ALASKAN HOTEL

4800 Spenard Road, Anchorage, 907-243-2300, 866-866-8086;
www.millenniumhotels.com

The spectacular lobby of this 248-room lakefront hotel sets the tone for the whole property, which is filled with dark woods, slate tiles, leather furniture and a massive rock fireplace in the lobby. The hotel has its own floatplane dock for sport fishing and flight seeing trips. For those looking for upscale accommodations, excellent service and a scenic location in Anchorage, few properties can rival what this hotel has to offer. 248 rooms. Restaurant. Fitness center. High-speed Internet access. $$$

★PARKWOOD INN

4455 Juneau St., Anchorage, 907-563-3590, 800-478-3590; www.parkwoodinn.net
50 rooms. $

★★RAMADA INN

115 E. Third Ave., Anchorage, 907-272-7561, 800-272-6232; www.ramada.com
90 rooms. Restaurant, bar. Complimentary continental breakfast. High-speed Internet access. Fitness center. Pets accepted. $$

★★★SHERATON ANCHORAGE HOTEL

401 E. Sixth Ave., Anchorage, 907-276-8700, 800-478-8700;
www.sheratonanchoragehotel.com

Right in downtown Anchorage, the Sheraton is a short walk to the Anchorage Museum of History and Art, the Fifth Avenue Mall and the Egan Convention and Civic Center. Most of the large, comfortable guest rooms have terrific views of the mountain ranges and tidal flats that surround the city Because the Sheraton caters to business professionals, however, it is not as kid-friendly as most other large downtown hotels. 370 rooms. Complimentary continental breakfast. Restaurant, bar. High-speed Internet access. Spa. $$$

★SPRINGHILL SUITES

3401 A St., Anchorage, 907-562-3247, 800-314-0783; www.marriott.com
101 rooms. Complimentary continental breakfast. Pool. Fitness center. High-speed Internet access. $$

★SUPER 8 MOTEL

3501 Minnesota Drive, Anchorage, 907-276-8884, 800-800-8000; www.super8.com
85 rooms. Complimentary continental breakfast. High-speed Internet access, pets accepted. Restaurant. $

★★THE VOYAGER HOTEL

501 K St., Anchorage, 907-277-9501, 800-247-9070; www.voyagerhotel.com
40 rooms. Complimentary continental breakfast. Restaurant. High-speed Internet access. $$

★★WESTMARK ANCHORAGE HOTEL

720 W. Fifth Ave., Anchorage, 907-276-7676, 800-544-0970;
www.westmarkhotels.com
200 rooms. Restaurant, bar. High-speed Internet access. Fitness center. **$$**

SPECIALTY LODGINGS

ALASKAN LEOPARD BED & BREAKFAST

16136 Sandpiper Drive, Anchorage, 907-868-1594, 877-454-3046;
www.alaskanleopard.com
Seven rooms. Bar. **$**

FIFTEEN CHANDELIERS BED & BREAKFAST INN

14020 Sabine St., Anchorage, 907-345-3032; www.15chandeliers.com
Five rooms. **$$**

MAHOGANY MANOR BED & BREAKFAST INN

204 E. 15th Ave., Anchorage, 907-278-1111, 888-777-0346;
www.mahoganymanor.com
Six rooms. High-speed Internet access. **$$$**

THE OSCAR GILL HOUSE HISTORIC BED & BREAKFAST

1344 W. 10th Ave., Anchorage, 907-279-1344; www.oscargill.com
Three rooms. **$**

SUSITNA SUNSETS BED & BREAKFAST

9901 Conifer St., Anchorage, 907-360-3983; www.bedandbreakfastcenter.com
Features views of Mt. McKinley with breakfast served in-room or on one of the decks. Three rooms. **$**

RESTAURANTS

★★★CLUB PARIS

417 W. Fifth Ave., Anchorage, 907-277-6332; www.clubparisrestaurant.com
The grand belle of Anchorage's downtown restaurant scene, Club Paris is considered by many to be the best steakhouse in the city. Opened in 1957, it's part French bistro, part Alaskan saloon. The local landmark has weathered earthquakes, blizzards and urban renewal, and still manages to be enduringly charming and idiosyncratic. Seafood, steak menu. Lunch, dinner. Bar. Casual attire. **$$$**

★★★CORSAIR RESTAURANT

944 W. Fifth Ave., Anchorage, 907-278-4502; www.corsairrestaurant.com
Featuring ultra-private wraparound booths, discreet soft lighting and a well-trained and knowledgeable staff, Corsair is an ideal destination for anyone looking for a sophisticated dining experience in the heart of Anchorage. The gourmet menu emphasizes French haute cuisine and Alaskan seafood dishes prepared with fresh local ingredients. Considered one of the top three wine cellars in Alaska, Corsair is above all a wine connoisseur's paradise, with more than 700 vintages in its 10,000 bottle cellar. French, seafood menu. Dinner. Closed Sunday; holidays. Bar. Casual attire, reservation recommended. **$$$**

ALASKA

★★★CROW'S NEST RESTAURANT

Fourth Avenue and K Street, Anchorage, 907-343-2217

Featuring one of the best views in Anchorage, this restaurant is known for its five-course prix-fixe menu and an impressive wine list. American menu. Dinner. Closed Sunday-Monday. $$$

★★GLACIER BREWHOUSE

737 W. Fifth Ave., Anchorage, 907-274-2739; www.glacierbrewhouse.com

American menu. Lunch, dinner. Closed holidays. Bar. Casual attire. Reservations recommended. $$

★★GWENNIE'S OLD ALASKA RESTAURANT

4333 Spenard Road, Anchorage, 907-243-2090; www.gwenniesrestaurant.com

American menu. Breakfast, lunch, dinner. Bar. Casual attire. $$

★★HOOPER BAY CAFÉ

500 W. Third Ave., Anchorage, 907-272-7411; www.hilton.com

American menu. Breakfast, lunch, dinner. Children's menu. Casual attire. $$

★★JENS' RESTAURANT

701 W. 36th Ave., Anchorage, 907-561-5367; www.jensrestaurant.com

French menu. Lunch, dinner. Closed Sunday. Bar. $$$

★★★MARX BROS. CAFÉ

627 W. Third Ave., Anchorage, 907-278-2133; www.marxcafe.com

A local favorite, this café was built in 1916 and features progressive American cuisine with an award-winning wine list. American menu. Dinner. Closed Sunday. Reservation recommended. $$$

★★ORSO

737 W. Fifth Ave., Anchorage, 907-222-3232; www.orsoalaska.com

Mediterranean menu. Lunch, dinner. Bar. Casual attire. $$$

★★PEPPER MILL

4101 Credit Union Drive, Anchorage, 907-561-0800;
www.seagalleyalaska.com/peppermill

Steak menu. Dinner. Closed holidays. Bar. Children's menu. Casual attire. $$$

★★PTARMIGAN BAR & GRILL

401 E. Sixth Ave., Anchorage, 907-276-8700;
www.sheratonanchoragehotel.com

American menu. Breakfast, lunch, dinner. Bar. Casual attire. $$

★★★SACK'S CAFÉ & RESTAURANT

328 G St., Anchorage, 907-274-4022; www.sackscafe.com

This is an award-winning restaurant specializing in eclectic New American cuisine. The menu includes everything from salt-crusted, grilled beef tenderloin to penne pasta with gorgonzola. American menu. Lunch, dinner. Saturday-Sunday brunch. $$

★★SEA GALLEY
4101 Credit Union Drive, Anchorage, 907-563-3520; www.seagalleyalaska.com
Seafood menu. Lunch, dinner. Bar. Children's menu. Casual attire. **$$**

★★SIMON & SEAFORT'S SALOON & GRILL
420 L St., Anchorage, 907-274-3502; www.simonandseaforts.com
American menu. Lunch, dinner, bar. **$$**

★★SNOW CITY CAFÉ
1034 W. Fourth Ave., Anchorage, 907-272-2489; www.snowcitycafe.com
American menu. Breakfast, lunch. Casual attire. Outdoor seating. **$**

★★SNOW GOOSE RESTAURANT & SLEEPING LADY BREWING COMPANY
717 W. Third Ave., Anchorage, 907-277-7727; www.alaskabeers.com
American menu. Lunch, dinner, late-night. Bar. Children's menu. Casual attire. Outdoor seating. **$$**

★UNCLE JOE'S PIZZERIA
428 G St., Anchorage, 907-279-3799; www.unclejoespizzeria.com
Pizza. Lunch, dinner. Casual attire, bar, children's menu. **$**

CORDOVA

Accessible only by boat or plane, Cordova sits on the eastern edge of Prince William Sound, close to the largest and most important migratory bird habitats in North America. Originally developed as the southern terminus of the Copper River and Northwestern Railroad, which transported copper from the Kennecott Mine 200 miles to the north, Cordova flourished from 1911 until the mine shut down in 1938. Eventually, the railroad track was torn up and the bed used as a makeshift roadway until the 1964 Good Friday earthquake destroyed the northernmost span of the Million Dollar Bridge across the Copper River, effectively cutting off Cordova's only land-based link to the outside world. The geographic isolation of the town has turned out to be one of its biggest assets, as it remains largely unaffected by the summer tourists who use it as a home base while they hunt, fish, hike, kayak and explore the vast wilderness that surrounds the town.
Information: www.alaskatravel.com/alaska/cordoval.html

WHAT TO SEE AND DO
POINTS NORTH HELI ADVENTURES
Cordova, 877-787-6784; www.alaskaheliski.com
Operating out of the Orca Adventure Lodge, this tour company helicopters brave skiers and snowboarders into the Chugach Mountains, dropping them directly onto the slopes for amazing runs in exceptional powder. Most skiers average 20,000-25,000 vertical feet in a day, with five to eight runs.

SPECIAL EVENT
COPPER RIVER WILD! SALMON FESTIVAL
Copper River Watershed Project, Cordova, 907-424-3334
Cordova's newest tourist draw, the Salmon Festival pays homage to the annual run of salmon up the Copper River. The festival features an assortment of outdoor activities,

including nature hikes, community barbecues and fundraising dinners. One of the main events is the King Salmon Marathon Run, which begins 27 miles up the Copper River Highway and ends in the middle of town.

HOTEL
★PRINCE WILLIAM MOTEL
501 Second St., Cordova, 907-424-3201, 888-796-6835; www.pwmotel.com
16 rooms. $

DENALI NATIONAL PARK AND PRESERVE
Like Alaska and Mount McKinley, Denali is big—really big. It ranks among the largest national parks, covering more than—6 million acres of pristine wilderness, a broad expanse of land roughly the same size as Massachusetts. Situated within the 600-mile-long Alaska Range, the park's sharp-edged mountains were carved by sprawling glaciers, many of which are still at work—the park contains more than 20 glaciers that are longer than five miles, including one, Kahiltna, which stretches 43 miles. Denali also possesses abundant wildlife, including moose, caribou, Dall sheep and grizzly bears, as well as smaller mammals such as marmots and snowshoe hares.

Hiking and camping are among the most popular activities at Denali. Although the park has few trails, one worth exploring is the Mount Healy Overlook Trail, a 2 1/2-mile trek that leads to a stellar view of the fast-flowing Nenana River and majestic peaks of the Alaska Range. The Nenana River offers incredible whitewater rafting, with stretches of the river categorized as Class IV rapids. Bicycling is another favorite activity, particularly on the 90-mile-long Park Road. Bikes may be transported on the Park Road shuttle bus, allowing for a one-way bike ride to the center of Denali followed by a one-way bus ride back to the visitor center. For those seeking to truly test their mettle, Mount McKinley stands as one of the most difficult climbs in the world. While not a technically difficult climb, bitterly cold temperatures, fierce winds and 16,000 feet of snowline make for a daunting expedition. The park is open year-round, and a surprising number of visitors arrive in the winter months to go cross-country skiing or dog sledding.

Native Alaskans have lived at Denali for many centuries. In fact, Mount McKinley (named for President William McKinley) was originally named Denali, which among the indigenous Athabascan people means "Great One." With the stroke of a pen, President Woodrow Wilson established Mount McKinley National Park in 1917. Congress changed the park's name to Denali National Park and Preserve 63 years later.

Denali is accessible by car. The parks headquarters sit on Highway 3, 125 miles south of Fairbanks and 240 miles north of Anchorage. Denali's mountaineering headquarters are in Talkeetna, about 100 miles north of Anchorage. The highly regarded Alaska Railroad runs the Denali Star line between Anchorage and Fairbanks, with stops in Talkeetna and Denali. Information: Denali Park, 907-683-2294; www.nps.gov/dena

SPECIALTY LODGING
THE CORDOVA LIGHTHOUSE INN
212 Nicholoff Way, Cordova, 907-424-7080, 888-424-7080;
www.cordovalighthouseinn.com
Six rooms. Restaurant. High-speed Internet access. **$**

HOTELS
★★DENALI BLUFFS HOTEL
George Parks Highway, Denali National Park and Preserve,
907-683-7000, 866-683-8500; www.denalialaska.com/bluffs
112 rooms. Closed October-April. Wireless Internet access. Restaurant, bar. **$$**

★★DENALI CROW'S NEST LOG CABINS
George Parks Highway, Denali National Park and Preserve,
907-683-2723, 888-917-8130; www.denalicrowsnest.com
39 rooms. Closed early September-mid-May. Restaurant, bar. Whirlpool. **$**

★DENALI PARK HOTEL
George Parks Highway, Healy, 907-683-1800, 866-683-1800;
www.denaliparkhotel.com
42 rooms. Closed mid-September-mid-May. High-speed Internet access. Pets accepted; fee. **$**

★★DENALI PRINCESS WILDERNESS LODGE
George Parks Highway, Denali National Park and Preserve,
907-683-2282, 800-426-0500; www.princesslodges.com
656 rooms. Closed mid-September-mid-May. Restaurants, bar. High-speed Internet access. **$$**

★★GRANDE DENALI LODGE
George Parks Highway, Denali National Park and Preserve,
907-683-8500, 866-683-8500; www.denalialaska.com
166 rooms. Closed mid-September-mid-May. Restaurant, bar. **$$**

★★MCKINLEY CHALET RESORT
George Parks Highway, Denali National Park and Preserve,
907-683-8200, 800-276-7234; www.denaliparkresort.com
345 rooms. Closed mid-September-mid-May. Restaurant, bar. **$$**

★★MCKINLEY VILLAGE LODGE
Mile Post 231, Denali National Park and Preserve,
907-683-8900, 800-276-7234; www.denaliparkresort.com
151 rooms. Closed mid-September-late May. Restaurant, bar. **$**

★★TALKEETNA ALASKAN LODGE
Talkeeta Spur Road,Talkeetna, 907-733-9500, 888-959-9590;
www.talkeetnalodge.com
212 rooms. Closed early October-mid-April. Restaurant, bar. **$$$**

RESTAURANTS
★★ALPENGLOW RESTAURANT
George Parks Highway, Denali National Park and Preserve,
907-683-8500, 866-683-8500; www.denalialaska.com
American menu. Breakfast, lunch, dinner. Closed mid-September-mid-May. Bar.
Children's menu. Casual attire. Reservations recommended. $$$

★CREEKSIDE CAFÉ
Mile 224 George Parks Highway, Denali National Park and Preserve,
907-683-2277; www.mckinleycabins.com
American menu. Breakfast, lunch, dinner. Closed mid-September-mid-May. Children's menu. Casual attire. Outdoor seating. $$

★★★NENANA VIEW GRILLE
Mile 23825 George Parks Highway, Denali National Park and Preserve,
907-683-8200, 800-276-7234; www.denaliparkresorts.com
Located at the McKinley Chalet Resort with sweeping views of the Nenana River, this sophisticated eatery offers some of the best fine dining in the Denali area. Featuring an open kitchen and a large stone pizza oven, the dining area is filled with beautiful wood furniture and striking artwork that gives the room an air of rustic elegance. The menu is a mix of haute cuisine, popular Alaskan dishes and lighter fare—all complemented by an extensive wine selection. American menu. Breakfast, lunch, dinner, late-night. Closed mid-September-mid-May. Bar. Children's menu. Casual attire. Reservations recommended. Outdoor seating. $$$

★★THE OVERLOOK BAR AT THE CROW'S NEST
George Parks Highway, Denali National Park and Preserve, 907-683-2723
American menu. Lunch, dinner. Bar. Casual attire. Outdoor seating. $

★PANORAMA PIZZA PUB
George Parks Highway, Denali National Park and Preserve,
907-683-2523, 888-322-2523; www.denaliparkresorts.com
Pizza menu. Breakfast, lunch, dinner. Children's menu. Casual attire. Outdoor seating. $

★★THE PERCH
George Parks Highway, Denali National Park and Preserve,
907-683-2523, 888-322-2523; www.denaliperchresort.com
American menu. Dinner. Bar. Children's menu. Casual attire. Outdoor seating. $$

EAGLE RIVER
A small town 20 minutes north of downtown Anchorage, Eagle River serves as a bedroom community for the city and as a friendly, relaxing and inexpensive home base for travelers wanting to explore the Anchorage area. It's also the one of the main gateways to Chugach State Park, which at nearly half a million acres ranks as the third-largest state park in the United States, and contains part of the Iditarod National Historic Trail. Twelve miles up Eagle River Road is the Eagle River Nature Center, offering self-guided hiking trails and hands-on interpretive exhibits. Regardless of the season, visitors to Eagle River can find outdoor recreational activities to suit their

ages and fitness levels: hiking, biking, fishing, canoeing, rafting, camping and rock climbing during the summer, ice climbing, dog mushing, downhill skiing and ice skating during winter. There are also numerous scenic parks and lakes within a short drive of the downtown area that provide excellent family-friendly spots for relaxing. *Information: www.cer.org*

WHAT TO SEE AND DO
EAGLE RIVER NATURE CENTER
32750 Eagle River Road, Eagle River, 907-694-2108; www.ernc.org
The Eagle River Nature Center serves as a gateway to the 500,000-acre Chugach State Park. Indoor and outdoor programs offered by the center teach visitors about the kinds of flora, fauna and geographic features they might encounter inside the park. June-August, Sunday-Thursday 10 a.m.-5 p.m., Friday-Saturday 10 a.m.-7 p.m.; October-April, Friday-Sunday 10 a.m.-5 p.m.; May, September, Tuesday-Sunday 10 a.m.-5 p.m.

SPECIAL EVENT
BEAR PAW FESTIVAL
Eagle River, 907-694-4702; www.cer.org
First held in 1985, the Bear Paw Festival was created to celebrate the beauty and diversity of the Eagle River and Chugiak area. Visitors to the festival can wander from the Renaissance Village, past the highly popular teddy bear picnic, and end up with prime seats at the Slippery Salmon Olympics. Carnival rides and a grand parade top the list of things to do at this unique small-town event.

HOTELS
★EAGLE RIVER MOTEL
11111 Old Eagle River Road, Eagle River, 907-694-5000, 866-256-6835; www.eaglerivermotel.com
14 rooms. Complimentary continental breakfast. Pets accepted. $

★MICROTEL INN & SUITES
13049 Old Glenn Highway, Eagle River, 907-622-6000, 800-771-7171; www.microtelinn.com
60 rooms. Complimentary continental breakfast. High-speed Internet access. Pets accepted. $

FAIRBANKS
The Fairbanks North Star Borough is about the same size as New Jersey but contains fewer than 90,000 people, a third of whom live in Fairbanks. Centrally located 120 miles north of Denali National Park and 200 miles south of the Arctic Circle, Fairbanks remains today the largest and most important commercial, social and tourist center in the Interior.

The origins of modern day Fairbanks can be traced to a series of mishaps that happened to a would-be goldfield merchant named E. T. Barnette. In 1901, in an attempt to capitalize on the need for supplies at the Tanacross goldfields far up the Tanana River, Barnette loaded a sternwheeler with supplies and set out. After the boat ran aground in the Tanana's shallow waters, Barnette decided to try to reach the area via the nearby Chena River, which proved equally unsuccessful. In defeat, he unloaded the boat on the banks of the Chena and set up a small trading post on the spot, very close

ALASKA

★
★★
★★
★

to where Italian prospector Felix Pedro struck gold the following year. In the ensuing gold rush, Barnette's business prospered and a town eventually grew up around it.

Today, Fairbanks is still very much a river city, with parks and walkways scattered along the Chena River and tour boats and rental kayaks plying the waters. One of the most popular attractions in the downtown area is a historic sternwheeler that takes passengers for scenic rides on the river during the summer.

One of Fairbanks's main distinctions is that it is subject to some of the widest temperature variations of any city on earth. Summertime temperatures occasionally hit the 90-degree mark, while winter temperatures have dipped as low as 62 below zero. Despite this, tourists still visit Fairbanks during winter, primarily because the long hours of darkness and cold night air provide excellent viewing of the aurora borealis, Alaska's northern lights. During the summer, the aurora is not visible, since the area is under nearly constant daylight.

Information: Convention and Visitors Bureau, 550 First Ave., 800-327-5774; www.explorefairbanks.com

WHAT TO SEE AND DO
CREAMER'S FIELD MIGRATORY WATERFOWL REFUGE
1300 College Road, Fairbanks, 907-459-7307; www.creamersfield.org
This 1,800-acre site on the northern edge of Fairbanks serves as an important stopover point for thousands of Canada geese, pintails, golden plovers and other birds on their spring and fall migrations. Although spring is the best time to see large numbers and varieties of birds at the refuge, sandhill cranes, shovelers and mallards remain in the area all summer. Admission to the refuge is free, as are nature walks departing from the visitor center. Farmhouse Visitor Center: Summer, daily 10 a.m.-5 p.m.; Winter, Saturday noon-4 p.m.

EL DORADO GOLD MINE
Elliott Highway, Fairbanks, 907-479-6673, 866-479-6673; www.eldoradogoldmine.com
Run by the same family that operates the Riverboat Discovery, the El Dorado Gold Mine provides visitors with a chance to watch a real Alaskan gold mine in operation. The two-hour tour begins with a narrated ride on the Tanana Valley Railroad, a narrow-gauge line that travels through some of Fairbanks's original gold fields. Upon arrival at El Dorado mine, guests are given a guided tour of the facility and are taught how to pan for gold. Mid-May-mid-September, 9:45 a.m. and 3 p.m., Saturday 3 p.m.

RIVERBOAT DISCOVERY
1975 Discovery Drive, Fairbanks, 907-479-6673, 866-479-6673; www.riverboatdiscovery.com
Run by members of an Alaskan family with more than a century of river boating experience, this classic sternwheeler carries tourists on a 3.5-hour narrated cruise on the Chena and Tanana rivers. Reservations are required. Mid-May-mid-September, Sunday-Friday 8:45 a.m. and 2 p.m., Saturday 2 p.m.

UNIVERSITY OF ALASKA MUSEUM OF THE NORTH
907 Yukon Drive, Fairbanks, 907-474-7505; www.uaf.edu/museum
Located on the campus of the University of Alaska Fairbanks, the Museum of the North houses more than a million artifacts relating to Alaska's history and culture.

Exhibits in the galleries range from a mummified Ice Age bison, affectionately known as Blue Babe, to intricately woven Aleut baskets and Eskimo ivory carvings. Mid-May-mid-September, daily 9 a.m.-7 p.m.; mid-September-mid-May, Monday-Friday 9 a.m.-5 p.m., Saturday-Sunday noon-5 p.m.

SPECIAL EVENTS

WORLD ESKIMO-INDIAN OLYMPICS
Big Dipper Ice Arena, 19th Avenue and Lathrop Street, Fairbanks, 907-452-6646; www.weio.org
Since 1961, this annual four-day gathering of Native Alaskans has celebrated the skills, traditions, artistry and spirit of Alaska's six major tribes. Each event in the Olympics is based on a traditional Eskimo or Indian hunting, fishing or survival activity and is designed to measure the competitor's athletic prowess and mental toughness. Third Wednesday in July.

WORLD ICE ART CHAMPIONSHIPS
Philips Field Road, Fairbanks, 907-451-8250; www.icealaska.com
At the beginning of March each year, ice sculptors from around the world descend on Fairbanks to compete for the title of World Ice Art Champion. The 11-day event consists of three separate contests: single block sculpting, multi-block sculpting and the Fairbanks Open, a less competitive event open to amateurs. While the competition is underway, visitors can wander around the Ice Park watching the artists at work. At the conclusion of the contest, the sculptures are outfitted with electric lights and the finished works remain on display until the last Sunday.

HOTELS

★★★ALL SEASONS BED & BREAKFAST
763 Seventh Ave., Fairbanks, 907-451-6649, 888-451-6649; www.allseasonsinn.com
You might feel like you're visiting Grandma's farmhouse at this bed and breakfast decorated with floral bedding, wallpaper borders and wood paneling. The inn conveniently provides a private bath with each of the eight rustic guest rooms, which feature wireless Internet access. Wake up to a full hot breakfast of quiche, apple pancakes, egg puffs or fruit-filled crepes. Just order it to go the night before if you have a flight or caribou to catch. Eight rooms. Wireless Internet access. Complimentary full breakfast. $$

★★BRIDGEWATER HOTEL
723 First Ave., Fairbanks, 907-452-6661, 800-528-4916; www.fountainheadhotels.com
94 rooms. Closed mid-September-mid-May. Restaurant. Airport transportation available. Wireless Internet access. $$

★★THE CAPTAIN BARTLETT INN
1411 Airport Way, Fairbanks, 907-452-1888, 800-478-7900; www.captainbartlettinn.com
197 rooms. Restaurant, bar. Airport transportation available. $

★★CHENA HOT SPRINGS RESORT
565 Chena Hot Springs Road, Fairbanks, 907-451-8104, 800-478-4681; www.chenahotsprings.com
90 rooms. Restaurant, bar. Indoor pool, whirlpool. $$

★COMFORT INN CHENA RIVER
1908 Chena Landings Loop, Fairbanks, 907-479-8080, 877-424-6423;
www.choicehotels.com
74 rooms. Complimentary continental breakfast. High-speed Internet access. Pool.
Pets accepted. **$**

★EXTENDED STAY DELUXE
4580 Old Airport Road, Fairbanks, 907-457-2288; www.extendedstaydeluxe.com
97 rooms. Complimentary continental breakfast. High-speed Internet access. Indoor
pool. Airport transportation available. Wireless Internet access. Pets accepted. **$**

★★★FAIRBANKS PRINCESS RIVERSIDE LODGE
4477 Pikes Landing Road, Fairbanks, 907-455-4477, 800-426-0500;
www.princesslodges.com
Set along the banks of the Chena River, this large, semi-secluded hotel is one of the
most upscale in Fairbanks. Painted a striking blue, its huge open deck overlooks the
river and is perfect for wildlife viewing. The interior, in contrast, is much more lodge-
like, with intimate dining and lounge areas, log and stone architectural features and
soft, plush furniture. Open year-round, the hotel is a popular spot for cruise ship passengers during the summer months and northern lights watchers in the winter. 325 rooms.
Airport transportation available. Fitness center. Wireless Internet access. **$$**

★★PIKE'S WATERFRONT LODGE
1850 Hoselton Road, Fairbanks, 907-479-6500, 877-774-2400; www.pikeslodge.com
208 rooms. Restaurant, bar. Fitness center. Wireless Internet access. **$$**

★★REGENCY FAIRBANKS HOTEL
95 10th Ave., Fairbanks, 907-459-2700, 800-478-1320;
www.regencyfairbankshotel.com
128 rooms. High-speed Internet access. Restaurant, bar. Fitness center. **$$**

★★RIVER'S EDGE RESORT
4200 Boat St., Fairbanks, 800-770-3343; www.riversedge.net
94 rooms. Closed mid-September-early May. Restaurant, bar. **$$**

★★SOPHIE STATION HOTEL
1717 University Ave., Fairbanks, 907-479-3650, 800-528-4916;
www.fountainheadhotels.com
148 rooms, all suites. Restaurant, bar. **$$**

★★SPRINGHILL SUITES BY MARRIOTT FAIRBANKS
575 First Ave., Fairbanks, 907-451-6552, 1-800-314-0858; www.marriott.com
140 rooms, all suites. Complimentary continental breakfast. High-speed Internet
access. Restaurant, bar. Airport transportation available. Fitness center. **$$**

★★WEDGEWOOD RESORT
212 Wedgewood Drive, Fairbanks, 907-452-1442, 800-528-4916;
www.fountainheadhotels.com
157 rooms. Closed mid-September-mid-May. Restaurant, bar. **$$**

★★WESTMARK FAIRBANKS HOTEL

813 Noble St., Fairbanks, 907-456-7722, 800-544-0970; www.westmarkhotels.com
400 rooms. High-speed Internet access. Restaurant, bar. Airport transportation available. Fitness center. $$

RESTAURANTS
★★CHENA HOT SPRINGS RESTAURANT

565 Chena Hot Springs Road, Fairbanks, 907-451-8104; www.chenahotsprings.com
American menu. Breakfast, lunch, dinner. Bar. Children's menu. Casual attire. Reservations recommended. Outdoor seating. $$

★GAMBARDELLA'S

706 Second Ave., Fairbanks, 907-457-4992; www.gambardellas.com
Italian menu. Lunch, dinner. Children's menu. Casual attire. Reservations recommended. Outdoor seating. $$

★★THE RIVER'S EDGE

4200 Boat St., Fairbanks, 907-474-0286, 800-770-3343; www.riversedge.net
American menu. Breakfast, lunch, dinner. Closed mid-September-early May. Bar. Children's menu. Casual attire. Reservations recommended. Outdoor seating. $$

GIRDWOOD

This ski town outside Anchorage lies in a valley of the Chugach Mountains. The city was moved 2 1/2 miles up the valley following the Good Friday Earthquake of 1964.
Information: www.girdwoodalaska.com

HOTEL
★★★ALYESKA RESORT

1000 Arlberg Ave., Girdwood, 907-754-1111, 800-880-3880; www.alyeskaresort.com
Located in the town of Girdwood, about 45 minutes south of Anchorage on the Seward Highway, the resort is surrounded by the Chugach Mountains and the waters of Turnagain Arm. It includes a ski area, a golf course (in Anchorage) and the Alyeska Hotel—a blend of Swiss chateau and modern architecture. Everything about this resort is first-rate: deluxe guest rooms; world-class skiing, snowboarding and heli-skiing in winter; extensive hiking and mountain biking in summer; fine-dining restaurants; state-of-the-art fitness facilities; and all-around spectacular views of hanging glaciers, soaring mountains and miles and miles of pristine wilderness. 307 rooms. Restaurant, bar. Pool. Golf. $$

RESTAURANTS
★THE BAKE SHOP

Alyeska Boardwalk, Girdwood, 907-783-2831; www.thebakeshop.com
Deli menu, pizza. Breakfast, lunch, dinner. Casual attire. Outdoor seating. $

★THE DOUBLE MUSKIE INN

Third Crow Creek Road, Girdwood, 907-783-2822
Cajun menu. Lunch, dinner. Closed Sunday. $$

ALASKA

★
★★
★★★
★★
☆

★★THE POND CAFÉ

1000 Arlberg Ave., Girdwood, 907-754-2236; www.alyeskaresort.com

American menu. Breakfast, lunch, dinner. Bar. Children's menu. Casual attire. Outdoor seating. $$

★★★SEVEN GLACIERS

1000 Arlberg Ave., Girdwood, 907-754-2237; www.alyeskaresort.com

Located 2,300 feet above the Girdwood valley floor, the ultra-chic Seven Glaciers restaurant is only accessible by gondola from the Alyeska Resort. From this mountainside perch, it provides guests with views to the north of seven hanging glaciers on a nearby mountain and, to the south, the waters of Turnagain Arm. The restaurant features award-winning Alaskan cuisine in an exceptionally warm and intimate environment and has a well-deserved reputation for flawless service. Northwest menu. Dinner. Closed mid-April-mid-May and October-mid-November. Bar. Children's menu. Business casual attire. $$$

★★★TEPPANYAKI SAKURA

1000 Arlberg Ave., Girdwood, 907-754-2237; www.alyeskaresort.com

Located inside the Alyeska Resort, Teppanyaki Sakura serves world-class Japanese cuisine with flair and features a u-shaped seating arrangement from which guests can watch the master chef prepare their food. With reservations limited to only 18 diners per seating and a menu of four set courses to choose from, the emphasis here is on creating a unique and memorable dining experience. Japanese menu. Dinner. Closed Tuesday-Wednesday. Bar. Casual attire. $$$

HAINES

Haines is a town rich in history and natural beauty. Located near the northern end of the Inside Passage, it's surrounded on all sides by soaring mountains, deepwater inlets and miles of rugged forests and massive glaciers. In 1898, the Klondike Gold Rush flooded the town with prospectors heading up the nearby Dalton Trail on their way north. Soon after the rush ended, the U.S. Army decided to build its first permanent army post in Alaska on the outskirts of town. In 1972, the fort was listed on the National Register of Historic Places and in 1978 it was designated a National Historic Landmark. To this day, it remains a fascinating visual link to Haines's storied past. Visitors interested in learning more about the area can visit the Sheldon Museum, home to a fascinating mix of pioneer and Gold Rush memorabilia as well as an extensive collection of Chilkat Tlingit art and artifacts.

One of the highlights of Haines's event calendar is its annual Alaska Bald Eagle Festival. Held during the middle of November, the festival celebrates the thousands of bald eagles that congregate in the area to feed on late spawning salmon in the Chilkat River. Photographers and bird-watchers can enjoy the spectacle from any number of highway pullouts adjacent to the 48,000-acre Alaska Chilkat Bald Eagle Preserve northwest of town.

Information: Convention and Visitors Bureau, 122 Second Ave., Haines, 907-766-2234; www.haines.ak.us

WHAT TO SEE AND DO

AMERICAN BALD EAGLE FOUNDATION MUSEUM

113 Haines Highway, Haines, 907-766-3094; www.baldeagles.org

Protecting and preserving bald eagles and their habitat is the mission of this nonprofit foundation. Located only 20 miles from the Chilkat Bald Eagle Preserve, where more than 3,000 eagles congregate each winter, the interpretive center has incorporated more than 180 specimens of fish and wildlife from the preserve into a massive indoor diorama that depicts the interaction of each species in the local ecosystem.

SHELDON MUSEUM AND CULTURAL CENTER

First Avenue and Main Street, Haines, 907-766-2366;
www.sheldonmuseum.org

Established in 1924, the Sheldon Museum houses a wide variety of historical and artistic artifacts relating to the different cultures that reside in the Chilkat Valley. Through onsite displays and exhibits of rare and elaborate Native handicrafts, visitors are able to learn about the Tlingit culture that predominated the area before the arrival of European settlers. The museum also focuses on the role Haines played in the Klondike Gold Rush, with exhibits and memorabilia that tell the story of the miners who set off on the nearby Dalton Trail leading into the interior and the gold fields of the Klondike. Most summer afternoons, visitors have the chance to observe master Native craftsmen fashioning totem poles in the front yard of the museum. Summer, Monday-Friday 11 a.m.-6 p.m., Saturday-Sunday 2-6 p.m.; winter, Monday-Friday 1-4 p.m.

SPECIAL EVENTS

ALASKA BALD EAGLE FESTIVAL

113 Haines Highway, Haines, 907-766-3094;
www.baldeagles.org

In October, the world's largest number of bald eagles gather in Haines to take advantage of the late salmon run. This amazing gathering of eagles is the basis of this annual festival that is held in the eagles' honor. October.

SOUTHEAST ALASKA STATE FAIR

Southeast Alaska Fairgrounds, 296 Fair Drive, Haines,
907-766-2476; www.seakfair.org

This old-fashioned regional fair is held over five days at the Southeast Alaska Fairgrounds on the northern edge of town. Friendly, lively and full of small-town appeal, it features contests to determine everything from the most lovable dog to the best zucchini, plus logging competitions, exhibits and live music.

HOTELS

★CAPTAIN'S CHOICE MOTEL

108 Second Ave. North, Haines, 907-766-3111, 800-478-2345; www.capchoice.com

40 rooms. Complimentary breakfast. Restaurant. $

★★HOTEL HÄLSINGLAND

13 Fort Seward Drive, Haines, 907-766-2000, 800-542-6363;
www.hotelhalsingland.com

60 rooms. Closed in winter. Restaurant, bar. $

ALASKA

★
★ ★
★ ★
★ ★
★

SPECIALTY LODGING
FORT SEWARD LODGE
39 Mud Bay Road, Haines, 907-766-2009, 877-617-3418; www.ftsewardlodge.com
10 rooms. Restaurant. Pets accepted. Closed October-April. **$**

RESTAURANTS
★THE BAMBOO ROOM
11 Second Ave. N., Haines, 907-766-2800; www.bamboopioneer.net
Seafood menu. Breakfast, lunch, dinner. Bar. Children's menu. Casual attire. Reservations recommended. Outdoor seating. **$$**

★★FORT SEWARD RESTAURANT
39 Mud Bay Road, Haines, 907-766-2009, 877-617-3418; www.ftsewardlodge.com
Seafood menu. Breakfast, lunch, dinner, brunch. Closed in winter. Bar. Children's menu. Casual attire. **$$**

HOMER

Homer bills itself as the Halibut Capital of the World and is known for having some of the best fishing on the Kenai Peninsula. Set on a hillside overlooking Kachemak Bay and Cook Inlet, it plays host to an enormous number of visitors each year, including hundreds who spend the whole summer camped out on the Homer Spit, a five-mile-long sliver of land that juts out into the waters of the bay, providing unrestricted access to great halibut and salmon fishing.

That said, Homer offers a range of other diversions for those uninterested in hooks, bait and flies. In May, the Kachemak Bay Shorebird Festival takes place, celebrating the tens of thousands of shorebirds that stop over on the local mudflats during their annual migration north. Throughout the summer, boats are available to shuttle passengers across the bay to the small fishing villages and artist communities that dot the rugged coastline. For more athletic types, a network of hiking and biking trails throughout the area provides spectacular views of the mountains, waters and wildlife that make up this region.
Information: Chamber of Commerce, 201 Sterling Highway, Homer,
907-235-7740; www.homeralaska.org

WHAT TO SEE AND DO
ALASKA ISLANDS AND OCEAN VISITOR CENTER
95 Sterling Highway, Homer, 907-235-6961; www.islandsandocean.org
Opened in December 2003, the Alaska Islands and Ocean Visitor Center is an educational and research facility that offers visitors an opportunity to learn about the Alaska Maritime National Wildlife Refuge and the Kachemak Bay Research Reserve through interactive exhibits, guided tours and video presentations. One of the primary goals of the center is to enhance people's awareness of the beauty, fragility and diversity of the remote 4.9-million-acre refuge, which stretches from the Arctic Ocean all the way to Alaska's southeast panhandle. Memorial Day-Labor Day, daily 9 a.m.-6 p.m.

PRATT MUSEUM
3779 Bartlett St., Homer, 907-235-8635; www.prattmuseum.org
Pratt Museum is home to native and contemporary culture exhibits, natural history artifacts, a gallery of contemporary regional art and a small room filled with live

marine plants and wildlife. Outside, the museum grounds include botanical gardens, forest trails teeming with birds and other wildlife and historical structures and artifacts from Homers pioneer days. Mid-May-mid-September, daily 10 a.m.-6 p.m.; mid-September-mid-May, Tuesday-Sunday noon-5 p.m.; closed January.

SPECIAL EVENT
KACHEMAK BAY SHOREBIRD FESTIVAL
Homer, 907-235-7740; www.homeralaska.org
First held in 1993, this festival was designed as a way to shake off winter's grip and celebrate the annual migration of hundreds of thousands of shorebirds through the Kachemak Bay region. Since then, it has evolved into a four-day event to track bird migrations, monitor the health of bird populations and educate the public about shorebirds and the need for habitat conservation. Throughout the festival, there are guest lectures and workshops, guided bird walks and boat tours to remote migration sites. Mid-May.

HOTELS
★★BELUGA LAKE LODGE
204 Ocean Drive Loop, Homer, 907-235-5995; www.belugalakelodging.com
32 rooms. Restaurant. Wireless Internet access. $

★★LAND'S END RESORT
4786 Homer Spit Road, Homer, 907-235-0400, 800-478-0400; www.lands-end-resort.com
80 rooms. Complimentary continental breakfast. Restaurant. Spa. $$

SPECIALTY LODGINGS
DRIFTWOOD INN
135 W. Bunnell Ave., Homer, 907-235-8019, 800-478-8019; www.thedriftwoodinn.com
20 rooms. $

HOMER INN & SPA
895 Ocean Drive, Homer, 907-235-2501, 800-294-7823; www.homerinn.com
Five rooms. Wireless Internet access. $$

VICTORIAN HEIGHTS BED & BREAKFAST
1585 Race Road, Homer, 907-235-6357; www.victorianheightsbedandbreakfast.com
Four rooms. $

RESTAURANTS
★★CHART ROOM
4786 Homer Spit Road, Homer, 907-235-0400, 800-478-0400; www.endofthespit.com
Seafood, steak menu. Breakfast, lunch, dinner. Bar. Children's menu. Casual attire. Outdoor seating. $$$

★TWO SISTERS BAKERY & CAFÉ
233 E. Bunnell Ave., Homer, 907-235-2280; www.twosistersbakery.net
American, deli menu, bakery. Breakfast, lunch. Casual attire. Outdoor seating. $

33

ALASKA

★
★
★
★
★

JUNEAU

Squeezed onto a narrow slip of land between the waters of Gastineau Channel and the base of 3,576-foot-tall Mount Juneau, Alaska's capital city is literally and figuratively overshadowed by the vast wilderness that surrounds it. Located in the middle of the Tongass National Forest two-thirds of the way up the Inside Passage, Juneau is a former Gold Rush town that has managed to strike it rich with tourists. Because no roads connect Juneau to the outside world, all visitors must arrive by air or sea. This is an enormous benefit for the city, as it is most striking when viewed against a backdrop of massive glaciers, dense forests, towering peaks and meandering waterways. In 2002, more than 750,000 visitors came to this remote region of Alaska, most arriving by cruise ship.

The city was originally called Harrisburg, in recognition of Richard Harris, one of the first prospectors to stake a claim in the area. The town's name was later changed to Rockwell for a short time, before being changed in 1881 to Juneau in honor of Joe Juneau, Harris's partner and cofounder of the settlement. In 1906, the government was moved from Sitka to Juneau, and it has remained the state capital ever since, despite its geographic isolation from the rest of the state. Although Juneau's population is about 31,000, making it the third-largest city in Alaska, it has managed to retain a small-town feel, due in large part to the preservation of the historic district around Front and Franklin streets and the casual, friendly attitude of its residents. And with an average of 222 days of rain each year, it's not surprising that the city is brimming with bookstores, coffeehouses, restaurants and bars.

Information: Juneau Convention & Visitors Bureau, 1 Sealaska Plaza,
Juneau, 907-586-1737, 800-587-2201; www.traveljuneau.com

WHAT TO SEE AND DO

ALASKA STATE MUSEUM
395 Whittier St., Juneau, 907-465-2901; www.museums.state.ak.us
Permanent collections and traveling exhibits highlight Alaska's native peoples, its natural history, the Alaska-Yukon gold rushes and the American period of Alaska's history. A children's room features a one-third scale model of the stern of the ship *Discovery*, used by Captain George Vancouver during his famous explorations of Alaska. Mid-May-mid-September, daily 8:30 a.m.-5:30 p.m.; mid-September-mid-May, Tuesday-Saturday 10 a.m.-4 p.m.; closed holidays.

JUNEAU-DOUGLAS CITY MUSEUM
Fourth Avenue and Main Street, Juneau, 907-586-3572;
www.juneau.org/parksrec/museum
Located across the street from the State Capitol, the Juneau-Douglas City Museum was founded to preserve and display materials relating to the cultural and historical development of the Juneau-Douglas area. The small galleries are packed with artifacts and memorabilia of the groups and events that have influenced the development of the Juneau and Douglas region, from ancient Tlingit tribes to turn-of-the-century mining corporations to modern-day tour companies. Mid-May-September, Monday-Friday 9 a.m.-5 p.m., Saturday-Sunday 10 a.m.-5 p.m.; October-mid-May, Tuesday-Saturday noon-4 p.m.

THE LAST CHANCE MINING MUSEUM

1001 Basin Road, Juneau, 907-586-5338; www.museumsusa.org

Listed on the National Register of Historic Places and Alaska Gold Rush Properties, this museum is housed in an historic compressor building associated with the former Alaska Juneau Gold Mining Company, which operated in Juneau from 1912 until 1944. The museum explores the history of the region's mining industry with exhibits of industrial artifacts associated with hard rock gold mining. Daily 9:30 a.m.-12:30 p.m., 3:30-6:30 p.m.

MENDENHALL GLACIER

8510 Mendenhall Loop Road, Juneau, 907-789-0097; www.fs.fed.us

Mendenhall Glacier is located about 12 miles from downtown Juneau at the northern end of the Mendenhall Valley. The glacier originates in the Juneau Icefield and stretches for 13 miles before terminating at the northern end of Mendenhall Lake, the waters of which conceal roughly half of the glacier's 200-foot-thick toe. Five trails originate in and around the visitor center, providing scenic walks during the summer months. Summer, daily 8 a.m.-6:30 p.m.

MOUNT ROBERTS TRAMWAY

490 S. Franklin St., Juneau, 907-463-3412, 888-461-8726; www.alaska.net/~junotram

The Mount Roberts Tramway runs from the cruise ship dock in downtown Juneau up the side of Mount Roberts to an elevation of about 1,800 feet, providing passengers with magnificent views of Juneau, Douglas Island and the Gastineau Channel. May-September, daily 9 a.m.-9 p.m.

WICKERSHAM STATE HISTORICAL SITE

213 Seventh St., Juneau, 907-586-9001; www.dnr.state.ak.us

A beautiful Victorian house dating from 1898, this site was home to James Wickersham, one of the most influential men in the development of Alaska during its pioneer days. As a district court judge, Wickersham was responsible for bringing law and order to more than a quarter-million square miles of Alaska's interior at the turn-of-the-century. The list of his other accomplishments is equally amazing. He served as a congressional delegate to Congress, helping to create Mount McKinley National Park, the Alaska Railroad and the territory's first college, later renamed the University of Alaska. He also won Home Rule for Alaska in 1912, which gave the territory an elected legislature, was one of the first to introduce a statehood bill for Alaska and was the first white man to attempt to climb Mount McKinley. His home is now a museum filled with artifacts, photographs and furnishings that tell the story of Wickersham's pioneering spirit and devotion to the territory. Summer, daily 10 a.m.-noon, 1-5 p.m.

HOTELS

★BEST WESTERN COUNTRY LANE INN

9300 Glacier Highway, Juneau, 907-789-5005, 888-7836; www.bestwestern.com

55 rooms. Complimentary continental breakfast. High-speed Internet access. $

★★BREAKWATER INN

1711 Glacier Ave., Juneau, 99801, 907-586-6303, 888-586-6303; www.breakwaterinn.com

49 rooms. Restaurant. $

★★★GOLDBELT HOTEL
51 Egan Drive, Juneau, 907-586-6900, 888-478-6909; www.goldbelthotel.com

Next door to the Centennial Convention and Visitors' Center, Goldbelt Hotel is one of the largest in town and has some of the best waterfront views around. A native-owned property, it boasts one of the most extensive collections of Tlingit art found anywhere in Alaska including shields, masks, necklaces, jewelry, baskets and bowls. The guest rooms are large and offer a level of comfort and style unsurpassed in Juneau. 105 rooms. Restaurant. Wireless Internet access. $$

SPECIALTY LODGING
ALASKA WOLF LODGE
1900 Wickersham Ave., Juneau, 907-586-2422, 888-425-9653;
www.alaskawolfhouse.com

Five rooms. $

RESTAURANTS
★★HANGAR ON THE WHARF
Second Marine Way, Juneau, 907-586-5018; www.hangaronthewharf.com

American menu. Lunch, dinner. $

★PARADISE CAFÉ
245 Marine Way, Juneau, 907-586-2253; www.paradisecafeyeehaw.com

American menu. Breakfast, lunch. Casual attire. Outdoor seating. $

★PIZZERIA ROMA
Second Marine Way, Juneau, 907-463-5020; www.pizzeriaroma.hangaronthewharf.com

Pizza menu. Lunch, dinner. Casual attire. $

★★T. K. MAGUIRE'S
375 Whittier St., Juneau, 907-586-3711; www.prospectorhotel.com/restaurant.htm

International menu. Breakfast, lunch, dinner. Children's menu. Casual attire. Outdoor seating. $$

★★★THE GOLD ROOM
127 N. Franklin St., Juneau, 907-463-6222; www.westmarkhotels.com

An historic restaurant at the Westmark Baranof Hotel, the Gold Room is one of the most architecturally and artistically attractive restaurants in Alaska. From the Art Deco skylight rediscovered after a fire in the 1980s to the huge wall mural by Alaskan artist Sydney Lawrence, the restaurant is filled with historical, artistic and architectural accents that give it an elegant air. The restaurant's menu is topnotch, too. American menu. Dinner. Bar. Children's menu. Casual attire. $$$

KENAI

As the oldest settlement on the Alaskan mainland, Kenai has been witness to some of the most significant events in Alaska's history. Originally the home of the Dena'ina Athabascan Indians, the area became a Russian fur trading post in 1791 and remained so for the next 80 years until Alaska was purchased by the U.S. government in 1869. Old Town Kenai, two blocks southeast of the Kenai Visitor Center, contains many artifacts from this period and includes a self-guided walking tour that explores the different cultural and economic influences that have shaped the lives of the Russian, Indian and American residents of the town over the past two-hundred years. In 1947, the Sterling Highway was completed, opening Kenai and the entire Peninsula up to the world and prompting the development of what has become one of the major industries in the area: tourism. Ten years after the Highway was built, oil was discovered at Swanson River northeast of town, opening up a new chapter in the town's history. Despite two centuries of dramatic social, economic and political change, the Kenai area remains an undeniably appealing place to visit. Set on the edge of Cook Inlet near the mouth of the Kenai River, the town is surrounded on all sides by untamed wilderness, from the muddy shores and frigid waters of the inlet to the pristine lakes, streams, hills and forests that make up the Kenai National Wildlife Refuge.

With panoramic views across Cook Inlet to three of Alaska's most active volcanoes, Mt. Redoubt, Mt. Spurr and Mt. Iliamna, few places can match Kenai's ability to put on a show, most recently a series of eruptions of Mt. Redoubt in 1990 and similar eruptions of Mt. Spurr in 1992. Visitors not fortunate enough to witness one of these events should plan on being in town for the annual Kenai River Festival, held in the Green Strip Park the second weekend in June. The festival celebrates the Kenai River and offers an appealing blend of arts and crafts, traditional dance and music and Alaskan food.

Information: Kenai Convention & Visitors Bureau, 11471 Kenai Spur Highway, 907-283-1991; www.visitkenai.com

WHAT TO SEE AND DO
ALAGNAK WILD RIVER

King Salmon, 907-246-3305; www.hikercentral.com/parks/alag
The Alagnak Wild River twists and turns across 67 miles of pristine wilderness in the Aleutian Range of southwestern Alaska. The braided river begins at Kukaklek Lake in the Katmai National Preserve and then flows west, widening along the Way, before spilling out into Bristol Bay. In 1980, the Alagnak was included in the national Wild and Scenic Rivers System. White-water rafters are drawn to the river's Class III rapids and ever-changing landscape, ranging from boreal forest to wet sedge tundra. The Alagnak's western stretch, shallow and marked by numerous sandbars, has become a favored destination for fly-fishing. The cool waters of the Alagnak teem with rainbow trout and all five species of Pacific salmon, including the prodigious king salmon, the largest of which can exceed 70 pounds. The Alagnak's designation as a Wild River helps protect the area's abundant wildlife, most notably a large population of brown bears that feed on the salmon. The Alagank Wild River is accessible only by boat or seaplane.

ALASKA

★
★
★
★
★

CLAM GULCH STATE RECREATION AREA

Kenai Spur Highway, Soldotna, 907-262-5581; www.dnr.state.ak.us
This area is famous for the thousands of razor clams harvested annually from the sandy beaches adjacent to the State Recreation Area. Visitors may dig clams during any low tide, although an Alaska sport fishing license is required. Clam Gulch is located on steep bluffs overlooking Cook Inlet, with sweeping views of the Aleutian Mountains and their three tallest peaks: Mount Iliamna, Mount Redoubt and Mount Spurr. The park offers camping and picnic areas.

HISTORIC OLD TOWN KENAI

Kenai Visitors & Cultural Center, 11471 Kenai Spur Highway, Kenai, 907-283-1991; www.visitkenai.com

In an effort to maintain a link with its rich cultural heritage, the city of Kenai has preserved some of its oldest, most historic buildings. Located within sight of the visitor center, the Old Town district consists of everything from grand churches to humble log cabins, each of which helps tell the story of the town's growth and development. Walking maps of the Historic Old Town district are available at the Visitors & Cultural Center on the Kenai Spur Highway. Mid-May-mid-September, Monday-Friday 9 a.m.-7 p.m., Saturday 10 a.m.-6 p.m., Sunday 11 a.m.-6 p.m.; mid-September-mid-May, Monday-Friday 9 a.m.-7 p.m.

KATMAI NATIONAL PARK AND PRESERVE

King Salmon, 907-246-3305; www.nps.gov/katm

Put simply, Katmai is bear country. Katmai National Park and Preserve has one of the world's highest concentrations of brown bears, with more than 2,000 of the giant furry mammals clambering within this remote wilderness along the Alaska Peninsula. The bears are drawn to the area's lakes and rivers, which teem with sockeye salmon. During the months of July and September, it's not uncommon to see dozens of bears gathered at Brooks Falls, feeding on salmon that have migrated up the Naknek River. While the salmon attract bears, the bears in turn attract tourists, thousands of whom make the trip to Katmai via air taxi or boat (no roads lead to the park) to witness North America's largest land predator in its natural habitat. A viewing platform at Brooks Camp provides a safe spot to photograph the brown bears, some of which weigh over 900 pounds.

Katmai is also famous for its 14 active volcanoes located in the park. In 1912, the largest volcanic eruption of the 20th century occurred here when the Novarupta Volcano blew its top, launching a plume of smoke and ash 20 miles skyward. The cataclysmic eruption was more powerful than Mount St. Helens's and created a 40-square-mile ash flow within the Valley of Ten Thousand Smokes, so named by botanist Robert Griggs during a 1916 expedition for *National Geographic*. Today, the area still resembles a lifeless moonscape, possessing a gray landscape devoid of grasses, trees and shrubs. Aside from wildlife viewing, popular activities at Katmai include hiking, sea kayaking and sport fishing.

LAKE CLARK NATIONAL PARK AND PRESERVE

Field Headquarters, 1 Park Place, Port Alsworth, 907-781-2218; www.nps.gov/lacl

Lake Clark National Park & Preserve encompasses 4 million acres of pristine wilderness, extending from Cook Inlet, across the craggy peaks of the Chigmit Mountains, farther west to the tundra-covered hills of Interior Alaska. Two active volcanoes can be found in the park: Mount Redoubt and Mount Iliamna. The park's namesake, Lake Clark, stretches for 40 miles. Teeming with red salmon, grayling, Dolly Varden and northern pike, Lake Clark offers tremendous fishing opportunities, as do the park's many other lakes and rivers—three of which have been designated National Wild and Scenic Rivers. Fishing season runs from May until October, although a few of the lakes may not fully thaw until June. Hiking is another popular activity, but it requires considerable backcountry experience and know-how. The park contains no trails, and even the most fit hikers will be challenged by streams and dense vegetation,

★
★ ★
★ ★
★

particularly near the coast. For those willing to take on the challenge, spectacular rewards await: awe-inspiring scenery, incomparable solitude and frequent wildlife sightings. Dall sheep, moose and black and brown bears live in the park, as do more than 125 species of birds. Beluga whales, harbor seals and sea lions can be seen in Chinitna Bay and Tuxedni Bay. No roads lead to the park, but floatplanes regularly shuttle visitors to the waters of Lake Clark from Anchorage, about 150 miles to the northeast.

SPECIAL EVENT
KENAI RIVER FESTIVAL
Soldotha Creek Park, Soldotha, 907-260-5449; www.kenaiwatershed.org
This community-wide event celebrates the Kenai River and seeks to raise awareness of the need to protect the river's watershed area. Take in the festival's parade (led by a 29-foot salmon), along with live local music, a 5K foot race, local foods and handicrafts by Alaskan artists, and a long list of free activities for children. Second weekend in June.

HOTEL
★★UPTOWN MOTEL
47 Spur View Drive, Kenai, 907-283-3660, 800-777-3650; www.uptownmotel.com
49 rooms. Restaurant. $

KETCHIKAN

Ketchikan is a town of about 8,500 people, but it hosts nearly 750,000 visitors during the summer. It's the first Alaskan stop for most cruise ships touring the Inside Passage and proudly declares itself to be Alaska's First City. Deep in the heart of the Tongass National Forest, the town has one of the highest rainfall totals in the state, with 162 inches of rain falling in an average year. It is also the closest community to Misty Fjords National Monument, a 2.3 million-acre wilderness of massive glaciers, deep saltwater fjords, pristine forests and abundant wildlife.

Closer to town, the protected waters of the Inside Passage attract massive runs of salmon each year (hence Ketchikan's claim to be the Salmon Capital of the World). The most famous section of the old-town area is Creek Street, a former red-light district that now houses an appealing blend of restaurants, art galleries and small shops built on pilings over Ketchikan Creek. It's a pedestrian-only zone and a great place to wander around, do a bit of shopping and grab a bite to eat. The Ketchikan area is also rich in native culture. Totem Bight State Park, eight miles north of town, contains a historic collection of totem poles set along a scenic trail. Saxman Totem Park, located two miles south of town, contains totem poles as well as workshops where visitors can watch native carvers create poles, canoes and other artwork using the same techniques employed by their ancestors. The Totem Heritage Center in town offers classes in traditional art forms and preserves totems from abandoned villages, and the Southeast Alaska Discovery Center in the middle of downtown has a wide range of exhibits, including a selection of contemporary poles, samples of native basketry and a model of a traditional fish camp.

Information: Ketchikan Visitors Bureau, 131 Front St., 907-225-6166, 800-770-3300; www.visit-ketchikan.com

★
★
★
★
★

WHAT TO SEE AND DO
SAXMAN NATIVE VILLAGE
South Tongass Highway, Ketchikan, 907-225-4846; www.capefoxtours.com
A short drive south of Ketchikan, the Village offers a window on the cultural and artistic heritage of the Tlingit tribe of southeast Alaska. It includes a park filled with 28 totems recovered from surrounding villages and restored by members of the Civilian Conservation Corps during the early part of the 20th century. Also onsite is the Beaver Clan House, a replica of a traditional winter house once used by the Tlingits. At the Saxman Carving Center, observe master totem carvers and their apprentices at work.

SOUTHEAST ALASKA DISCOVERY CENTER
50 Main St., Ketchikan, 907-228-6220; www.fs.fed.us
As one of four Public Lands Information Centers in Alaska, this center's mission is to provide information about the cultures, people, ecosystems and history of Alaska's southeast. Throughout the day, the onsite theater shows *Mystical Southeast Alaska,* a short multimedia presentation that provides a general introduction to the region. In the center's exhibit halls, life-size ecosystem displays, historic artifacts and scenic and wildlife photographs give visitors a more detailed view of the region's beauty and diversity. May-September, daily 8 a.m.-5 p.m.; October-April, Tuesday-Saturday 10 a.m.-4:30 p.m.

TOTEM BIGHT STATE HISTORICAL PARK
9883 N. Tongass Highway, Ketchikan, 907-247-8574; www.dnr.state.ak.us
In 1938, the U.S. Forest Service began salvaging and reconstructing magnificent examples of Tlingit, Haida and Tsimshian symbolic carvings. Decaying totem poles were copied in freshly cut cedar logs using traditional tools and techniques; even the paints used were made of natural materials like clam shells and salmon eggs. Today, this state park houses the largest collection of totem poles in the world.

HOTELS
★★GILMORE HOTEL
326 Front St., Ketchikan, 907-225-9423, 800-275-9423; www.gilmorehotel.com
42 rooms. Complimentary continental breakfast. Restaurant. High-speed Internet access. Business Center. $

★SUPER 8
2151 Sea Level Drive, Ketchikan, 907-225-9088, 800-800-8000; www.super8.com
82 rooms. Complimentary continental breakfast. High-speed Internet access. Pets accepted. $

★★WESTCOAST CAPE FOX LODGE
800 Venetia Way, Ketchikan, 907-225-8001; www.westcoasthotels.com
72 rooms. Restaurant, bar. $$

RESTAURANTS
★★ANNABELLE'S
326 Front St., Ketchikan, 907-225-6009; www.gilmorehotel.com
American, seafood menu. Lunch, dinner. Bar. Casual attire. $$

★★★HEEN KAHIDI

800 Venetia Way, Ketchikan, 907-225-8001, 866-225-8001; www.capefoxlodge.com

Heen Kahidi, which translates as "house by the river," is perched on the side of a bluff overlooking downtown Ketchikan and the waters of the Tongass Narrows. The dining area has the feel of an après ski lodge, with massive wooden roof beams, a river rock fireplace, subtle lighting and soft colors that enhance the stylish ambience of the place. Towering literally and figuratively above all of its competitors, this restaurant serves truly succulent seafood, chicken and pasta dishes prepared by chef Timothy Frank, the creative mastermind behind the restaurant's success. American, seafood menu. Breakfast, lunch, dinner. Bar. Casual attire. **$$**

★★THE NARROWS RESTAURANT

4871 N. Tongass Highway, Ketchikan, 907-247-2600; www.narrowsinn.com

Seafood menu. Breakfast, lunch, dinner. Bar. Children's menu. Casual attire. Reservations recommended. **$$**

★★NEW YORK CAFÉ

207 Stedman St., Ketchikan, 907-225-0246, 866-225-0246;
www.thenewyorkhotel.com

American menu. Breakfast, lunch, dinner. Bar. Children's menu. Casual attire. Reservations recommended. Outdoor seating. **$$**

★★SALMON FALLS RESTAURANT

16707 N. Tongass Highway, Ketchikan, 907-225-2752, 800-247-9059;
www.salmonfallsresort.com

Seafood menu. Breakfast, lunch, dinner. Closed winter. Bar. Casual attire. Outdoor seating. **$$**

KODIAK

Located on Chiniak Bay at the northeastern tip of Kodiak Island, the town of Kodiak is home to more than 770 commercial fishing vessels that ply the waters of the Gulf of Alaska and the Bering Sea in search of king crab, salmon, halibut, cod, shrimp and many other varieties of seafood. Although the Alutiit people have called the island their home for nearly 8,000 years, it wasn't until the arrival of Alexander Baranov in 1792 that a permanent settlement was established next to the sheltered natural harbor he christened St. Paul. In creating a fur trading outpost on the site, he also founded what was to become the first capital of Russian America. By 1804, just 12 years after the Russians' arrival, the sea otters had been hunted to near extinction, so Baranov moved the company's operations far to the west, where he founded a new settlement known today as Sitka.

★
★
★
★
★

With the demise of the fur trade and the 1867 purchase of Alaska by the United States, the local economy shifted to commercial salmon fishing, which has remained a mainstay ever since. Two-hundred years after the departure of Baranov and his workers, Kodiak still maintains ties to its Russian heritage, most notably in the Holy Resurrection Russian Orthodox Church, with its blue onion-dome spire and Russian cross; the Baranov Museum nearby, which was built by Baranov's men as an otter pelt warehouse; and in numerous street, place and business names throughout the town.

Kodiak today offers far more than just fresh Alaskan seafood, liquid sunshine and spectacular views. An estimated 3,000 Kodiak brown bears live on the island along with large numbers of deer, foxes, mountain goats, bald eagles and shore birds, and the waters near shore are home to orcas, humpback whales, sea otters and Stellar sea lions. Visitors need only walk the shores, hike the trails, drive the roads or paddle the rivers and bays to immerse themselves in the natural wonders that make Kodiak such an extraordinary destination in Alaska.

Information: Kodiak Island Convention & Visitors Bureau,
907-486-4782, 800-789-4782; www.kodiak.org

WHAT TO SEE AND DO

ANIAKCHAK NATIONAL MONUMENT AND PRESERVE

King Salmon, 907-246-3305; www.nps.gov/ania

The Aniakchak Caldera, a volcanic crater measuring almost six miles in diameter, is a spectacular sight and a truly awesome example of nature's power. Created over the last 3,400 years by a series of volcanic eruptions—the most recent occurring in May 1931—the caldera has explosion pits, lava flows and cinder cones. The largest cone, Vent Mountain, rises 1,400 feet above the caldera floor. The walls of the caldera vary in height, generally ranging between 2,000 and 4,400 feet. Surprise Lake glistens within the caldera and serves as the source of the Aniakchak River, which offers an unparalleled white-water rafting experience. The river cuts a 1,500-foot opening (known as the Gates) in the caldera wall, and then briskly flows east, winding around the mountains of the Aleutian Range, before spilling out into Aniakchak Bay and the Pacific Ocean. With its remote location along the Alaska Peninsula, the Aniakchak National Monument and Preserve can be accessed only via floatplane.

BARANOV MUSEUM

101 Marine Way, Kodiak, 907-486-5920; www.baranov.us

Housed in the oldest wooden building in Alaska, this historical museum was built by the Russian-American Company as an otter pelt warehouse during Kodiak's heyday as a Russian fur trading post. Now, its home to a collection of photographs, exhibits, artworks and artifacts tracing Kodiak's history from the time the Alutiit Indian culture thrived in the area through the Russian fur trading frenzy and into Alaska's territorial era and early statehood years. Summer, Monday-Saturday 10 a.m.-4 p.m., Sunday noon-4 p.m.; winter, Tuesday-Saturday 10 a.m.-3 p.m.; special openings on request.

FORT ABERCROMBIE STATE HISTORIC PARK

Kodiak District Office, 1400 Abercrombie Drive, Kodiak,
907-486-6339; www.dnr.state.ak.us

This scenic Oceanside park on 186 acres north of downtown Kodiak was the site of a defensive military installation during World War II and still contains visual reminders of its wartime function. Today the site plays a completely different role—that of scenic park, crisscrossed by a ribbon of trails passing through meadows, trout-filled lakes and seaside cliffs with excellent whale-watching vantage points. Only 3 1/2 miles from downtown and connected to it by a paved bike trail, the park is a popular spot for outdoor enthusiasts. Hiking and camping are available onsite, as is a visitor center run by the Alaska Department of Natural Resources.

KODIAK ISLAND

907-486-4782, 800-789-4782; www.kodiak.org

Unlike the frozen wilderness that's usually associated with Alaska, Kodiak Island is known as the state's Emerald Isle thanks its tree-lined fjords. Located off the southern coast of Alaska, it is one of the largest commercial fishing ports in the nation and is famous for its Kodiak brown bears. Outdoor activities include fishing, kayaking, hiking, biking and wildlife viewing.

KODIAK NATIONAL WILDLIFE REFUGE VISITOR CENTER

1390 Buskin River Road, Kodiak, 907-487-2600; www.kodiak.fws.gov

Located beside the Buskin River a half mile from Kodiak Airport, this visitor center explains the animals, plants and ecosystems that make up the 1.9-million-acres Kodiak National Wildlife Refuge. Encompassing two-thirds of Kodiak Island and a few neighboring islands, the refuge is a haven for red foxes, river otters, weasels, Sitka deer, mountain goats and 250 species of birds, including an estimated 600 pairs of bald eagles. The most famous inhabitants, though, are the approximately 3,000 Kodiak brown bears that roam the island. The largest of the brown bears, they average 10 feet tall and weigh as much as 1,600 pounds. The refuge is accessible only by boat or floatplane, so the visitor center also serves as an invaluable resource for travelers planning trips into the area. Memorial Day-Labor Day, Monday-Friday 8 a.m.-7 p.m., Saturday-Sunday noon-4 p.m.; rest of year, Monday-Friday 8 a.m.-4:30 p.m.

SPECIAL EVENTS

BEAR COUNTRY MUSIC FESTIVAL

State Fair and Rodeo Grounds, West Rezanof Drive, Kodiak,
907-486-4782; www.kodiak.org/bearcountry.html

An annual musical event featuring live performances of folk, country, bluegrass, soft rock and native Alaskan music by bands from all around the state. The festival draws thousands of visitors each year and features performances on three stages, one of which is indoors to hedge against Kodiak's unpredictable weather. Camping is available nearby, and shuttle service is provided between downtown and the festival site. Early August.

KODIAK STATE FAIR AND RODEO

★
★
★
★
☆

Kodiak State Fair & Rodeo Grounds, West Rezanof Drive, Kodiak,
907-486-6380; www.kodiakrodeoandstatefair.com

This local version of the larger state fair held in Palmer retains much of the old-fashioned, hometown charm of a traditional county fair. Rodeo events include calf roping, barrel racing and bull and bronco riding, while pony rides, a petting zoo, pie eating, seed spitting and bubble gum blowing competitions keep the kids entertained. Live local music and vendor booths selling everything from local artwork to kettle corn round out the fair's attractions. Labor Day weekend.

HOTELS

★★COMFORT INN KODIAK

1395 Airport Way, Kodiak, 907-487-2700, 800-424-6423; www.choicehotels.com

50 rooms. Restaurant, bar. Airport transportation available. Complimentary continental breakfast. Wireless Internet access. Pets accepted; fee. $

★★SHELIKOF LODGE

211 Thorsheim Ave., Kodiak, 907-486-4141; www.shelikoflodgealaska.com

38 rooms. Restaurant, bar. Airport transportation available. **$**

RESTAURANTS
★SHELIKOF LODGE RESTAURANT

211 Thorsheim Ave., Kodiak, 907-486-4141; www.shelikoflodgealaska.com

American, Italian menu. Breakfast, lunch, dinner. Bar. Children's menu. Casual attire. **$**

★★THE CHART ROOM

236 Rezanof Drive, Kodiak, 907-486-5712; www.kodiakinn.com

American menu. Breakfast, lunch, dinner. Bar. Children's menu. Casual attire. **$$$**

MOOSE PASS

This tiny hamlet of 200 people on the southern shores of Trail Lake in the middle of the Kenai Peninsula is renowned for its scenic beauty and its laid-back, rustic charm. Throughout the summer, floatplanes skim in over the mountains and land on the lake, dropping off hikers, hunters and fishermen. From mid-May-mid-September, the Alaska Railroad winds down the eastern side of the lake, stopping in Moose Pass each day on its journey to and from Seward, 29 miles to the south. In winter, when heavy snows close the rail line, the town remains accessible via the Seward Highway, which passes by the edge of town, connecting Anchorage with Seward. Located less than 20 miles from Cooper Landing and the spectacular fishing of the Kenai River, Moose Pass is a popular spot for travelers looking for beauty and tranquility in the heart of one of Alaska's most popular regions.

Information: www.moosepassalaska.com

SPECIAL EVENT
SUMMER SOLSTICE FESTIVAL

Main Street, Moose Pass, www.moosepass.net/solstice.html

Despite having a population of only 200 people, Moose Pass throws a lively festival to celebrate the summer solstice each year. Held on the weekend of or immediately preceding June 21, the two-day event features live music from local bands, arts and crafts booths, a community barbecue and a huge bake sale by local residents. Sponsored by the local Sportsmans Club, the festival proceeds are used to support community projects and organizations.

HOTEL
★★TRAIL LAKE LODGE

Seward Highway, Moose Pass, 907-288-3101, 888-395-3624; www.traillakelodge.com

35 rooms. Restaurant, bar. **$**

RESTAURANT
★★TRAIL LAKE LODGE RESTAURANT

Seward Highway, Moose Pass, 907-288-3101, 888-395-3624; www.traillakelodge.com

Breakfast, lunch, dinner. Closed October; Tuesday-Thursday in November-April. Bar. Children's menu. Casual attire. **$$**

PALMER

Tucked into a fertile valley between the rugged Talkeetna Range to the north and the towering Chugach Range to the south, Palmer was originally established as a trading post on the Matanuska River by George Palmer around 1890. It remained a sleepy little town until 1935 when it was chosen as the site of a New Deal agricultural experiment called the Matanuska Valley Colony. Two-hundred farm families from the American Midwest arrived in the area that year and were given 40-acre tracts of land in the hopes of establishing a permanent agricultural colony that would help in the development of Alaska. Although the colony ultimately proved unsuccessful, descendents of the original colonists continue to live in the area and many of the original buildings are listed on the National Register of Historic Places. Today, Palmer is home to the Alaska State Fair, a 12-day event that begins in late August and runs through Labor Day. The Palmer area also offers a broad array of activities year-round, ranging from fishing, hiking and berry picking during the summer to ice-fishing, cross-country skiing and dogsled racing during the winter.

Information: Greater Palmer Chamber of Commerce, 723 S. Valley Way,
907-745-2880; www.palmerchamber.org

WHAT TO SEE AND DO
MUSK OX FARM
Glenn Highway, Palmer, 907-745-4151; www.muskoxfarm.org

For more than four decades, this one-of-a-kind nonprofit farm has been raising domesticated musk oxen in the Matanuska Valley. Visitors to the farm can tour the grounds and learn about the history of these shaggy holdovers from the last ice age. The farm is more than just a tourist attraction, it's an important player in a thriving cottage industry. Each spring, the musk oxens' soft underwool, called qiviut, is combed out and shipped to native communities in Alaska's far north, where it's fashioned into traditional wool garments which are then sold in stores throughout the state. Guided tours are given every half hour until 5:30 p.m. Mother's Day-late September, daily 10 a.m.-6 p.m.

SPECIAL EVENT
ALASKA STATE FAIR
Alaska State Showgrounds, 2075 Glenn Highway, Palmer,
907-745-4827, 800-850-3247; www.alaskastatefair.org

One of the highlights of Alaska's summer season, this fair includes 12 days of live entertainment, carnival rides, rodeo events and exhibitors displaying everything from handcrafted jewelry and local artwork to homemade quilts, cakes, pies, jams and jellies. One of the most popular events is the agricultural weigh-off, where locally grown cabbages frequently top 100 pounds, and carrots have tipped the scales at more than 70 pounds. Located less than 45 miles from downtown Anchorage, the fair makes for an easy day trip for visitors to the Anchorage area. Late August-early September.

PETERSBURG

Petersburg is both geographically and culturally far removed from the rest of the towns and villages that dot the Inside Passage. In a region with centuries-old ties to Russian and native cultures, this remote fishing port at the northern tip of Mitkof Island proudly celebrates its rich Norwegian heritage. Founded at the end of the

19th century by businessman Peter Buschmann, Petersburg soon attracted other Norwegian immigrants who felt at home amid the snowy mountains and deep fjords of the area. Set in the heart of the Tongass National Forest, Mitkof Island features a landscape dominated not by shady forests and craggy peaks but by muskeg bogs, dense brush and rolling hills. The best time to visit is around May 17, when the town holds its annual Little Norway Festival to coincide with Norway's Constitution Day. Visitors can enjoy traditional Norwegian music, dancing and food, view the works of local artists and even get their pictures taken with real Vikings and Valkyries.

Information: Visitor Information Center, Petersburg,
907-772-4636; www.petersburg.org

WHAT TO SEE AND DO
CLAUSEN MEMORIAL MUSEUM

203 Fram St., Petersburg, 907-772-3598;www.clausenmuseum.net

This small city-run museum in the center of town focuses on the historical development of Petersburg and Mitkof Island, on which the town is located. Exhibits and artifacts relating to Tlingit culture introduce visitors to the earliest society that lived in the region while fishing gear and nautical memorabilia bring to life the history of the Norwegian fishermen who settled in the region during the latter part of the 19th century. Logging tools and artifacts also are on display, providing insight into another industry that helped fuel Petersburg's economy during the 20th century. May-mid-September, Monday-Saturday 10:30 a.m.-4:30 p.m.; winter hours vary.

PETROGLYPH BEACH STATE HISTORIC PARK

Wrangell, 907-874-2381; www.wrangell.com

Petroglyphs (or rock carvings) were artistic works by Native Americans, and Petroglyph Beach offers some of the best examples that still survive today.

SPECIAL EVENT
LITTLE NORWAY FESTIVAL

Petersburg, 907-772-3646; www.petersburg.org

All of Petersburg turns out to celebrate Norwegian Constitution Day—an event filled with live performances of Norwegian music, songs and dances, a Scandinavian pageant, downtown arts and crafts booths and the annual Fish-O-Rama Seafood Feast. The festival's colorful parade is a highlight of the weekend, with the Viking ship *Valhalla*-sailing through downtown to the sound of traditional Norwegian songs. Third full weekend in May.

HOTELS
★★SCANDIA HOUSE

110 N. Nordic Drive, Petersburg, 907-772-4281, 800-722-5006;
www.scandiahousehotel.com

33 rooms. Complimentary continental breakfast. Restaurant. Airport transportation available. $

★TIDES INN

307 N. First St., Petersburg, 907-772-4288, 800-665-8433; www.tidesinnalaska.com

47 rooms. Complimentary continental breakfast. Airport transportation available. $

SEWARD

This town of 3,000 people on the shores of Resurrection Bay is named after William H. Seward, the U.S. Secretary of State who was responsible for negotiating the purchase of Alaska from Russia in 1867. The town sits on the eastern side of the Kenai Peninsula, 127 miles from Anchorage via the Seward Highway. Founded in 1903 as an ocean terminus for the Alaska Railroad, the town's economy originally relied almost exclusively on the fishing and railroad industries. With the opening of the Seward and Sterling Highways on the Kenai Peninsula after World War II, Seward's economy gradually shifted, making tourism and fishing the leading industries. Throughout the summer, the town vibrates with life as thousands of visitors arrive each day by road, sea and rail. From the bustling small boat harbor, visitors can join halibut and salmon fishing charters, take tour boats to view the abundant wildlife and magnificent tidewater glaciers of Kenai Fjords National Park, or rent kayaks and paddle the shores of Resurrection Bay. After a day on the water, visitors leaving the harbor can either head directly downtown via Fourth Avenue or opt to walk part of the Iditarod National Historic Trail that parallels the shoreline all the way to one of Seward's newest and most impressive attractions, the Alaska SeaLife Center. Opened in 1998, it's a combination marine research station, wildlife rehabilitation center and hands-on interpretive venue. The highlight of the summer is the town's Fourth of July celebration, the largest in Alaska. A multiday event, it's capped off by the Mount Marathon run, a grueling three miles out-and-back course in which runners race through downtown, claw their way to the top of 3,022-foot-high Mount Marathon and then turn around and come pounding back down the hillside, ending up in the center of town to the cheers of thousands of spectators lining the streets.

Information: Chamber of Commerce, 907-224-8051; www.sewardak.org

WHAT TO SEE AND DO

ALASKA SEALIFE CENTER

301 Railway Ave., Seward, 907-224-6300, 800-224-2525; www.alaskasealife.org
The Alaska SeaLife Center offers an unrivaled up-close experience with Gulf of Alaska marine wildlife. Witness 1,500-pound Stellar sea lions gliding past underwater viewing windows, puffins diving in a carefully crafted naturalistic habitat and harbor seals hauled out on rocky beaches. Alaskan king crab, sea stars and Pacific octopus also await you, as well as a variety of intertidal creatures and deep-sea fish. Daily 10 a.m.-5 p.m.

EXIT GLACIER

Glacier Road (Herman Leirer Road), Seward, 907-224-7500, www.nps.gov/kefj
Originating in the massive Harding Icefield that dominates the landscape on the eastern side of the Kenai Peninsula, Exit Glacier flows for three miles before coming to an end in a scenic river valley just north of Seward. Visitors can walk from the nature center to the foot of the glacier via the Outwash Plain Trail or branch off onto the relatively easy Overlook Loop Trail, which arrives at a small plateau very close to the jagged blue glacier ice. Park Service rangers lead one-hour interpretive tours from the Nature Center to the glacier along these trails twice a day during the summer, at 11 a.m. and 3 p.m. Nature Center: summer, daily 9 a.m.-7:30 p.m.

ALASKA

★
★★
★★
★★
★

HOTELS

★HARBORVIEW INN

804 Third Ave., Seward, 907-224-3217, 888-224-3217; www.sewardhotel.com
37 rooms. $

★HOTEL SEWARD

221 Fifth Ave., Seward, 99664, 907-224-8001, 800-655-8785;
www.hotelsewardalaska.com
38 rooms. $$

★MARINA MOTEL

Seward Highway, Seward, 907-224-5518; www.sewardmotel.com
18 rooms. $

★THE VAN GILDER HOTEL

308 Adams St., Seward, 907-224-3079, 800-204-6835; www.vangilderhotel.com
24 rooms. $

RESTAURANTS

★★BREEZE INN RESTAURANT

1306 Seward Highway, Seward, 907-224-5238, 888-224-5237;
www.breezeinn.com
American menu. Breakfast, lunch, dinner. Bar. Children's menu. Casual attire. $$

★CHRISTO'S PALACE

133 Fourth Ave., Seward, 907-224-5255; www.christospalace.com
American menu. Lunch, dinner. Bar. Children's menu. Casual attire. $$

SITKA

One of the oldest Western settlements in Alaska, Sitka was established at the beginning of the 19th century as a fur trading outpost and fort by the Russian American Company under the leadership of Alexander Baranov. Originally called New Archangel, it served as the capital of Russian Alaska until 1867, when a waning fur trade and domestic economic upheaval led the Russian government to sell its stake in the New World. The transfer of ownership of Alaska from Russia to the United States took place on Castle Hill, and a series of plaques on the site now provide visitors with a detailed account of that event. Modern Sitka retains strong ties to its past as evidenced by the Russian architecture of Saint Michael's Cathedral in the middle of downtown (a replica of the original that burned to the ground in 1966), the restored Russian Bishops house across from Crescent harbor and Russian Cemetery at the end of Observatory Street. Evidence of the older, Tlingit civilization can be found on the east end of town at the Sheldon Jackson Museum, which contains a stunning display of native arts and crafts. Further down the road is Sitka National Historic Park, which features a collection of 15 totem poles set along a meandering forest trail. The park's visitor center houses an extensive native history museum, a collection of delicate wood carvings that could not survive outdoors in Sitka's rainy climate and a woodworking shop where native Alaskan crafts are fashioned and art classes are taught.
Information: Sitka Convention and Visitors Bureau, 907-747-5940; www.sitka.org

★
★★★
★★
★

WHAT TO SEE AND DO
OLD SITKA STATE HISTORICAL SITE
Halibut Point Road, Sitka, www.dnr.state.ak.us

Seven miles north of downtown, Old Sitka is where the original 1799 Russian-American Company settlement was located. After the Russian fort was destroyed during fighting with the local Tlingit tribe in 1803, the Russians responded by attacking and capturing the nearby Tlingit settlement of Shee Atika. The Russians then built another settlement on the site, naming it New Archangel. When the United States purchased Alaska from the Russians in 1867, the town's name was changed to Sitka, a European version of the area's Tlingit name. The Old Sitka site contains numerous outdoor displays that tell the history of the native and Russian settlements that once thrived in the area. Visitors with time to spare can walk the site's trail network, which includes the Forest and Muskegs Trail, the Estuary Life Trail and the slightly longer Mosquito Cove Loop Trail. Overnight visitors can stay at Starrigavan Campground, a U.S. Forest Service facility on the northern edge of the historic site.

SHELDON JACKSON MUSEUM
104 College Drive, Sitka, 907-747-8981; www.museums.state.ak.us

A small, oddly shaped museum on the Sheldon Jackson College campus near downtown Sitka, it houses what is generally regarded as one of the best collections of native arts and crafts in the state. It is also Alaska's oldest museum, founded in 1887 by Reverend Sheldon Jackson, who sought to create a museum in Alaska that would preserve and exhibit the cultural and artistic history of Native Alaskan cultures. Highlights of the collection include Eskimo masks, Tlingit and Haida headdresses and a full-sized Aleut baidarka, a specialized form of sea kayak. Mid-May-mid-September, daily 9 a.m.-5 p.m.; mid-September-mid-May, Tuesday-Saturday 10 a.m.-4 p.m.

SITKA NATIONAL HISTORICAL PARK
103 Monastery St., Sitka, 907-747-0110; www.nps.gov/sitk

Sitka National Historical Park is one of Alaska's smallest but most popular national parks, with nearly 300,000 visitors making the trip every year. Located in a temperate rainforest at the mouth of the Indian River on Baranof Island, the park marks the site of the 1804 Battle of Sitka, a fight that pitted the native Tlingit Indians against the Russians. Another popular attraction is the Russian Bishop's House, constructed in 1843 when the Tsar ruled Alaska. The log structure survives as one of four remaining examples of Russian-period architecture in North America. The park also features a remarkable collection of original and replica totem poles from villages throughout southeastern Alaska. The park's visitor center offers talks, exhibits and slide programs. Alaska's oldest federally designated park, Sitka National Historical Park is a short drive from downtown Sitka. The Alaska Marine Highway serves Sitka, and the town is a 10-hour ferry ride from Juneau to the north.

ST. MICHAEL'S CATHEDRAL
240 Lincoln St., Sitka, 907-747-8120; www.sitka.org

A local landmark since its construction in 1848, this beautiful Russian Orthodox cathedral is actually a replica of the original, which burned in 1966. Featuring classic Russian Orthodox architectural elements like a large onion dome and three-bar crosses, the cathedral houses an exquisite collection of historic icons and religious artifacts dating back to the days when Russian culture dominated the region. Because

49

ALASKA

★
★
★
★
★

the cathedral is still in use, visitors are permitted to wander around inside only during posted hours, when religious services are not being conducted. Hours vary depending on cruise ship schedules and time of year and are posted on the cathedral door.

TONGASS NATIONAL FOREST

204 Siginaka Way, Sitka, 907-747-6671; www.fs.fed.us/r10/tongass

Tongass National Forest, the largest national forest in the United States, is the very definition of "wilderness." In fact, one-third of the Tongass (5.7 million acres) is managed as wilderness so that Alaska retains its undeveloped character. Expect to see eagles, bears, deer and a variety of other animals, birds and fish in this vast national forest.

SPECIAL EVENT
SITKA SUMMER MUSIC FESTIVAL

Harrigan Centennial Hall, Sitka, 907-277-4852; www.sitkamusicfestival.org

Although many towns in Alaska host summer music festivals, Sitka is the only place that features classical music. First held in 1972 as an informal reunion event for musicians from around the world, the festival begins on the first Friday in June and ends on the last Friday of the month, with concerts held on Tuesday and Friday evenings and one Saturday evening. Special fundraising events are also part of the festivities, with a pair of concerts aboard a tour boat drawing some of the biggest crowds.

HOTELS
★★SITKA HOTEL

118 Lincoln St., Sitka, 907-747-3288; www.sitkahotel.com

63 rooms. Restaurant. Wireless Internet access. $

★★WESTMARK SITKA

330 Seward St., Sitka, 907-747-6241, 800-544-0970; www.westmarkhotels.com

101 rooms. Restaurant, bar. High-speed Internet access. $$

RESTAURANTS
★BAYVIEW RESTAURANT

407 Lincoln St., Sitka, 907-747-5440

American menu. Breakfast, lunch, dinner. Children's menu. Casual attire. $$

★★RAVEN DINING ROOM & KADATAAN LOUNGE

330 Seward St., Sitka, 907-747-6241; www.westmarkhotels.com

Seafood menu. Breakfast, lunch, dinner. Bar. Casual attire. $$$

SKAGWAY

Skagway is located at the northernmost point of the Inside Passage near the Canadian border and derives its name from the Tlingit word skaqua, meaning "windy place." It was a hunting and fishing camp for local Indian tribes for centuries until the discovery of gold 600 miles north at Bonanza Creek in 1896. By 1898, the town had grown to nearly 10,000 people and had become an important staging area for gold prospectors preparing to make the arduous trek through White Pass north of town to seek their fortunes in the Klondike. The nearby settlement of Dyea offered a different route, through Chilkoot Pass, but both routes merged at Bennett Lake just inside the Canadian border and formed a single route, now referred to as the Trail of 98. Skagway's fortunes declined with the end of the gold rush, but its downtown area still retains its late 1890s charm, with wooden sidewalks, false-fronted wooden buildings and the restored turn-of-the-century White Pass & Yukon Railroad passenger depot and steam engine. Much of downtown Skagway is now part of Klondike Gold Rush National Historic Park and well-prepared adventurers can once again hike the 33-miles Chilkoot Trail, beginning at the long-abandoned Dyea town site.

Information: Skagway Convention & Visitors Bureau, 907-983-2854, 888-762-1898; www.skagway.com

WHAT TO SEE AND DO
ARCTIC BROTHERHOOD HALL
Broadway Street, Skagway, 907-983-2854, 888-762-1898; www.skagway.org
Easily the most recognizable structure in Skagway, if not all of Alaska, this two-story wooden building dating to 1899 features an exterior covered with more than 10,000 pieces of driftwood. Built by the Fraternal Order of the Arctic Brotherhood, the building served as a social, cultural and charitable center for its members during Skagway's heyday as a boomtown. In its current incarnation, it is home to the Skagway Visitor Center and an excellent place to begin a sightseeing tour of the area. Mid-May-mid-September, Sunday-Friday 8 a.m.-6 p.m., Saturday 9 a.m.-6 p.m.; mid-September-mid-May, call for hours.

KLONDIKE GOLD RUSH NATIONAL HISTORICAL PARK
Second Avenue and Broadway Street, Skagway, 907-983-2921; www.nps.gov/klgo
Today, the 33-mile-long Chilkoot Trail is administered by the park, and it makes for a challenging but rewarding three- to five-day hike. Most stampeders abandoned Skagway, along with dreams of instant riches, in 1898. The town now has a year-round population of only 800, although the historical park receives around 750,000 annual visits. Nestled within the Taiya Inlet and surrounded by snow-capped mountains, the park offers guided tours of the Skagway Historic District. Many visitors arrive in Skagway by boat, as the town is served by the Alaska Marine Highway.

WHITE PASS AND YUKON ROUTE OF THE SCENIC
RAILWAY OF THE WORLD
White Pass & Yukon Route Depot, Second Avenue and Spring Street, Skagway, 907-983-2217, 800-343-7373; www.whitepassrailroad.com
Built in only 20 months during the Klondike Gold Rush, the White Pass & Yukon Route connecting Skagway with Whitehorse, Yukon Territory remains one of the most spectacular railways in the world. (It's been designated an International Historic Civil Engineering Landmark.) Modern travelers on this rail line can choose from four different excursions. The White Pass Summit Excursion is a three-hour, 40-mile round-trip that climbs 2,865 feet from Skagway to the summit at White Pass. Covering many of the railway's most scenic sections, this tour is the least expensive from Skagway and the most popular. The Lake Bennett Excursion takes 8.5 hours and travels an additional 20 miles on the line to Canada's Lake Bennett, where the Chilkoot Trail comes to an end. The railway also offers a Chilkoot Trail Hikers Service for those interested in hiking up the 33-mile historic Chilkoot Trail and then hopping aboard the train as it heads back to Skagway. Another option is the combination bus and train

ALASKA

★
★
★
★
★

service which transports travelers from Skagway to Whitehorse. Prices and departure times vary, and reservations are required for all excursions.

HOTEL
★SGT. PRESTON'S LODGE
370 Sixth Ave., Skagway, 907-983-2521, 866-983-2521;
www.sgtprestons.eskagway.com
30 rooms. **$**

RESTAURANT
★HAVEN CAFÉ
Ninth Avenue and State Street, Skagway, 907-983-3553; www.haven-cafe.com
Deli menu. Breakfast, lunch, dinner. Closed holidays. Casual attire. Outdoor seating. **$**

SOLDOTNA

Soldotna exists thanks to the confluence of two events in 1947: the granting of home-steading rights on the Kenai Peninsula to veterans of World War II; and the selection of Soldotna as the site for a highway bridge across the Kenai River. When the Sterling Highway was completed soon after, Soldotna was suddenly connected to the Alaskan road system and rapidly became a major stopping point for travelers and outdoor enthusiasts on the Kenai Peninsula. Today, Soldotna's enormous popularity stems from its greatest natural asset, the Kenai River, from whose waters the world record king salmon, weighing in at 97.2 pounds, was pulled in 1985. Other highlights of Soldotna are its two campgrounds, nine parks and network of trails and walks that provide visitors with plenty of opportunities to enjoy the natural beauty of the area. During summer, it's possible to go hiking, canoeing, biking, wildlife viewing and berry picking without straying far from town. In winter, snow machining and cross-country skiing keep locals and off-season visitors active.

Information: 44790 Sterling Highway, 907-262-9814; www.soldotnachamber.com

WHAT TO SEE AND DO
KENAI NATIONAL WILDLIFE REFUGE
Refuge Visitor Center, 2139 Ski Hill Road, Soldotna, 907-262-7021; www.kenai.fws.gov
Originally created as the 1.7-million-acre Kenai National Moose Range in 1941, this refuge now totals nearly 2 million acres, covering much of the western half of the Kenai Peninsula. Containing every type of Alaskan habitat and supporting an enormous amount of wildlife including moose, bears, caribou, eagles and lynxes, the refuge is visited by more than half a million travelers each year, many of whom come to try their luck fishing in the nine rivers that run through it. The Refuge's visitor center in Soldotna is open year-round and contains exhibits about local wildlife, information about recreational activities available in the area and a range of displays explaining the geological and ecological makeup of the refuge. Summer, Monday-Friday 8 a.m.-4:30 p.m., Saturday-Sunday 9 a.m.-6 p.m.; winter, Monday-Friday 8 a.m.-4:30 p.m.; Saturday-Sunday 10 a.m.-5 p.m.

HOTELS
★ASPEN HOTEL SOLDOTNA
326 Binkley Circle, Soldotna, 907-260-7736, 888-308-7848; www.aspenhotelsak.com
63 rooms. Complimentary continental breakfast. Pool. **$**

★★BEST WESTERN KING SALMON MOTEL

35546A Kenai Spur Highway, Soldotna, 907-262-5857, 800-780-7234;
www.bestwestern.com
49 rooms. Restaurant. Fitness center. High-speed Internet access. **$$**

★KENAI RIVER LODGE

393 Riverside Drive, Soldotna, 907-262-4292, 800-977-4292;
www.kenairiverlodge.com
25 rooms. Complimentary continental breakfast. **$**

★★SOLDOTNA INN

35041 Kenai Spur Highway, Soldotna, 907-262-9169, 866-262-9169;
www.thesoldotnainn.com
28 rooms. Complimentary continental breakfast. Restaurant. Pool. Wireless Internet access. Pets accepted. **$**

RESTAURANT
★★MYKEL'S RESTAURANT & LOUNGE

35041 Kenai Spur Highway, Soldotna, 907-262-4305; www.mykels.com
American menu. Lunch, dinner. Bar. Children's menu. Casual attire. **$$$**

TALKEETNA

Located about a 2 1/2 hours north of Anchorage, this community of less than 800 people centers around a picturesque downtown that's been designated a National Historic Site. Talkeetna is the embarkation point for most treks into Denali National Park, and superb fishing abounds in the area.

Information: Talkeetna/Denali Visitor Center, 907-733-2499, 800-660-2688;
www.talkeetnadenali.com

RESTAURANT
★★★FORAKER RESTAURANT

Talkeetna Spur Road, Talkeetna, 907-733-9500, 877-777-4067;
www.talkeetnalodge.com
Earthy elegance characterizes this upscale spot named after 17,400-foot Mount Foraker, visible in the distance beside Mount McKinley. With an award-winning wine selection, fresh Alaskan seafood and panoramic views of the Alaska Range, Foraker offers fine dining in the heart of the wilderness. As part of the Native-owned Talkeetna Alaskan Lodge, the restaurant features original Native Alaskan artwork in the dining area. American menu. Dinner. Closed September-April. Bar. Casual attire. Reservations recommended. Outdoor seating. **$$$**

VALDEZ

Valdez was founded in the spring of 1898 by a group of hucksters who printed advertisements touting the speedy, established All-American Route from Prince William Sound to the Klondike gold fields. Upon arriving, thousands of prospectors discovered that said route was little more than a rough-hewn trail up and over a glacier. Despite its ignominious beginnings, Valdez is today the Gateway to the Interior, providing a vital link between the interior and the rest of the world. As North America's northernmost ice-free port, it also serves as the terminus for the Alaska Pipeline. With an average of 325 inches of snow per year, the town boasts some of the best snowcat, helicopter and extreme skiing in the world, as well as world-class ice climbing in nearby Keystone Canyon. In recent years, an extensive network of hiking trails has been developed to provide better access to the wild beauty of the area.

Information: Valdez Convention and Visitors Bureau, 200 Chenega St.,
907-835-2984; www.valdezalaska.org

WHAT TO SEE AND DO
HISTORIC AND SCENIC HIKING TRAILS
Valdez, 907-835-4636; www.valdezalaska.org/maps/maps.html
With mountains and rugged wilderness surrounding it on all sides, Valdez is graced with some of the best hiking trails in Alaska, some of which follow historic gold prospector routes through the mountains. Of the seven main trails in or near town, the easiest is the Dock Point Trail, a scenic 3/4-mile round-trip beginning at the east end of the dock harbor and looping around a narrow peninsula jutting out into Valdez Bay. Hikers looking for more of a challenge can try the historic lower section of the Keystone Canyon Pack Trail, running for 2.6 miles from the Old Richardson Highway Loop to Bridal Veil Falls. Rated easy to moderate, this 1899 trail was abandoned for nearly a century before being hand cleared and reopened to foot traffic in the late 1990s. This trail provides excellent views of the canyon and the waterfalls, river and forests. Another easy to moderate hike nearby is the Goat Trail and Wagon Road, which replaced the northern part of the Keystone Canyon Pack Trail. This 4.8-mile hike takes travelers from Bridal Veil Falls north to mile 18 on the Richardson Highway and offers spectacular views of Snowslide Gulch, Bear Creek and the Lowe River. Other trails in the Valdez area are equally scenic, though not as historic. One runs up Mineral Creek, another along Shoup Bay and a third through Solomon Gulch. The **Valdez Convention & Visitors Bureau** *(200 Fairbanks St.)* offers free maps and detailed information about each of the trails in the area.

VALDEZ MUSEUM AND ANNEX
217 Egan Drive, Valdez, 907-835-2764; www.valdezmuseum.org
This museum is full of exhibits that tell the story of Valdez and the Prince William Sound area, starting with the area's origins as a trailhead supply depot during the Klondike Gold Rush of 1897-1898. Other exhibits focus on the 1989 *Exxon Valdez* oil spill that occurred in Prince William Sound and detail both the massive cleanup effort that was made and the steps that have been taken locally and nationally to learn from the accident. Museum: summer, Monday-Saturday 9 a.m.-6 p.m., Sunday 8 a.m.-5 p.m.; winter, Monday-Friday 1-5 p.m., Saturday noon-4 p.m. Annex: summer, Daily 9 a.m.-4 p.m.

SPECIAL EVENTS
GOLD RUSH DAYS
Valdez, 907-835-2987; www.valdezalaska.org
Held for five days at the start of August, Valdez's Gold Rush Days festival celebrates the town's rich Gold Rush history. Highlights include the coronation of the king and queen of Gold Rush Days, a fashion show put on by local residents, roaming costumed can-can dancers and a free community halibut and salmon fish fry held outdoors in one of the town's parks.

LAST FRONTIER THEATER CONFERENCE

Prince William Sound Community College, Valdez, 907-834-1614;
www.pwscc.edu/conference

Co-hosted each year by Prince William Sound Community College and Edward Albee, (the Pulitzer Prize-winning playwright best known for his work *Who's Afraid of Virginia Woolf*), this lively, highly social event begins in mid-June and runs for nine days. During this time, panel discussions and small-group seminars feature well-known actors, directors and playwrights talking about their craft and giving advice to conference attendees, some of whose plays are later read and critiqued. Evenings feature live performances of works with professional and amateur actors filling the roles. Past invitees have included playwrights Arthur Miller, Tony Kushner and Terrence McNally and actors Angela Bassett, Laura Linney and Chris Noth. Individual and multi-event tickets are available. Mid-June.

HOTELS

★★BEST WESTERN VALDEZ HARBOR INN

100 Harbor Drive, Valdez, 907-835-3434; www.valdezharborinn.com
88 rooms. Restaurant. Wireless Internet access. Fitness center. $

★L & L'S BED & BREAKFAST

533 W. Hanagita St., Valdez, 907-835-4447; www.lnlalaska.com
Five rooms. Complimentary continental breakfast. $

★★TOTEM INN HOTEL

144 E. Egan Drive, Valdez, 907-835-4443, 888-808-4431; www.toteminn.com
70 rooms. Restaurant. $

SPECIALTY LODGING

BROOKSIDE INN BED & BREAKFAST

1465 Richardson Highway, Valdez, 907-835-9130, 866-316-9130;
www.brooksideinnbb.com
Six rooms. Wireless Internet access. $

RESTAURANTS

★★ALASKAN BISTRO

100 Harbor Drive, Valdez, 907-835-3434; www.valdezharborinn.com
Mediterranean menu. Breakfast, lunch, dinner. Bar. Casual attire. $$

★★TOTEM INN RESTAURANT

144 E. Egan Drive, Valdez, 907-835-4443; www.toteminn.com
American menu. Breakfast, lunch, dinner. Bar. Children's menu. Casual attire. $$

WASILLA

Like many small towns in Alaska, Wasilla owes its existence to the Alaska Railroad. In 1917, the rail line between Anchorage and Fairbanks reached Wasilla. Practically overnight, the tiny community that had been little more than a wayside stop on the Carle Wagon Road became a vital, commercial and industrial center for the surrounding area. With the completion of the Parks Highway from Anchorage to Fairbanks in 1971, the area once again began an era of rapid growth as it suddenly became possible to live amid the scenic beauty and tranquility of the Wasilla area and work in Anchorage, 43 miles away.

These days, visitors can learn more about the characters, events and decisions that shaped the region at the Dorothy Page Museum and Historical Town Site, located in downtown Wasilla. Other noteworthy local attractions are the Iditarod Trail Sled Dog Race Headquarters and the Knik Museum and Dog Mushers' Hall of Fame, both of which spotlight the history and evolution of dog sledding through interpretive exhibits and historical artifacts.

Information: Greater Wasilla Chamber of Commerce, 415 E. Railroad Ave., 907-376-1299; www.wasillachamber.org

WHAT TO SEE AND DO
IDITAROD TRAIL SLED DOG RACE HEADQUARTERS
Knik Goose Bay Road, Wasilla, 907-376-5155; www.iditarod.com
This rustic log cabin headquarters and visitor center just south of the Parks Highway contains displays and historical artifacts relating to the Iditarod dogsled race. Visitors can view videos of past races, wander through the museum and take dogsled rides during summer months. Unlike many attractions in Alaska, the headquarters stays open all year and is most crowded in the weeks leading up to the race, which officially starts in Wasilla the day after its ceremonial—and much publicized—start in Anchorage. Hours change during the weeks surrounding the Iditarod Trail Sled Dog race, so call for details. Mid-May-mid-September, daily 8 a.m.-7 p.m.; mid-September-mid-May, Monday-Friday 8 a.m.-5 p.m.

SPECIAL EVENT
TESORO IRON DOG 2000 SNOWMOBILE RACE
Tesoro Iron Dog Headquarters, 7100 Old Seward Highway, Anchorage, 907-563-4414; www.irondog.org
The 2,000-mile race pits teams of two racers on separate snowmobiles against some of the harshest, most isolated terrain in Alaska. With temperatures dipping to 40 below, speeds as high as 93 mph and limited daylight for much of the journey, the race runs in segments over the course of a week and usually goes from Fairbanks west to Nome and then southeast to Wasilla, reversing direction in alternating years. Highlights of the competition include a 500-mile full-throttle dash down the frozen Yukon River, a pressure-ridge and snowdrift-plagued traverse across the ice pack on Norton Sound, and a forested climb through deep snow up and over the Alaska Range. Of the 25 teams that started out in 2004, only 12 finished the race, with the first team crossing the line in a cumulative time of 39 hours, three minutes. Mid-February.

HOTELS
★ALASKAN VIEW MOTEL
2650 E. Parks Highway, Wasilla, 907-376-6787; www.alaskanviewmotel.com
24 rooms. $

★★BEST WESTERN LAKE LUCILLE INN

1300 W. Lake Lucille Drive, Wasilla, 907-373-1776, 800-780-7234;
www.bestwestern.com/lakelucilleinn
54 rooms. Complimentary continental breakfast. Restaurant, bar. Whirlpool. Fitness
center. High-speed Internet access. Pets accepted. **$**

★★GRAND VIEW INN & SUITES

2900 Parks Highway, Wasilla, 907-357-7666, 866-710-7666; www.grandviewak.com
79 rooms. Complimentary continental breakfast. Restaurant. Pool. Fitness center. **$**

RESTAURANT
★★SHORELINE RESTAURANT

1300 W. Lake Lucille Drive, Wasilla, 907-373-1776;
www.bestwestern.com/lakelucilleinn
American menu. Lunch, dinner. Bar. Children's menu. Casual attire. Outdoor seating. **$$**

57

ALASKA

★
★
★
★
★

IDAHO

WHEN THE IDAHO TERRITORY WAS CREATED IT INCLUDED MUCH OF MONTANA AND WYOMING. President Abraham Lincoln had difficulty finding a governor who was willing to come to this wild and rugged land. Some appointees, including Gilman Marston and Alexander H. Conner, never appeared.

They had good reason to be tentative. The area was formidable and still is, for there is not just one Idaho; there are at least a half-dozen: a land of virgin forests; a high desert covering an area bigger than Rhode Island and Delaware combined; gently sloping farmland, where soft Pacific winds carry the pungency of growing alfalfa; an alpine region of icy, isolated peaks and densely forested valleys hiding more lakes and streams than have been named, counted, or even discovered; an atomic energy testing station only a few miles from the Craters of the Moon, where lava once poured forth and congealed in fantastic formations; and the roadless, nearly uninhabited, 2.3 million-acre Frank Church-River of No Return Wilderness, where grizzly bear, moose and bighorn sheep still run wild.

Stretching south from Canada for nearly 500 miles and varying dramatically in terrain, altitude and climate, Idaho has the deepest canyon in North America, Hell's Canyon, which is 7,913 feet deep. The largest stand of white pine in the world is in the Idaho Panhandle National Forests, and the finest big game areas in the country are the Chamberlain Basin and Selway. Idaho boasts the largest wilderness area in the United States in Frank Church-River of No Return Wilderness, and the largest contiguous irrigated area in the United States was created by the American Falls and several lesser dams. Idaho's largest county, named after the state itself, would hold the entire state of Massachusetts; its second-largest county, Owyhee, would hold New Jersey.

In addition to superlative scenery, fishing and hunting, visitors find diversions such as buried bandit treasure, lost gold mines, hair-raising boat trips down the turbulent Salmon River (the "River of No Return") and ghost mining towns. For those who prefer less strenuous activities, Sun Valley and Coeur d'Alene have luxurious accommodations.

Millions of years ago herds of mammoth, mastodon, camels and a species of enormous musk ox roamed the area. When Lewis and Clark entered the region in 1805, they found fur-bearing animals in such great numbers that they got in each other's way. The promise of riches in furs brought trappers and Native Americans. They were aided and abetted by the great fur companies, including the legendary Hudson's Bay Company. The first gold strike in the Clearwater country in 1860, followed by rich strikes in the Salmon

IDAHO

★
★★
★★★
★★★★
★★★★★

FUN FACTS

Rivers flow across 3,100 miles of Idaho, more than any other state.

Idaho's Hells Canyon is the deepest river gorge (7,913 feet) in North America.

Ernest Hemingway finished *For Whom the Bell Tolls* while living in Sun Valley, and he is buried in Ketchum.

River and Florence areas, the Boise Basin and Coeur d'Alene (still an important mining area in the state) brought hordes of miners who were perfectly willing to continue the no-holds-barred way of life initiated by fur trappers. Soon afterward the shots of warring sheepmen and cattlemen mingled with those of miners.

Mining, once Idaho's most productive and colorful industry, has yielded its economic reign, but the state still produces large amounts of silver, zinc, pumice, antimony and lead. It holds great reserves (268,000 acres) of phosphate rock. Copper, thorium, limestone, asbestos, graphite, talc, tungsten, cobalt, nickel, cinnabar, bentonite and a wealth of other important minerals are found here. Gems, some of the finest quality, include agate, jasper, garnets, opals, onyx, sapphires and rubies.

Today, Idaho's single largest industry is farming. On more than 3.5 million irrigated acres, the state produces an abundance of potatoes, beets, hay, vegetables, fruit and livestock. The upper reaches of the Snake River Valley, once a wasteland of sagebrush and greasewood, are now among the West's most fertile farmlands. Manufacturing and processing of farm products, timber and minerals is an important part of the state's economic base. Tourism is also important to the economy.
Information: www.visitid.org

AMERICAN FALLS

After a party of American Fur Company trappers was caught in the current of the Snake River and swept over the falls here, the fur company gave its name to both the community and the falls. American Falls boasts an important hydroelectric plant and is the capital of a vast dry-farming wheat belt; agricultural reclamation projects stretch westward for 170 miles.
Information: Chamber of Commerce, 239 Idaho St., 208-226-7214; www.americanfallschamber.org

WHAT TO SEE AND DO
MASSACRE ROCKS STATE PARK
3592 Park Lane, American Falls, 208-548-2672; www.seeidaho.org/massacrerock.html
Along the Old Oregon Trail, emigrants carved their names on Register Rock. Nearby, at Massacre Rocks, is the spot where a wagon train was ambushed in 1862. The area offers waterskiing, fishing, boating, hiking, bird-watching and picnicking.

ASHTON

Ashton's economy is centered on the flow of products from the rich agricultural area that extends to Blackfoot. Equally important to the town, which has a view of the Twin Teton Peaks in Wyoming, is the influx of vacationers bound for the Targhee National Forest, Warm River recreation areas and Bear Gulch winter sports area. A Ranger District office of the forest is located here.
Information: Chamber of Commerce, 714 Main St., Ashton, 208-652-3355; www.ashtonidaho.com

WHAT TO SEE AND DO
HENRY'S LAKE STATE PARK
3917 E. 5100 N., Island Park, 208-558-7532; www.henryslakeanglers.com
This 586-acre park offers waterskiing, boating, hiking, picnicking and 50 campsites. Mid-May-October, daily.

IDAHO

★
★★
★★
★

BLACKFOOT

Blackfoot is situated in southeast Idaho, halfway between Idaho Falls and Pocatello. The community bills itself as the Potato Capital of the World, a boast supported by the downtown presence of the Idaho Potato Expo, a museum celebrating the state's most famous export. Blackfoot was originally called Grove City, an homage to the town's abundance of trees. Its present name is derived from the Blackfoot River, which flows through town. The Fort Hall Indian Reservation sprawls across 544,000 acres to the south. Authentic Shoshone and Bannock arts and crafts are available at nearby stores, a favorite being the Clothes Horse, a marketplace located on the reservation.

Information: Chamber of Commerce, 130 N.W. Main, 208-785-0510;
www.blackfootchamber.org

SPECIAL EVENT
SHOSHONE-BANNOCK INDIAN FESTIVAL

Fort Hall Indian Reservation, Simplot Road; www.shoshonebannocktribes.com
Tribes from many Western states and Canada gather for this festival which features dancing, parades, a rodeo, a Native American queen contest, buffalo feast and other events. Early August.

BOISE

Capital and largest city in Idaho, Boise is also the business, financial, professional and transportation center of the state. It is home to Boise State University and the National Interagency Fire Center, the nation's logistical support center for wildland fire suppression. Early French trappers labeled this still tree-rich area as *les bois* (the woods). Established during gold rush days, Boise was overshadowed by nearby Idaho City until designated the territorial capital in 1864. Abundant hydroelectric power stimulated manufacturing, with electronics, steel fabrication, and mobile homes the leading industries. Several major companies have their headquarters here. Lumber, fruit, sugar beets and livestock are other mainstays of the economy; the state's main dairy region lies to the west of Boise. Natural hot water from the underground springs (with temperatures up to 170 F) heats some of the homes in the eastern portion of the city. A Ranger District office and the headquarters of the Boise National Forest are located here.

Extending alongside the Boise River is the Greenbelt, a trail used for jogging, skating, biking and walking. When complete, the 22-mile trail will connect Eagle Island State Park on the west side of the city with Lucky Peak State Park on the east side of the city.

Information: Convention and Visitors Bureau, 312 S. Ninth St.,
208-344-7777, 800-635-5240; www.boise.org

WHAT TO SEE AND DO
BASQUE MUSEUM AND CULTURAL CENTER

611 Grove St., Boise, 208-343-2671; www.basquemuseum.com
The only museum in North America dedicated solely to Basque heritage, it contains historical displays, paintings by Basque artists, changing exhibits and a restored boarding house used by Basque immigrants in 1900s. Tuesday-Saturday, limited hours.

EXPLORING DOWNTOWN BOISE

Boise is a high-spirited city that manages to meld the vestiges of the cowboy Old West with the sophistication of the urban Pacific Northwest. The downtown core is relatively small, which makes it fun to explore on foot.

Begin at the state capitol building, at Capitol Boulevard and Jefferson Street. This vast structure is constructed of local sandstone and faced on the interior with four kinds of marble and mahogany paneling. On the first floor, wander across the rotunda and gaze upward at the interior of the 200-foot dome, ringed with 43 stars (Idaho was the 43rd state in the Union). The legislative chambers are on the third floor. The Idaho capitol is the only geothermally heated statehouse in the country: water from hot springs five blocks away is pumped into the buildings radiators.

From the capitol, proceed down Capitol Boulevard to Main Street. From this corner east on Main Street to about Third Street is a district of fine old homes—many renovated into shops and restaurants—that recalls Boise's early 20th-century opulence. Referred to as Old Boise, this street is home to the Egyptian Theatre (at Main and Capital), an architecturally exuberant early vaudeville theater and movie palace in full King Tut garb.

One block farther west, at Grove and Eighth streets, is the Grove, Boise's unofficial city center. The grove is a brick-lined plaza with a large fountain, public art, and a pedestrian area. Summer concerts are held here, and it's the place to gather for skateboarders, cyclists and lunchtime office workers.

Continue down Grove to Sixth Street to the **Basque Museum and Cultural Center** *(611 Grove Street)*. Idaho contains one of the largest Basque settlements outside of Europe, and this interesting museum tells the story of their culture and settlement in southwest Idaho. Next door, and part of the museum, is the Cyrus Jacobs-Uberuaga House, built as a boarding house for Basque immigrants in 1864.

Continue up Capitol Boulevard to Julia Davis Park, a large park along the Boise River that contains many of the city's important museums and cultural institutions. Follow the posted sign trails to the **Idaho Historical Museum** *(610 N. Julia Davis Drive)*, which gives an excellent overview of the state's rich historic heritage. Especially good are the exhibits devoted to Idaho native Indian history and to Oregon Trail pioneers. Immediately next door is Pioneer Village, a re-created town with vintage buildings dating from the late 19th century. Also in the park is the **Boise Art Museum** *(670 Julia Davis Drive)*, with a permanent collection that focuses on American Realism.

At the center of Julia Davis Park is Zoo Boise. In addition to the traditional exotic zoo animal favorites from Africa, the zoo is home to a collection of large Rocky Mountain mammals like moose, mountain lions, elk and bighorn sheep. Zoo Boise has the largest display of birds of prey in the Northwest. Return to the downtown area along Fifth Street.

IDAHO

★
★★
★★
★
★

BOISE NATIONAL FOREST

1249 S. Vinnell Way, Boise, 208-373-4100; www.fs.usda.gov

This 2,646,341-acre forest includes the headwaters of the Boise and Payette rivers, two scenic byways, abandoned mines and ghost towns and access to the Sawtooth Wilderness and the Frank Church—River of No Return Wilderness. Visitors will find trout fishing, swimming, rafting, hunting, skiing, snowmobiling, mountain biking, motorized trail biking, hiking, picnicking and camping.

DISCOVERY CENTER OF IDAHO

131 W. Myrtle St., Boise, 208-343-9895; www.scidaho.org

Hands-on exhibits explore various principles of science at the Discovery Center, which features a large bubble maker, catenary arch and magnetic sand. Tuesday-Sunday.

IDAHO BLACK HISTORY MUSEUM

508 Julia Davis Drive, Boise, 208-443-0017; www.ibhm.org

Changing exhibits highlight the history and culture of African Americans, with special emphasis on Idaho African Americans. The museum features lectures, films, workshops, storytelling and musical performances. Summer, Tuesday-Sunday 10 a.m.-4 p.m.; winter, Wednesday-Saturday 10 a.m.-4 p.m.

IDAHO HISTORICAL MUSEUM

610 Julia Davis Drive, Boise, 208-334-2120; www.idahohistory.net

Detailing the history of Idaho and the Pacific Northwest, the museum features exhibits on Native Americans, fur trade, mining, ranching and forestry. Daily.

WORLD CENTER FOR BIRDS OF PREY

5668 W. Flying Hawk Lane, Boise, 208-362-3716; www.peregrinefund.org

Originally created to prevent the extinction of the peregrine falcon, the scope of the center has been expanded to include national and international conservation of birds of prey and their environments. Visitors can see the breeding chamber of California condors and other raptors at the interpretive center. Daily.

SPECIAL EVENT

IDAHO SHAKESPEARE FESTIVAL

5657 Warm Springs Ave., Boise, 208-429-9908; www.idahoshakespeare.org

Enjoy an outdoor summer performance of one of Shakespeare's famous tragedies or comedies. The 600-seat amphitheater is situated in a nature preserve in the scenic Boise foothills. June-September.

HOTELS

★★DOUBLETREE HOTEL

475 Parkcenter Blvd., Boise, 208-345-2002, 800-222-8733; www.doubletree.com

158 rooms. Restaurant, bar. Fitness center. Outdoor pool. Airport transportation available. High-speed Internet access. Pets accepted. Business Center. **$**

IDAHO

★
★★
★
★

★★DOUBLETREE HOTEL
2900 Chinden Blvd., Boise, 208-343-1871, 800-222-8733; www.doubletree.com

304 rooms. Pets accepted, some restrictions; fee. Restaurant, bar. Outdoor pool, children's pool, whirlpool. Airport transportation available. High-speed Internet access. Fitness center. **$**

★★★GROVE HOTEL
245 S. Capitol Blvd., Boise, 208-333-8000, 888-961-5000; www.grovehotelboise.com

Steps from the Boise Convention Center, this hotel situates guests in the heart of the downtown area. Rooms are comfortably appointed with modern furnishings. With over 17,000 square feet of flexible meeting space, The Grove Hotel has much to offer business travelers. The hotel is attached to the 5,000-seat Bank of America Centre, which hosts a variety of sporting and entertainment events. Fine dining is available at Emilios, which offers a menu of New American cuisine. Julia Davis Park and the Boise River are a short stroll away. 254 rooms. Wireless Internet access. Restaurants, bar. Fitness center. Indoor pool, whirlpool. Airport transportation available. **$**

★★HOLIDAY INN
3300 Vista Ave., Boise, 208-343-4900, 800-465-4329; www.holiday-inn.com

265 rooms. Pets accepted; fee. Restaurant, bar. Indoor pool, children's pool. Airport transportation available. High-speed Internet access. **$**

★★HOTEL 43
981 Grove St., Boise, 208-342-4622; www.hotel43.com

112 rooms. Complimentary full breakfast. Wireless Internet access. Restaurant, bar. Fitness center. Whirlpool. Airport transportation available. Business Center. Fitness center. **$**

★★OWYHEE PLAZA HOTEL
1109 Main St., Boise, 208-343-4611, 800-233-4611; www.owyheeplaza.com

100 rooms. Restaurant, bar. Wireless Internet access. Outdoor pool. Airport transportation available. Pets accepted, some restrictions; fee. **$**

★★RED LION
1800 Fairview Ave., Boise, 208-344-7691, 800-733-5466; www.redlion.com

182 rooms. Restaurant, bar. High-speed Internet access. Fitness center. Outdoor pool. Airport transportation available. Pets accepted. **$**

★SAFARI INN DOWNTOWN
1070 Grove St., Boise, 208-344-6556, 800-541-6556; www.safariinnboise.com

103 rooms. Complimentary continental breakfast. High-speed Internet access. Outdoor pool, whirlpool. Airport transportation available. **$**

★SHILO INN
3031 Main St., Boise, 208-344-3521, 800-222-2244; www.shiloinns.com

111 rooms. Pets accepted, some restrictions; fee. Complimentary continental breakfast. Indoor pool, whirlpool. Airport transportation available. **$**

IDAHO

★
★
★
★

SPECIALTY LODGING
IDAHO HERITAGE INN
109 W. Idaho St., Boise, 208-342-8066, 800-342-8445; www.idheritageinn.com
Six rooms. Complimentary full breakfast. Wireless Internet access. **$**

RESTAURANT
★BARDENAY RESTAURANT DISTILLERY
610 W. Grove St., Boise, 208-426-0538; www.bardenay.com
American menu. Lunch, dinner, late-night. Bar. Children's menu. Casual attire. Outdoor seating. **$**

BONNERS FERRY
E.L. Bonner offered ferry service from this point on the Kootenai River, near the northern tip of the state, and gave this community its name. Today, Bonners Ferry services the agricultural and lumbering districts of Boundary County, of which it is the county seat. From here the broad, flat and fertile Kootenai Valley stretches north to British Columbia. This scenic area features many lakes and streams; fishing, hunting and hiking are popular pastimes. A Ranger District office of the Idaho Panhandle National Forest-Kaniksu is located here.
Information: 208-267-5922; www.bonnersferrychamber.com

WHAT TO SEE AND DO
KOOTENAI NATIONAL WILDLIFE REFUGE
Riverside Road, Bonners Ferry, 208-267-3888; www.fws.gov/kootenai
This 2,774-acre refuge was created as a resting area for waterfowl during migration. Its wide variety of habitat supports many species of birds and mammals, including bald eagles.

HOTEL
★KOOTENAI VALLEY MOTEL
Highway 95, Bonners Ferry, 208-267-7567; www.kootenaivalleymotel.com
22 rooms. Pets accepted, some restrictions; fee. Whirlpool. **$**

BURLEY
Burley was created by a 210,000-acre irrigation project that turned a near-desert area into a thriving agricultural center ideal for alfalfa, grain, sugar beets and potatoes. The town is a center for potato processing and has one of the largest sugar beet processing plants in the world. A Ranger District office of the Sawtooth National Forest is located here.
Information: Mini-Cassia Chamber of Commerce, 1777 Seventh St., Heyburn, 208-679-4793; www.burleyidaho.org

WHAT TO SEE AND DO
CITY OF ROCKS NATIONAL RESERVE
3035 Elba-Almo Road Almo, 208-824-5519; www.nps.gov/ciro
A pioneer stopping place, this 25-square-mile area of granite spires and sculptured rock formations resembles a city carved from stone; granite walls are inscribed with messages and names of westward-bound settlers, and remnants of the California Trail are still visible. Well-known for technical rock climbing, it also offers hiking and picnicking.

IDAHO

★
★★
★★
★

SPECIAL EVENT
IDAHO POWERBOAT REGATTA
Burley Marina; www.idahoregatta.com

Boat racers from throughout the Western United States compete in this American Power Boat Association national championship series event. Last weekend in June.

HOTEL
★★BEST WESTERN BURLEY INN & CONVENTION CENTER
800 N. Overland Ave., Burley, 208-678-3501, 800-599-1849;
www.bestwestern.com

126 rooms. Pets accepted, some restrictions. Restaurant, bar. Outdoor pool, children's pool. High-speed Internet access. $

CALDWELL

Caldwell, seat of Canyon County, is situated in the triangle formed by the confluence of the Snake and Boise rivers. Founded by the Idaho and Oregon Land Improvement Company, the town was named for the company's president, C.A. Caldwell. Livestock, diversified agriculture and vegetable-processing plants are mainstays of the economy.
Information: Chamber of Commerce, 704 Blaine St., 208-459-7493;
www.cityofcaldwell.com

WHAT TO SEE AND DO
ALBERTSON COLLEGE OF IDAHO
2112 Cleveland Blvd., Caldwell, 208-459-5011; www.collegeofidaho.edu

Built in 1891, the college currently has 800 students and is the oldest four-year college in Idaho. It's a private liberal arts college. The Evans Mineral Collection, Orma J. Smith Natural Science Museum and a planetarium are in Boone Science Hall; Blatchley Hall houses the Rosenthal Gallery of Art. September-May, inquire for hours.

SPECIAL EVENTS
CANYON COUNTY FAIR & FESTIVAL
Equine & Event Center, 111 S. 22nd Ave., Caldwell, 208-455-8500;
www.canyoncountyfair.org

The Canyon County Fair hosts a carnival, music and comedy acts, and livestock exhibits. It also features several special events like a tractor driving contest, Barn Yard Game Show and the Ag Challenge. Late July-early August.

NIGHT RODEO
CNR Arena, 2301 Blaine St., Caldwell, 208-459-2060; www.caldwellnightrodeo.com

Caldwell's Night Rodeo features several PRCA and WPRA events, but the week also includes activities like the Buckaroo Breakfast and performances by the Horsemanship Drill Team. Second or third week in August.

HOTELS
★LA QUINTA INN
901 Specht Ave., Caldwell, 208-454-2222; www.lq.com

71 rooms. Pets accepted, some restrictions. Complimentary continental breakfast. Fitness center. Indoor pool, whirlpool. High-speed Internet access. $

★SUNDOWNER MOTEL

1002 Arthur St., Caldwell, 208-459-1585, 800-454-9487; www.sundownerinc.com

66 rooms. Pets accepted; fee. Complimentary continental breakfast. **$**

CHALLIS

Cloud-capped mountains, rocky gorges and the Salmon River make this village one of the most picturesque in the Salmon River "Grand Canyon" area. Challis is the seat of Custer County and the headquarters for Challis National Forest. Two Ranger District offices of the forest are located here.

Information: www.challischamber.com

WHAT TO SEE AND DO
SALMON-CHALLIS NATIONAL FOREST

1206 S. Challis St., Salmon, 208-756-5100; www.fs.fed.us

More than 2.5 million acres of forestland surrounds Challis on all sides, crossed by Highway 93 and Highway 75. Attractions include hot springs, ghost towns, nature viewing via trails; portion of the Frank Church—River of No Return Wilderness; trout fishing; camping, picnicking and hunting.

MIDDLE FORK OF THE SALMON WILD AND SCENIC RIVER

Highway 93, South Challis St., 208-879-4101; www.fs.fed.us

One of the premier whitewater rafting rivers in the U.S.; permits are required to float this river.

HOTEL
★★VILLAGE INN

310 S. Highway 93, Challis, 208-879-2239; www.challisvillageinn.com

54 rooms. Pets accepted, some restrictions; fee. Restaurant. Whirlpool. **$**

★
★
★
★
★

COEUR D'ALENE

Nestled amid lakes and rivers, Coeur d'Alene (cor-da-LANE) is a tourist and lumbering community, but particularly a gateway to a lush vacation area in the Idaho Panhandle. Irrigation has opened vast sections of nearby countryside for agricultural development; grass seed production is of major importance. The city is the headquarters for the three Idaho Panhandle National Forests, and there are three Ranger District offices here.

Information: Coeur d'Alene Visitor Bureau, 4199 W. Riverbend Ave., Post Falls, 208-664-3194; www.coeurdalene.org

WHAT TO SEE AND DO
LAKE COEUR D'ALENE

www.coeurdalene.org

Partially adjacent to the Idaho Panhandle National Forest, this lake is 26 miles long with a 109-miles shoreline. It is considered one of the loveliest in the country and is popular for boating, fishing, and swimming.

MUSEUM OF NORTH IDAHO

115 N.W. Blvd., Coeur d'Alene, 208-664-3448; www.museumni.org

Exhibits at this museum feature steamboating, the timber industry and Native American history. There is also a big game trophy collection. April-October, Tuesday-Saturday 11 a.m.-5 p.m.

SILVERWOOD THEME PARK

27843 N. Highway 95, Athol, 208-683-3400;
www.silverwoodthemepark.com

A turn-of-the-century park and village with Victorian buildings, Silverwood includes restaurants, a saloon, general store, theater featuring old newsreels and classic movies, aircraft museum, air shows and entertainment. Memorial Day weekend-Labor Day, daily.

SPECIAL EVENT
ART ON THE GREEN

1000 W. Garden Ave., North Idaho College Campus, Coeur d'Alene,
208-667-9346; www.artonthegreen.org

Art on the Green is an annual marketplace for more than 130 artists who sell their glass, metal and clay pieces to the more than 50,000 people who attend the festival each year. The event also hosts hands-on craft instruction for both children and adults. First weekend in August.

HOTELS
★AMERITEL INN

333 W. Ironwood Drive, Coeur d'Alene, 208-665-9000, 800-600-6001;
www.ameritelinns.com

118 rooms. Complimentary continental breakfast. High-speed Internet access. Fitness center. Indoor pool, whirlpool. $

IDAHO

★★BEST WESTERN COEUR D'ALENE INN

506 W Appleway Ave., Coeur d'Alene, 208-765-3200, 800-780-7234;
www.bestwestern.com

122 rooms. Pets accepted; fee. Restaurant, bar. High-speed Internet access. Fitness center. Indoor pool, outdoor pool. Airport transportation available. Business center. $

★
★
★
★
★

★★★THE COEUR D'ALENE RESORT

115 S. Second St., Coeur d'Alene, 208-765-4000, 800-688-5253; www.cdaresort.com

Northern Idaho's Coeur d'Alene Resort is a superb destination for active travelers. This lakeside resort enjoys a park-like setting filled with a multitude of outdoor activities. From boat cruises, waterskiing and marina access to downhill skiing, championship golf and nearby shopping, this resort has something to satisfy every guest. This spot is particularly notable for its golf, both for its premier golf academy and its amazing floating green, accessible by a small boat. A European-style spa primps and pampers, while five lounges and bars entertain. Sophisticated Northwestern regional cuisine is highlighted at Beverly's restaurant, and Tito Macaroni's enjoys a lively Italian spirit. 336 rooms. Pets accepted; fee. Restaurant, bar. Spa. Indoor pool, outdoor pool, children's pool, whirlpool. Golf, 18 holes. Airport transportation available. Tennis. $

★DAYS INN

2200 N.W. Blvd., Coeur d'Alene, 208-667-8668; www.daysinn.com

62 rooms. Pets accepted; fee. Complimentary continental breakfast. Whirlpool. Business center. High-speed Internet access. **$**

★★RED LION TEMPLIN'S HOTEL ON THE RIVER

414 E. First Ave., Post Falls, 208-773-1611, 800-733-5466; www.redlion.com

163 rooms. Pets accepted, some restrictions; fee. High-Speed Internet access. Restaurant, bar. Indoor pool, whirlpool. Airport transportation available. Tennis. **$**

★RIVERBEND INN

4105 W. Riverbend Ave., Post Falls, 208-773-3583, 800-243-7666; www.riverbend-inn.com

71 rooms. Complimentary continental breakfast. Outdoor pool, whirlpool. **$**

★SHILO INN

702 W. Appleway Ave., Coeur d'Alene, 208-664-2300, 800-222-2244; www.shiloinns.com

139 rooms. Pets accepted; fee. Complimentary continental breakfast. Indoor pool, whirlpool. High-speed Internet access. **$**

SPECIALTY LODGING
THE ROOSEVELT

105 E. Wallace Ave., Coeur d'Alene, 208-765-5200, 800-290-3358;
www.therooseveltinn.com

Built in 1905 and listed on the National Register of Historic Places, the four-story building was converted from a schoolhouse into a cozy bed and breakfast in 1994. The inn, named in honor of Theodore Roosevelt, features 15 antique-furnished rooms. A complimentary gourmet breakfast awaits guests each morning. 15 rooms. Pets accepted, some restrictions; fee. Children over six years only. Complimentary full breakfast. Whirlpool. Airport transportation available. **$**

RESTAURANT
★★★BEVERLY'S

115 S. Second St., Coeur d'Alene, 208-765-4000, 800-688-5253; www.cdaresort.com

This seventh-floor restaurant is the signature dining room at the Coeur d'Alene Resort. Enjoy great lake views, a fine wine cellar and Northwest-inspired cuisine including the popular firecracker prawns with angel hair. International menu. Breakfast, lunch, dinner, late-night, brunch. Bar. Children's menu. Casual attire. Valet parking. **$$$**

GRANGEVILLE

Grangeville is a light industrial and agricultural community. It was a focal point in the Nez Perce Indian War and a gold rush town in the 1890s, when rich ore was found in the Florence Basin and the Elk City areas. The seat of Idaho County is also the gateway to several wilderness areas. The headquarters and two Ranger District offices of the Nez Perce National Forest are located here.

Information: Chamber of Commerce, Highway 95 and Pine St., 208-983-0460;
www.grangevilleidaho.com

WHAT TO SEE AND DO
HELLS CANYON NATIONAL RECREATION AREA
541-426-5546; www.fs.fed.us/hellscanyon
Created by the Snake River, at the Idaho/Oregon border, Hell's Canyon is the deepest gorge in North America 1 1/2 miles from He Devil Mountain (elevation 9,393 feet) to the Snake River at Granite Creek (elevation 1,408 feet). The recreation area includes parts of the Nez Perce and Payette National Forests in Idaho and the Wallowa-Whitman National Forest in Oregon. Activities include float trips, jet boat tours, auto tours, backpacking, and horseback riding and boat trips into canyon from Lewiston, Grangeville and Riggins and via Pittsburg Landing or the Hells Canyon Dam. Be sure to inquire about road conditions before planning a trip; some roads are rough and open for a limited season.

NEZ PERCE NATIONAL FOREST
104 Airport Road, Grangeville, 208-983-1950; www.fs.fed.us
Nez Perce offers more than 2.2 million acres with excellent fishing, camping, picnicking, cross-country skiing and snowmobiling. The Salmon (the River of No Return), Selway, South Fork Clearwater and Snake rivers, all classified as wild and scenic, flow through or are adjacent to the forest. Pack and float trips are available.

IDAHO FALLS
An industrial, transportation and trading center in the upper Snake River Valley, Idaho Falls is a center of potato production and headquarters for the Idaho Operations Office of the Department of Energy. The Idaho National Engineering Laboratory is located on the Lost River Plains, 30 miles west on Highway 20. Potato processing is important; the stockyards here are the state's largest. Also, one of the nation's leading safety research centers for nuclear reactors is located here. A Ranger District office of Targhee National Forest can be found in Idaho Falls.
Information: Convention and Visitors Bureau, 630 W. Broadway,
866-365-6943; www.visitidahofalls.com

WHAT TO SEE AND DO
CARIBOU-TARGHEE NATIONAL FOREST
1405 Hollipark Drive, Idaho Falls, 208-524-7500; www.fs.fed.us
Approximately 1.8 million acres includes two wilderness areas: Jedediah Smith (West slope of the Tetons, adjacent to Grand Teton National Park) and Winegar Hole (grizzly bear habitat, bordering Yellowstone National Park). Attractions include fishing, big game hunting, camping, picnicking and winter sports at the Grand Targhee Resort ski area. Float trips are available on the Snake River and the Palisades Reservoir offers boating, sailing, waterskiing and canoeing.

HOTELS
★AMERITEL INN IDAHO FALLS
645 Lindsay Blvd., Idaho Falls, 208-523-1400, 800-600-6001; www.ameritelinns.com
126 rooms. Complimentary full breakfast. Indoor pool, whirlpool. Airport transportation available. High-speed Internet access. **$**

★★RED LION HOTEL ON THE FALLS

475 River Parkway, Idaho Falls, 208-523-8000, 800-733-5466; www.redlion.com
138 rooms. Wireless Internet access. Restaurant, bar. Outdoor pool, whirlpool. Fitness center. Pets accepted. $

★SHILO INN

780 Lindsay Blvd., Idaho Falls, 208-523-0088, 800-222-2244; www.shiloinns.com
161 rooms. Pets accepted, some restrictions. Complimentary full breakfast. Restaurant, bar. Indoor pool, whirlpool. Airport transportation available. High-speed Internet access. Business Center. $

RESTAURANT
★JAKERS

851 Lindsay Blvd., Idaho Falls, 208-524-5240; www.jakers.com
American menu. Lunch, dinner. Bar. Children's menu. Casual attire. $$

KELLOGG

In this rich mining region are the country's largest silver and lead mines. One of the state's most violent miners' strikes took place here in 1899. Today, the former mining town is being transformed into a ski resort.
Information: Historic Silver Valley Chamber of Commerce, 10 Station Ave.,
208-784-0821; www.silvervalleychamber.com

WHAT TO SEE AND DO
OLD MISSION STATE PARK

Cataldo, 10 miles West off I-90, 208-682-3814; www.visitidaho.org
Visitors can tour the Coeur d'Alene Mission of the Sacred Heart, a restored Native American mission, which is the oldest existing building in the state. Daily 9 a.m.-5 p.m.

SUNSHINE MINE DISASTER MEMORIAL

Frontage Road, Highway 90, Kellogg, 208-784-0821; www.visitidaho.org
A double-life-size statue constructed of steel serves as a memorial to all miners. Created by Ken Lonn, a native of Kellogg, the helmet's light burns perpetually and the miner holds a typical jackleg drill.

SPECIAL EVENT
CHRISTMAS DICKENS FESTIVAL

208-784-0821; www.silvervalleychamber.com
The entire town dresses in period costume for this festival, which features plays, skits, puppet shows and a parade. Second weekend in December.

HOTEL
★BAYMONT INN & SUITES

601 Bunker Ave., Kellogg, 208-783-1234
61 rooms. Pets accepted, some restrictions; fee. Complimentary continental breakfast. Indoor pool, whirlpool. Wireless Internet access. $

KETCHUM

While Ketchum may not receive as much attention as its sister city, Sun Valley, it's not for a lack of charm or beauty. Main Street is a pleasant stretch of shops, restaurants and art galleries. The town sits just to the south of the Sawtooth National Recreation Area, a four-season playground for outdoor enthusiasts. Trapper and guide David Ketchum, the town's namesake, settled here in 1879. Writer Ernest Hemingway spent his final years in Ketchum and is buried in the town cemetery.

Information: Sun Valley/Ketchum Chamber & Visitors Bureau,
866-305-0408; www.visitsunvalley.com

HOTELS

★★BEST WESTERN KENTWOOD LODGE

180 S. Main St., Ketchum, 208-726-4114, 800-780-7234; www.bestwestern.com
57 rooms. Restaurant. Indoor pool, whirlpool. High-speed Internet access. Fitness center. Business Center. **$$**

★★★KNOB HILL INN

960 N. Main St., Ketchum, 208-726-8010, 800-526-8010;
www.knobhillinn.com
This country-style inn draws skiers who flock to Sun Valley for its top-notch slopes, as well as summer vacationers who come to take advantage of the area's golf courses, hiking trails and river rafting. Each guest room has a balcony, enabling guests to revel in the mountain views. You'll also find a dressing room and a separate tub and shower. The inn prides itself on serving healthy breakfasts using no artificial ingredients; coffee, tea, wine and pastries are available at the Knob Hill Cafe in the afternoons. 26 rooms. Indoor pool, whirlpool. **$$**

★TAMARACK LODGE

291 Walnut Ave., North Ketchum, 208-726-3347, 800-521-5379;
www.tamaracksunvalley.com
26 rooms. Wireless Internet access. Indoor pool, whirlpool. **$**

RESTAURANT

★★★CHANDLER'S RESTAURANT

200 S. Main St., Ketchum, 208-726-1776; www.chandlersrestaurant.com
This restaurant is set in a 1940s home with antique furnishings and open beamed ceilings. American menu. Dinner. Bar. Children's menu. Casual attire. Reservations recommended. Outdoor seating. **$$$**

LAVA HOT SPRINGS

Hot water pouring out of the mountains and bubbling up in springs, believed to be the most highly mineralized water in the world, makes Lava Hot Springs a busy year-round resort. Fishing, swimming, hunting, camping and golf are available in the surrounding area.

Information: www.lavahotsprings.org

★
★
★
★

WHAT TO SEE AND DO
LAVA HOT SPRINGS
430 E. Main Lava Hot Springs, 208-776-5221; www.lavahotsprings.org

Outdoor mineral pools, fed by 30 different springs, range from 104 to 112 F. The springs also include an Olympic-size swimming pool with diving tower. Memorial Day-Labor Day, daily.

SOUTH BANNOCK COUNTY HISTORICAL CENTER
110 Main St., Lava Hot Springs, 208-776-5254

Museum artifacts, photographs, transcripts and memorabilia trace the town's history from the era of Native Americans and fur trappers to its development as a resort area. Daily.

LEWISTON

The Clearwater River, starting in the Bitterroot Mountains and plunging through the vast Clearwater National Forest, joins the Snake River at Lewiston. The two rivers and the mountains that surround the town give it one of the most picturesque settings in the state. A thriving tourist trade supplements Lewiston's grain, lumber and livestock industries.

Information: Chamber of Commerce, 111 Main St., 208-743-3531, 800-473-3543; www.lewistonchamber.org

WHAT TO SEE AND DO
CLEARWATER NATIONAL FOREST
12730 Highway 12, Orofino, 208-476-4541; www.fs.fed.us

Clearwater National Forest stretches about 1,850,000 acres with trout fishing, hunting, skiing and snowmobiling trails, camping, picnicking and lookout towers.

HELLS GATE STATE PARK
5100 Hells Gate Road, Lewiston, 208-799-5015; www.visitidaho.org

Hells Gate State Park draws visitors with swimming, fishing, boating, hiking, paved bicycle trails, a horseback riding area, picnicking and a playground. March-November.

NEZ PERCE NATIONAL HISTORICAL PARK
Highway 95 S., Spalding, 208-843-7001; www.nps.gov

The park is composed of 38 separate sites scattered throughout Washington, Oregon, Montana and Idaho. All of the sites relate to the culture and history of the Nez Perce; some relate to the westward expansion of the nation into homelands.

SPECIAL EVENT
LEWISTON ROUNDUP
2100 Tammany Creek Road, Lewiston, 208-746-6324; www.lewistonroundup.org

The Lewiston Roundup has a longstanding tradition of excellence and entertainment. It is a top 50 PRCA rodeo, and several world champions have participated in the event since it began in 1935. Weekend after Labor Day.

★
★★
★★
★

HOTELS
★GUESTHOUSE INN & SUITES
1325 Main St., Lewiston, 208-746-3311, 800-214-8378; www.guesthouseintl.com
75 rooms. Complimentary continental breakfast. Outdoor pool. Fitness center. **$**

★★INN AMERICA
702 21st St., Lewiston, 208-746-4600, 800-469-4667; www.innamerica.com
61 rooms. Restaurant. High-speed Internet access. Outdoor pool. Airport transportation available. **$**

★★RED LION HOTEL LEWISTON
621 21st St., Lewiston, 208-799-1000, 800-733-5466; www.redlion.com
183 rooms. Restaurant, bar. High-speed Internet access. Fitness center. Indoor pool, outdoor pool, whirlpool. Airport transportation available. Business center. Pets accepted, some restrictions. **$**

MCCALL
At the southern tip of Payette Lake, McCall is a resort center for one of the state's chief recreational areas. Fishing, swimming, boating and waterskiing are available on Payette Lake. McCall is also the headquarters for Payette National Forest, and three Ranger District offices of the forest are located here.
Information: Chamber of Commerce, 102 N. Third St.,
208-634-7631, 800-260-5130; www.mccallchamber.org

WHAT TO SEE AND DO   73
PONDEROSA STATE PARK
Huckleberry Loop, McCall, 208-634-2164; www.visitidaho.org
Approximately 1,280 acres, Ponderosa takes its name from a large stand of ponderosa pines located in the park. Other draws include swimming, waterskiing, fishing, boating, hiking, cross-country skiing, picnicking and camping.

SPECIAL EVENT
WINTER CARNIVAL
102 N. 3rd St., McCall, 208-634-7631; www.mccallchamber.org
The winter celebration features parades, fireworks, ice sculptures, snowmobile and ski races, a snowman-building contest and carriage and sleigh rides. 10 days in early February.

HOTEL
★THE WESTERN MOUNTAIN LODGE
415 N. Third St., McCall, 208-634-6300, 800-780-7234;
www.westernmountainlodge.com
79 rooms. High-speed Internet access. Indoor pool, whirlpool. Pets accepted, some restrictions. **$**

SPECIALTY LODGING
HOTEL MCCALL
1101 N. Third St., McCall, 208-634-8105, 866-800-1183; www.hotelmccall.com
32 rooms. Complimentary full breakfast. **$**

IDAHO

★
★
★
★
★

RESTAURANT
★★MILL STEAKS & SPIRITS
324 N. Third St., McCall, 208-634-7683; www.themillmccallidaho.com
Steak menu. Dinner. Bar. Children's menu. Casual attire. Reservations recommended. **$$**

MONTPELIER
Located in the highlands of Bear Lake Valley, Montpelier is surrounded by lakes, rivers, creeks and grazing ranges. The average yearly temperature is 46 F. First called Clover Creek, then Belmont, it was finally designated by the Mormon leader, Brigham Young, as Montpelier, after the capital of Vermont. There are Mormon tabernacles throughout this area. Phosphate is mined extensively nearby. A Ranger District office of the Caribou National Forest is located here.
Information: Bear Lake Convention & Visitors Bureau, Fish Haven,
208-945-3333, 800-448-2327; www.bearlake.org

★★CLOVER CREEK INN
243 N. Fourth St., Montpelier, 208-847-3519; www.visitidaho.org
65 rooms. Pets accepted, some restrictions; fee. Complimentary continental breakfast. Restaurant. Whirlpool. **$**

MOSCOW
This northern Idaho town is nestled between Moscow Mountain and the scenic rolling hills of the Palouse. A quaint college town, Moscow is home to the University of Idaho, and Washington State University is only a 15-minute drive west, just across the state line in Pullman. Moscow bills itself as the Heart of the Arts, an appropriate moniker given the town's well-attended arts festivals, renowned summer theater program, and vibrant live music scene. The nearby Palouse hills possess rich soils, producing high yields of dry peas and lentils. The U.S.A. Dry Pea and Lentil Council is headquartered in Moscow.
Information: Chamber of Commerce, 411 S. Main St.,
208-882-1800, 800-380-1801; www.moscowchamber.com

WHAT TO SEE AND DO
APPALOOSA MUSEUM AND HERITAGE CENTER
2720 W. Pullman Road, Moscow, 208-882-5578; www.appaloosamuseum.org
The museum features exhibits of paintings and artifacts relating to the appaloosa horse, early cowboy equipment, a saddle collection and Nez Perce clothing and tools. It also houses the national headquarters of the Appaloosa Horse Club, Inc. June-August, Monday-Saturday; September-May, Monday-Friday.

SPECIAL EVENT
LIONEL HAMPTON JAZZ FESTIVAL
University of Idaho Perimeter Drive and Rayburn Street, Moscow, 709 Deakin,
Moscow, 208-885-6765; www.visitidaho.org
Four-day festival Hosted by Lionel Hampton, the four-day festival features all-star headliners and student performers. Late February.

HOTELS
★★BEST WESTERN UNIVERSITY INN
1516 Pullman Road, Moscow, 208-882-0550, 800-780-7234; www.bestwestern.com
173 rooms. Restaurant, bar. High-speed Internet access. Indoor pool, children's pool, whirlpool. Airport transportation available. Fitness center. Pets accepted; fee. **$**

★★MARK IV MOTOR INN
414 N. Main St., Moscow, 208-882-7557; www.visitidaho.org
86 rooms. Pets accepted; fee. Restaurant, bar. Indoor pool, whirlpool. Airport transportation available. **$**

★SUPER 8
175 Peterson Drive, Moscow, 208-883-1503, 800-800-8000; www.super8.com
60 rooms. High-speed Internet access. Pets accepted. **$**

MOUNTAIN HOME
A transportation center in the Boise-Owyhee Valley of southwest Idaho, Mountain Home affords a fine starting point for side trips. Within a few hours' drive are forested ranges of the Boise National Forest, sand dunes, ghost towns, reservoirs and canyons; a Ranger District office of the forest is located here.
Information: Desert Mountain Visitor Center, 2900 American Legion Blvd.,
208-587-4464; www.mountain-home.org

WHAT TO SEE AND DO
BRUNEAU CANYON
3948 Development Ave., Bruneau, 208-384-3300; www.visitidaho.org
A 61-mile gorge, Bruneau Canyon is 800 feet deep but narrow enough in places to toss a rock across. Bruneau Dunes State Park has small lakes, sand dunes and the highest single-structured dune in North America at 470 feet. Attractions include fishing for bass and bluegill, boating, nature trails, picnicking, and a public observatory.

HOTEL
★BEST WESTERN FOOTHILLS MOTOR INN
1080 Highway 20, Mountain Home, 208-587-8477, 800-780-7234;
www.bestwestern.com
77 rooms. Complimentary continental breakfast. High-speed Internet access. Outdoor pool, whirlpool. Pets accepted; fee. **$**

NAMPA
Nampa, the most populous city in Canyon County, is located in southwestern Idaho's agriculturally rich Treasure Valley. Crops such as sweet corn, onions, mint and potatoes thrive in the area's sun-soaked, high-desert climate. Nampa is a short drive west of Boise on Interstate 84, a few miles north of the Snake River Birds of Prey National Conservation Area, home to North America's largest concentration of nesting raptors.
Information: Chamber of Commerce, 132 13th Ave. S.,
208-466-4641; www.nampa.com

WHAT TO SEE AND DO
CANYON COUNTY HISTORICAL SOCIETY MUSEUM
1200 Front St., Nampa, 208-467-7611; www.canyoncountyhistory.com
Historical artifacts and memorabilia are housed inside a 1903 train depot once used as offices of the Union Pacific Railroad. Tuesday-Saturday, limited hours.

DEER FLAT NATIONAL WILDLIFE REFUGE
13751 Upper Embankment Road, Nampa, 208-467-9278; www.fws.gov/deerflat
Thousands of migratory waterfowl pause at this 10,500-acre refuge while on their journey.

LAKE LOWELL
13751 Upper Embankment Road, Nampa, 208-467-9278; www.fws.gov
Approximately 8,800 acres, Lake Lowell offers boating, sailing, waterskiing and picnicking. Mid-April-September, daily.

HOTEL
★HAMPTON INN AT IDAHO CENTER
5750 E. Franklin Road, Nampa, 208-442-0036, 800-426-7866; www.hamptoninn.com
101 rooms. Complimentary continental breakfast. High-speed Internet access. Indoor pool, whirlpool. Pets accepted; fee. Airport transportation available. $

POCATELLO

At the heart of the intermontane transportation system is Pocatello. Once the site of a reservation, the city was named for the Native American leader who granted the railroad rights of way and building privileges. A Ranger District office and the headquarters of the Caribou National Forest are located here.
Information: Greater Pocatello Chamber of Commerce, 324 S. Main St., 208-233-1525; www.pocatelloidaho.com

★
★
★
★
★

WHAT TO SEE AND DO
IDAHO MUSEUM OF NATURAL HISTORY
Fifth Avenue and Dillon Street, Pocatello, 208-282-3168; www.imnh.isu.edu
Exhibits on Idaho fossils, especially large mammals of the ice age, are the highlight at this museum, which also shows Native American basketry and beadwork. Monday-Saturday.

BANNOCK COUNTY HISTORICAL MUSEUM
3000 Alvord Loop, Pocatello, 208-233-0434; www.visitidaho.org
Relics of the early days of Pocatello and Bannock County, Bannock and Shoshone are on display at the historical museum. Memorial Day-Labor Day, daily; October-April, Tuesday-Saturday, limited hours; closed mid-December-mid-January.

OLD FORT HALL REPLICA
3002 Alvord Loop, Upper Level Ross Park, Pocatello; www.forthall.net
A reproduction of a Hudson's Bay Trading Post houses period displays. June-mid-September, daily; April-May, Tuesday-Saturday.

SPECIAL EVENT

SHOSHONE-BANNOCK INDIAN FESTIVAL

10588 Fairgrounds Road, Pocatello, 208-237-1340;
www.shoshonebannocktribes.com/festival

Experience century-old traditions nightly at the tribal dancing, singing and drumming performances in the arbor. Other activities include an all-Indian rodeo, an arts and crafts fair, a juried art show and a softball tournament. Second weekend in August.

HOTELS

★★HOLIDAY INN

1399 Bench Road, Pocatello, 208-237-1400, 888-400-9714; www.holiday-inn.com

205 rooms. Complimentary continental breakfast. Restaurant, bar. High-speed Internet access. Indoor pool, whirlpool. Airport transportation available. Pets accepted, some restrictions. **$**

★★RED LION

1555 Pocatello Creek Road, Pocatello, 208-233-2200, 800-733-5466;
www.redlion.com

150 rooms. Pets accepted, some restrictions. Restaurant, bar. Indoor pool, children's pool, whirlpool. Fitness center. Business Center. Airport transportation available. **$**

REXBURG

Rexburg enjoys its position as a farm and trading center. Founded on instructions of the Mormon Church, the community was named for Thomas Ricks; common usage changed it to Rexburg.

Information: Chamber of Commerce Tourist & Information Center, 420 W. Fourth St.,
208-356-5700; www.rexcc.com

WHAT TO SEE AND DO

TETON FLOOD MUSEUM

51 N. Center, Rexburg, 208-359-3063; www.rexcc.com

Artifacts, photographs, and films document the 1976 flood caused by the collapse of the Teton Dam, which left 11 people dead and caused $1 billion in damage. May-August, Monday-Saturday; September-April, Monday-Friday, limited hours.

YELLOWSTONE BEAR WORLD

6010 S. 4300 W., Rexburg, 208-359-9688; www.yellowstonebearworld.com

This drive-through preserve near Yellowstone National Park features bears, wolves and other wildlife. "Cub Yard" shows bear cubs at play and "Duck Deck" is a waterfowl observation/feeding deck. May-October, daily.

SPECIAL EVENT

IDAHO INTERNATIONAL FOLK DANCE FESTIVAL

208-356-5700; www.visitidaho.org

Dance teams from around the world come to perform at this festival. Last week in July-first weekend in August.

HOTEL
★★BEST WESTERN COTTONTREE INN
450 W. Fourth St. S., Rexburg, 208-356-4646, 800-78-7234;
www.bestwestern.com
95 rooms. Restaurant. Indoor pool, whirlpool. Business center. High-speed Internet access. Pets accepted, some restrictions. $

RESTAURANT
★FRONTIER PIES RESTAURANT
460 W. Fourth St., Rexburg, 208-356-3600; www.frontierpies.com
American menu. Breakfast, lunch, dinner. Children's menu. Casual attire. $

SALMON
This town, at the junction of the Salmon and Lemhi rivers, serves as a doorway to the Salmon River country. It has towering mountains, lush farmland, timberland and rich mines. The Salmon River runs through the town on its way to the Columbia River and the Pacific Ocean. Fishing and boating are available along the Salmon and Lemhi rivers and in more than 250 lakes. The headquarters and two Ranger District offices of the Salmon National Forest are located here.
Information: Salmon Valley Chamber of Commerce, 200 Main St.,
208-756-2100, 800-727-2540; www.salmonchamber.com

HOTEL
★STAGECOACH INN MOTEL
201 Riverfront Drive, Salmon, 208-756-2919; www.stagecoachinnmotel.com
100 rooms. Complimentary continental breakfast. Wireless Internet access. Outdoor pool. Airport transportation available. Pets accepted. $

RESTAURANT
★SALMON RIVER COFFEE SHOP
608 Main St., Salmon, 208-756-3521; www.salmonrivercoffeeshop.com
American menu. Breakfast, lunch, dinner. Children's menu. Casual attire. $

SANDPOINT
At the point where the Pend Oreille River empties into Lake Pend Oreille (pon-da-RAY, from a Native American tribe given to wearing pendant ear ornaments), Sandpoint straddles two major railroads and three U.S. highways. All of these bring a stream of tourists into town. In the surrounding area are dozens of smaller lakes and streams. A Ranger District office of the Idaho Panhandle National Forests-Coeur d'Alene is located here.
Information: Chamber of Commerce, 900 N. Fifth Ave.,
208-263-0887, 800-800-2106; www.sandpointchamber.com

WHAT TO SEE AND DO
CEDAR STREET BRIDGE PUBLIC MARKET
334 N. First Ave., Sandpoint, 208-263-1685; www.cedarstreetbridge.com
Inspired by the Ponte Vecchio in Florence, Italy, the Cedar Street Bridge shops provide panoramic views of Lake Pend Oreille and nearby mountains. Daily.

★
★★
★★
★★
★★

ROUND LAKE STATE PARK

10 miles south on Highway 95, then two miles west,
208-263-3489; www.fishandgame.idaho.gov
Approximately 140 acres of coniferous woods, Round Lake State Park offers swimming, skin diving, fishing, ice fishing, ice-skating, boating, hiking, cross-country skiing, sledding, tobogganing and snowshoeing.

SPECIAL EVENTS

FESTIVAL AT SANDPOINT

Old Power House Building, 120 E. Lake St., Sandpoint,
208-265-4554, 888-265-4554; www.festivalatsandpoint.com
Since 1982, thousands have gathered in this arts town to enjoy music performed by internationally acclaimed musicians representing just about every genre imaginable. Past artists have included the likes of B.B. King, Shawn Colvin, Tony Bennett, Wynton Marsalis and Johnny Cash. August.

WINTER CARNIVAL

208-263-0887; www.sandpoint.org/wintercarnival
Two weekends of festivities include snow sculpture, snowshoe softball, other games, races and a torchlight parade. Mid-January.

HOTELS

★★BEST WESTERN EDGEWATER RESORT

56 Bridge St., Sandpoint, 208-263-3194, 800-635-2534; www.bestwestern.com
55 rooms. Complimentary full breakfast. Restaurant, bar. High-speed Internet access. Indoor pool, whirlpool. Pets accepted; fee. $

★★LA QUINTA INN

415 Cedar St., Sandpoint, 208-263-9581, 800-642-4271; www.lq.com
71 rooms. Complimentary continental breakfast. Restaurant, bar. High-speed Internet access. Outdoor pool, whirlpool. Fitness center. Pets accepted. $

SPECIALTY LODGING

THE COIT HOUSE BED & BREAKFAST

502 N. Fourth Ave., Sandpoint, 208-265-4035, 866-265-2648; www.coithouse.com
This charming bed and breakfast is located in downtown Sandpoint, steps away from shopping, restaurants and the City Beach at Lake Pend Oreille. Antiques and handmade crafts can be found throughout this restored Victorian manor. Each of the four bedrooms has a private bath. The upstairs master suite charms guests with a beautiful sleigh bed and clawfoot tub. A cheery sun room is the perfect place to relax before or after a day of outdoor fun in this year-round vacation community. Five rooms. Children over 10 years only. Complimentary full breakfast. Wireless Internet access. Pets accepted, some restrictions; fee. $

RESTAURANT

★★IVANO'S RISTORANTE

102 S. First Ave., Sandpoint, 208-263-0211; www.ivanos-sandpoint.com
Italian menu. Lunch, dinner. Bar. Children's menu. Casual attire. Reservations recommended. Outdoor seating. $$

IDAHO

SHOSHONE

Located in the Magic Valley region of south-central Idaho, Shoshone serves as the seat of Lincoln County. The town is surrounded by ranches and farms, and the area retains an aura of the untamed old West. Popular recreational activities include boating, fishing and big-game hunting. Shoshone marks the beginning of the Sawtooth Scenic Route, a stretch of State Highway 75 leading northward to the resort community of Sun Valley.

Information: City Hall, 207 S. Rail St. West, 208-886-2030; www.shoshonecity.com

WHAT TO SEE AND DO
SHOSHONE INDIAN ICE CAVES

1561 N. Highway 75, Shoshone, 208-886-2058; www.visitidaho.org

The caves function as a natural refrigerator, with temperatures ranging from 18 to 33 F. The cave is three blocks long, 30 feet wide and 40 feet high, and local legend has it that long ago a princess was buried under the ice. To this day, visitors report hearing strange voices and footsteps that seem to come from nowhere. On the grounds are a statue of Shoshone Chief Washakie and a museum of Native American artifacts, as well as minerals and gems. The caves are a good place to take children. 45-minute guided tours May-September, daily.

STANLEY

Situated on the Salmon River (the famous "River of No Return"), Stanley is located at the center of the Sawtooth Wilderness, Sawtooth Valley and scenic Stanley Basin. A Ranger District office of the Sawtooth National Forest is located here.

Information: Chamber of Commerce, 204-774-3411; www.stanleycc.org

SPECIAL EVENT
SAWTOOTH MOUNTAIN MAMAS ARTS AND CRAFTS FAIR

208-774-3411, 800-878-7950; www.stanleycc.org

The Mountain Mamas are a group of women who coordinate activities that raise money for local causes. This fair is their largest event, and it is also one of the best arts and crafts fairs in the state. Third weekend in July.

HOTEL
★★MOUNTAIN VILLAGE RESORT

Highways 75 and 21, Stanley, 208-774-3661; www.mountainvillage.com

61 rooms. Restaurant, bar. Pets accepted; fee. Airport transportation available. $

SPECIALTY LODGING
IDAHO ROCKY MOUNTAIN RANCH

HC 64 Box 9934, Stanley, 208-774-3544; www.idahorocky.com

21 rooms. Complimentary full breakfast. Restaurant. Outdoor pool. $

SUN VALLEY

Sheltered by surrounding ranges, Sun Valley attracts both winter and summer visitors and offers nearly every imaginable recreational opportunity. Powder snow lasts until late spring, allowing long skiing seasons, and there is hunting, mountain biking and

★
★ ★
★ ★
★

WANDERING THE SUN-DRENCHED SUN VALLEY AREA

Begin a tour of the resort towns of Ketchum and Sun Valley at the Ketchum-Sun Valley Heritage and Ski Museum, in Ketchum's Forest Service Park at First Street and Washington Avenue. The museum tells the story of the indigenous Tukudeka tribe, the early mining settlement and the building of Sun River Resort. There is also information about past and present residents like Ernest Hemingway, Olympic athletes and the Hollywood glitterati who come to ski. Walk north along Washington Avenue, passing coffee shops and gift boutiques, to the **Sun Valley Center for the Arts and Humanities** *(191 Fifth St. E.)*, the hub of the valley's art world. The center presents exhibits, lectures and films and is a great place to find out what's going on in Ketchum.

Walk one block east to Main Street. For a city of its size, downtown Ketchum has an enormous number of art galleries, restaurants and high-end boutiques. It would be easy to spend a day wandering the small town center, looking at art, trying on sheepskin coats and stopping for lattes. While you wander, be sure to stop at the **Chapter One Bookstore** *(160 Main St.)*, which offers a good selection of regional titles. **Charles Stuhlberg Furniture** *(571 East Ave. North)* is filled with the faux-rustic New West furniture and accessories popular with the area's upscale residents. For art galleries, go to the corner of Sun Valley Road and Walnut Avenue. **The Walnut Avenue Mall** *(620 Sun Valley Road)* is a boutique development with four independent galleries. Directly across the street is the **Colonnade Mill** *(601 Sun Valley Road)* with four more top-notch galleries.

Continue east on Sun Valley Road, picking up the walking and biking trail north of the road. Follow the trail one mile east through forest to the Sun Valley Resort, a massive complex with an imposing central lodge, condominium developments, home tracts and golf courses. The lodge was built in 1936 by Averill Harriman, chairman of the Union Pacific Railroad, and was modeled after European ski resorts in Switzerland and Austria. Harriman hired an Austrian count to tour the western United States in search of a suitable locale; the count chose the little mining town of Ketchum for the resort.

Wander the interior of the vast lodge, looking at the photos of the celebrities who have skied here. In its heyday, Sun Valley hosted the likes of Lucille Ball, the Kennedys, Gary Cooper and dozens of other stars of film and politics. Just west of the lodge, easily glimpsed through the windows that look out onto the Bald Mountain ski area, is an outdoor skating rink. Kept frozen even in summer, the rink is usually a spin with novice ice skaters. On Saturday evenings, professional ice skaters take to the ice to perform.

For a longer hike, return to Sun Valley Road and walking trail and continue east up Trail Creek, past golf courses and meadows. In a mile, the valley narrows. Here, in a grove of cottonwoods overlooking the river is the Hemingway Memorial, a simple stone bust that commemorates the author, who died in Ketchum in 1961. Etched in the stone are the words Hemingway wrote upon the death of a friend: "Best of all he loved the fall. The leaves yellow on the cottonwoods. Leaves floating on the trout streams. And above the hills the high blue windless skies... now he will be a part of them forever."

IDAHO

★
★★
★★
★

superb fly-fishing. Two Ranger District offices of the Sawtooth National Forest are located in nearby Ketchum.

Information: Sun Valley/Ketchum Chamber of Commerce, Sun Valley,
866-305-0408; www.visitsunvalley.com

SPECIAL EVENT
WAGON DAYS
866-305-0408; www.visitsunvalley.com

A celebration of the area's mining history Wagon Days features a large, non-motorized parade, band concerts, entertainment, arts and crafts fair and dramas. Labor Day weekend.

HOTEL
★★★SUN VALLEY LODGE
1 Sun Valley Road, 208-622-2001, 800-786-8259; www.sunvalley.com

Everyone from Ernest Hemingway to Clark Gable came to Sun Valley to enjoy the area's rustic luxury, and the Sun Valley Lodge has been this resort town's shining star since 1936. The guest rooms and suites are decorated in French-country style with oak furnishings and cozy fabrics, and modern amenities make guests feel at home. But the real draw is Sun Valley's legendary skiing and fishing. The Duchin Lounge's hot buttered rum hits the spot after a day on the slopes; Gretchen's pleases with casual fare; and the Lounge Dining Room is a standout with its epicurean delights. 148 rooms. Restaurant, bar. Outdoor pool, children's pool. Golf, 18 holes. Tennis. Airport transportation available. $$

★
★★
★★
★

RESTAURANT
★★★GRETCHEN'S
Sun Valley Road, Sun Valley, 208-622-2800; www.sunvalley.com

After a day on the slopes, guests can relax and unwind at this beautifully decorated restaurant located in the Sun Valley Lodge. Featuring a cozy, country-French atmosphere, Gretchen's serves a variety of specialty salads, pastas, seafood and poultry. Continental menu. Breakfast, lunch, dinner. Bar. Children's menu. Casual attire. Reservations recommended. Valet parking. Outdoor seating. $$

TWIN FALLS

After rising on the tide of irrigation that reached this valley early in the century, Twin Falls has become the major city of south central Idaho's "Magic Valley" region. Seat of agriculturally rich Twin Falls County, it is also a tourist center, boasting that visitors in the area can enjoy almost every known sport. The headquarters and a Ranger District office of the Sawtooth National Forest are located here.

Information: Chamber of Commerce, 858 Blue Lakes Blvd. N.,
208-733-3974, 800-255-8946; www.twinfallschamber.com

SPECIAL EVENT
TWIN FALLS COUNTY FAIR AND MAGIC VALLEY STAMPEDE
County Fairgrounds, 215 Fair Ave., Filer,
208-326-4396, 888-865-4398; www.tfcfair.com

Events at the fair include a PRCA rodeo, demolition derby and extreme motor cross races. One week starting the Wednesday before Labor Day.

HOTELS

★BEST WESTERN TWIN FALLS HOTEL

1377 Blue Lakes Blvd. N., Twin Falls, 208-736-8000, 800-822-8946;
www.bestwestern.com

118 rooms. Complimentary continental breakfast. Wireless Internet access. Indoor pool, whirlpool. Fitness center. Airport transportation available. Pets accepted. **$**

★★RED LION HOTEL CANYON SPRINGS

1357 Blue Lakes Blvd. N., Twin Falls,
208-734-5000, 800-733-5466; www.redlion.com

112 rooms. Restaurant, bar. Outdoor pool. Airport transportation available. Pets accepted. Fitness center. **$**

★SHILO INN

1586 Blue Lakes Blvd. N., Twin Falls,
208-733-7545, 800-222-2244; www.shiloinns.com

128 rooms. Complimentary continental breakfast. High-speed Internet access. Indoor pool, whirlpool. Business Center. Pets accepted; fee. **$**

RESTAURANT

★JAKER'S

1598 Blue Lakes Blvd. N., Twin Falls, 208-733-8400; www.jakers.com

American menu. Lunch, dinner. Bar. Children's menu. Casual attire. Outdoor seating. **$$**

WALLACE 83

Gold was discovered in streams near here in 1882; lead, zinc, silver and copper deposits were found in 1884. A Ranger District office of the Idaho Panhandle National Forests-Coeur d'Alene is located in nearby Silverton.
Information: Chamber of Commerce, 10 River St., 208-753-7151;
www.wallaceidahochamber.com

WHAT TO SEE AND DO

NORTHERN PACIFIC DEPOT RAILROAD MUSEUM

219 Sixth St., Wallace, 208-752-0111; www.visitidaho.org

Northern Pacific Depot Railroad Museum houses artifacts, photographs and memorabilia that portray the railroad history of the Coeur d'Alene Mining District. May-October, hours vary.

SIERRA SILVER MINE TOUR

420 Fifth St., Wallace, 208-752-5151; www.silverminetour.org

A 75-minute guided tour through an actual silver mine includes demonstrations of mining methods, techniques and operation of modern-day equipment. Tours depart every 30 minutes. May-mid-October, daily.

IDAHO

WALLACE DISTRICT MINING MUSEUM

509 Bank St., Wallace, 208-556-1592; www.visitidaho.org

The museum hosts material on the history of mining including a 20-minute video, old mining machinery and information on mine tours and old mining towns in the area. May-September, daily; October-April, Monday-Saturday.

HOTEL

★★WALLACE INN

100 Front St., Wallace, 208-752-1252; www.wallaceinn.net

63 rooms. Restaurant, bar. Indoor pool, whirlpool. Pets accepted; fee. $

WEISER

Located at the confluence of the Weiser and Snake rivers, the town of Weiser (WEE-zer) is both a center for tourism for Hells Canyon National Recreation Area to the north and the center for trade and transportation for the vast orchards, onion, wheat and sugar beet fields of the fertile Weiser Valley to the east. Lumbering, mining, the mobile home manufacturing and cattle raising also contribute to the town's economy. A Ranger District office of the Payette National Forest is located in Weiser.

Information: Chamber of Commerce, 309 State St.,
208-414-0452; www.weiserchamber.com

WHAT TO SEE AND DO

HELLS CANYON NATIONAL RECREATION AREA

55 miles northwest via Highway 95, to Cambridge then via Highway 71;
www.fs.fed.us/hellscanyon

Spanning the Idaho/Oregon border, this canyon, the deepest in North America, was created by the Snake River, which rushes nearly 8,000 feet below Seven Devils rim on the Idaho side. Three dams built by the Idaho Power Company have opened up areas that were once inaccessible and created man-made lakes that provide boating, fishing and waterskiing. Whitewater rafting and jet boat tours are available below the dams, on the Snake River.

SPECIAL EVENT

NATIONAL OLDTIME FIDDLERS' CONTEST

115 W. Idaho, Weiser, 208-414-0255; www.visitidaho.org

One of the oldest such contests in the country, it attracts some of the nation's finest fiddlers. The contest also includes a parade, barbecue and arts and crafts. Monday-Saturday, third full week in June.

MONTANA

THIS MAGNIFICENT STATE TOOK ITS NAME FROM THE SPANISH *MONTAÑA* WHICH MEANS "mountain." The altitude of about half the state is more than 5,000 feet, and the sprawling ranges of the Continental Divide rise more than two miles into air that is so clear, photographers must use filters to avoid overexposure. The names of many towns, though, indicate that Montana has more than mountains. Grass Range, Roundup and Buffalo tell of vast prairie regions, where tawny oceans of wheat stretch to the horizon and a cattle ranch may be 30 miles from front gate to front porch. Big Timber and Highwood suggest Montana's 22 million acres of forests; Gold Creek and Silver Gate speak of the roaring mining days (the roaring is mostly over, but you can still pan for gold in almost any stream); and Jim Bridger reminds us of the greatest mountain man of them all. Of special interest to vacationing visitors are Antelope, Lame Deer and Trout creeks, which offer excellent hunting and fishing.

First glimpsed by French traders Louis and Francois Verendrye in 1743, Montana remained unexplored and largely unknown until Lewis and Clark crossed the region in 1805. Two years later, Manuel Lisa's trading post at the mouth of the Big Horn ushered in a half-century of hunting and trapping.

The Treasure State's natural resources are enormous. Its hydroelectric potential is the greatest in the world—annual flow of the four major rivers is enough to cover the whole state with six inches of water. The 25 major dams include Fort Peck, one of the world's largest hydraulic earth-fill dams. Near Great Springs, one of the world's largest freshwater springs, pours out nearly 400-million gallons of water every day. In more than 1,500 lakes and 16,000 miles of fishing streams, the water is so clear, you may wonder if it's there at all.

For a hundred years, the state has produced gold and silver, with Virginia City (complete with Robber's Roost situated within convenient raiding distance) probably the most famous mining town. Montana produces about $1 billion worth of minerals a year. Leading resources are coal, copper, natural gas, silver, platinum and palladium. Montana also produces more gem sapphires than any other state. Farms and ranches totaling 67-million acres add $2 billion a year to the state's economy.

Along with the bounty of its resources, Montana's history has given us Custer's Last Stand (June 25, 1876); the last spike in the Northern Pacific Railroad (September 8, 1883); the country's first Congresswoman (Jeannette Rankin of Missoula, in 1916); the Dempsey-Gibbons fight (July 4, 1923) and a state constitution originally prefaced by the Magna Carta, the Declaration of Independence, the Articles of Confederation and the United States Constitution.

MONTANA

FUN FACTS

Montana has the largest grizzly bear population in the lower 48.

Montana is the 48th most densely populated state in the country.

The Roe River in Great Falls is the world's shortest river.

ANACONDA

Chosen by Marcus Daly, a copper king, as the site for a copper smelter, the city was first dubbed with the tongue-twisting name of Copperopolis, but was later renamed. In 1894, the "war of the copper kings" was waged between Daly and W. A. Clark over the location of the state capital. Clark's Helena won by a small margin. After his rival's death, the world's largest copper smelter was built here, standing 585 feet.

Information: Chamber of Commerce, 306 E. Park Ave.,
406-563-5458; www.anacondamt.org

WHAT TO SEE AND DO
COPPER VILLAGE MUSEUM AND ARTS CENTER
401 E. Commercial St., Anaconda, 406-563-2422; coppervillageartcenter.com
Located in the Anaconda City Hall Cultural Center, this museum and arts center features local and traveling art exhibitions, theater, music, films and a museum of local pioneer and industrial history. The building is on the National Register of Historic Places. Tuesday-Saturday 10 a.m.-4 p.m.; closed holidays.

VISITOR CENTER
306 E. Park St., Anaconda, 406-563-5458; www.anacondamt.org
Housed in a replica of a turn-of-the-century railroad station, Anaconda's visitor center has a display of smelter works photographs, an outdoor railroad exhibit and a video presentation highlighting area attractions. Mid-May-mid-September, Monday-Saturday 9 a.m.-5 p.m.; October-April, Monday-Friday 9 a.m.-5 p.m.

HOTEL
★★★FAIRMONT HOT SPRINGS RESORT
1500 Fairmont Road, Anaconda, 406-797-3241,
800-332-3272; www.fairmontmontana.com
The four hot springs-fed swimming and soaking pools are the pride of this resort. Filled with 155-degree naturally hot spring water and cooled to varying comfortable temperatures, the pools (open 24 hours to guests and until 9:30 p.m. to the general public for a fee) also include a 350-foot enclosed water slide. Conference and convention facilities accommodate groups of up to 500—making this a popular place for family reunions. 153 rooms. Restaurant, bar. Fitness center. Two indoor pools, two outdoor pools, whirlpool. Golf, 18 holes. Tennis. Wireless Internet access. **$**

BIG SKY

Located 45 miles southwest of Bozeman in the Gallatin National Forest, Big Sky is a resort community developed by the late newscaster and commentator Chet Huntley. Golf, tennis, skiing, fishing, whitewater rafting and horseback riding are among the many activities available in the area.

Information: Big Sky Montana Resort, 406-995-5000,
800-548-4486; www.bigskyresort.com

HOTELS
★★★BIG EZ LODGE
7000 Beaver Creek Road, Big Sky, 406-995-7000, 877-244-3299; www.bigezlodge.com
This luxurious lodge features beautifully decorated rooms with plush beds topped with colorful country quilts. After a day of skiing in winter or horseback riding in summer,

sink into a chair in the cozy dining room and sample ranch country cuisine like stilton and walnut-crusted elk with a chokecherry and port wine reduction. 13 rooms. Closed mid-October-mid-November and mid-April-mid-May. Complimentary full breakfast. Restaurant, bar. Fitness center. Whirlpool. $$$

★★★BIG SKY RESORT

1 Lone Mountain Trail, Big Sky, 406-995-5000, 800-548-4486; www.bigskyresort.com

This resort, established by famed newscaster Chet Huntley, features condos of various layouts and themes. Daily programs are available for kids, in addition to plenty of seasonal recreational offerings. 666 rooms. Closed mid-April-May and mid-October-late November. Restaurants, bar. Fitness center. Spa. Outdoor pool, children's pool, two whirlpools. Golf. Tennis. Airport transportation available. $$

★★BUCK'S T-4 LODGE

46621 Gallatin Road, Big Sky, 406-995-4111, 800-822-4484; www.buckst4.com

74 rooms. Closed early-mid-May. Pets accepted; fee. Complimentary continental breakfast. Restaurant. Whirlpool. Wireless Internet access. $

★★RAINBOW RANCH LODGE

42950 Gallatin Road, Big Sky, 406-995-4132, 800-937-4132; www.rainbowranch.com

16 rooms. Closed mid-December-April. Pets accepted. Complimentary continental breakfast. Restaurant. Whirlpool. $$

SPECIALTY LODGING

LONE MOUNTAIN RANCH

750 Lone Mountain Ranch Road, Big Sky, 406-995-4644,
800-514-4644; www.lmranch.com

Discover nature at the Lone Mountain. The log cabins are rustic with modern touches. Great fishing, water sports and nature activities are available, or just relax with a therapeutic massage. 30 rooms. Closed mid-April-May and mid-October-November. Restaurant, bar. Whirlpool. Airport transportation available. Wireless Internet access. $$$

RESTAURANT

★★★LONE MOUNTAIN RANCH DINING ROOM

750 Lone Mountain Ranch Road, Big Sky, 406-995-2782; www.lmranch.com

Dine in a spacious log cabin complete with elk antler chandeliers, a large stone fireplace and spectacular views at this Big Sky restaurant. More exotic cuts—such as elk, bison and pheasant—are featured on the menu, alongside traditional pasta, beef and fish entrées. American menu. Breakfast, lunch, dinner. Closed April-May and October-November. Bar. Children's menu. Casual attire. Reservations recommended. $$$

BIG TIMBER

Some of the tall cottonwoods that gave this settlement its name remain. Livestock ranches make Big Timber their selling and shopping center. It is also a popular dude ranch area, with good hunting and fishing facilities. The Yellowstone and Boulder rivers are popular for trout fishing. The first dude ranch in the state was started here around 1911. Natural bridge and falls area is located approximately 25 miles south of town.

Information: www.bigtimber.com

MONTANA

★
★
★
★
★

HOTEL
★SUPER 8
Interstate 90 and Highway 10 West, Big Timber,
406-932-8888, 800-800-8000; www.super8.com
41 rooms. Pets accepted; fee. Complimentary continental breakfast. High-speed Internet access. $

RESTAURANT
★★THE GRAND
139 McLeod St., Big Timber, 406-932-4459; www.thegrand-hotel.com
American menu. Breakfast, dinner. Bar. Children's menu. Casual attire. Reservations recommended. $$

BIGFORK
Surrounded by lakes, a river and a dam, Bigfork's businesses are electric power and catering to tourists who visit the east shore of Flathead Lake, the largest freshwater lake west of the Mississippi. The quaint downtown offers art galleries, specialty shops and an array of restaurants. The Bob Marshall and Swan wilderness areas lie in the town's backyard.
Information: Billings Area Chamber of Commerce,
815 S. 27th St., 406-245-4111; www.billingscvb.visitmt.com

WHAT TO SEE AND DO
SWAN LAKE
200 Ranger Station Road, Bigfork, 406-837-7500; www.fs.fed.us
A slender finger of water 20 miles long and a mile wide, Swan Lake is one of a chain of lakes on the Clearwater River. It's known as a fishing destination—in the spring, northern pike are the prime catch, and in the summer and fall it's Kokanee salmon and bull trout. Swan Lake is also popular with boaters; there are campsites and hiking trails near its shores, as well as in the village of the same name on its southern tip.

SPECIAL EVENT
BIGFORK SUMMER PLAYHOUSE
526 Electric Ave., Bigfork, 406-837-4886; www.bigforksummerplayhouse.com
One of Montana's most acclaimed summer stock theaters, the Bigfork Summer Playhouse began in the 1960s and today is a popular cultural draw in the Flathead Valley. It stages Broadway musicals every summer, with recent productions of "*Always...Patsy Cline*" and "*Carousel*" under its belt. In the off-season, a children's theater company performs regularly. Mid-May-mid-September, Monday-Saturday 8 p.m.

HOTEL
★★MARINA CAY RESORT & CONFERENCE CENTER
180 Vista Lane, Bigfork, 406-837-5861, 800-433-6516; www.marinacay.com
180 rooms. Restaurant, bar. Outdoor pool, whirlpool. Airport transportation available. $

MONTANA

SPECIALTY LODGINGS

AVERILL'S FLATHEAD LAKE LODGE

150 Flathead Lake Lodge Road, Bigfork, 406-837-4391; www.averills.com

Resting on 2,000 acres on the eastern shores of Montana's largest freshwater lake, this lodge is a paradise for outdoor enthusiasts. Anglers can fly fish, and the lake is perfect for sailing and canoeing, but the focus is on horseback riding at this authentic dude ranch. From riding instruction and horse competition to team roping and guest rodeos, this resort gives city slickers a taste of cowboy culture. Young riders learn about horse care and barn duties as part of the Junior Wranglers program. The log lodges capture the essence of the Old West with buffalo-hide couches and river-rock fireplaces, and the family-style meals feature roasted meats and other classic Western dishes. 38 rooms. Closed early September-early June. Complimentary full breakfast. Wireless Internet access. Bar. Outdoor pool. Tennis. Airport transportation available. $$$$

O'DUACHAIN COUNTRY INN

675 Ferndale Drive, Bigfork, 406-837-6851, 800-837-7460; www.montanainn.com

This bed and breakfast is housed in a log cabin. Rooms are decorated with log beds and furniture and feature private baths. Five rooms. Pets accepted, some restrictions; fee. Complimentary full breakfast. Whirlpool. $

RESTAURANTS

★★BIGFORK INN

604 Electric Ave., Bigfork, 406-837-6680; www.bigforkinn.com

International menu. Dinner. Bar. Children's menu. Casual attire. Outdoor seating. $$

★★★COYOTE ROADHOUSE

602 Three Eagle Lane, Bigfork, 406-837-4250,
406-837-1233; www.coyoteroadhouse.com

This restaurant, located just outside of Bigfork and inside the Coyote Roadhouse Inn, offers an elegant dining experience. The menu reflects chef-owner Gary Hastings' travels, with internationally influenced fare that features Southwestern, Tuscan, Cajun and Mexican flavors in dishes like jambalaya with scampi and petrale sole with red peppers, pea pods, yellow squash and a five-citrus sauce. International menu. Dinner. Closed Monday-Tuesday. Children's menu. Casual attire. Outdoor seating. $$

★★★SHOWTHYME

548 Electric Ave., Bigfork, 406-837-0707; www.showthyme.com

Located in an old bank building, this restaurant has original brick walls and molded tin ceilings. The menu includes steak, fresh seafood and chicken, and the desserts are homemade (and delicious). American menu. Dinner. Closed January. Bar. Children's menu. Casual attire. Reservations recommended. Outdoor seating. $$$

BILLINGS

On the west bank of the Yellowstone River, Billings, the seat of Yellowstone County, was built by the Northern Pacific Railway and took the name of the railroad president Frederick K. Billings. Today, Billings is a major distribution point for Montana's and Wyoming's vast strip-mining operations. Billings offers excellent medical facilities

MONTANA

★
★
★
★
★

and is a regional convention center. It is also the headquarters of the Custer National Forest.

Information: Billings Area Chamber of Commerce,
815 S. 27th St., 406-252-4111; www.billingscvb.visitmt.com

WHAT TO SEE AND DO
YELLOWSTONE ART MUSEUM
401 N. 27th St., Billings, 406-256-6804; www.yellowstone.artmuseum.org
The standout attraction in Billings, the one-time Yellowstone County Jail was renovated in the 1960s into this museum. After a significant expansion in the late 1990s, it emerged as the top art museum in Montana and is among the best in the Rocky Mountain region. The focus is on works by Montana artists with a strong emphasis on contemporary art. Temporary exhibitions tend toward the edgy and modern, but not exclusively: a recent exhibition showcased art depicting Montana as seen by Lewis and Clark. Monday 10 a.m.-5 p.m., Tuesday-Saturday 10 a.m.-5 p.m., Sunday noon-5 p.m., Thursday noon-8 p.m. Memorial Day-Labor Day 10 a.m.-5 p.m.; closed January.

ZOOMONTANA
2100 S. Shiloh Road, Billings, 406-652-8100; www.zoomontana.org
The state's only wildlife park features a homestead petting zoo. May 1-September 4, Daily 10 a.m.-5 p.m.; September 24-April 30, weekends 10 a.m.-4 p.m.

HOTELS
BEST WESTERN CLOCKTOWER INN
2511 First Ave. North, Billings, 406-259-5511, 800-780-7234; www.bestwestern.com
127 rooms. Pets accepted, some restrictions. Complimentary continental breakfast. Fitness center. Outdoor pool. Airport transportation available. High-speed Internet access. **$**

★BOOTHILL INN AND SUITES
242 E. Airport Road, Billings, 406-245-2000, 866-266-8445; www.boothillinn.com
69 rooms. Complimentary continental breakfast. Fitness center. Indoor pool, whirlpool. **$**

★COUNTRY INN & SUITES-BILLINGS
231 Main St., Billings, 406-245-9995, 888-201-1746; www.countryinns.com
67 rooms. Complimentary continental breakfast. High-speed Internet access. Fitness center. Indoor pool, whirlpool. **$**

★★★CROWNE PLAZA HOTEL
27 N. 27th St., Billings, 406-252-7400, 800-496-7621; www.ichotelsgroup.com
From families to business travelers, everyone will feel welcome at this branch of the national chain. Rooms at this downtown hotel are modern, with brick and dark wood accents, and offer great views of the city and mountains. 282 rooms. Pets accepted. High-speed Internet access. Restaurant, bar. Fitness center. Indoor pool, children's pool, whirlpool. Airport transportation available. **$**

★FAIRFIELD INN

2026 Overland Ave., Billings, 406-652-5330, 888-236-2427; www.fairfieldinn.com

63 rooms. Complimentary continental breakfast. Wireless Internet access. Indoor pool, whirlpool. Fitness center. **$**

★HOLIDAY INN EXPRESS

430 Cole St., Billings, 406-259-8600, 888-465-4329; www.hiexpress.com

66 rooms. Complimentary continental breakfast. High-speed Internet access. Fitness center. Indoor pool, whirlpool. **$**

★QUALITY INN

2036 Overland Ave., Billings, 406-652-1320, 877-424-6423; www.qualityinn.com

119 rooms. Pets accepted; fee. Complimentary full breakfast. Wireless Internet access. Indoor pool, whirlpool. Airport transportation available. **$**

RESTAURANTS

★★REX

2401 Montana Ave., Billings, 406-245-7477; therexrestaurant.com

American menu. Lunch, dinner. Closed holidays. Bar. Casual attire. Reservations recommended. Outdoor seating. **$$**

★★★WALKER'S GRILL

2700 First Ave. N., Billings, 406-245-9291; www.walkersgrill.com

This restaurant attracts locals and visitors alike. The menu changes seasonally and features a variety of meat, seafood and pasta dishes. The Southwest tapas tables are popular, and an extensive wine list is offered. American menu. Dinner. Bar. Children's menu. Casual attire. Reservations recommended. **$$**

BOZEMAN

Blazing a trail from Wyoming, pioneer John M. Bozeman led a train of immigrants who settled here and named the town for their leader. The first settlements in the Gallatin Valley were agricultural, but they were economically surpassed by the mines nearby. Today, small grain farming, livestock, dairying, tourism and the state university are important sources of income.

Information: Chamber of Commerce, 2000 Commerce Way,
406-586-5421, 800-228-4224; www.bozemanchamber.com

WHAT TO SEE AND DO

BRIDGER BOWL SKI AREA

15795 Bridger Canyon Road, Bozeman, 406-587-2111,
800-223-9609; www.bridgerbowl.com

Founded in the 1950s, Bridger Bowl is the perfect low-key antidote to today's overcrowded ski resort. It's the locals' favorite and a nonprofit enterprise, which translates to an emphasis on good skiing rather than the almighty dollar. There are no on-mountain accommodations, but the lift tickets are inexpensive, the lift lines are short and the snow is so dry, it's called "powder smoke." On the 2,200 acres of terrain, there are 69 trails (25 percent beginner, 35 percent intermediate, 30 percent expert and 10 percent extreme) spread over 2,600 vertical feet and served by seven lifts (one quad, two triples and four doubles). Perched 400 feet above the top of the lifts, "The Ridge" is known as some of the steepest, most extreme terrain within the boundaries of any resort in the West. Mid-December-April, daily 9 a.m.-4 p.m. Ticket rates: adult $45, children 6-12 $16, seniors free.

GALLATIN NATIONAL FOREST

Bozeman, 406-587-6701; www.fs.fed.us/r1/gallatin

One of the crown jewels of the National Forest system, the 1.8 million-acre Gallatin National Forest is part of the Greater Yellowstone ecosystem and is home to endangered grizzly bears, bald eagles and gray wolves. There are six mountain ranges, countless trout streams and two wilderness areas—the Lee Metcalf and the Absaroka-Beartooth—within Gallatin's boundaries. One of the best hiking areas is the Hyalite Drainage, south of Bozeman, with trails for every level of ability. Right outside West Yellowstone is the Rendezvous Ski Trails, a 20-miles groomed cross-country ski trail system. Bridger Bowl and Lone Mountain Ranch are ski resorts with leases on forest land. There are also nearly 40 developed campgrounds as well as two-dozen bare-bones rental cabins (with stoves but, no running water) once occupied by rangers.

SPECIAL EVENT

MONTANA WINTER FAIR

Fergus County Fairgrounds, Bozeman, 406-538-3007; www.visitmt.com

Enjoy the Montana scenery while at this state winter fair. Attractions include a livestock show, horse show and sale, fiddlers contest, art swap and shop, death-by-chocolate competition, quilts and leather-working divisions and farm equipment displays. Late January or early February.

HOTELS

★★BEST WESTERN GRANTREE INN

1325 N. Seventh Ave., Bozeman, 406-587-5261, 800-780-7234; www.bestwestern.com

120 rooms. Pets accepted. Wireless Internet access. Restaurant, bar. Fitness center. Indoor pool, whirlpool. Airport transportation available. **$**

★★GALLATIN GATEWAY INN

76405 Gallatin Road, Bozeman, 406-763-4672,

800-676-3522; www.gallatingatewayinn.com

33 rooms. Pets accepted. Complimentary continental breakfast. Restaurant, bar. Outdoor pool, whirlpool. Tennis. Airport transportation available. Wireless Internet access. **$$**

★HAMPTON INN

75 Baxter Lane, Bozeman, 406-522-8000, 800-426-7866; www.hamptoninn.com

70 rooms. Complimentary continental breakfast. Wireless Internet access. Fitness center. Indoor pool, whirlpool. Airport transportation available. **$**

★★HOLIDAY INN

5 E. Baxter Lane, Bozeman, 406-587-4561, 800-315-2621; www.holiday-inn.com

178 rooms. Pets accepted, some restrictions. Wireless Internet access. Restaurant, bar. Fitness center. Indoor pool, whirlpool. Airport transportation available. **$**

★LA QUINTA INN & SUITES BELGRADE

6445 Jackrabbit Lane, Belgrade, 406-388-2222, 800-642-4241; www.lq.com

65 rooms. Pets accepted. Complimentary continental breakfast. Fitness center. Indoor pool, whirlpool. Wireless Internet access. **$**

★MICROTEL

612 Nikles Drive, Bozeman, 406-586-3797, 800-771-7171; www.microtelinn.com

61 rooms. Pets accepted; fee. Complimentary continental breakfast. Indoor pool, whirlpool. **$**

SPECIALTY LODGING

GALLATIN RIVER LODGE

9105 Thorpe Road, Bozeman, 406-388-0148, 888-387-0148; www.grlodge.com

This modern bed and breakfast is set on a lake on a 350-acre ranch just outside Bozeman. Rooms are crisp and uncluttered and some have whirlpool baths. Six rooms. Pets accepted; fee. Complimentary full breakfast. Restaurant, bar. Whirlpool. **$$**

RESTAURANTS

★★BOODLES

215 E. Main St., Bozeman, 406-587-2901

Continental menu. Lunch, dinner. Closed Sunday; holidays. Bar. Casual attire. **$$**

★★★GALLATIN GATEWAY INN

76405 Gallatin Road, Bozeman, 406-763-4672,
800-676-3522; www.gallatingatewayinn.com

Impeccable service and an outstanding wine list are some of the features of this eatery, located in a restored, historic railroad hotel. American menu. Dinner. Bar. Children's menu. Reservations recommended. **$$**

★★JOHN BOZEMAN'S BISTRO

125 W. Main St., Bozeman, 406-587-4100; www.johnbozemansbistro.com

International menu. Lunch, dinner. Closed Sunday-Monday, holidays. Children's menu. Casual attire. Reservations recommended. **$$**

BUTTE

Settled more than 100 years ago, Butte has more than 1,000 acres of mines that produce copper along with by-product gold, silver and other metals. Although mined for more than a century, this treasure chest seems to be inexhaustible. Butte's famous old properties continue to produce high-grade ores, and modern mining techniques have exposed vast new low-grade mineral resources.

Butte was born as a bonanza silver camp. When the silver ores became lower grade at comparatively shallow depths, copper ores were discovered. Although development of the copper mines was a slow process, fortunes were made and lost, and battles were fought in court for control of ore on the surface and underground.

Information: Butte-Silver Bow Chamber of Commerce, 1000 George
St., 406-723-3177, 800-735-6814; www.buttechamber.com

MONTANA

★
★
★
★
☆

WHAT TO SEE AND DO
BERKELEY PIT
200 Shields St., Butte, 406-723-3177

A mile-long, man-made gash that's allegedly visible from the moon, the Berkeley Pit is a reminder of the world's richest hill, a former mountain of copper adjacent to downtown Butte. An estimated 290 million tons of copper ore were pulled from the ground here, leaving the 1,780-foot deep pit and thousands of miles of underground tunnels. Groundwater, seeping into the pit since mining operations ended in 1983, has been made toxic by tailings left over from the mining days. (Entire flocks of birds have met their fates by merely landing in the acidic water.) A water treatment plant went into operation in 2003 to combat the pit's pollution. Just east of downtown, a tunnel leads to an observation platform that's open from March-November; the spot is Butte's most visited tourist attraction.

COPPER KING MANSION
219 W. Granite St., Butte, 406-782-7580; www.thecopperkingmansion.com

This restored 34-room structure was built in 1888 and was the home of Senator W. A. Clark, a prominent political figure of Montana's early mining days. May-September, daily.

HOTELS
★COMFORT INN
2777 Harrison Ave., Butte, 406-494-8850, 877-424-6423; www.comfortinn.com

145 rooms. Pets accepted; fee. Complimentary continental breakfast. Fitness center. Indoor pool, two whirlpools. Airport transportation available. High-speed Internet access. $

★HOLIDAY INN EXPRESS
1 Holiday Park Drive, Butte, 406-494-6999, 800-315-2621; www.hiexpress.com

83 rooms. Complimentary continental breakfast. Wireless Internet access. Fitness center. Airport transportation available. $

RESTAURANTS
★★LYDIA'S
4915 Harrison Ave., Butte, 406-494-2000

This local standby's Victorian décor features many antique stained-glass windows. Menu selections include steak and Italian dishes, which are presented by an attentive staff. Italian, American menu. Dinner. Closed holidays. Bar. Children's menu. Casual attire. Reservations recommended. $$

★★UPTOWN CAFÉ
47 E. Broadway, Butte, 406-723-4735; www.uptowncafe.com

Paintings by local artists adorn the walls at this contemporary American bistro in the historic Uptown district. Wonderfully fresh seafood, steaks, pasta and poultry are all creatively prepared with home-style flair and served by a knowledgeable and attentive staff. American menu. Lunch, dinner. Closed holidays. Casual attire. Reservations recommended. $$

BIG HOLE NATIONAL BATTLEFIELD

A memorial to those who died in a battle between the U.S. Army and the Nez Perce tribe, Big Hole National Battlefield is part of a larger system of parklands known as the Nez Perce National Historic Park. The Nez Perce, or Nimiipuu, people lived in a vast wilderness stretching from Washington to Idaho for generations before the westward expansion of the U.S. The federal policy as of 1877 was to force tribes onto reservations to clear the way for white settlers, but a contingent of 750 Nez Perce resisted and escaped into what is now Montana, stopping in Big Hole to rest and possibly settle. Six weeks later, on August 9, 1877, U.S. soldiers ambushed the camp, and casualties were high. The surviving Nez Perce fled east, and most surrendered two months later. More than 655 acres of the battlefield are preserved today. Facilities here include two visitor centers with exhibits and hiking trails.

Fees are collected from late May-late September; some access roads are closed in winter.

Information: Southwest of Butte near Wisdom, 406-689-3155; www.nps.gov/biho/; summer 9 a.m.-6 p.m., fall 9 a.m.-5 p.m., winter and spring 10 a.m.-5 p.m.

COLUMBIA FALLS

A gateway to Glacier National Park and the North Fork of the Flathead River, this is an area of superb hunting and fishing. Also located here is the *Hungry Horse News,* Montana's only Pulitzer Prize-winning newspaper.

Information: Flathead Convention & Visitor Bureau, 15 Depot Park, Kalispell, 406-756-9091; www.columbiafallschamber.com

HOTEL

★★MEADOW LAKE GOLF AND SKI RESORT

100 St. Andrews Drive, Columbia Falls, 406-892-8700, 800-321-4653; www.meadowlake.com

24 rooms. Pets accepted; fee. Restaurant, bar. Fitness center. Indoor pool, outdoor pool, children's pool, whirlpool. Golf, 18 holes. Tennis. Airport transportation available. $$

EAST GLACIER PARK

This tiny community of fewer than 400 people serves as a gateway to Glacier National Park.

Information: 1121 E. Broadway, Missoula, 406-532-3234; www.glaciermt.com/pub/

HOTELS

★GLACIER PARK LODGE

Midville Drive, East Glacier Park, 406-892-2525; www.bigtreehotel.com

161 rooms. Closed October-mid-May. Restaurant, bar. Outdoor pool. Golf, nine holes. Spa. $$

★
★
★
★
★

★★SAINT MARY LODGE

Highway 89 and Going-to-the-Sun Road, St. Mary, 888-788-6279;
www.stmarylodgeandresort.com

122 rooms. Closed mid-October-April. Pets accepted, some restrictions; fee. Restaurant, bar. **$**

RESTAURANT
★★GLACIER VILLAGE

304 Highway 2 E., East Glacier Park, 406-226-4464; www.glaciervillagecafe.com
American menu. Breakfast, lunch, dinner Closed late September-early May. **$$**

GARDINER

Gardiner was established as the original entrance to Yellowstone Park. Named for a trapper who worked this area, Gardiner is the only gateway to Yellowstone National Park open year-round. A Ranger District office of the Gallatin National Forest is located here.

Information: www.gardinerchamber.com

HOTELS
★★BEST WESTERN MAMMOTH HOT SPRINGS

Highway 89 West, Gardiner, 406-848-7311, 800-828-9020; www.bestwestern.com
85 rooms. Pets accepted; fee. Restaurant, bar. Indoor pool, whirlpool. High-speed Internet access. **$**

★★COMFORT INN

Highway 89, Gardiner, 406-848-7536, 800-424-6423; www.choicehotels.com
77 rooms. Complimentary continental breakfast. Restaurant, bar. Whirlpool. **$**

★YELLOWSTONE VILLAGE INN

Yellowstone Park North Entrance, Gardiner, 406-848-7417,
800-228-8158; www.yellowstonevinn.com
43 rooms. Complimentary continental breakfast. Indoor pool. **$**

SPECIALTY LODGING
YELLOWSTONE SUITES B&B

506 Fourth St., Gardiner, 406-848-7937, 800-948-7937; www.yellowstonesuites.com
Four rooms. Complimentary full breakfast. **$**

GREAT FALLS

Great Falls's growth has been powered by thriving industry, agriculture and livestock, construction, and the nearby Malmstrom Air Force Base. The city takes its name from the falls of the Missouri River, a source of electric power.

Information: Chamber of Commerce, 100 First Ave. N.,
406-761-4434; www.greatfallschamber.org

WHAT TO SEE AND DO
C. M. RUSSELL MUSEUM COMPLEX AND ORIGINAL LOG CABIN STUDIO
400 13th St. N., Great Falls, 406-727-8787; www.cmrussell.org
Born in St. Louis, Charles Marion Russell (1864-1926) worked as a wrangler in Montana's Judith Basin before he found his true calling: painting the inhabitants and landscapes of the West. He was the first well-known western artist to live in the West, and his life's work includes more than 4,000 pieces. On the site of Russell's former home (and adjacent log studio), an impressive museum houses 2,000 of Russell's artworks, personal possessions and other relevant artifacts. May-September, Monday-Saturday 9 a.m.-6 p.m., Sunday noon-5 p.m.; October-April, Tuesday-Saturday 10 a.m.-5 p.m., Sunday 1-5 p.m.

LEWIS AND CLARK NATIONAL FOREST
1101 15th St. N., Great Falls, 406-791-7700; www.fs.fed.us/r1/lewisclark
More than 1.8 million acres of canyons, mountains, meadows and wilderness can be viewed here. Activities include scenic drives, stream and lake fishing, big-game hunting, hiking, camping, picnicking and winter sports.

LEWIS AND CLARK NATIONAL HISTORICAL TRAIL INTERPRETIVE CENTER
4201 Giant Springs Road, Great Falls, www.nps.gov/lecl/
No facility better tells the story of Meriwether Lewis and William Clark's legendary journey than this attractive structure perched on a bluff above the banks of the Missouri River. What is now Great Falls was in 1805 the site of the most arduous leg of the expedition, where the waterfalls (which have since been subdued by hydroelectric projects) forced the Corps of Discovery to portage their riverboats and other supplies across 18 miles of often rugged terrain. A variety of interactive exhibits tell this story and others, tracing the fascinating history of Lewis and Clark, chronologically and from both the explorers' perspectives and that of the Native Americans they encountered. Throughout the day, interpreters lecture on topics ranging from the medical techniques used on the expedition to the ecology of the land in the early 19th century. There are also costumed actors demonstrating skills of the era and a theater with regular screenings of an excellent documentary. Summer, Monday-Friday 8 a.m.-5 p.m., Saturday and Sunday 9 a.m.-5 p.m.; winter, Monday-Friday 8 a.m.-4.30 p.m., Saturday and Sunday closed.

HOTELS
★★BEST WESTERN HERITAGE INN
1700 Fox Farm Road, Great Falls, 406-761-1900,
800-548-8256; www.bestwestern.com
231 rooms. Pets accepted. High-speed Internet access. Restaurant, bar. Fitness center. Indoor pool, whirlpool. Airport transportation available. $

★DAYS INN
101 14th Ave. N.W., Great Falls, 406-727-6565,
800-329-7466; www.daysinngreatfalls.com
61 rooms. Pets accepted; fee. Complimentary continental breakfast. Restaurant, bar. High-speed Internet access. $

97

MONTANA

★
★
★
★
★

★FAIRFIELD INN
1000 Ninth Ave. S., Great Falls, 406-454-3000, 800-276-7415; www.fairfieldinn.com
63 rooms. Complimentary continental breakfast. Indoor pool, whirlpool. **$**

★★HOLIDAY INN
400 10th Ave. S., Great Falls, 406-727-7200, 800-315-2621; www.holiday-inn.com
168 rooms. Pets accepted; fee. High-speed Internet access. Restaurant, bar. Fitness center. Indoor pool, whirlpool. Airport transportation available. **$**

★★TOWNHOUSE INNS
1411 10th Ave. S., Great Falls, 406-761-4600,
800-442-4667; www.montana-motels.com
109 rooms. Pets accepted; fee. Restaurant, bar. Indoor pool, whirlpool. Airport transportation available. **$**

RESTAURANT
★★JAKER'S STEAK, RIBS & FISH HOUSE
1500 10th Ave. S., Great Falls, 406-727-1033; www.jakers.com
American menu. Lunch Monday-Friday, dinner Monday-Thursday; closed holidays. Bar. Children's menu. Casual attire. Reservations recommended. **$$**

HAMILTON
Hamilton is the county seat and main shopping center for Ravalli County and the headquarters for the Bitterroot National Forest.
Information: Bitterroot Valley Chamber of Commerce, 105 E. Main,
406-363-2400; www.bitterrootvalleychamber.com

WHAT TO SEE AND DO
DALY MANSION
251 Eastside Highway, Hamilton, 406-363-6004; www.dalymansion.org
This 42-room mansion built in 1890 was the home of Marcus Daly, an Irish immigrant who became one of Montana's "copper kings" through the copper mines near Butte. Tours: May-October, daily 10 a.m.-5 p.m.; November-April, by appointment.

HOTEL
★★★TRIPLE CREEK RANCH
5551 W. Fork Road, Darby, 406-821-4600, 800-654-2943; www.triplecreekranch.com
With the mountains of Montana as a backdrop, this ranch allows guests to experience the wilderness in its natural setting. Log cabins, trout-filled lakes, horseback riding and hiking trails keep guests coming back, as does the fresh mountain air and relaxing atmosphere. 19 rooms. Pets accepted, some restrictions. Children over 16 years only. Complimentary full breakfast. Restaurant, bar. Fitness center. Outdoor pool, whirlpool. Tennis. Wireless Internet access. **$$$$**

LITTLE BIGHORN BATTLEFIELD NATIONAL MONUMENT

As the U.S. government looked westward after the Civil War, the construction of roads and forts threatened the traditional way of life of the Cheyenne and Sioux tribes, among others. In the late 1860s and early 1870s, a series of skirmishes between Native warriors and U.S. soldiers escalated, and Lieutenant Colonel George Custer was dispatched to lead 12 companies of the Seventh Cavalry against the uprising. At a ridge above the Little Bighorn River, Custer's party was surprised and overwhelmed by a far larger contingent of Sioux and Cheyenne warriors, and 220 men were killed on June 25 and 26, 1876. The battlefield became a memorial for the fallen U.S. soldiers soon thereafter, and an Indian Memorial was dedicated in 2003. The visitor center includes historical displays, and the park has walking trails, self-guided auto routes and guided bus tours. National Park Service personnel provide interpretive programs (Memorial Day-Labor Day) and guided tours of Custer National Cemetery. Also here are a national cemetery, established in 1879, and the Reno-Benteen Battlefield, five miles southeast, where the remainder of the Seventh Cavalry withstood until late on June 26. Headstones show where the soldiers fell, and a large obelisk marks the mass grave of the Seventh Cavalry.

Information: Third St., Hardin, 406-638-3204; www.nps.gov/libi/; Memorial Day-August, 8 a.m.-9 p.m., August-Labor Day, 8 a.m.-8 p.m.; September-October, 8 a.m.-6 p.m.; November-March, 8 a.m.-4 p.m., April-May, 8 a.m.-6 p.m.

HARDIN

Hardin became the seat of Big Horn County after the area was opened to white settlers in 1906. It is the trading center for ranchers, farmers and Native Americans from the Crow Reservation. Nearby is the Little Bighorn National Monument.

Information: City of Hardin, 406 N. Cheyenne, Hardin;
www.hardinmt.com, www.custerslaststand.org

HELENA

The state capital and its fourth-largest city, Helena was the site of one of the state's largest gold rushes. In 1864, a party of discouraged prospectors decided to explore a gulch—now Helena's Main Street—as their "last chance" at striking it rich. This gulch and the area surrounding it produced more than $20 million in gold. A hundred cabins soon appeared. The mining camp, known as "Last Chance," was renamed Helena, after a town in Minnesota. Besides being the governmental center for Montana, today's Helena hosts agriculture and industry.

Information: Helena Area Chamber of Commerce,
225 Cruse Ave., 406-442-4120, 800-743-5362;
www.helenachamber.com

WHAT TO SEE AND DO
GATES OF THE MOUNTAINS
Highway 15, Helena, 406-458-5241; www.gatesofthemountains.com
This 12-mile, two-hour Missouri River cruise explores the deep gorge in Helena National Forest, discovered and named by Lewis and Clark. Memorial Day weekend-mid-September, daily.

MONTANA HISTORICAL SOCIETY MUSEUM
225 N. Roberts St., Helena, 406-444-2694; www.montanahistoricalsociety.org
Adjacent to the Montana State Capitol, this museum's exhibits cover the last 12,000 years of the area's history. On display are artifacts relating to everything from agriculture to transportation, as well as a collection of art by Montana's own Charles Russell and a special display about Big Medicine, a rare albino buffalo who lived in the National Bison Range in northwest Montana. His mounted hide is the centerpiece of the exhibit. Memorial Day-Labor Day, daily; rest of year, closed Sunday and holidays, Monday-Saturday 9 a.m.-5 p.m., Thursday until 8 p.m.

HOTELS
★★JORGENSON'S INN AND SUITES
1714 11th Ave., Helena, 406-442-1770; www.jorgensonsinn.com
117 rooms. Restaurant, bar. Indoor pool. Airport transportation available. Business center. High-speed Internet access. Indoor pool. $

★★RED LION COLONIAL HOTEL
2301 Colonial Drive, Helena, 406-443-2100, 800-743-5466; www.redlion.com
149 rooms. Pets accepted, some restrictions; fee. Wireless Internet access. Restaurant, bar. Fitness center. Indoor pool, outdoor pool, whirlpool. Airport transportation available. Business center. $

SPECIALTY LODGING
THE SANDERS-HELENA'S BED AND BREAKFAST
328 N. Ewing, Helena, 406-442-3309; www.sandersbb.com
This bed and breakfast was built in 1875 by Senator Wilbur Fisk Sanders. The guest rooms feature elegant furnishings. Seven rooms. Complimentary full breakfast. High-speed Internet access. $

RESTAURANTS
★JADE GARDEN
3128 N. Montana Ave., Helena, 406-443-8899; www.jadegardenhelena.com
Chinese menu. Lunch, dinner. Closed holidays. Bar. Children's menu. Casual attire. $

★★ON BROADWAY
106 E. Broadway, Helena, 406-443-1929; www.onbroadwayinhelena.com
International, Italian menu. Dinner. Closed Sunday, holidays. Bar. Casual attire. $$

MONTANA

KALISPELL

The center of a mountain vacationland, Kalispell is located in the Flathead Valley. Seed potatoes and sweet cherries are grown here and recreational activities abound.
Information: www.kalispellchamber.com

WHAT TO SEE AND DO
CONRAD MANSION
Woodland Ave. E., Kalispell, 406-755-2166; www.conradmansion.com
A 23-room Norman-style mansion built in 1895, this house is authentically furnished and restored. Tours: mid-May-mid-October, Tuesday-Sunday 10 a.m.-5 p.m.

HOTELS
★BEST WESTERN WHITE OAK GRAND
4824 Highway 93 S., Kalispell, 406-857-2400, 800-780-7234;
www.bestwestern.com
59 rooms. Complimentary continental breakfast. Wireless Internet access. Fitness center. Indoor pool, whirlpool. Airport transportation available. Business Center. $

★DAYS INN
1550 Highway 93 N., Kalispell, 406-756-3222, 800-329-7466; www.daysinn.com
53 rooms. Pets accepted, some restrictions; fee. Complimentary continental breakfast. High-speed Internet access. Business Center. $

★★OUTLAW HOTEL
1701 Highway 93 S., Kalispell, 406-755-6100, 800-804-6835;
www.outlawhotel.com
220 rooms. Pets accepted; fee. Wireless Internet access. Restaurant, bar. Fitness center. Two indoor pools, whirlpool. Tennis. Casino. Airport transportation available. $

SPECIALTY LODGING
FLATHEAD LAKE SUITES
829 Angel Point Road, Lakeside, 406-844-2204, 800-214-2204;
www.angelpoint.com
On Flathead Lake near Glacier National Park, this hotel offers spectacular views of the Rockies from private balconies in the suites. Along with 300 feet of private beach for swimming and canoeing, it is also close to many ski areas. Three rooms, all suites. No credit cards accepted. $

LIVINGSTON

Railroading has been key to the town's history and economy since railroad surveyors first named it Clark City. The present name was later adopted to honor a director of the Northern Pacific Railway. Today agriculture, ranching and tourism are the main industries. In recent years, celebrities such as Peter Fonda and Margot Kidder have bought houses here.
Information: Visitor Information Center, 303 E. Park,
406-222-0850; www.yellowstone-chamber.com

MONTANA

★
★
★
★
★

HOTELS
★★BEST WESTERN YELLOWSTONE INN
1515 W. Park St., Livingston, 406-222-6110,
800-780-7234; www.theyellowstoneinn.com
99 rooms. Pets accepted; fee. Complimentary continental breakfast. Restaurant, bar. Indoor pool. Wireless Internet access. $

★★CHICO HOT SPRINGS RESORT
1 Old Chico Road, Pray, 406-333-4933, 800-468-9232; www.chicohotsprings.com
102 rooms. Pets accepted, some restrictions; fee. Restaurant, bar. Fitness center. Spa. Outdoor pool, whirlpool. $

SPECIALTY LODGING
MOUNTAIN SKY GUEST RANCH
Big Creek Road, Emigrant, 406-333-4911, 800-548-3392; www.mtnsky.com
Mountain Sky is a family-friendly ranch offering a variety of activities. Enjoy the beautiful countryside while horseback riding or gaze at it by the outdoor pool. 30 rooms. Closed mid-October-April. Complimentary full breakfast. Outdoor pool, whirlpool. Tennis. Airport transportation available. $$$$

MISSOULA
Since the days of the Lewis and Clark Expedition, Missoula has been a trading and transportation crossroads. It is a lumber and paper manufacturing center, the hub of large reserves of timber, and the regional headquarters of the U.S. Forest Service and Montana State Forest Service.
Information: Missoula Convention and Visitors Bureau, 1121 E. Broadway St.,
406-532-3250; www.missoulachamber.com, www.exploremissoula.com

WHAT TO SEE AND DO
LOLO NATIONAL FOREST
Missoula, 406-329-3750; www.fs.fed.us
Located in West-Central Montana, Lolo National Forest is a popular recreation destination in both summer and winter, with hiking and cross-country skiing. Foot trails to 100 lakes and peaks in the more than two-million acres of forest, which include the Welcome Creek Wilderness and Rattlesnake National Recreation Area and Wilderness, part of Scapegoat Wilderness and Selway-Bitterroot Wilderness. Fishing is another big draw here, with four excellent rivers and their myriad tributaries running through the Lolo. The historic Lolo Trail and Lewis and Clark Highway (Highway 12) over the Bitterroot Mountains take visitors along the route of famed exploration. In the town of Huson, the Forest Service operates the unique Nine Mile Wildlands Training Center, where visitors can enroll in classes covering such skills as horsemanship, backcountry survival and historic preservation.

MONTANA SNOWBOWL
Snow Bowl Road, Missoula, 406-549-9777; www.montanasnowbowl.com
Spread over two mountains linked by a skiable saddle, Montana Snowbowl is an underrated resort with an impressive 2,600-foot vertical drop. There are plenty of close-in runs for experienced skiers on Snowbowl's 950 acres (20 percent beginner,

MONTANA

★
★★
★★
★★
★

40 percent intermediate and 40 percent expert). The backside Lavelle Creek Area is ideal for families, with runs for all ski levels in close proximity. There is a restaurant and a ski school, and in-mountain accommodations are available at a European-style lodge. Late November-April, Monday, Wednesday-Sunday.

SPECIAL EVENT
INTERNATIONAL WILDLIFE FILM FESTIVAL
Missoula, 406-728-9380; www.wildlifefilms.org
The biggest event of its kind, this weeklong film fest in May showcases the best wildlife films the world has to offer, with a strong emphasis on conservation of wildlife and its habitat. Held at several downtown venues, it kicks off with a parade and an outdoor community festival and continues with numerous public screenings, as well as workshops and lectures. Mid-May.

HOTELS
★BEST WESTERN GRANT CREEK INN
5280 Grant Creek Road, Missoula, 406-543-0700,
888-780-7234; www.bestwestern.com
126 rooms. Pets accepted; fee. Complimentary continental breakfast. Wireless Internet access. Fitness center. Indoor pool, whirlpool. Airport transportation available. Business center. $

★★DOUBLETREE HOTEL
100 Madison, Missoula, 406-728-3100, 800-222-8733; www.doubletree.com
172 rooms. Pets accepted, some restrictions; fee. Wireless Internet access. Restaurant, bar. Fitness center. Outdoor pool, whirlpool. Business Center. Airport transportation available. $

★HAMPTON INN
4805 N. Reserve St., Missoula, 406-549-1800, 800-426-7866; www.hamptoninn.com
61 rooms. Pets accepted; fee. Complimentary continental breakfast. Wireless Internet access. Fitness center. Indoor pool, whirlpool. Airport transportation available. $

★★HOLIDAY INN DOWNTOWN AT THE PARK
200 S. Pattee St., Missoula, 406-721-8550, 800-399-0408; www.himissoula.com
200 rooms. Pets accepted; fee. Wireless Internet access. Restaurant, bar. Fitness center. Indoor pool, whirlpool. Airport transportation available. Business Center. $

★QUALITY INN
3803 Brooks St., Missoula, 406-251-2665; www.choicehotels.com
81 rooms. Pets accepted; fee. Complimentary continental breakfast. Whirlpool. Airport transportation available. High-speed Internet access. $

★RED LION
700 W. Broadway, Missoula, 406-728-3300, 800-733-5466; www.redlion.com
76 rooms. Pets accepted; fee. Complimentary continental breakfast. Wireless Internet access. Fitness center. Outdoor pool, whirlpool. Airport transportation available. $

103

MONTANA

★
★
★
★
★

POLSON

At the south edge of Flathead Lake, Polson is the trade center for a productive farming area and a provisioning point for mountain trips. According to legend, Paul Bunyan dug the channel from Flathead Lake to Flathead River.

Information: Chamber of Commerce, 7 Third Ave. West,
406-883-5969; www.polsonchamber.com

WHAT TO SEE AND DO
FLATHEAD LAKE BIOLOGICAL STATION
311 Bio Station Lane, Polson, 406-982-3301; www.umt.edu/flbs
Run by the University of Montana, this state-of-the-art ecological research and education center has free public seminars for adults and children as well as natural laboratories for teaching and research, a museum and self-guided nature trips. Monday-Friday; closed holidays.

NINEPIPE AND PABLO NATIONAL WILDLIFE REFUGES
132 Bison Range Road, Moiese, 406-644-2211; www.fws.gov/bisonrange/ninepipe
More than 180 species of birds have been observed in these waterfowl refuges, including ducks, geese, grebes, great blue herons and cormorants. Fishing is permitted at certain times and in areas in accordance with tribal and state regulations. Joint state tribal recreation permit and fishing stamp are required. Portions of (or all) refuges may be closed during waterfowl season and nesting period.

POLSON-FLATHEAD HISTORICAL MUSEUM
708 Main St., Polson, 406-883-3049; www.polsonflatheadmuseum.org
This museum has Native American artifacts and farm and household items from the opening of the Flathead Reservation in 1910. It's the home of Rudolph, a Scotch-Highland steer, who appeared in more than 136 parades in five states and Canada; a wildlife display; and an old stagecoach. Memorial Day-Labor Day, Sunday 10 a.m.-3 p.m., Monday-Saturday 9 a.m.-5 p.m.

HOTEL
★★BEST WESTERN KWATAQNUK RESORT
49708 Highway 93 E., Polson, 406-883-3636, 800-882-6363; www.kwataqnuk.com
112 rooms. Pets accepted; fee. Restaurant, bar. Indoor pool, outdoor pool, whirlpool. High-speed Internet access. $

RED LODGE

The seat of Carbon County and a busy resort town, Red Lodge was (according to legend) named for a Native American tribe whose tepees were painted red. It offers a magnificent approach to Yellowstone National Park and is the gateway to the half-million-acre Beartooth-Absaroka Wilderness Area. A Ranger District office of the Custer National Forest is located here.

Information: www.redlodge.com

HOTELS

★COMFORT INN
612 N. Broadway, Red Lodge, 406-446-4469, 877-424-6423; www.comfortinn.com
53 rooms. Pets accepted; fee. Complimentary continental breakfast. Fitness center. Indoor pool, whirlpool. Wireless Internet access. **$**

★★POLLARD HOTEL
2 N. Broadway, Red Lodge, 406-446-0001, 800-765-5273; www.pollardhotel.com
39 rooms. Complimentary continental breakfast. Restaurant, bar. Fitness center. **$**

★★ROCK CREEK RESORT
Highway 212, Red Lodge, 406-446-1111, 800-667-1119; www.rockcreekresort.com
39 rooms. Restaurant, bar. Fitness center. Indoor pool, whirlpool. Tennis. **$**

RESTAURANT

★★OLD PINEY DELL
Highway 212, Red Lodge, 406-446-1196, 800-667-1119; www.rockcreekresort.com
American menu. Dinner, Sunday brunch. Bar. Winter: closed Sunday. Children's menu. Casual attire. Reservations recommended. **$$**

VIRGINIA CITY

This ghost town was revived and restored beginning in the 1950s and now serves as a great example of an old west mining town. On May 26, 1863, gold was found in the area. Ten-thousand gold miners arrived within a month, followed by bands of desperadoes—190 murders were committed in seven months. Vigilantes hunted down 21 road agents and discovered that the sheriff was the leader of the criminals. Nearly $300 million in gold was washed from Alder Gulch, but the area faded as the diggings became less productive. The restoration program has brought back much of the early mining-town atmosphere.
Information: Chamber of Commerce, 800-829-2969; www.virginiacitychamber.com

WHAT TO SEE AND DO

GILBERT'S BREWERY
Virginia City; www.virginacitymt.com
Virginia City's first brewery was built in 1864. The main building has been restored and the original brewery is still inside. Musical variety shows: mid-June-mid-September, Monday, Wednesday-Sunday.

WEST GLACIER

This Northwestern Montana town is an entry point for exploring Glacier National Park. The town has coffee houses, restaurants and any kind of supplies needed for camping and mountaineering trips.
Information: www.npc.gov/glac

WHAT TO SEE AND DO

SPERRY AND GRINNELL GLACIERS
Going-to-the-Sun Road and Highland Trail, West Glacier,
406-888-7800; www.nrmsc.usgs.gov
The largest glaciers in the park can be found here.

105

MONTANA

★
★
★
★
★

GLACIER NATIONAL PARK

Big, rugged and primitive, Glacier National Park is nature's unspoiled domain. This is the place for a snowball fight in midsummer, glacial solitude, alpine flowers and lonely and remote campgrounds along fir-fringed lakes. The park is also a living textbook in geology.

Declared a national park on May 11, 1910, these more than 1 million acres of spectacular scenery are preserved year after year, much as they were when Meriwether Lewis saw them in the distance in 1806. The United States and Canada share the area—the 204 square miles of Canada that are linked to Glacier are known as the Waterton-Glacier International Peace Park. Glacier National Park contains 50 glaciers, among the few in the United States, some of which are relatively accessible. There are more than 200 lakes and 1,400 varieties of plants, 63 species of animals—from mice to moose—and 272 varieties of birds.

Spectacular views of the park can be glimpsed from a car, particularly when crossing the Continental Divide on Going-to-the-Sun Road. It is 50 miles long and one of the most magnificent drives in the world (open approximately mid-June-mid-October). As of January 1994, vehicles longer than 21 feet (including trailers) and wider than 8 feet (including mirrors) are prohibited from Going-to-the-Sun Road between Avalanche and Sun Point. The road continuously winds up and down in tight curves. This unforgettable ride links the east and west sides of the park, passing over Logan Pass for a 100-mile view from an elevation of 6,646 feet. It connects with Highway 89 at St. Mary and with Highway 2 at West Glacier. Highway 89 on the east side of the park is called the Blackfeet Highway, extending from Browning to Canada. The road to Many Glacier Valley branches from Highway 89, nine miles north of St. Mary. The road to Two Medicine Lake leaves Highway 49, four miles north of East Glacier Park. Chief Mountain International Highway (Highway 17) leads to Waterton Lakes National Park in Canada.

Most of the park, including the glaciers, is accessible only by trail. There are 732 miles of maintained trails penetrating to remote wilderness areas. Whether you're going by foot or on horseback, magnificent and isolated parts of Glacier await discovery.

There are eight major and five semi-primitive campgrounds. The camping limit is seven days. Most campgrounds are available on a first-come, first-served basis. Fish Creek and St. Mary campgrounds may be reserved ahead of time through the National Park Reservation System by calling 877-444-6777. Visitors planning to camp overnight in Glacier's backcountry must obtain a Backcountry User Permit and camp in designated sites.

Information: Park Headquarters, West Glacier, 406-888-7800; www.nps.gov/glac/; open daily.

HOTELS

★★IZAAK WALTON INN

290 Izaak Walton Inn Road, Essex, 406-888-5700; www.izaakwaltoninn.com

33 rooms. Complimentary continental breakfast. Restaurant, bar. **$**

★★LAKE MCDONALD LODGE

Going-to-the-Sun Road, West Glacier, 406-892-2525; www.glacierparkinc.com
100 rooms. Restaurants, bar. $

★VILLAGE INN

Going-to-the-Sun Road, Apgar, 406-892-2525; www.glacierparkinc.com
36 rooms. $

WEST YELLOWSTONE

At the west entrance to Yellowstone National Park, this town serves as a hub for incoming tourists. Not long ago, West Yellowstone was abandoned and snowbound in the winter. Today, winter sports and attractions keep the town busy year-round. A Ranger District office of the Gallatin National Forest is located here.

Information: Chamber of Commerce, 30 Yellowstone Ave.,
406-646-7701; www.westyellowstonechamber.com

WHAT TO SEE AND DO

XANTERRA PARKS & RESORTS

West Yellowstone, 307-344-7311; www.xanterra.com
Xanterra offers guided snow coach tours and cross-country ski trips through Yellowstone National Park departing from West Yellowstone and other locations surrounding the park. Mid-December-early March. Summer season offers full-day bus tours, boat tours and horseback rides in the park. June-August. Reservations recommended.

YELLOWSTONE IMAX THEATRE

101 S. Canyon St., West Yellowstone,
406-646-4100, 888-854-5862; www.yellowstoneimax.com
A six-story-high screen shows "Yellowstone," a film interpreting the history, wildlife, geothermal activity and grandeur of America's first national park. Exhibits include wildlife photography, props used in the film and "Effects of the Yellowstone Hot Spot." Daily, shows hourly.

HOTELS

★BEST WESTERN DESERT INN

133 Canyon St., West Yellowstone, 406-646-7376,
800-780-7234; www.bestwestern.com
74 rooms. Complimentary continental breakfast. Pets accepted; fee. Wireless Internet access. Indoor pool. $

★GRAY WOLF INN & SUITES

250 S. Canyon St., West Yellowstone, 406-646-0000,
800-852-8602; www.graywolf-inn.com
102 rooms. Pets accepted, some restrictions. Complimentary continental breakfast. Indoor pool, whirlpool. Airport transportation available. $

MONTANA

★
★
★
★
★

★★HOLIDAY INN SUNSPREE RESORT WEST YELLOWSTONE

315 Yellowstone Ave., West Yellowstone,
406-646-7365, 800-646-7365; www.doyellowstone.com
123 rooms. Restaurant, bar. Fitness center. Indoor pool, whirlpool. Airport transportation available. High-speed Internet access. $$

★★STAGE COACH INN

209 Madison Ave., West Yellowstone,
406-646-7381, 800-842-2882; www.yellowstoneinn.com
83 rooms. Pets accepted, some restrictions. Restaurant, bar. Whirlpool. Complimentary continental breakfast. Wireless Internet access. $

RESTAURANT
★★THREE BEAR

207 Yellowstone Ave., West Yellowstone,
406-646-7353, 800-646-7353; www.threebearlodge.com
American menu. Breakfast, dinner. Closed holidays; late March-early May, late October-mid-December. Bar. Children's menu. Casual attire. $$

WHITEFISH

Located on the shore of Whitefish Lake, this community headquarters a four-state summer vacation area and is a winter ski center, as well. A growing forest products industry and the railroad constitute the other side of Whitefish's economy.

Information: Flathead Convention & Visitor Bureau, 15 Depot Park,
Kalispell, 406-756-9091, 800-543-3105; www.fcvb.org

★
★ ★
★ ★
★

WHAT TO SEE AND DO
BIG MOUNTAIN SKI AND SUMMER RESORT

County 487, Flathead National Forest, Whitefish, 800-858-4152;
www.skiwhitefish.com
This ski resort has a double, four triple, two high-speed quad chairlifts, T-bar, platter lift and ski patrol. The longest run is 3 1/2 miles, and the vertical drop is 2,500 feet.

HOTELS
★★GROUSE MOUNTAIN LODGE

2 Fairway Drive, Whitefish, 406-862-3000, 800-321-8822; www.grmtlodge.com
153 rooms. Restaurant, bar. Fitness center. Indoor pool, two whirlpools. Airport transportation available. Business Center. Wireless Internet access. $$

★★KANDAHAR THE LODGE AT BIG MOUNTAIN

3824 Big Mountain Road, Whitefish,
406-862-6098, 800-862-6094; www.kandaharlodge.com
50 rooms. Closed mid-April-May and October-late November. Complimentary full breakfast. Wireless Internet access. Restaurant, bar. Fitness center. $$

★PINE LODGE

920 Spokane Ave., Whitefish, 406-862-7600, 800-305-7463; www.thepinelodge.com

76 rooms. Pets accepted, some restrictions. Complimentary continental breakfast. Fitness center. Indoor pool, outdoor pool, whirlpool. Airport transportation available. High-speed Internet access. **$**

SPECIALTY LODGING

GOOD MEDICINE LODGE

537 Wisconsin Ave., Whitefish, 406-862-5488,

800-860-5488; www.goodmedicinelodge.com

This small, cozy bed and breakfast has rooms decorated with rustic furnishings and Native American-influenced fabrics. Some rooms have balconies. Nine rooms. Complimentary full breakfast. Wireless Internet access. Whirlpool. **$**

109

MONTANA

★
★
★
★
★

OREGON

THIS IS THE END OF THE FAMOUS OREGON TRAIL FROM WHICH CAME SCORES OF PIONEERS in covered wagons. The state abounds in the romance of the country's westward expansion. Meriwether Lewis and William Clark, sent by President Thomas Jefferson to explore the vast area bought in the Louisiana Purchase, ended their explorations here. This was also the scene of John Jacob Astor's fortune-making fur trade and that of Hudson's Bay Company, which hoped to keep the area for England.

English Captain James Cook was the first European to see the coast in 1778, but it remained for Lewis and Clark to discover what a prize Oregon was. When they returned to St. Louis in 1806, they spread the word. In 1811, Astor's Pacific Fur Company built its post at Astoria, only to be frightened into selling it to the British North West Company during the War of 1812. Other fur traders, missionaries, salmon fishermen and travelers followed them, but the Oregon country was hard to reach. The first true settlers did not arrive until 1839, four years before a great wagon train blazed the Oregon Trail.

Cattle and sheep were driven up from California, and land was cleared for farms. Oregon was settled by pioneers looking for good land that could support them. Local Native Americans resented the early settlers and fought them until 1880. The Oregon Territory, established in 1848, received a flood of immigrants. More arrived after President James Buchanan proclaimed statehood 11 years later.

The rich forests that flourished in the moist climate west of the Cascade Mountains produced much lumber. The streams provided fish, and the woods also offered nuts and berries. The Columbia, Willamette, Rogue and other rivers offered transportation to the sea. Steamboats coasted on the Willamette and Columbia rivers as early as 1850. The first ship's wheat cargo traveled from Portland to Liverpool in 1868. When the railroad reached Portland in 1883, the state shipped out fish, grain, lumber and livestock.

Oregon's vast rivers provided electric power and water to irrigate farms east of the Cascades. Timber is still important: One quarter of Oregon is national forest land. Sustained yield practices by lumber companies ensure a continuing supply.

One of the most beautiful drives in Oregon extends from Portland to The Dalles, the end of the Oregon Trail, along the Columbia River. Here is the Columbia Gorge, designated a National Scenic Area, where waterfalls, streams and mountains abound. The area offers many recreational activities such as camping, skiing, snowmobiling, windsurfing and hiking.

The visitor who loves the outdoors or the American West loves Oregon. Each year, millions of tourists enjoy the state's magnificent coastline, blue lakes, mountains and forests.

Information: www.traveloregon.com

FUN FACTS

At 1,932 feet, Crater Lake is the deepest lake in the United States.

Oregon has more ghost towns than any other state.

ALBANY

The gateway to Oregon's covered bridge country, Albany was founded by Walter and Thomas Monteith and named for their former home, Albany, N.Y. The city boasts the state's largest collection of Victorian homes. The seat of Linn County, Albany is nestled in the heart of the Willamette Valley along the Interstate 5 corridor of the Cascades. The Calapooia River joins the Willamette here.

Information: Albany Visitors Association, 250 Broadalbin S.W., Albany, 541-928-0911, 800-526-2256; www.albanyvisitors.com

WHAT TO SEE AND DO
SPECIAL EVENT
HISTORIC INTERIOR HOMES TOURS

300 Second Ave., S.W., Albany, 541-928-0911, 800-526-2256; www.albanyhistorictours.zoomshare.com

Last Saturday of July and second Sunday of December.

HOTEL
★LA QUINTA INN

251 Airport Road S.E., Albany, 541-928-0921, 800-642-4271; www.laquinta.com

62 rooms. Complimentary continental breakfast. High-speed Internet access. Fitness center. Indoor pool, whirlpool. Pets accepted, some restrictions. **$**

ASHLAND

When the pioneers climbed over the Siskiyou Mountains and saw the green expanse of the Rogue River Valley ahead, many decided to go no further and settled here. Later, when mineral springs were found, their Lithia water was piped in; it now gushes from fountains on this city's plaza. Tourism, education and small industry support the town. Southern Oregon University College makes Ashland a regional education center. The Rogue River National Forest is on three sides; a Ranger District office is located here.

Information: Chamber of Commerce, 110 E. Main St., Ashland, 541-482-3486; www.ashlandchamber.com

WHAT TO SEE AND DO
LITHIA PARK

E. 59 Winburn Way (at E. Main St.), Ashland, 541-488-5340 (band shell performances), 541-482-3486 (nature walks); www.nps.gov/nr/travel/ashland/lit.htm

Adjacent to City Plaza, the park has 100 acres of woodlands and ponds along with nature trails, tennis, concerts, picnicking, sand volleyball, and rose and Japanese gardens. Daily.

MOUNT ASHLAND SKI AREA

693 Washington St., Ashland, eight miles south on I-5, then nine miles west on access road, 541-482-2897; www.mtashland.com

The ski area has two triple and two double chairlifts, school, rentals and a cafeteria and bar. The longest run is one mile and the highest vertical drop is 1,150 feet. Thanksgiving-April.

★
★★
★★★
★★★★
★★★★★

SPECIAL EVENTS
OREGON CABARET THEATRE
241 Hargadine St., Ashland, 541-488-2902; www.oregoncabaret.com
The Oregon Cabaret Theatre presents musicals, revues and comedies in a dinner club setting. Schedule varies. February-December.

OREGON SHAKESPEARE FESTIVAL
15 S. Pioneer St., Ashland, 541-482-4331, 800-219-8161; www.orshakes.org
From its humble beginnings with a 1935 staging of *Twelfth Night,* this repertory theater has evolved in size and scope, earning a reputation for excellent productions and making Ashland a must-stop destination for drama lovers. *Time* magazine recognized the festival in 2003, naming the company as one of the five best regional theaters in the United States. Running from February to early November, the festival features a variety of drama from Shakespeare to modern plays. OSF actually consists of three separate theaters: the New Theatre, Angus Bowmer Theatre and the open-air Elizabethan Stage. February-early November.

HOTELS
★★ASHLAND SPRINGS HOTEL
212 E. Main St., Ashland, 541-488-1700, 888-795-4545; www.ashlandspringshotel.com
70 rooms. Complimentary continental breakfast. Wireless Internet access. Restaurant, bar. Pets accepted, some restrictions; fee. **$$**

★BEST WESTERN BARD'S INN
132 N. Main St., Ashland, 541-482-0049, 800-780-7234; www.bestwestern.com
91 rooms. Complimentary continental breakfast. Outdoor pool, whirlpool. Pets accepted; fee. **$**

★★★MT. ASHLAND INN
550 Mt. Ashland Road, Ashland, exit six from I-5, five miles west,
541-482-8707, 800-830-8707; www.mtashlandinn.com
Sandwiched between slopes and cliffs and mountain ranges, the Mt. Ashland Inn provides guests with a breathtaking view no matter where they look. Guests will enjoy activities such as hiking, skiing, rafting, sledding and fishing. Five rooms. Children over 10 years only. Complimentary full breakfast. **$$**

★STRATFORD INN
555 Siskiyou Blvd., Ashland, 541-488-2151, 800-547-4741;
www.stratfordinnashland.com
55 rooms. Complimentary continental breakfast. Wireless Internet access. Indoor pool, whirlpool. Spa. **$**

★★★THE WINCHESTER INN & RESTAURANT
35 S. Second St., Ashland, 541-488-1113, 800-972-4991; www.winchesterinn.com
Located one block from downtown Ashland, this restored Victorian house once served as the area's first hospital. The individually decorated rooms boast several pieces of antique furniture along with plush bedding that includes feather beds and down blankets. Some bathrooms feature claw foot tubs, and others have Jacuzzi tubs and

separate showers. Rooms feature flat screen TVs, stereos and fireplaces. 19 rooms. Complimentary full breakfast. Wireless Internet access. Restaurant, bar. **$$**

★★WINDMILL INN AND SUITES OF ASHLAND
2525 Ashland St., Ashland, 541-482-8310, 800-547-4747; www.windmillinns.com
230 rooms. Complimentary continental breakfast. Wireless Internet access. Fitness center. Outdoor pool, whirlpool. Tennis. Airport transportation available. Pets allowed. **$**

SPECIALTY LODGINGS
CHANTICLEER INN
120 Gresham St., Ashland, 541-482-1919, 800-898-1950; www.ashlandbnb.com
This inn is convenient to many area attractions such as the Shakespeare Festival, Cascade volcanoes and the Oregon Caves. Antiques, fine art and a beautifully manicured garden welcome guests for a romantic getaway. Six rooms. Complimentary full breakfast. Wireless Internet access. **$$**

COUNTRY WILLOWS BED & BREAKFAST INN
1313 Clay St., Ashland, 541-488-1590, 800-945-5697; www.willowsinn.com
This restored 1890s farmhouse is surrounded by 5 acres of farmland in the Siskiyou and Cascade mountains. Breakfast is served every morning at private tables. Nine rooms. Children over 12 years only. Complimentary full breakfast. High-speed Internet access. Outdoor pool, whirlpool. **$$**

OAK HILL BED & BREAKFAST
2190 Siskiyou Blvd., Ashland, 888-482-1554; www.oakhillbb.com
Six rooms. Children over 12 years only. Complimentary full breakfast. **$**

ROMEO INN BED & BREAKFAST
295 Idaho St., Ashland, 541-488-0884, 800-915-8899; www.romeoinn.com
Established in 1982, this bed and breakfast property has amenities to help guests relax and enjoy their time away from the hustle and bustle of life. Six rooms. Children over 12 years only. Complimentary full breakfast. Restaurant. Outdoor pool, whirlpool. **$**

RESTAURANTS
★ASHLAND BAKERY & CAFÉ
38 E. Main St., Ashland, 541-482-2117; www.ashlandbistrocafe.com
American menu. Breakfast, lunch, dinner. Closed Tuesday in winter. Children's menu. Casual attire. **$**

★★CHATEAULIN
50 E. Main St., Ashland, 541-482-2264; www.chateaulin.com
French menu. Dinner. Closed Monday, Tuesday in winter. Bar. Business casual attire. Reservations recommended. **$$$**

★★WINCHESTER COUNTRY INN
35 S. Second St., Ashland, 541-488-1113, 800-972-4991; www.winchesterinn.com
International menu. Dinner, brunch. Closed January; and Sunday, Monday February-March. Bar. Business casual attire. Reservations recommended. Outdoor seating. **$$**

★
★
★
★
★

ASTORIA

John Jacob Astor's partners sailed around Cape Horn and picked this land 10 miles from the Pacific, overlooking the mouth of the Columbia River, for a fur-trading post. The post lost its importance eventually, but the location and natural resources attracted immigrants and the town grew. A four-mile bridge crosses the mouth of the Columbia here.

Information: Astoria-Warrenton Chamber of Commerce, 111 W. Marine Drive, Astoria, 503-325-6311, 800-875-6807; www.oldoregon.com

WHAT TO SEE AND DO

ASTORIA COLUMN
Follow scenic drive signs to Coxcomb Hill, 503-325-7275; www.astoriacolumn.org

A 125-foot tower commemorates the first settlement with a gift shop, information booth and an observation deck at the top. Memorial Day-Labor Day, daily.

COLUMBIA RIVER MARITIME MUSEUM
1792 Marine Drive, Astoria, 503-325-2323; www.crmm.org

The museum features rare maritime artifacts and memorabilia of the Columbia River, its tributaries and the Northwest coast. Visitors can browse exhibits on the fishing industry, discovery and exploration, steamships, shipwrecks, the Coast Guard, Navy, navigation and steamboats. Daily 9:30 a.m.-5 p.m.

FLAVEL HOUSE
441 Eighth St., Astoria, 503-325-2203; www.cumtux.org

Flavel House is built by Captain George Flavel, a pilot and shipping man. It is an outstanding example of Queen Anne architecture. The restored Victorian home houses antique furnishings and fine art, along with a collection of 19th- and 20th-century toys. Visitors can also visit the carriage house, site of the museum store and orientation film. Daily 10 a.m.-5 p.m.

★
★★
★★
★☆

FORT CLATSOP NATIONAL MEMORIAL
92343 Fort Clatsop Road, Astoria, 503-861-2471; www.nps.gov/lewi

This site marks the Western extremity of the territory explored by Meriwether Lewis and William Clark in their expedition of 1804-1806. The fort is a reconstruction of their winter quarters. The original fort was built here because of its excellent elk-hunting grounds, easy access to ocean salt, protection from the westerly coastal storms and the availability of fresh water. The expedition set out on May 14, 1804 to seek "the most direct and practicable water communication across this continent" under orders from President Thomas Jefferson. The company left Fort Clatsop March 23, 1806 on their return trip and was back in St. Louis on September 23 of the same year. The Lewis and Clark Expedition was one of the greatest explorations in the history of the United States. The visitor center has museum exhibits and provides audiovisual programs. The canoe landing has replicas of dugout canoes of that period. Ranger talks and living history demonstrations are presented mid-June-Labor Day. Daily April-September.

FORT STEVENS STATE PARK

Astoria, five miles west on Highway 101, then five miles north on Ridge Road, 503-861-1671, 800-551-6949; www.oregonstateparks.org

A 3,763-acre park, Fort Stevens State Park is adjacent to an old Civil War fort and includes the wreck of the *Peter Iredale* on the ocean shore. Fort Stevens is the only military post in the lower 48 states to be fired upon by foreign forces since 1812. There is a visitor center and self-guided tour at the Old Fort Stevens Military Complex along with ocean beach and lake swimming, fishing, clamming, boating, bicycling and picnicking at Coffenbury Lake. Daily.

SPECIAL EVENTS

ASTORIA REGATTA

Astoria, 503-325-6311, 800-875-6807; www.astoriaregatta.org

The Regatta features a parade, arts festival, public dinner, barbecue and boating competition. Mid-August.

ASTORIA-WARRENTON CRAB AND SEAFOOD FESTIVAL

Clatsop County Fairgrounds, Hammond, 503-325-6311; www.clatsopfairgrounds.com

Carnival goers can enjoy a crab feast, Oregon wines, food and craft booths and carnival. Last weekend in April.

GREAT COLUMBIA CROSSING BRIDGE RUN

Port of Astoria, 1 Portway St., Astoria, 503-325-6311; www.greatcolumbiacrossing.com

One of the most unusual and scenic runs, the eight-mile course begins in Chinook, Wash., and ends at Astoria port docks. Mid-October.

SCANDINAVIAN MIDSUMMER FESTIVAL

Astoria, 503-338-0046; www.astoriascanfest.com

The festival features a parade, folk dancing, display booths, arts and crafts demonstrations and Scandinavian food. Mid-June.

HOTELS

★★★★★

★BEST WESTERN LINCOLN INN

555 Hamburg Ave., Astoria, 503-325-2205, 800-780-7234; www.bestwestern.com

76 rooms. Pets accepted; fee. Complimentary continental breakfast. High-speed Internet access. Indoor pool, whirlpool. $

★★RED LION

400 Industry St., Astoria, 503-325-7373, 800-733-5466; www.redlion.com

124 rooms. Restaurant, bar. Airport transportation available. Pets accepted; fee. $

★★SHILO INN

1609 E. Harbor Drive, Warrenton, 503-861-2181, 800-222-2244; www.shiloinns.com

62 rooms. Restaurant, bar. Fitness room. Indoor pool, whirlpool. Pets accepted; fee. Airport transportation available. $

SPECIALTY LODGING
ROSEBRIAR HOTEL
636 14th St., Astoria, 800-487-0224; www.rosebriar.net
12 rooms. Complimentary full breakfast.

RESTAURANT
★★SILVER SALMON GRILLE
1105 Commercial St., Astoria, 503-338-6640; www.silversalmongrille.com
American, seafood menu. Lunch, dinner. $$

BAKER CITY
The Baker City Historic District includes more than 100 commercial and residential buildings, many built from stone quarried in town at the same place where gold was found. A 15-block area, from the Powder River to Fourth Street and from Estes to Campbell streets, has many structures built between 1890 and 1910 that are being restored. Baker City, on the "old Oregon trail," is also the home of the 80-ounce Armstrong Gold Nugget found by George Armstrong on June 19, 1913.
Information: Baker County Visitor & Convention Bureau, 490 Campbell St., Baker City, 541-523-3355, 800-523-1235; www.visitbaker.com

WHAT TO SEE AND DO
ANTHONY LAKES SKI AREA
47500 Anthony Lake Highway, North Powder, 35 miles northwest, off I-84, 541-856-3277; www.anthonylakes.com
The ski area features a triple chairlift, cross country trails, a school, rentals, nursery, day lodge, cafeteria, concession area and bar. The longest run is 1 1/2 miles, and the peek vertical drop is 900 feet. Skiing mid-November-mid-April Thursday-Sunday. Fishing, hiking, cabin rentals, store open summer.

EASTERN OREGON MUSEUM
610 Third St., Haines, 541-856-3233; www.hainesoregon.com
The museum exhibits a large collection of relics and implements used in the development of the West, turn-of-the-century logging and mining tools, period rooms, a doll collection and children's antique furniture. On the grounds is an 1884 railroad depot. Mid-April-Labor Day Thursday-Monday.

NATIONAL HISTORIC OREGON TRAIL INTERPRETIVE CENTER
22267 Highway 86, Baker City, 541-523-1843, 800-523-1235; www.blm.gov
Learn about the Oregon Trail through exhibits, living history presentations and multimedia displays. Daily.

OREGON TRAIL REGIONAL MUSEUM
2490 Grove St., Baker City, 541-523-9308, 800-523-1235; www.bakercounty.org
The Oregon Trail Regional Museum houses one of the most outstanding collections of rocks, minerals and semiprecious stones in the West along with housing an elaborate sea life display, wildlife display, period clothing and artifacts of early Baker County. Late March-October daily.

SUMPTER VALLEY RAILWAY
Baker City, 30 miles southwest on Highway 7, 541-894-2268, 866-894-2268;
www.svry.com

A restored gear-driven Heisler steam locomotive and two observation cars travel seven miles on a narrow-gauge track through a wildlife game habitat area where beavers, muskrats, geese and other animals can be seen. The train also passes through the Sumpter mining district, the location of the Sumpter Dredge. The dredge recovered more than $10 million in gold between 1913 and 1954. Memorial Day-September weekends and holidays.

UNITY LAKE STATE PARK
Highway 26, Mount Vernon, 45 miles southwest on Highway 245, near junction
Highway 26, 541-932-4453, 800-551-6949; www.oregonstateparks.org/park_10.php

A 39-acre park with swimming, fishing, camping and a boat ramp on Unity Lake.

WALLOWA-WHITMAN NATIONAL FOREST
1550 Dewey Ave., Baker City, 541-523-6391; www.fs.fed.us/r6/w-w

Located on more than 2 million acres, the national forest has a variety of areas explore including the 14,000-acre North Fork John Day Wilderness, 7,000-acre Monument Rock Wilderness, 358,461-acre Eagle Cap Wilderness, 215,500-acre Hells Canyon Wilderness. Visitors will find snowcapped peaks, alpine meadows and rare wildflowers. Take a scenic drive to Hells Canyon Overlook, which overlooks the deepest canyon in North America. Other diversions include stream and lake trout fishing, elk, deer and bear hunting, float and jet boat trips and saddle and pack trips.

HOTELS
★★BEST WESTERN SUNRIDGE INN
1 Sunridge Lane, Baker City, 541-523-6444,
800-780-7234; www.bestwestern.com

154 rooms. High-speed Internet access. Restaurant, bar. Outdoor pool, whirlpool. Pets accepted; fee. **$**

★★GEISER GRAND HOTEL
1996 Main St., Baker City, 541-523-1889, 888-434-7374;
www.geisergrand.com

30 rooms. Wireless Internet access. Restaurant, bar. Pets accepted; fee. **$**

OREGON

BANDON

A picturesque beach, legendary rocks and a harbor at the mouth of the Coquille River attract many travelers to Bandon. From November through March, the town is known for its short-lived storms followed by sunshine: It even has a group called the Storm Watchers. Popular seashore activities include beachcombing, hiking, fishing from the south jetty and crabbing from the docks. Summer and early autumn bring the salmon run in the Coquille River. Geology lovers can search for agate, jasper and petrified wood.

Information: Chamber of Commerce, 300 Second St., Bandon, 514-347-9616;
www.bandon.com

WHAT TO SEE AND DO
BANDON HISTORICAL SOCIETY MUSEUM
270 Filmore Ave., Bandon, 541-347-2164; www.bandonhistoricalmuseum.org
History buffs will find exhibits on maritime activities of early Bandon and Coquille River, coastal shipwrecks, Coast Guard operations and an extensive collection of Native American artifacts and old photos. Schedule varies.

BULLARDS BEACH STATE PARK
52470 Highway 101, Bandon, 541-347-3501; www.oregonstateparks.org
A 1,266-acre park with four miles of ocean beach, Bullards Beach State Park brings in visitors for fishing, boating and picnicking. If you're curious about local history the Coquille River Lighthouse includes interpretive plaques. May-October daily.

FACE ROCK STATE PARK
Bandon, four miles south on Highway 101, then one mile west on Bradley Lake Road, 800-551-6949; www.oregonstateparks.org
An 879-acre park on coastal dune area, Face Rock offers beach access, fishing and picnicking.

WEST COAST GAME PARK
Highway 101, Bandon, seven miles south on Highway 101, 541-347-3106; www.gameparksafari.com
A 21-acre park with more than 450 exotic animals and birds, allows visitors to the game park meet and walk with free-roaming wildlife. Animal keepers demonstrate the personalities of many large predators residing at the park. March-November, daily; December-February, weekends and holidays.

SPECIAL EVENTS
CRANBERRY FESTIVAL
Bandon, 541-347-9616; www.bandon.com
The fall festival features a parade, barbecue, square dances, harvest ball and sports events. September.

WINE & FOOD FESTIVAL
Bandon, 541-347-9616; www.bandon.com
Featuring handmade crafts as well as a variety of Oregon wines, the festival also offers regional foods and music. Memorial Day weekend.

HOTELS
★★BEST WESTERN INN AT FACE ROCK RESORT
3225 Beach Loop Road, Bandon, 541-347-9441, 800-638-3092, 800-780-7234; www.facerock.net, www.bestwestern.com
74 rooms. Restaurant. Fitness center. Beach. Indoor pool, whirlpool. Pets accepted, some restrictions; fee. $$

OREGON

★
★
★
★
★

★★★LODGE AT BANDON DUNES

57744 Round Lake Drive, Bandon, 541-347-4380, 888-345-6008;
www.bandondunesgolf.com

The Lodge at Bandon Dunes sits alongside the windswept coast of the Pacific Ocean. The property offers luxurious accommodations for the Bandon Dunes Golf Resort, home to two of the northwest's premiere 18-hole courses. All guest rooms feature scenic views, and some have fireplaces and private balconies. Just off the lobby, Gallery Restaurant serves three meals a day, specializing in fresh seafood. 153 rooms. Restaurant, bar. High-speed Internet access. Fitness center. Whirlpool. Airport transportation available. $$

★★SUNSET OCEANFRONT LODGING

1865 Beach Loop Drive, Bandon, 541-347-2453, 800-842-2407;
www.sunsetmotel.com

71 rooms. Restaurant, bar. Indoor pool, whirlpool. Spa. Pets accepted; fee. $

BEAVERTON

Nestled amid the scenic rolling hills and lush forests of the Tualatin Valley, Beaverton appeals to those who love to explore the great outdoors, offering more than 100 public parks, 30 miles of hiking trails and a 25-mile network of bike paths. Every home in the city is within a half mile of a park. Beaverton is situated midway between the beaches of the Pacific Ocean and the ski slopes at Mount Hood, either destination within an hour's drive. Oregon's fifth most populous city, Beaverton boasts strong public schools and close-knit residential neighborhoods. Economically, the city has been strengthened by the tremendous success of Nike, which is headquartered here. Each July, Beaverton's SummerFest features a parade, live music, freshly prepared food and an arts and crafts marketplace. The event draws thousands to this friendly community seven miles west of Portland.

Information: Beaverton Area Chamber of Commerce, 12655 S.W. Center St.,
Beaverton, 503-644-0123; www.beaverton.org

HOTELS

★★COURTYARD BY MARRIOTT

8500 S.W. Nimbus Drive, Beaverton, 503-641-3200, 888-236-2427;
www.courtyard.com

137 rooms. Bar. High-speed Internet access. Fitness center. Indoor pool, whirlpool. $

★FAIRFIELD INN & SUITES PORTLAND WEST/BEAVERTON

15583 N.W. Gateway Court, Beaverton, 503-972-0048, 888-236-2427;
www.marriott.com

106 rooms. Complimentary continental breakfast. Indoor pool, whirlpool. $

BEND

The early town was named Farewell Bend after a beautiful wooded area on a sweeping curve of the Deschutes River, where pioneer travelers had their last view of the river. The U.S. Post Office shortened it, but there was a good reason for this nostalgic name. As westward-bound settlers approached, they found the first lush, green forests and good water they had seen in Oregon. Tourists are attracted to the region year-round by its streams, lakes, mountains, great pine forests, ski slopes and golf courses. There is also much of interest to geologists and rock hounds in this area. Movie and television producers often take advantage of the wild western scenery. Two Ranger District offices of the Deschutes National Forest are located here.

Information: Chamber of Commerce, 777 N.W. Wall St., Bend,
541-382-3221; www.bendchamber.org

WHAT TO SEE AND DO

DESCHUTES NATIONAL FOREST
1001 S.W. Emkay Drive, Bend, 541-383-5300; www.fs.fed.us
The Deschutes National Forest encompasses 1.6 million acres of rugged wilderness, with snow-capped mountains, craggy volcanic formations, old-growth forests and deep rivers running through high-desert canyons. Established as a national forest in 1908, Deschutes has become one of the Pacific Northwest's most popular year-round tourist destinations, attracting more than eight million visitors annually. The winter months bring hordes of skiers and snowmobilers. Oregon's largest ski resort can be found alongside the 9,065-foot-high Mt. Bachelor. Hikers arrive after the spring thaw, eager to take advantage of the area's 1,388 miles of trails. Paddlers head to the Deschutes River, which has been designated both a National Scenic River and a National Recreational River. Anglers are drawn to the forest's 157 trout-filled lakes and reservoirs.

HIGH DESERT MUSEUM
59800 S. Highway 97, Bend, 541-382-4754; www.highdesertmuseum.org
A regional museum with indoor and outdoor exhibits featuring live animals and cultural history of the intermountain northwest arid lands, visitors at High Desert Museum can enjoy hands-on activities and ongoing presentations. The galleries house wildlife, western art and Native American artifacts. Walk-through dioramas depict the opening of the American west. The desertarium showcases seldom-seen bats, burrowing owls, amphibians and reptiles. Daily 9 a.m.-5 p.m.

LAPINE STATE PARK
15800 State Recreation Road, Bend, 541-536-2071, 800-551-6949;
www.oregonstateparks.org
A 2,333-acre park on the Deschutes River in the Ponderosa pine forest, LaPine offers scenic views, swimming, bathhouse, fishing, boating, picnicking and improved trailer campsites.

LAVA BUTTE AND LAVA RIVER CAVE
11 miles south on Highway 97, 541-593-2421; vulcan.wr.usgs.gov
Lava Butte is an extinct cinder cone. A paved road to the top provides a view of the Cascades and there are interpretive trails through the pine forest and lava flow. One mile south, Lava River Cave features a lava tube 1.2 miles long. The visitor center has audiovisual shows. May-September, daily.

MOUNT BACHELOR SKI AREA

22 miles southwest on Southwest Century Drive/Cascade Lakes Scenic Byway
(Highway 46), Bend, 541-382-2442, 800-829-2442; www.mtbachelor.com

Panoramic views of forests, lakes and Cascade Range await visitors to Mount Bachelor, with facilities at a base of 6,000 feet. With 56 miles of cross-country trails, the area has 10 chairlifts, ski patrol, school, rentals, cafeterias, concession areas, bars, lodges and day care. The longest run is 1 1/2 miles with the steepest vertical drop at 3,365 feet. Mid-November-May daily.

NEWBERRY NATIONAL VOLCANIC MONUMENT

24 miles south on Highway 97, then 14 miles east on Forest Road 21,
in Deschutes National Forest, 541-383-5300; www.fs.fed.us

This monument, an active volcano, has a wide range of volcanic features and deposits similar to those of Mount Etna such as obsidian flow and pumice deposits. On the same road are East and Paulina lakes, both of which have excellent fishing.

PILOT BUTTE STATE SCENIC VIEWPOINT

Pilot Butte Summit Drive, off Highway 20, Bend, one mile east on
Highway 20, 800-551-6949; www.oregonstateparks.org

A 101-acre park noted for a lone-cinder cone rising 511 feet above the city, the summit at the Pilot Butte affords an excellent view of the Cascade Range.

PINE MOUNTAIN OBSERVATORY

26 miles southeast via Highway 20, turn right at Millican, then eight miles
south on dirt road, Bend, 541-382-8331; www.pmo-sun.uoregon.edu

Visitors to the University of Oregon's astronomical research facility may view stars, planets and galaxies through telescopes. Memorial Day-September Friday and Saturday.

TUMALO

5 1/2 miles northwest off Highway 20, Bend, 541-382-3586, 800-551-6949;
www.oregonstateparks.org

A 320-acre park situated along the banks of the Deschutes River, Tumalo offers hiking, tent and trailer campsites, solar-heated showers and swimming and fishing nearby.

WHITEWATER RAFTING

Sun Country Tours, 531 S.W. 13th St., Bend, 541-382-6277, 800-770-2161;
www.suncountrytours.com

Thrill seekers can choose from two-hour or all-day rafting trips or try canoeing. May-September.

HOTELS

★★★INN OF THE SEVENTH MOUNTAIN

18575 S.W. Century Drive, Bend, 541-382-8711, 800-452-6810; www.7thmtn.com

With breathtaking views, this oasis is set in Deschutes National Forest. Activities such as whitewater rafting, horseback riding, golfing and canoeing make it Oregon's premiere resort destination. 250 rooms. Restaurant, bar. Outdoor pool, children's pool, whirlpool. Tennis. $

OREGON

★
★
★
★
★

★★RED LION
1415 N.E. Third St., Bend, 541-382-7011, 800-733-5466; www.redlion.com
75 rooms. Restaurant. Outdoor pool, whirlpool. Pets accepted. **$**

★★THE RIVERHOUSE
3075 N. Highway 97, Bend, 541-389-3111, 866-453-4480; www.riverhouse.com
220 rooms. Restaurant. Indoor pool, outdoor pool. Golf. Pets accepted. **$**

★★SHILO INN
3105 N.E. O. B. Riley Road, Bend, 541-389-9600, 800-222-2244; www.shiloinns.com
120 rooms. Restaurant, bar. Fitness center. Indoor pool, outdoor pool, whirlpool. Airport transportation available. Pets accepted, some restrictions; fee. **$**

★★★SUNRIVER RESORT
17600 Center Drive, Sunriver, 541-593-1000, 800-801-8765; www.sunriver-resort.com
This full-service, all-season resort on the sunny side of the scenic Cascade Mountain Range offers visitors a complete getaway with an endless supply of recreational opportunities, including sparkling pools, three 18-hole golf courses, fitness center and elegant spa. Recreational opportunities include canoe and kayak trips and biking trails. The Sunriver Nature Center and Observatory offers stargazing, botanical garden and nature trails. 441 rooms. Restaurant, bar. Fitness Center. Spa. Outdoor pool, children's pool, whirlpool. Airport transportation available. Tennis. **$**

SPECIALTY LODGINGS
DIAMOND STONE GUEST LODGE
16693 Sprague Loop, La Pine, 541-536-6263, 866-626-9887; www.diamondstone.com
This lodge sits adjacent to Quail Run Golf Course at the gateway to Newberry National Volcanic Monument with the Cascade Mountains as a backdrop. Surrounded by open meadows and pines, there are plenty of trails for hiking and exploring. Five rooms. Pets accepted, some restrictions. **$**

ROCK SPRINGS GUEST RANCH
64201 Tyler Road, Bend, 541-382-1957, 800-225-3833; www.rocksprings.com
26 rooms. Restaurant. Fitness center. Outdoor pool, whirlpool. Tennis. Airport transportation available. **$$**

RESTAURANTS
★★COWBOY DINNER TREE
Silver Lake, 4 1/2 miles south on East Bay Road (County 4-12 and Forest Service Road 28), 541-576-2426; cowboydinnertree.homestead.com
American menu. Dinner. Closed Monday, Tuesday, Thursday. No credit cards accepted. **$$**

★★★ERNESTO'S ITALIAN RESTAURANT
1203 N.E. Third St., Bend, 541-389-7274; www.ernestositalian.com
This former church is now a family restaurant featuring basic Italian fare. Italian menu. Dinner. Bar. Children's menu. **$$**

★★★MEADOWS AT THE LODGE

17600 Center Drive, Sunriver, 541-593-3740; www.sunriver-resort.com

This casual family restaurant is nestled in the Sunriver Resort. Its lovely, rustic dining room features large windows, which offer beautiful views of the golf course and Mt. Bachelor. The restaurant calls its menu Oregon's first indigenous cuisine with a western flair. Starters may include seared crab cakes with roasted red peppers, chipotle aioli and Asian slaw, while featured entrées are dishes such as ribs with a house barbecue sauce and mashed potatoes or a vegetarian walnut-and-mushroom loaf with creamy mushroom gravy. Kids are made to feel at home with their own menu and kids-only station at Sunday brunch. American menu. Dinner. Bar. **$$**

★★PINE TAVERN

967 N.W. Brooks St., Bend, 541-382-5581; www.pinetavern.com

Seafood, steak menu. Lunch, dinner. Bar. Children's menu. Outdoor seating. **$$**

BROOKINGS

Beachcombers, whale-watchers and fishermen find this coastal city a haven for their activities. A commercial and sport fishing center, Brookings lies in an area that produces a high percentage of the nation's Easter lily bulbs. A Ranger District office of the Siskiyou National Forest is located here.

Information: Brookings-Harbor Chamber of Commerce and Information Center, 16330 Lower Harbor Road, Brookings, 541-469-3181, 800-535-9469; www.brookingsor.com

WHAT TO SEE AND DO

ALFRED A. LOEB STATE PARK

1601 Highway 101 N. Brookings, 541-469-2021, 800-551-6949; www.oregonstateparks.org

A 320-acre park on the Chetco River with an area of old myrtle trees and redwoods, Alfred E. Load State Park offers swimming, fishing and improved camping.

AZALEA PARK

Highway 101 and North Bank Chetco River Road, Brookings, 541-469-1100; www.brookings.or.us

The name of the 36-acre city park comes from five varieties of large native azaleas found there, some blooming twice a year. Other features include an observation point, hiking and picnicking.

HARRIS BEACH STATE PARK

1655 Highway 101 N. Brookings, 541-469-2021, 800-551-6949; www.oregonstateparks.org

This is a 171-acre park with scenic rock cliffs along the ocean. Visitors come for the ocean beach, fishing, hiking trails, sights from the observation point, picnicking and improved tent and trailer campsites.

SAMUEL H. BOARDMAN STATE SCENIC CORRIDOR

4655 Highway 101 N. Brookings, 541-469-2021, 800-551-6949; www.oregonstateparks.org

A 1,473-acre park with observation points along 11 miles of spectacular coastline, the scenic corridor also features fishing, clamming, hiking and picnicking.

OREGON

★
★
★
★
★

SPECIAL EVENTS
AZALEA FESTIVAL
Azalea Park, Brookings, 541-469-3181; www.brookingsor.com
The annual Azalea Festival features a parade, seafood, art exhibits, street fair, crafts fair and music. Memorial Day weekend.

HOTEL
★★BEST WESTERN BROOKINGS INN
1143 Chetco Ave., Brookings, 541-469-2173, 800-780-7234; www.bestwestern.com
68 rooms. Complimentary continental breakfast. Wireless Internet access. Restaurant, bar. Indoor pool, whirlpool. $

BURNS
This remote trading center and county seat serves a livestock-raising and forage production area bigger than many eastern states. Ranger District offices of the Malheur National Forest and Ochoco National Forest are located here.
Information: Harney County Chamber of Commerce, 18 W. D St., Burns, 541-573-2636; www.harneycounty.com

WHAT TO SEE AND DO
HARNEY COUNTY HISTORICAL MUSEUM
76 E. Washington St., Burns, 541-573-5618; www.burnsmuseum.com
Displays include arrowheads, quilts, wildlife, cut glass and Pete French's safe and spurs. The Hayes Room contains a bedroom and dining room furnished in antiques. April-October, Monday-Saturday.

MALHEUR NATIONAL WILDLIFE REFUGE
36391 Sodhouse Lane, Princeton, 32 miles south on Highway 205,
541-493-2612; www.fws.gov/malheur
Established in 1908 by Theodore Roosevelt, the 185,000-acre refuge was set aside primarily as a nesting area for migratory birds. It is also an important fall and spring gathering point for waterfowl migrating between the northern breeding grounds and the California wintering grounds. More than 320 species of birds and 58 species of mammals have been recorded in the refuge. Daily dawn-dusk.

SPECIAL EVENT
JOHN SCHARFF MIGRATORY BIRD FESTIVAL
76 E. Washington St., Burns, 541-573-2636; www.migratorybirdfestival.com
This festival includes birding and historical tours, films and arts and crafts. First weekend in April.

HOTEL
★DAYS INN
577 W. Monroe St., Burns, 541-573-2047, 800-329-7466; www.daysinn.com
52 rooms. Complimentary continental breakfast. Pets accepted, some restrictions; fee. $

CANNON BEACH

The cannon and capstan from the survey schooner *USS Shark*, which washed ashore in 1846, are now a small monument four miles south of this resort town. Swimming, surfing and surf fishing can be enjoyed here. Among the large rocks offshore is the 235-foot Haystack Rock, the third-largest monolith in the world. Migrating gray whales often can be spotted heading south from mid-December to early February and returning in early to mid spring.

Information: Cannon Beach Chamber of Commerce Visitor Information Center,
207 N. Spruce, Cannon Beach, 503-436-2623; www.cannonbeach.org

WHAT TO SEE AND DO
ECOLA STATE PARK
Ecola Road, Cannon Beach, two miles north off Highway 101,
503-436-2844, 800-551-6949; www.oregonstateparks.org

Lewis and Clark ended their expedition in what is now a 1,303-acre park with six miles of ocean frontage. Visitors can spot sea lion and bird rookeries on rocks and offshore islands and do whale-watching at observation points. October 1-April 30, daily day use $3, yearly day use $25; May 1-September 30, Daily day use $3, yearly day use $25.

OSWALD WEST STATE PARK
9500 Sandpiper Lane, Nehalem, 10 miles south on Highway 101,
800-551-6949; www.oregonstateparks.org/park_195.php

A 2,474-acre park with outstanding coastal headland, Oswald West features towering cliffs, low dunes and rain forest with massive spruce and cedar trees. The road winds 700 feet above sea level and 1,000 feet below the peak of Neahkahnie Mountain. Visitors come for surfing, fishing and hiking trails. October 1-April 30 tent site $10, extra vehicle $5; May 1-September 30 tent site $14, extra vehicle $5.

HOTELS
★HALLMARK RESORT
1400 S. Hemlock St., Cannon Beach, 503-436-1566, 888-448-4449;
www.hallmarkinns.com

142 rooms. Indoor pool, children's pool, whirlpool. Pets accepted, some restrictions; fee. $

★★SURFSAND RESORT
148 W. Gower, Cannon Beach, 503-436-2274, 800-547-6100;
www.surfsand.com

82 rooms. Restaurant, bar. Indoor pool, whirlpool. Pets accepted, some restrictions; fee. Reservations recommended. $$

★TOLOVANA INN
3400 S. Hemlock, Cannon Beach, 503-436-2211, 800-333-8890;
www.tolovanainn.com

175 rooms. Pets accepted, some restrictions; fee. Indoor pool, whirlpool. Restaurants. Fitness center. Wireless Internet access. Reservations recommended. $

OREGON

★
★
★
★
★

RESTAURANT

★★DOOGER'S

1371 S. Hemlock, Cannon Beach, 503-436-2225; www.cannon-beach.net/doogers
Seafood, steak menu. Breakfast, lunch, dinner. Bar. Children's menu. **$$$**

CAVE JUNCTION

This small, rural community in the picturesque Illinois Valley is the gateway to the Oregon Caves National Monument. Surrounding forest lands offer opportunities for fishing, hiking and backpacking. A Ranger District office of the Siskiyou National Forest is located here.

Information: Illinois Valley Chamber of Commerce, 201 Caves Highway,
Cave Junction, 541-592-3326; www.cavejunction.com

SPECIAL EVENT

WILD BLACKBERRY FESTIVAL

535 East River St., Cave Junction, 541-592-3326; www.wildblackberry.org
Berry fans can celebrate the season with blackberry foods, cooking, games, crafts and music. Mid-August.

HOTEL

★★OREGON CAVES CHATEAU

20000 Caves Highway, Cave Junction, 541-592-3400, 877-245-9022;
www.oregoncavesoutfitters.com
22 rooms. Closed November-April. Restaurant. **$**

COOS BAY

This charming port town borders a bay that shares its name. The bay itself is the largest natural harbor between San Francisco and Seattle. It is the state's second-busiest maritime center, supported by forestry, shipbuilding and fishing industries. Outdoor enthusiasts appreciate the area's mild climate and the terrific recreational opportunities available at three local state parks: Cape Arago, Shore Acres and Sunset Bay. Anglers flock to the shores of the nearby Coos River, which is considered one of best places in Oregon to catch salmon and steelhead.

Information: Bay Area Chamber of Commerce, 145 Central Ave., Coos Bay,
541-266-0868, 800-824-8486; www.oregonsbayareachamber.com

WHAT TO SEE AND DO

CAPE ARAGO

Cape Arago Highway, Coos Bay, 15 miles southwest off Highway 101,
541-888-8867, 800-551-6949; www.oregonstateparks.org
This 134-acre promontory juts into the ocean and features two beaches, fishing, hiking and an observation point for whale and seal watching.

CHARLESTON MARINA COMPLEX

63534 Kingfisher Drive, Charleston, nine miles southwest, 541-888-2548;
www.charlestonmarina.com
Boating enthusiasts can come to Charleston Marina to charter boats or to use the launching and moorage facilities, car and boat trailer parking, dry boat storage and

travel park. The complex includes a motel, marine fuel dock, tackle shops and restaurants. Monday-Friday.

SHORE ACRES STATE PARK
89814 Cape Arago Highway, Coos Bay, 541-888-2472, 800-551-6949;
www.oregonstateparks.org
The former grand estate of a Coos Bay lumberman is now noted for its unusual botanical and Japanese gardens and spectacular ocean views. The park offers an ocean beach, hiking and picnicking. October 1-April 30, daily day use $3, yearly day use $25; May 1-September 30, daily day use $3, yearly day use $25.

SOUTH SLOUGH NATIONAL ESTUARINE RESEARCH RESERVE
61907 Seven Devils Road, Charleston, 541-888-5558;
www.oregon.gov
A 4,400-acre area reserved for the study of estuarine ecosystems and life, Previous studies here include oyster culture techniques and water pollution. An interpretive center offers special programs, lectures and exhibits. Daily. Guided trail walks and canoe tours: June-August. Interpretive Center: June-August, daily; September-May, Monday-Friday.

SUNSET BAY
Cape Arago Highway, Coos Bay, 12 miles southwest off Highway 101,
541-888-4902, 800-551-6949; www.oregonstateparks.org
A 395-acre park, Sunset Bay features a swimming beach on a sheltered bay, fishing, hiking, observation point, picnicking, and tent and trailer sites.

SPECIAL EVENTS
BAY AREA FUN FESTIVAL
Coos Bay, 541-266-0868, 800-824-8486; www.oregonsbayareachamber.com
The festival features activities for all ages including a quilt show, duck derby, sock hop, vendor booths and car shows. Third weekend in September.

OREGON COAST MUSIC FESTIVAL
Coos Bay, 541-267-0938, 877-897-9350; www.oregoncoastmusic.com
Festival goers come for a variety of musical presentations ranging from jazz and dance to chamber and symphonic music, along with free outdoor picnic concerts. Two weeks in July.

HOTEL
★★RED LION HOTEL
1313 N. Bayshore Drive, Coos Bay, 541-267-4141, 800-733-5466; www.redlion.com
145 rooms. Wireless Internet access. Restaurant, bar. Outdoor pool, whirlpool. Airport transportation available. Pets accepted; fee. $

RESTAURANT
★★PORTSIDE
63383 Kingfisher Road, Charleston, 541-888-5544; www.portsidebythebay.com
Seafood menu. Lunch, dinner. Bar. Children's menu. Outdoor seating. Reservations recommended. $$

OREGON

★
★
★
★
★

CORVALLIS

Located in the heart of Oregon's fertile Willamette Valley and built on the banks of the Willamette River, Corvallis is a center for education, culture and commerce. It is the home of Oregon State University, the state's oldest institution of higher education. The Siuslaw National Forest headquarters is here.

Information: Convention & Visitors Bureau, 553 N.W. Harrison Blvd., Corvallis, 541-757-1544, 800-334-8118; www.visitcorvallis.com

WHAT TO SEE AND DO
AVERY PARK
1310 S.W. Avery Park Drive, Corvallis, 541-766-6918; www.ci.corvallis.or.us
A 75-acre park on the Marys River Avery Park features bicycle, cross-country and jogging trails, picnicking, a playground, ball field, and rose, rhododendron and community gardens, along with a 1922 Mikado locomotive. Daily.

BENTON COUNTY HISTORICAL MUSEUM
1101 Main St., Philomath, 541-929-6230;
www.bentoncountymuseum.org
Located in the former Philomath College building, the museum features displays on the history of the county an art gallery and a reference library by appointment. Tuesday-Saturday.

OREGON STATE UNIVERSITY
1500 S.W. Jefferson Way, Corvallis, 541-737-1000; www.oregonstate.edu
This university was founded in 1868 and enrolls 14,500 students. On its 400-acre campus is the Memorial Union Concourse Gallery. Daily.

SIUSLAW NATIONAL FOREST
4077 S.W. Research Way, Corvallis, 541-750-7000; www.fs.fed.us
Siuslaw includes 50 miles of ocean frontage with more than 30 campgrounds, public beaches, sand dunes and overlooks. A visitor center and nature trails are located in the Cape Perpetua Scenic Area. Mary's Peak, highest peak in the Coast Range, has a road to picnic grounds and campground near the summit. Camping and dune buggies are allowed in designated areas. The forest contains 630,000 acres including the Oregon Dunes National Recreation Area.

TYEE WINE CELLARS
26335 Greenberry Road, Corvallis, 541-753-8754; www.tyeewine.com
Located on a 460-acre Century farm, Tyee Wine Cellars offers tastings, tours, interpretive hikes and picnicking. July-August, Friday-Monday; April-June and October-December, weekends and by appointment.

SPECIAL EVENTS
BENTON COUNTY FAIR AND RODEO
110 S.W. 53rd St., Corvallis, 541-766-6521; www.bentoncountyfair.com
The festival features activities for all ages including a quilt show, pony show and livestock show. Late July-early August.

DA VINCI DAYS

760 S.W. Madison Ave., Corvallis, 541-757-6363; www.davinci-days.org

The festival celebrates the relationship between art, science and technology. Third weekend in July.

FALL FESTIVAL

568 S.W. Third St., Corvallis, 541-752-9655; www.corvallisfallfestival.com

The festival features over 150 arts and crafts booths, including original designs in a variety of art such as textiles, wearable art, handcrafted ceramics, decorative and functional wood, jewelry, leather, photography, paintings, drawings, prints and metalwork. Last weekend in September.

HOTEL

★BEST WESTERN GRAND MANOR INN

925 N.W. Garfield Ave., Corvallis, 541-758-8571, 800-780-7234;
www.bestwestern.com

55 rooms. Complimentary continental breakfast. High-speed Internet access. Outdoor pool. Pets allowed, restrictions; fee. $

RESTAURANTS

★★THE GABLES

1121 N.W. Ninth St., Corvallis, 541-752-3364, 800-815-0167;
www.thegablessteakhouse.com

American menu. Dinner. Bar. Children's menu. $$

★★MICHAEL'S LANDING

603 N.W. Second St., Corvallis, 541-754-6141; www.michaelslanding.com

American menu. Breakfast (Sunday), lunch, dinner. Bar. Children's menu. $$

SPECIALTY LODGING

HARRISON HOUSE BED & BREAKFAST

2310 N.W. Harrison Blvd., Corvallis, 541-752-6248, 800-233-6248;
www.corvallis-lodging.com

Located within walking distance of Oregon State University, this bed and breakfast is convenient to area kayaking, rafting and hiking opportunities. Four rooms. Complimentary full breakfast. Restaurant. $

COTTAGE GROVE

Cottage Grove is the lumber, retail and distribution center for southern Lane County. A Ranger District office of the Umpqua National Forest is located here.

Information: Cottage Grove Area Chamber of Commerce, 400 E. Main St.,
Cottage Grove, 541-942-3346; www.cottagegrove.org

WHAT TO SEE AND DO

CHATEAU LORANE WINERY

27415 Siuslaw River Road, Lorane, 541-942-8028; www.chateaulorane.com

A 30-acre vineyard is located on this 200-acre wooded estate. The winery features a lakeside tasting room serving a great variety of traditional, rare and handmade wines.

June-October, daily; March-May and November-December, weekends, holidays, by appointment.

DORENA LAKE

Five miles east on Row River Road, Cottage Grove; www.dorenalake.com

A five-mile-long lake, Schwarz Park on Row River has fishing, picnicking and camping. Baker Bay Park, on the south shore, offers swimming, waterskiing, fishing and boating. Harms Park, on the north shore, offers boat launching and picnicking.

SPECIAL EVENT
BOHEMIA MINING DAYS CELEBRATION

North 12th and East Main streets, Cottage Grove, 541-942-5064;
www.bohemiaminingdays.org

Commemorating the area's gold-mining days, the celebration includes parades, flower and art shows, a rodeo and other entertainment. Third week in July.

HOTEL
★★VILLAGE GREEN RESORT

725 Row River Road, Cottage Grove, 541-942-2491, 800-343-7666;
www.villagegreenresortandgardens.com

96 rooms. Complimentary full breakfast. Restaurant, bar. Outdoor pool, whirlpool. Tennis. Airport transportation available. Pets accepted, some restrictions. **$**

CRATER LAKE
WHAT TO SEE AND DO
CRATER LAKE NATIONAL PARK

57 miles north of Klamath Falls on Highways 97 and 62, 541-594-3000;
www.nps.gov/crla

★
★★
★★★
★★

Surrounded by 25 miles of jagged rim rock, the 21-square-mile lake is broken only by Wizard and Phantom Ship islands. The park, established in 1902, covers 286 square miles. The 33-mile Rim Drive leads to all observation points, park headquarters and a visitor center at Rim Village (June-September, daily). The park can be explored on foot or by car following spurs and trails extending from Rim Drive. Depending on snow, the campground is open from late June to mid-October. There are six picnic areas on Rim Drive. Conservation measures may dictate the closing of certain roads and recreational facilities.

HOTEL
★★★CRATER LAKE LODGE

565 Rim Village Drive, Crater Lake, 541-594-2255, 888-774-2728; www.crater-lake.com

This grand lodge has been welcoming guests to its lakeside location since 1915. Guests can relax with a good book in front of the Great Hall's massive stone fireplace. The dining room restaurant prepares dishes using Oregon-grown ingredients. Guest rooms are without TVs and phones. 71 rooms. Breakfast, lunch, dinner. Closed mid-October-mid-May. Restaurant. **$**

DEPOE BAY

The world's smallest natural navigable harbor, the 6-acre Depoe Bay is a base for the Coast Guard and a good spot for deep-sea fishing. The shoreline is rugged. Seals and sea lions inhabit the area, and whales are seen so often that Depoe Bay claims to be the "whale watching capital of the Oregon coast." In the center of town are the "spouting horns," natural rock formations throwing geyser-like sprays into the air. There are nine state parks within a few miles of this resort community.

Information: Chamber of Commerce, 223 S.W. Highway 101, Depoe Bay,
541-765-2889, 877-485-8348; www.depoebaychamber.org

WHAT TO SEE AND DO
FOGARTY CREEK STATE PARK
Depoe Bay, two miles north on Highway 101, 800-551-6949;
www.oregonstateparks.org
A 142-acre park, Fogarty Creek includes a beach area and creek, swimming, fishing, hiking and picnicking.

SPECIAL EVENTS
CLASSIC WOODEN BOAT SHOW AND CRAB FEED
Depoe Bay, 541-765-2889; www.depoebaychamber.org
Boat exhibitors display handcrafted boats of original designs and explain boat-building techniques, boat renovation history, and hull and power plant design. Crab dinners are available at the Community Hall. Last weekend April.

FLEET OF FLOWERS CEREMONY
Depoe Bay, 541-765-2889; www.depoebaychamber.org
After services on shore, flowers are cast on the water to honor those who lost their lives at sea. Memorial Day.

SALMON BAKE
Depoe Bay Park, Depoe Bay, 541-765-2889; www.depoebaychamber.org
Try salmon prepared in the Native American manner. Third Saturday in September.

HOTELS
★★INN AT OTTER CREST
301 Otter Crest Drive, Otter Rock, 541-765-2111, 866-869-4291;
www.innatottercrest.com
120 rooms. Restaurant, bar. Wireless Internet access. Outdoor pool, whirlpool. Tennis. Fitness center. **$**

★★SURFRIDER RESORT
3115 N.W. Highway 101, Depoe Bay, 541-764-2311, 800-662-2378;
www.surfriderresort.com
52 rooms. Restaurant, bar. Wireless Internet access. Indoor pool, whirlpool. Airport transportation available. **$**

131

OREGON

SPECIALTY LODGING
CHANNEL HOUSE
35 Ellingson St., Depoe Bay, 541-765-2140, 800-447-2140; www.channelhouse.com
14 rooms. Restaurant. Children over 16 years only. Complimentary full breakfast. Reservations recommended. **$$**

EUGENE
Eugene sits on the west bank of the Willamette River, facing its sister city Springfield on the east bank. The Cascade Range rises to the east, mountains of the Coast Range to the west. Bicycling, hiking and jogging are especially popular here with a variety of trails available. Eugene-Springfield is at the head of a series of dams built for flood control of the Willamette River Basin. Willamette National Forest headquarters is located here.
Information: Lane County Convention & Visitors Association, 754 Olive St.,
541-484-5307, 800-547-5445; www.visitlanecounty.org

WHAT TO SEE AND DO
ARMITAGE COUNTY PARK
90064 Coburg Road, six miles north off I-5 on Coburg Road, Eugene,
541-682-2000; www.lanecounty.org/parks/armitage.htm
A 57-acre park on partially-wooded area on the south bank of the McKenzie River, Armitage features fishing, boating, hiking and picnicking.

HENDRICKS PARK RHODODENDRON GARDEN
Summit and Skyline drives, Eugene, 541-682-5324;
www.friendsofhendrickspark.org
A 20-acre, internationally known garden features more than 6,000 aromatic plants, including rare species and hybrid rhododendrons from the local area and around the world. The park includes walking paths, hiking trails and a picnic area Peak bloom mid-April-mid-May. Daily.

HULT CENTER FOR THE PERFORMING ARTS
1 Eugene Center, Eugene, Seventh Avenue and Willamette Street,
541-682-5000; www.hultcenter.org
The Performing arts center offers more than 300 events each year ranging from Broadway shows and concerts to ballet.

JORDAN SCHNITZER MUSEUM OF ART
1223 University of Oregon, 1430 Johnson Lane, Eugene,
541-346-3027; uoma.uoregon.edu
Diverse collections include a large selection of Asian art representing cultures of China, Japan, Korea and Cambodia and American and British works of Asian influence. The museum also features Persian miniatures and ceramics, photography and works by contemporary artists and craftsmen from the Pacific Northwest, including those of Morris Graves. Wednesday-Sunday afternoons.

132

OREGON

★
★★
★★
★★

KNIGHT LIBRARY

University of Oregon Library, 1501 Kincaid, Eugene, 541-346-3053;
www.libweb.uoregon.edu/knight

With more than 2 million volumes, this is the largest library in Oregon. The main lobby features changing exhibits of rare books and manuscripts with an Oregon zcollection on the second floor. Daily.

LANE COUNTY HISTORICAL MUSEUM

740 W. 13th Ave., Eugene, 541-682-4242; www.lanecountyhistoricalsociety.org

Changing exhibits depict the history of the county from mid-19th century to the 1930s. The museum includes artifacts of pioneer and Victorian periods; textiles; and a local history research library. Wednesday-Friday 10 a.m.-4 p.m., Saturday-Sunday noon-4 p.m.

OWEN MUNICIPAL ROSE GARDEN

North end of Jefferson Street along the Willamette River, Eugene,
541-682-4800; www.eugene-or.gov

The 5-acre park includes more than 300 new and rare varieties of roses, as well as wild species and is a recognized test garden for experimental roses. Best blooms are late June-early July. Daily.

SCIENCE FACTORY CHILDREN'S MUSEUM & PLANETARIUM

2300 Leo Harris Parkway, Eugene, 541-682-7888; www.sciencefactory.org

A participatory science center, Science Factory encourages hands-on learning and features planetarium shows and exhibits illustrating physical, biological and earth sciences and related technologies. Wednesday-Sunday.

SOUTH BREITENBUSH GORGE NATIONAL RECREATION TRAIL

Eugene, from Detroit Ranger Station, east on Highway 22 one mile, left onto
Breitenbush Road 46, travel about 14 miles, turn right on Forest Road 4685,
access one is a half-mile up Road 4685; access two is two miles on Road
4685 at Roaring Creek; and access three is 1/4 mile further, 541-225-6300;
www.fs.fed.us/r6/willamette/recreation

Meandering through giant trees in an old-growth grove, this popular trail follows the South Breitenbush River. A small Forest Service operated campground is near the trailhead.

SPENCER BUTTE PARK

Ridgeline and Willamette streets, Eugene, 541-682-4800; www.eugene-or.gov

The park has 305 acres of wilderness, with Spencer Butte Summit, at 2,052 feet, dominating the scene. Daily.

UNIVERSITY OF OREGON

1205 University of Oregon, Eugene, 541-346-1000; www.uoregon.edu

The 250-acre campus includes more than 2,000 varieties of trees. Points of interest include the Museum of Natural History, Robinson Theatre, Beall Concert Hall, Hayward Field and the Erb Memorial Union. Campus tours depart from Information and Tour Services, Oregon Hall. Monday-Saturday.

WILLAMETTE NATIONAL FOREST

East via Highways 20, 126 or 58, 541-225-6300;
www.fs.fed.us

Covering more than 1.5 million acres, Wilamette National Forest is home to more than 300 species of wildlife and the Cascade Mountain Range summit. Attractions include fishing, hunting, hiking, skiing, snowmobiling and camping.

WILLAMETTE PASS SKI AREA

Cascade Summit, south via Interstate 5, east on Highway 58, 541-345-7669;
www.willamettepass.com

The ski area features double andtriple chairlifts, ski patrol and school, ski and snowboard rentals, a lodge, lounge and restaurant. The longest run is 2.1 miles, and the peak vertical drop is 1,583 feet. Night skiing is allowed in late December-late February Friday-Saturday. Late-November-mid-April.

SPECIAL EVENTS

BACH FESTIVAL

Eugene, 541-682-5000, 800-457-1486; www.oregonbachfestival.com

Celebrate classical music with numerous concerts by regional and international artists, master classes and family activities. Late June-early mid-July.

LANE COUNTY FAIR

796 W. 13th Ave., Eugene, 541-682-4292; www.atthefair.com

The fair features local talents in art, baking, photography and livestock. Mid-August.

HOTELS

★★★HILTON EUGENE AND CONFERENCE CENTER

66 E. Sixth Ave., Eugene, 541-342-2000, 800-445-8667; www.hiltoneugene.com

In the heart of downtown Eugene, the Hilton is adjacent to the Hult Center for the Performing Arts, which offers Broadway shows, concerts and other performances. At the hotel, the Big River Grille serves Pacific Northwest cuisine and the lobby bar offers local microbrews. 269 rooms. Wireless Internet access. Restaurant, bar. Fitness center. Business center. Indoor pool, whirlpool. Airport transportation available. Pets accepted. **$**

★PHOENIX INN SUITES EUGENE

850 Franklin Blvd., Eugene, 541-344-0001, 800-344-0131;
www.phoenixinn.com/eugene

97 rooms. Complimentary continental breakfast. Wireless Internet access. Indoor pool, whirlpool. Fitness center. Business center. Airport transportation available. **$**

★★RED LION

205 Coburg Road, Eugene, 541-342-5201, 800-733-5466; www.redlion.com

137 rooms. Pets accepted; fee. Wireless Internet access. Restaurant, bar. Fitness center. Outdoor pool, whirlpool. Airport transportation available. **$**

★★★VALLEY RIVER INN

1000 Valley River Way, Eugene, 541-743-1000, 800-543-8266; www.valleyriverinn.com

Adjacent to Valley River Center, Eugene's largest shopping mall, the Valley River Inn offers an attractive riverside setting on the north bank of the Willamette River. Accommodations are non-smoking and comfortable with triple-sheeted beds with duvets, bath robes and wireless Internet access. Many of the rooms also feature lovely river views. 257 rooms. Pets accepted, some restrictions. Wireless Internet access. Restaurant, bar. Outdoor pool, children's pool, whirlpool and sauna. Fitness center. Airport transportation available. Business center. **$$**

SPECIALTY LODGING
THE CAMPBELL HOUSE

252 Pearl St., Eugene, 541-343-1119, 800-264-2519; www.campbellhouse.com

Comfort and elegance await guests at this intimate bed and breakfast, which offers views of the city from a hill. 20 rooms. Complimentary full breakfast. **$$**

RESTAURANTS
★★AMBROSIA

174 E. Broadway, Eugene, 541-342-4141; www.ambrosiarestaurant.com

Italian menu. Lunch, dinner. Bar. Outdoor seating. **$$**

★EXCELSIOR INN

754 E. 13th Ave., Eugene, 541-342-6963, 800-321-6963; www.excelsiorinn.com

Italian menu. Breakfast, lunch, dinner, Sunday brunch. Bar. Children's menu. Outdoor seating. **$$**

★★NORTH BANK

22 Club Road, Eugene, 541-343-5622; www.casado.net/northbank

Seafood, steak menu. Lunch Monday-Friday, dinner. Bar. Reservations recommended. **$$**

★★OREGON ELECTRIC STATION

27 E. Fifth Ave., Eugene, 541-485-4444; www.oesrestaurant.com

American menu. Lunch Monday-Friday, dinner. Bar. Children's menu. Outdoor seating. Reservation recommended. **$$**

★★★SWEETWATERS

1000 Valley River Way, Eugene, 541-743-1000, 800-543-8266; www.valleyriverinn.com

With a beautiful view of the Willamette River, this casually elegant restaurant serves northwest cuisine and Mediterranean-inspired dishes. Fresh seafood, game meats, exotic fruits and local ingredients make up the majority of the menu. Breakfast, lunch, dinner, Sunday brunch. Bar. Children's menu. Outdoor seating. Reservation recommended. **$$**

FLORENCE

With some of the highest sand dunes in the world, Florence is within reach of 17 lakes for fishing, swimming and boating. River and ocean fishing, crabbing and clamming are also popular. Along the Siuslaw River is "Old Town," a historic area with galleries, restaurants and attractions.

Information: Florence Area Chamber of Commerce, 290 Highway 101, Florence, 541-997-3128; www.florencechamber.com

WHAT TO SEE AND DO

C&M STABLES

90241 Highway 101 N. Florence, 541-997-7540;
www.oregonhorsebackriding.com

Experience the spectacular scenery of Oregon coast on horseback. Rides cover beach and dune trails, including sunset rides. Children must be eight or older. Daily 10 a.m.-5 p.m.

CARL G. WASHBURNE MEMORIAL

93111 Highway 101, Florence, 14 miles north on Highway 101,
541-547-3416, 800-551-6949; www.oregonstateparks.org

This 1,089-acre park is a good area for the study of plant life. Features include a two-mile beach, swimming, fishing and clamming. Elk may be seen in campgrounds and nearby meadows.

DARLINGTONIA STATE NATURAL SITE

Florence, five miles north on Highway 101, 541-997-3641, 800-551-6949;
www.oregonstateparks.org

An 18-acre park with short loop trail through a bog area, the natural site is named for Darlingtonia, a carnivorous, insect-eating plant also known as cobra lily that makes its home there.

DEVILS ELBOW STATE PARK

13 miles north on Highway 101, Florence below Heceta Head Lighthouse
in Heceta State Park, 541-997-3641; www.oregonstateparks.org

A 545-acre park, Devils Elbow includes ocean beach, fishing, hiking, picnicking and an observation point.

HECETA HEAD LIGHTHOUSE

12 miles north on Highway 101, Yachats, 541-547-3416; www.oregonstateparks.org

Built in 1894, Heceta Head Lighthouse is a picturesque beacon set high on rugged cliff. Tours: May, daily 11 a.m.-3 p.m.; June-September, daily 11 a.m.-5 p.m.; March, April and October, Friday-Monday 11 a.m.-3 p.m.; November-February, call for tour schedule.

JESSIE M. HONEYMAN MEMORIAL STATE PARK

Three miles south on Highway 101, Florence, 541-997-3641, 800-551-6949;
www.oregonstateparks.org

Honeyman Memorial State Park has 522 coastal acres with wooded lakes and sand dunes, an abundance of rhododendrons and an excellent beach. Features include swimming, waterskiing, fishing, boat dock and ramps, hiking and picnicking.

OREGON

★
★
★
★
★

SAND DUNES FRONTIER

3 1/2 miles south on Highway 101, Florence, 541-997-3544;
www.sanddunesfrontier.com

Take an excursions aboard a 20-passenger dune buggy, or drive yourself. Sand Dunes Frontier also offers miniature golf, a flower garden, gift shop and snack bar. Daily, weather permitting.

SEA LION CAVES

91560 Highway 101 N., Florence, 541-547-3111;
www.sealioncaves.com

Descend 208 feet under basaltic headland into a 1,500-foot-long cavern that is home to wild sea lions. These mammals are generally seen on rocky ledges outside the cave in spring and summer and inside the cave in fall and winter. Self-guided tours. Daily from 9 a.m.

SIUSLAW PIONEER MUSEUM

278 Maple St., Florence, 541-997-7884; www.florencechamber.com

Exhibits at Siuslaw Pioneer Museum preserve the history of the area with Impressive display of artifacts and items from early settlers and Native Americans. Tuesday-Sunday noon to 4 p.m.; closed January, Easter Sunday, Thanksgiving Day, Christmas.

SPECIAL EVENT
RHODODENDRON FESTIVAL

Florence, 541-997-3128; www.florencechamber.com

Activities at the festival include the crowning of the Rhododendron Queen, parades, carnival rides and entertainment. Third weekend in May.

HOTELS
★BEST WESTERN PIER POINT INN

85625 Highway 101, Florence, 541-997-7191, 800-780-7234;
www.bestwestern.com

55 rooms. Complimentary continental breakfast. Wireless Internet access. Whirlpool. Pets accepted; fee. **$**

★★DRIFTWOOD SHORES RESORT & CONFERENCE CENTER

88416 First Ave., Florence, 541-997-8263, 800-422-5091;
www.driftwoodshores.com

127 rooms. Wireless Internet access. Restaurant, bar. Indoor pool, whirlpool. Restaurant. **$**

OREGON

★
★
★
★
★

FOREST GROVE

Forest Grove traces its beginning to missionaries who brought religion to what they called the "benighted Indian." The town is believed to have been named for a forest of firs that met a grove of oaks.

Information: Chamber of Commerce, 2417 Pacific Ave., Forest Grove,
503-357-3006; www.fgchamber.org

WHAT TO SEE AND DO
PACIFIC UNIVERSITY
2043 College Way, Forest Grove,
503-352-6151, 877-722-8648; www.pacificu.edu
Founded as Tualatin Academy, Pacific University is one of the Northwest's oldest schools. On campus is an art gallery and Old College Hall. Tours: academic year, Tuesday, Thursday and by appointment.

SCOGGINS VALLEY PARK AND HENRY HAGG LAKE
50250 S.W. Scoggins Valley Road, Gaston, 503-846-8715; www.co.washington.or.us
With 11 miles of shoreline, Scoggins Valley attracts visitors with swimming, windsurfing, fishing, boating, bird-watching, and hiking and bicycling trails. March-November, daily sunrise to sunset.

SPECIAL EVENTS
CONCOURS D'ELEGANCE
Pacific University, 2043 College Way, Forest Grove, 503-357-3006, 800-359-2510;
www.forestgroveconcours.org
View classic and vintage cars on display. Third Sunday in June.

HAWAIIAN LUAU
Pacific University, 2043 College Way, Forest Grove, 503-357-6151, 877-722-8648;
www.pacificu.edu/studentlife/luau/
Hawaiian traditions are celebrated in food, fashions and dance. Mid-April.

HOTEL
★BEST WESTERN UNIVERSITY INN AND SUITES
3933 Pacific Ave., Forest Grove, 503-992-8888, 800-780-7234; www.bestwestern.com
54 rooms. Complimentary continental breakfast. Fitness center. Indoor pool, whirlpool. Business center. High-speed Internet access. Pets accepted, some restrictions. $

GLENEDEN BEACH
RESTAURANT
★★THE DINING ROOM AT SALISHAN
7760 N. Highway 101, Gleneden Beach, 541-764-3000, 800-452-2300;
www.salishan.com
American menu. Breakfast, lunch, dinner, Sunday brunch. Children's menu. Valet parking. $$$

GOLD BEACH
Gold Beach is situated at the mouth of the Rogue River on the south shore. Agate hunting is popular at the mouth of the Rogue River. The river is also well-known for steelhead and salmon fishing. Surf fishing and clamming are possible at many beaches. The Siskiyou National Forest is at the edge of town and a Ranger District office of the forest is located here.
Information: Chamber of Commerce & Visitors Center, 94080 Shirley Lane, Gold Beach,
541-247-7526, 800-525-2334; www.goldbeach.org

WHAT TO SEE AND DO

CAPE SEBASTIAN STATE SCENIC CORRIDOR

Seven miles south on Highway 101, 800-551-6949; www.oregonstateparks.org

Part of approximately 1,143 acres of open and forested land, Cape Sebastian is a precipitous headland, rising more than 700 feet above the tide with a view of many miles of coastline. A short roadside through the forest area is marked by wild azaleas, rhododendrons and blue ceanothus in season.

CURRY COUNTY HISTORICAL MUSEUM

29419 Ellensburg Ave., Gold Beach, 541-247-9396; www.curryhistory.com

The historical museum features collections and interpretive displays of early life in Curry County. February-December, Tuesday-Saturday afternoons.

JERRY'S ROGUE RIVER JET BOAT TRIPS

Gold Beach, south end of Rogue River Bridge at port of Gold Beach Boat Basin,
541-247-4571, 800-451-3645; www.roguejets.com

Take a six-hour, 64-mile round trip into wilderness area with a two-hour lunch or dinner stop at Agness. There are also eight-hour (104-mile) and six-hour (80-mile) round-trip whitewater excursions. May-October, daily.

MAIL BOAT WHITEWATER TRIPS

94294 Rouge River Road, Gold Beach, Mail Boat Dock,
541-247-7033, 800-458-3511; www.mailboats.com

Options at Mail Boat include a 104-mile (round trip) jet boat ride into the wilderness and whitewater of the upper Rogue Rivera; 80-mile round trip to the middle of Rogue River; and a 64-mile round trip by jet boat with a two-hour lunch stop at Agness. Reservations are recommended. May-October, daily.

HOTELS

★GOLD BEACH INN

29346 Ellensburg Ave., Gold Beach, 541-247-7091, 888-663-0608;
www.goldbeachinn.com

40 rooms. Complimentary continental breakfast. Pets accepted; fee. $

★★★TU TU' TUN LODGE

96550 N. Bank Rogue, Gold Beach, 541-247-6664, 800-864-6357; www.tututun.com

From its flower-filled gardens to its scenic location on the banks of the Rogue River, the Tu Tu' Tun Lodge offers a peaceful atmosphere. Guest rooms feature wood-burning fireplaces, deep-soaking tubs, overstuffed furnishings and soft bed linens. Inventive Pacific Northwest cuisine is available in the restaurant. 18 rooms. Restaurant, bar. Outdoor pool. Airport transportation available. $$

OREGON

GRANTS PASS

Grants Pass was named by rail constructors who were there when news reached them of General Grant's victorious siege of Vicksburg in 1863. Tourism is the chief source of income, and fishing in the Rogue River is a popular activity. A Ranger District office and headquarters of the Siskiyou National Forest is located here.

Information: Visitor & Convention Bureau, 1995 N.W. Vine St., Grants Pass, 541-476-5510; www.visitgrantspass.org

WHAT TO SEE AND DO

GRANTS PASS MUSEUM OF ART

229 S.W. G St., Grants Pass, 541-479-3290; www.gpmuseum.com

The Museum of Art features permanent and changing exhibits of photography, paintings and art objects. Tuesday-Saturday afternoons.

HELLGATE JETBOAT EXCURSIONS

966 S.W. Sixth St., depart from Riverside Inn, Grants Pass, 541-479-7204, 800-648-4874; www.hellgate.com

Interpretive jet boat trips down the Rogue River include two-hour scenic excursions, four-hour country dinner excursions, five-hour whitewater trips and four-hour champagne brunch excursions.

ROGUE RIVER RAFT TRIPS

8500 Galice Road, Merlin, 800-826-1963; www.rogueriverraft.com

Serious rafting enthusiasts can take three- to four-day whitewater trips through the wilderness past abandoned gold-mining sites with overnight lodges or camping en route.

SISKIYOU NATIONAL FOREST

2164 N.E. Spalding Ave., 541-471-6500;
www.fs.fed.us

Covering more than 1 million acres, Siskiyou is famous for salmon fishing in the lower Rogue River gorge and early-day gold camps. Many species of trees and plants are relics of past ages. An 84-mile stretch of Rogue River between Applegate River and Lobster Creek Bridge is designated a National Wild and Scenic River, nearly half of which is in the forest.

VALLEY OF THE ROGUE STATE PARK

3792 N. River Road, Grants Pass, eight miles south on I-5, 541-582-1118, 800-551-6949; www.oregonstateparks.org

The 275-acre Valley of the Rogue State Park includes fishing, a boat ramp to Rogue River and picnicking. Daily.

SPECIAL EVENTS

BOATNIK FESTIVAL

Riverside Park, Grants Pass, 541-476-7717; www.boatnik.com

A 25-mile whitewater hydroplane race from Riverside Park to Hellgate Canyon and back is the focal point of this festival, which also features a parade, concessions, carnival rides and a square dance festival at Josephine County Fairgrounds. Memorial Day weekend.

HOTELS

★BEST WESTERN INN AT THE ROGUE

8959 Rogue River Highway, Grants Pass, 541-582-2200, 800-780-7234;
www.bestwestern.com

54 rooms. Pets accepted, some restrictions; fee. Complimentary continental breakfast. Wireless Internet access. Fitness center. Outdoor pool. **$**

★COMFORT INN

1889 N.E. Sixth St., Grants Pass, 541-479-8301, 877-424-6423;
www.choicehotels.com

59 rooms. Pets accepted; fee. Complimentary continental breakfast. Wireless Internet access. Outdoor pool. **$**

★HOLIDAY INN EXPRESS

105 N.E. Agness Ave., Grants Pass, 541-471-6144, 800-315-2621;
www.holiday-inn.com

80 rooms. Pets accepted, some restrictions; fee. Complimentary continental breakfast. Airport transportation available. **$**

★★MORRISON'S ROGUE RIVER LODGE

8500 Galice Road, Merlin, 541-476-3825, 800-826-1963; www.morrisonslodge.com

22 rooms. Closed December-April. Restaurant. Wireless Internet access. Outdoor pool. Tennis. **$**

SPECIALTY LODGINGS

FLERY MANOR

2000 Jumpoff Joe Creek Road, Grants Pass, 541-476-3591; www.flerymanor.com

Set on 7 rural acres about 10 miles north of Grants Pass, Flery Manor is an elegant country bed and breakfast. The grounds include gardens, three ponds, a small waterfall and a gazebo. Guest rooms are furnished with antiques, canopied feather beds and clawfoot tubs. Five rooms. Children over 11 years only. Complimentary full breakfast. **$**

WEASKU INN

5560 Rogue River Highway, Grants Pass, 541-471-8000, 800-493-2758;
www.weasku.com

A secluded setting on the Rogue River amid towering pine trees lends this 1924 inn an air of tranquility. Originally a vacation spot for Hollywood stars, including Clark Gable, Bing Cosby and Carole Lombard, the Weasku is a high-end lodge that offers guests the opportunity to fish for salmon, go river rafting or relax on the expansive lawn. All rooms feature pine furnishings and beamed ceilings with ceiling fans. Guests enjoy an evening wine-and-cheese reception, nightly milk and cookies and summertime barbecues. 17 rooms. Complimentary continental breakfast. High-speed Internet access. **$$**

HOOD RIVER

Hood River, located in the midst of a valley producing apples, pears and cherries, boasts a scenic view of Oregon's highest peak, Mount Hood; its slopes are accessible

in all seasons by road. Highway 35, called the Loop Highway, leads around the mountain and up to the snowline. The Columbia River Gorge provides perfect conditions
for windsurfing in the Hood River Port Marina Park.

Information: Chamber of Commerce Visitor Center, 405 Portway Ave., Hood River,
541-386-2000, 800-366-3530; www.hoodriver.org

WHAT TO SEE AND DO

BONNEVILLE LOCK & DAM

U.S. Army Corp of Engineers Bonneville Lock & Dam,
23 miles west on I-84, Cascade Locks, 541-374-8442;
www.corpslakes.usace.army.mil/visitors

The dam consists of three parts, one spillway and two powerhouses. It has an overall
length of 3,463 feet and extends across the Columbia River to Washington. It was
a major hydroelectric project of the U.S. Army Corps of Engineers. On the Oregon
side is a five-story visitor center with underwater windows into the fish ladders and
new navigation lock with viewing facilities which offers audiovisual presentations
and tours of fish ladders and the original powerhouse. The state salmon hatchery is
adjacent, and fishing is allowed in salmon and sturgeon ponds.

HOOD RIVER COUNTY MUSEUM

Port Marina Park, 300 E. Port Marina Drive, Hood River,
541-386-6772; www.co.hood-river.or.us

Hood River County Museum shows off items from early settlers to modern residents.
An outdoor display includes a sternwheeler paddle wheel, beacon light used by air
pilots in the Columbia Gorge and a steam engine from the *Mary*. April-October, daily.

MOUNT HOOD SCENIC RAILROAD

110 Railroad Ave., Hood River, 541-386-3556, 800-872-4661;
www.mthoodrr.com

This historic railroad makes 44-mile round-trip excursions. Dinner, brunch and mur-
der mystery and comedy excursions are available. Reservations are recommended.
March-December, schedule varies.

HOTELS

★★BEST WESTERN HOOD RIVER INN

1108 E. Marina Way, Hood River, 541-386-2200, 800-828-7873;
www.hoodriverinn.com

149 rooms. Pets accepted, some restrictions; fee. Restaurant, bar. Outdoor pool. **$**

★★★COLUMBIA GORGE HOTEL

4000 Westcliff Drive, Hood River, 541-386-5566, 800-345-1921;
www.columbiagorgehotel.com

Nestled in the Columbia Gorge National Scenic Area, this hotel is surrounded by trees
and mountain peaks. The grounds feature a waterfall, beautiful scenic gardens and a
Jazz Age atmosphere. 40 rooms. Pets accepted, some restrictions; fee. Complimentary
full breakfast. Restaurant, bar. Spa. **$$**

★★★DOLCE SKAMANIA LODGE

1131 S.W. Skamania Lodge Way, Stevenson, 509-427-7700, 800-221-7117;
www.skamania.com

Tucked among the mountain peaks, waterfalls and canyons of the Columbia River Gorge 45 minutes north of Portland, this resort is an ideal spot for large groups or couples seeking rest and recreation. It offers many recreational opportunities such as golf and tennis. The guest rooms and suites pay tribute to the area's Native American heritage with distinctive decorative accents. 254 rooms. Wireless Internet access. Restaurant, bar. Spa. Fitness center. Indoor pool, whirlpool. Tennis. $

★★★HOOD RIVER HOTEL

102 Oak St., Hood River, 541-386-1900, 800-386-1859;
www.hoodriverhotel.com

Charm and elegance await guests at the Hood River Hotel, which is listed on the National Register of Historic Places. Each room is decorated uniquely with antique reproductions and artwork illustrating the hotel's history, dating back to its construction in 1913. Cornerstone Cuisine restaurant specializes in organic and locally grown Pacific Northwest dishes. 41 rooms. Complimentary continental breakfast. Restaurant, bar. Fitness center. $$

SPECIALTY LODGING
INN OF THE WHITE SALMON

172 W. Jewett Blvd., White Salmon, 509-493-2335, 800-972-5226;
www.innofthewhitesalmon.com

16 rooms. Pets accepted, some restrictions; fee. Complimentary full breakfast. Outdoor pool. $

RESTAURANT
★★★COLUMBIA GORGE DINING ROOM

4000 Westcliff Drive, Hood River, 541-386-5566, 800-345-1921;
www.columbiagorgehotel.com

Located in the historic Columbia Gorge Hotel. Visitors are urged to try the signature "farm" breakfast, a five-course extravaganza. Evening meals focus on northwest cuisine, especially salmon, lamb and venison. International menu. Breakfast, lunch, dinner, brunch. Bar. $$

JACKSONVILLE

The discovery of gold here in 1851 brought prospectors by the thousands. An active town until the gold rush waned in the 1920s, Jacksonville lost its county seat to the neighboring town of Medford in 1927. Now a national historic landmark, Jacksonville is one of the best preserved pioneer communities in the Pacific Northwest. A Ranger District office of the Rogue River National Forest is located about 20 miles southwest of town in Applegate Valley.

Information: Historic Jacksonville Chamber of Commerce, 185 N. Oregon St.,
Jacksonville, 541-899-8118; www.jacksonvilleoregon.org

OREGON

★
★
★
★
★

WHAT TO SEE AND DO
JACKSONVILLE MUSEUM
206 N. Fifth St., Jacksonville, 541-773-6536; www.sohs.org
Located in Old County Courthouse, this museum has exhibits of Southern Oregon history, pioneer relics, early photographs, Native American artifacts, quilts and natural history. Wednesday-Sunday.

OREGON VORTEX LOCATION OF THE HOUSE OF MYSTERY
4303 Sardine Creek L Fork Road, Gold Hill, 541-855-1543; www.oregonvortex.com
The Vortex is a spherical field of force half above the ground, half below. Natural, historical, educational and scientific phenomena are found in a former assay office and surrounding grounds. March-October, daily.

SPECIAL EVENT
BRITT MUSICAL FESTIVALS
216 W. Main St., Medford, 541-779-0847, 800-882-7488; www.brittfest.org
The Hillside estate of pioneer photographer Peter Britt forms a natural amphitheatre used for classical, jazz, folk, country, dance and musical theater performances. Mid-June-September.

RESTAURANT
★★★MCCULLY HOUSE
240 E. California St., Jacksonville, 541-899-1942, 800-367-1942; www.mccullyhouseinn.com
Housed in a historic Gothic Revival mansion—one of the first houses built in town—that is now the McCully House Inn, the dining room features contemporary Pacific Northwest cuisine. Emphasizing only the freshest ingredients, chef Mark Bender provides tempting selections, including pan-seared scallops with cilantro crème fraîche and an extensive wine list. American menu. Dinner. Bar. Outdoor seating. $$

JOHN DAY
John Day, named for a heroic scout in the first Astor expedition, was once a Pony Express stop on trail to The Dalles. Logging and cattle raising are the major industries in the area. Headquarters for the Malheur National Forest is located here.
Information: Grant County Chamber of Commerce, 281 W. Main St., John Day, 541-575-0547, 800-769-5664; www.grantcounty.cc

WHAT TO SEE AND DO
GRANT COUNTY HISTORICAL MUSEUM
101 S. Canyon City Blvd., Canyon City, 541-5750-0362; www.ortelco.net
The museum features mementos of gold-mining days and exhibits on Joaquin Miller cabin and Greenhorn jail. Mid-May-September, daily.

JOHN DAY FOSSIL BEDS NATIONAL MONUMENT
32651 Kimberly, John Day, 541-987-2333; www.nps.gov/joda
The monument consists of three separate units in Wheeler and Grant counties of north central Oregon. No collecting is allowed within the monument.

CLARNO UNIT

32651 Kimberly, 541-763-2203; www.nps.gov/joda

The Clarno Unit consists of hills, bluffs, towering rock palisades and pinnacles. A self-guided tour on the trail features abundant plant fossils visible in the 35-50 million-year-old rock.

KAM WAH CHUNG STATE HERITAGE SITE

725 Summer St., Northeast, John Day, 541-575-2800, 800-551-6949; www.oregonstateparks.org

Originally constructed as a trading post on The Dalles Military Road in 1866, it now houses a Chinese medicine herb collection, shrine, kitchen and picture gallery. May-October: Monday-Thursday, Saturday-Sunday.

MALHEUR NATIONAL FOREST

431 Patterson Bridge Road, John Day, 541-575-3000; www.fs.fed.us/r6/malheur

With nearly 1.5 million acres in the southwestern part of Blue Mountains, Malheur National Forest includes Strawberry Mountain and Monument Rock wilderness areas. Visitors can find hiking, trout fishing in Magone Lake and Yellowjacket Reservoir, stream fishing and elk and deer hunting.

PAINTED HILLS UNIT

37375 Bear Creek Road, Mitchell, 541-462-3961; www.nps.gov/joda

Painted Hills displays a colorful, scenic landscape of buff and red layers in the John Day Formation with two self-guided trails.

SHEEP ROCK UNIT

Highways 19 and 26, Kimberly, 541-987-2333; www.nps.gov/joda

Here are outstanding examples of the buff and green layers of the fossil-bearing John Day Formation, Mascall Formation and Rattlesnake Formation. The visitor center offers picnicking and fossil displays. Self-guided trails include exhibits.

HOTEL

★BEST WESTERN JOHN DAY INN

315 W. Main St., John Day, 541-575-1700, 800-780-7234; www.bestwestern.com

39 rooms. Complimentary continental breakfast. High-speed Internet access. Fitness center. Pool. Pets accepted. **$**

JOSEPH

Joseph is located in the isolated wilderness of Northeast Oregon. Remote from industry, the town attracts vacationers with its beautiful surroundings. There are fishing lakes and hunting in the surrounding area. At the north end of Wallowa Lake is Old Joseph Monument, a memorial to the Nez Perce chief who resisted the U.S. government. A Ranger District office of the Wallowa-Whitman National Forest is located in nearby Enterprise.

Information: Wallowa County Chamber of Commerce, 115 Tejaka Lane, Enterprise, 541-426-4622, 800-585-4121; www.wallowacountychamber.com

OREGON

VALLEY BRONZE OF OREGON

307 W. Alder St., Joseph, 541-432-7551; www.valleybronze.com

Valley Bronze produces finished castings of bronze, fine and sterling silver and stainless steel and the showroom displays finished pieces. Tours of foundry are available by reservation. May-November, daily; December-April, by appointment.

WALLOWA LAKE STATE PARK

725 Summer St., N.E., Joseph, 541-432-4185, 800-551-6949;
www.oregonstateparks.org

This park has 201 forested acres in an alpine setting formed by a glacier at the base of the rugged Wallowa Mountains. Features include swimming, water sport equipment rentals, fishing, boating, hiking and riding trails and picnicking. Horse stables are nearby.

SPECIAL EVENT
CHIEF JOSEPH DAYS

102 E. First St., Joseph, 541-432-1015; www.chiefjosephdays.com

The weekend celebration includes a rodeo, parades, Native American dances and cowboy breakfasts. Last full weekend in July.

HOTEL
★★WALLOWA LAKE LODGE

60060 Wallowa Lake Highway, Joseph, 541-432-9821; www.wallowalake.com

22 rooms. Restaurant. $

★
★
★
★

KLAMATH FALLS

With more than 100 good fishing lakes nearby, Klamath Falls appeals to those who love to fish. Upper Klamath Lake, the largest body of fresh water in Oregon, runs north of town for 30 miles. White pelicans, protected by law, nest here each summer, and a large concentration of bald eagles winter in the Klamath Basin. Headquarters and a Ranger District office of the Fremont-Winema National Forest are located here.

Information: Klamath County Department of Tourism, 205 Riverside Drive, Klamath Falls, 541-882-1501, 800-445-6728; www.klamathcountytourism.com

WHAT TO SEE AND DO
COLLIER MEMORIAL STATE PARK AND LOGGING MUSEUM

46000 Highway 97, Chiloquin, 541-783-2471, 800-551-6949;
www.oregonstateparks.org

A 655-acre park located at the confluence of Spring Creek and Williamson River, Collier includes an open-air historic logging museum with display of tools, machines and engines; various types of furnished 1800s-era pioneer cabins and a gift shop.

JACKSON F. KIMBALL STATE RECREATION SITE

46000 Highway 97, Chiloquin, 541-783-2471, 800-551-6949;
www.oregonstateparks.org

A 19-acre pine- and fir-timbered area, the recreation site is at the headwaters of the Wood River, which is noted for its transparency and deep blue appearance. Mid-April-October.

KLAMATH COUNTY BALDWIN HOTEL MUSEUM

31 Main St., Klamath Falls, 541-883-4207; www.co.klamath.or.us

This restored turn-of-the-century hotel contains many original furnishings and offers guided tours. June-September, Tuesday-Saturday; closed holidays.

KLAMATH COUNTY MAIN MUSEUM

1451 Main St., Klamath Falls, 541-883-4208; www.co.klamath.or.us

The museum features local geology, history, wildlife and Native American displays and a research library with books on history, natural history and anthropology of the Pacific Northwest. Tuesday-Saturday; closed holidays.

WINEMA NATIONAL FOREST

2819 Dahlia St., Highway 62 or Highway 140, Klamath Falls,
541-883-6714; www.fs.fed.us/r6/frewin

This forest stretches more than one million acres and includes former reservation lands of the Klamath Tribe, high country of Sky Lakes, portions of Pacific Crest National Scenic Trail and recreation areas in Lake of the Woods, Recreation Creek, Mountain Lakes Wilderness and Mt. Theilson Wilderness.

HOTELS

★BEST WESTERN OLYMPIC INN

2627 S. Sixth St., Klamath Falls, 541-882-9665, 800-600-9665, 800-780-7234;
www.klamathfallshotelmotel.com

92 rooms. Complimentary full breakfast. High-speed Internet access. Outdoor pool, whirlpool. Airport transportation available. $

★HOLIDAY INN EXPRESS

2500 S. Sixth St., Klamath Falls, 541-884-9999, 800-315-2621; www.hiexpress.com

58 rooms. Complimentary continental breakfast. High-speed Internet access. Fitness center. Indoor pool, whirlpool. $

OREGON

★★★THE RUNNING Y RANCH RESORT

5500 Running Y Road, Klamath Falls, 541-850-5500,
888-850-0275; www.runningy.com

This 3,600-acre resort is set amid wooded hills and open meadows at the edge of the Cascade Range. The Running Y Ranch overlooks Klamath Lake, the largest natural lake in the northwest. The resort's lodge has comfortably appointed rooms with golf course views. Guests can take advantage of the resort's fitness center, pool complex and Sandhill Spa. An Arnold Palmer-designed golf course is the best among the public links in the nation. 350 rooms. Restaurant, bar. Fitness center. Spa. Indoor pool, whirlpool. Airport transportation available. $

★
★
★
★
★

SPECIALTY LODGINGS

CRYSTAL WOOD LODGE

38625 Westside Drive, Klamath Falls, 541-381-2322, 866-381-2322;
www.crystalwoodlodge.com

Seven rooms. Wireless Internet access. $

PROSPECT HOTEL
391 Mill creek Drive, Prospect, 541-560-3664, 800-944-6490; www.prospecthotel.com
24 rooms. $

LA GRANDE

Located in the heart of Northeast Oregon amid the Blue and Wallowa mountains, La Grande offers visitors breathtaking scenery and numerous exhilarating activities. Rafting and fishing enthusiasts enjoy the Grande Ronde River; hikers and mountain bikers navigate the Eagle Cap Wilderness and the tracks of the Oregon Trail. A Ranger District office of the Wallowa-Whitman National Forest is located here.
Information: La Grande/Union County Visitors & Conventions Bureau, 102 Elm St.,
La Grande, 541-963-8588, 800-848-9969; www.visitlagrande.com

WHAT TO SEE AND DO
CATHERINE CREEK STATE PARK
Eight miles southeast on Highway 203, 800-551-6949; www.oregonstateparks.org
A 160-acre park in a pine forest along the creek, Catherine Creek State Park features fishing, biking, hiking and picnicking. Mid-April-October.

EASTERN OREGON UNIVERSITY
One University Blvd., La Grande, 541-962-3378; www.eou.edu
There is a rock and mineral collection displayed in the free-admission science building of this small liberal arts college. The Nightingale Gallery hosts changing art exhibits. Monday-Friday; closed holidays.

HILGARD JUNCTION STATE PARK
Eight miles west off Interstate 84 N. 800-551-6949;
www.oregonstateparks.org
A 233-acre park on the old Oregon Trail, Hilgard Junction features fishing, picnicking, and exhibits at the Oregon Trail Interpretive Center. Memorial Day-Labor Day, daily.

SPECIALTY LODGING
STANG MANOR BED AND BREAKFAST
1612 Walnut St., La Grande, 541-963-2400, 888-286-9463;
www.stangmanor.com
Four rooms. Children over 10 years only. Complimentary full breakfast. $

RESTAURANTS
★★FOLEY STATION
1114 Adams, La Grande, 541-963-7473; www.foleystation.com
American menu. Breakfast, lunch, dinner. Closed Monday. $$

★★TEN DEPOT STREET
10 Depot St., La Grande, 541-963-8766; www.tendepotstreet.com
American menu. Lunch, dinner. Closed Sunday. $$

★
★
★
★
★

LAKEVIEW

General John C. Fremont and Kit Carson passed through what is now Lake County in 1843. There are antelope and bighorn sheep in the area, as well as many trout streams and seven lakes nearby. A supervisor's office of the Fremont National Forest is located in Lakeview. There is also a district office of the Bureau of Land Management and an office of the U.S. Department of Fish and Wildlife.

Information: Lake County Chamber of Commerce, 126 N.E. St., Lakeview, 541-947-6040; www.lakecountychamber.org

WHAT TO SEE AND DO

FORT ROCK VALLEY HISTORICAL HOMESTEAD MUSEUM

Fort Rock, 541-576-2207; www.fortrockmuseum.com

The purpose of this village museum is to preserve some of the homestead era structures by moving them from original locations to the museum site, just west of the town of Fort Rock. The Webster cabin and Dr. Thom's office were the two buildings that were in place for the opening in 1988. Since then, several homes and a church have been moved to the village, as well as pieces of equipment. More structures and other pieces will be moved in the future. The moving of the buildings has been accomplished by volunteers from the community, the Lake County Road Department and the Midstate Electric Cooperative. Restoration has been done by a few local members. Memorial Day-Labor Day, Friday-Sunday 10 a.m.-4 p.m.

FREMONT NATIONAL FOREST

1301 S. G St., 541-947-2151; www.fs.fed.us/r6/frewin

More than 5 million acres, this forest includes remnants of ice-age lava flows and the largest and most defined exposed geologic fault in North America, Abert Rim, on east side of Lake Abert. Abert Rim is most spectacular at the east side of Crooked Creek Valley. Many of the lakes are remnants of post glacial Lake Lahontan. Gearhart Mountain Wilderness is rough and forested with unusual rock formations, streams and Blue Lake.

HART MOUNTAIN NATIONAL ANTELOPE REFUGE

65 miles northeast via Highway 140; www.fws.gov/sheldonhartmtn/Hart

The 275,000-acre Hart Mountain National Antelope Refuge was established in 1936 to provide spring, summer and fall range for remnant antelope herds. These herds usually winter in Catlow Valley to the east and on the Sheldon National Wildlife Refuge about 35 miles southeast in Nevada. Since then, the purpose of the refuge has been expanded to include management of all wildlife species characteristic of this high-desert habitat and to preserve natural, native ecosystems for the enjoyment, education and appreciation of the public. Most refuge roads are not maintained for passenger vehicles and require high-clearance and four-wheel drive.

HOTEL

★BEST WESTERN SKYLINE MOTOR LODGE

414 N. G St., Lakeview, 541-947-2194, 800-780-7234; www.bestwestern.com

38 rooms. Pets accepted, some restrictions; fee. Complimentary continental breakfast. High-speed Internet access. Indoor pool, whirlpool. $

OREGON

★
★
★
★
★

LINCOLN CITY

Nicknamed the "kite capital of the world," Lincoln City is a popular recreation, art and shopping area offering many accommodations with ocean-view rooms.
Information: Visitor & Convention Bureau, 4039 N.W. Logan Road, Lincoln City, 541-994-3070; www.el.com/to/lincolncity

WHAT TO SEE AND DO
ALDER GLASS
611 Immonen Road, Lincoln City; www.alderhouse.com
Set in a grove of alder trees, this is the oldest glass-blowing studio in Oregon. Mid-March-November, daily.

CHINOOK WINDS CASINO & CONVENTION CENTER
1777 N.W. 44th St., Lincoln City, 541-996-5825, 888-244-6665; www.chinookwindscasino.com
About 80 miles south of the Washington border on the scenic Oregon coast, Chinook Winds is the largest convention facility between Seattle and San Francisco. With more than 1,200 machines and tables, the modern casino has all the requisite games-slots, blackjack, keno, poker, roulette, craps, even bingo—with a betting limit of $500. The cavernous showroom sees regular performances by classic rock bands, country artists and comedians, many of them household names. There are also three restaurants (an upscale room, a buffet and a deli), a lounge, childcare services and an arcade for the kids. Best of all, the casino's beachfront location is serene, and there's plenty of public access in the area.

DEVILS LAKE STATE PARK
1452 N.E. 6th Dr., Lincoln City, 541-994-2002, 800-551-6949; South of town, off Highway 101; www.oregonstateparks.org
Devils Lake is a 109-acre park with swimming, fishing and boating.

THEATRE WEST
3536 S.E. Highway 101, Lincoln City, 541-994-5663; www.theatrewest.com
The community theater features comedies and dramas. Thursday-Saturday 8 p.m.

HOTELS
★BEST WESTERN LINCOLN SANDS SUITES
535 N.W. Inlet Ave., Lincoln City, 541-994-4227, 800-780-7234; www.bestwestern.com
33 rooms. Complimentary continental breakfast. Fitness center. High-speed Internet access. Outdoor pool, whirlpool. **$**

★COHO INN
1635 N.W. Harbor Ave., Lincoln City, 541-994-3684, 800-848-7006; www.thecohoinn.com
50 rooms. Pets accepted, some restrictions; fee. Whirlpool. **$**

★
★★
★★★
★

★★INN AT SPANISH HEAD

4009 S.W. Highway 101, Lincoln City, 541-996-2162, 800-452-8127;
www.spanishhead.com
120 rooms. Restaurant, bar. Fitness center. Outdoor pool, whirlpool. $$

★★★SALISHAN LODGE & GOLF RESORT

7760 Highway 101, Gleneden Beach, 541-764-2371, 800-452-2300;
www.salishan.com
Carved out of a scenic stretch of Oregon coastline, the Salishan Lodge & Golf Resort
is desirable to nature lovers who appreciate creature comforts. This traditional Pacific
Northwest lodge is perhaps best loved for its magnificent views of the region's rug-
ged landscape. Private beach access and an 18-hole, Scottish-style golf course rank
among the property's favorite amenities, which also include an indoor tennis center,
fitness center and two indoor pools. 205 rooms. Pets accepted; fee. Restaurant, bar.
Fitness center. Indoor pool, whirlpool. Spa. Tennis. $

SPECIALTY LODGING
THE O'DYSIUS HOTEL

120 N.W. Inlet Court, Lincoln City, 541-994-4121, 800-869-8069;
www.odysius.com
The O'dysius Hotel appeals to water lovers, with the Pacific Ocean to the immediate
west, the D-River (the world's shortest river) bordering to the south and Devils Lake
a short walk to the east. Each room has a fireplace, whirlpool tub and custom décor.
30 rooms. No children allowed. Complimentary continental breakfast. Whirlpool. $$

RESTAURANT
★★★BAY HOUSE

5911 S.W. Highway 101, Lincoln City, 541-996-3222; www.bayhouserestaurant.com
Located at the south end of the city, the restaurant offers spectacular views of Siletz
Bay. American menu. Dinner, brunch. Bar. $$

MADRAS

White settlement in Madras proceeded slowly at first because of territorial issues
relating to a wall of separation between local Native Americans and new settlers. In
1862, the first road was built across the Cascades to provide a passage for traders.
Information: Chamber of Commerce, 274 S.W. Fourth St., Madras,
541-475-2350, 800-967-3564; www.madraschamber.com

WHAT TO SEE AND DO
COVE PALISADES STATE PARK

7300 S.W. Jordan Road, Madras, 541-546-3412, 800-551-6949;
www.oregonstateparks.org
This 4,130-acre park is on Lake Billy Chinook behind the Round Butte Dam. It fea-
tures a scenic canyon of geological interest and spectacular views of the confluence
of the Crooked, Deschutes and Metolius rivers forming Lake Billy Chinook in a steep
basaltic canyon.

OREGON

JEFFERSON COUNTY MUSEUM

34 S.E. D St., Madras, 541-475-3808; www.madraschamber.com/museums.cfm
Located in the old courthouse, the museum features old-fashioned doctor's equipment, military memorabilia, and homestead and farm equipment. Daily 9 a.m.-5 p.m.; closed New Year's Day, Thanksgiving Day and Christmas.

RICHARDSON'S ROCK RANCH

6683 N.E. Haycreek Road, Madras, 541-475-2680, 800-433-2680; www.richardsonrockranch.com
The highlight of the ranch is famous agate beds, featuring thunder eggs and ledge agate material. Daily 7 a.m.-5 p.m. Closed November-March.

SPECIAL EVENT
COLLAGE OF CULTURE

274 S.W. Fourth St., Madras, 541-475-2350, 800-967-3564; www.collageofculture.com
A music and balloon festival celebrates cultural diversity in the Jefferson County Fair Complex. Mid-May.

HOTELS
★★★KAH-NEE-TA LODGE

1-250 Highway, Highway 26 north to Warm Springs, Warm Springs, 541-553-1112, 800-554-4786; www.kah-nee-taresort.com
Overlooking the Warm Springs River, this resort gives each guest a view of the sunrise from their room. Authentic Native American dances are featured on Sundays from May-September. 139 rooms. Restaurant, bar. High-speed Internet access. Fitness center. Outdoor pool. Golf. Tennis. Casino. Spa. Pets accepted, some restrictions. **$**

★SONNY'S MOTEL

1539 S.W. Highway 97, Madras, 541-475-7217; www.sonnysmotel.net
44 rooms. Complimentary continental breakfast. Outdoor pool, whirlpool. Pets accepted; fee. **$**

★
★★
★★
★

MCKENZIE BRIDGE

McKenzie Bridge and the neighboring town of Blue River are located on the beautiful McKenzie River with covered bridges, lakes, waterfalls and wilderness trails of the Cascades nearby. Fishing, float trips, skiing and backpacking are some of the many activities available. Ranger District offices of the Willamette National Forest are located here and in Blue River.
Information: McKenzie River Chamber of Commerce and Information Center, 44643 McKenzie Highway East (Highway 126), Leaburg; 541-896-3330; www.el.com/to/mckenzierivervalley

WHAT TO SEE AND DO
BLUE RIVER DAM AND LAKE

500 E. Fourth Ave., Eugene, 541-937-2131, 877-444-6777; www.corpslakes.usace.army.mil/visitors
The area offers boating, swimming, fishing and camping.

COUGAR DAM AND LAKE

Five miles west on Highway 126, then south on Forest Road 19 (Aufderheide Forest Drive), in Willamette National Forest, 541-937-2131, 877-444-6777; www.corpslakes.usace.army.mil/visitors

A six-mile-long reservoir, Cougar Dam and Lake features swimming, waterskiing and fishing.

HOTELS

★ALL SEASONS MOTEL

130 Breitenbush Road, Detroit, 503-854-3421, 877-505-8779; www.allseasonsmotel.net

12 rooms. Wireless Internet access. Pets accepted. $

★★★HOLIDAY FARM RESORT

54455 McKenzie River Drive, Blue River, 541-822-3725; www.holidayfarmresort.com

Eight cottages. Wireless Internet access. Restaurant. Spa. $$

SPECIALTY LODGINGS

BELKNAP LODGE & HOT SPRINGS

59296 N. Belknap Springs Road, McKenzie Bridge, 541-822-3512; www.belknaphotsprings.com

Extensive grounds and perennial gardens make this mountain retreat on the banks of the McKenzie River one of the state's most enjoyable. 26 rooms. Pool. $$

MCKENZIE RIVER INN

49164 McKenzie River Highway, Vida, 541-822-6260; www.mckenzieriverinn.com

Built in 1929, this inn is one of the oldest bed and breakfasts on the river. Six rooms. $

METOLIUS RIVER RESORT

25551 S.W. Forest Service Road, Camp Sherman, 800-818-7688; www.metoliusriverresort.com

Located on one of Oregon's premier fly-fishing rivers, this area offers fully furnished cabins with kitchens and private decks. 12 rooms. $$

WAYFARER RESORT

46725 Goodpasture Road, Vida, 541-896-3613, 800-627-3613; www.wayfarerresort.com

13 rooms. Pets accepted; fee. $$

RESTAURANTS

★THE CEDARS RESTAURANT & LOUNGE

200 Detroit Ave., Detroit, 503-854-3636; www.thecedarsrestaurant.com

American menu. Breakfast, lunch, dinner. $

★KORNER POST RESTAURANT

100 Detroit Ave., Detroit, 503-854-3735; www.cornerpost.com

American menu. Breakfast, lunch, dinner. $

153

OREGON

★
★
★
★
★

★THE LAKESIDE BISTRO

12930 Hawks Beard Road, Black Butte Ranch, 541-595-1264, 866-901-2961;
www.blackbutteranch.com
American menu. Lunch, dinner. **$**

★★THE LODGE RESTAURANT

12930 Hawks Beard Road, Black Butte Ranch, 541-595-1260, 866-901-2961;
www.blackbutteranch.com
French menu. Lunch, dinner. **$**

MCMINNVILLE

McMinnville is in the center of a wine-producing area. Many of the wineries offer tours.
Information: Chamber of Commerce, 417 N.W. Adams St., McMinnville,
503-472-6196; www.mcminnville.org

WHAT TO SEE AND DO

EVERGREEN AVIATION & SPACE MUSEUM

500 N.E. Capt. Michael King Smith Way, McMinnville, 503-434-4180;
www.sprucegoose.com
This museum is the home of Howard Hughes's "Spruce Goose" aircraft. Daily 9 a.m.-5 p.m.; closed Thanksgiving, Christmas and Easter Sunday.

GALLERY THEATER

210 N. Ford St., McMinnville, 503-472-2227; www.gallerytheater.org
The theater features musical, comedy and drama productions by the Gallery Players of Oregon. Friday-Sunday.

LINFIELD COLLEGE

900 S.E. Baker St., McMinnville, 503-883-2200; www.linfield.edu
On the 100-acre campus are the Miller Fine Arts Center, Linfield Anthropology Museum and Linfield Theater. The music department offers concerts and lectures and events are scheduled throughout the year.

HOTEL

★BEST WESTERN VINEYARD INN

2035 S. Highway 99 West, McMinnville, 503-472-4900, 800-780-7234;
www.bestwestern.com
65 rooms. Complimentary continental breakfast. High-speed Internet access. Fitness center. Indoor pool, whirlpool. Pets accepted, some restrictions. **$**

SPECIALTY LODGINGS

STEIGER HAUS BED AND BREAKFAST

360 S.E. Wilson St., McMinnville, 503-472-0821; www.steigerhaus.com
Five rooms. Children over 10 years only. Complimentary full breakfast. **$**

YOUNGBERG HILL VINEYARDS INN

10660 S.W. Youngberg Hill Road, McMinnville, 503-472-2727, 888-657-8668;
www.youngberghill.com

Set on a hillside above the Willamette Valley, this cozy inn overlooks Youngberg Hills' award-winning pinot noir vineyards. Guests can relax in the library and lounging salon. Covered decks wrap the inn's perimeter, affording breathtaking views of the valley below and nearby mountain peaks. Four rooms. Whirlpool. **$$**

MEDFORD

Medford is known for its pears: Comice, Bartlett, Winter Nellis, Bosc and Anjou. The city is surrounded by orchards. Trees make the city park-like and supply the lumber industry. Mild winters and warm summers encourage outdoor sports such as boating and fishing on the Rogue River, camping and hunting. The Rogue River National Forest headquarters is here.

Information: Visitors and Convention Bureau, 101 E. Eighth St., Medford,
541-779-4847, 800-469-6307; www.visitmedford.org

WHAT TO SEE AND DO
BUTTE CREEK MILL

402 Royal Ave. N., Eagle Point, 541-826-3531;
www.buttecreekmill.com

This water-powered gristmill dating to 1872 grinds whole-grain products with original millstones. Museum: Summer, Saturday. Mill: Monday-Saturday 9 a.m.-5 p.m., Sunday 11 a.m.-5 p.m.; closed holidays.

155

CRATER ROCK MUSEUM

2002 Scenic Ave., Central Point, 541-664-6081; www.craterrock.com
The museum features gem and mineral collections, Native American artifacts, fossils, geodes and crystals. Tuesday-Saturday 10 a.m.-4 p.m.; closed holidays.

OREGON

ROGUE RIVER NATIONAL FOREST

333 W. Eighth St., Medford, 541-858-2200; www.fs.fed.us/r6/rogue-siskiyou
The National Forest has 632,045 acres with extensive stands of Douglas fir, ponderosa and sugar pine. Rogue-Umpqua National Forest Scenic Byway offers a day-long drive through southern Oregon's dramatic panorama of mountains, rivers and forest viewpoints. A part of the Pacific Crest National Scenic Trail and portions of three wilderness areas are included in the forest. For fishermen, the upper reaches of the Rogue River and other streams and lakes yield rainbow, cutthroat and brook trout. Union Creek Historic District is on Highway 62 near Crater Lake National Park.

SOUTHERN OREGON HISTORICAL SOCIETY

106 N. Central Ave., Medford, 541-858-1724; www.sohs.org
More than 2,000 items from Southern Oregon Historical Society's cultural history collection are on display here. Monday-Friday.

TOUVELLE STATE RECREATION SITE

Three miles northeast on I-5, then six miles north on Table Rock Road,
541-582-1118, 800-551-6949; www.oregonstateparks.org

The 51-acre TouVelle State Recreation Site features fishing on the Rogue River, swimming, hiking, bird-watching and picnicking.

SPECIAL EVENTS
JACKSON COUNTY FAIR

Jackson County Fairgrounds, 1 Peninger Road, Central Point, 541-774-8270;
www.jcfairgrounds.com

Along with a 4-H fair, the county celebration includes entertainment, dance and music. Third weekend in July.

PEAR BLOSSOM FESTIVAL

541-779-4847; www.pearblossomparade.org

The celebration features a parade, 10-mile run and band festival. Second weekend in April.

HOTELS
★★RED LION

200 N. Riverside Ave., Medford, 541-779-5811, 800-733-5466; www.redlion.com

185 rooms. High-speed Internet access. Restaurants, bar. Fitness center. Outdoor pool. Airport transportation available. Pets accepted; fee. $

★★ROGUE REGENCY INN

2300 Biddle Road, Medford, 541-770-1234, 800-535-5805; www.rogueregency.com

203 rooms. High-speed Internet access. Restaurant, bar. Fitness center. Spa. Indoor pool, whirlpool. Airport transportation available. $

MOUNT HOOD NATIONAL FOREST
WHAT TO SEE AND DO
MOUNT HOOD MEADOWS

11 miles northeast of Government Camp on Highway 35,
503-337-2222; www.skihood.com

Skiing enthusiasts will find quad, triple and double chairlifts, ski school and rentals a restaurant, cafeteria, concessions, bar, day care and two day lodges at Mount Hood. The longest run is three miles and the highest vertical drop is 2,777 feet. The area also features 550 acres of expert canyon skiing, groomed and ungroomed cross-country trails and night skiing. November-May.

MOUNT HOOD NATIONAL FOREST

16400 Champion Way, Sandy, 503-668-1700; www.fs.fed.us/r6/mthood

Mount Hood is the natural focal point of this 1,064,573-acre forest with headquarters in Sandy. Its white-crowned top, the highest point in Oregon, can be seen for miles on a clear day. It is also popular with skiers, who know it has some of the best slopes in the northwest. There are five winter sports areas. Throughout the year, however, visitors can take advantage of the surrounding forest facilities for camping, hunting, fishing, swimming, mountain climbing, golfing, horseback riding, hiking and tobogganing. The Columbia Gorge, which cuts through the Cascades here, has many spectacular waterfalls, including Multnomah. There are nine routes to the summit, which has fumed and smoked several times since the volcanic peak was discovered. Only experienced climbers should try the ascent and then only with a guide.

RIVER CRUISE

45 miles east of Portland via Interstate 84, 503-224-3900, 800-224-3901; www.sternwheeler.com

Take a two-hour narrated cruise of Columbia Gorge aboard the 599-passenger *Columbia Gorge*, an authentic sternwheeler. Mid-June-September, three departures daily; reservations required for dinner cruise.

TIMBERLINE LODGE

Timberline Ski Area, six miles north of Highway 26, on Timberline Highway, 503-622-7979; www.timberlinelodge.com

Timberline Lodge features quads, triple, and double chairlifts, ski school and rentals, a restaurant, cafeteria, bar and lodge. The longest run is more than two miles and the peak vertical drop is 3,580 feet.

HOTELS

★MT. HOOD INN

87450 E. Government Camp Loop, Government Camp, 503-272-3205, 800-443-7777; www.mthoodinn.com

56 rooms. Complimentary continental breakfast. Wireless Internet access. Whirlpool. Pets accepted, some restrictions; fee. **$**

★★★THE RESORT AT THE MOUNTAIN

68010 E. Fairway Ave., Welches, 503-622-3101, 800-669-7666; www.theresort.com

160 rooms. Restaurant, bar. High-speed Internet access. Outdoor pool, whirlpool. Golf. Tennis. **$**

★★TIMBERLINE LODGE

Timberline Ski Area, six miles north of Highway 26, 503-622-7979; www.timberlinelodge.com

70 rooms. Restaurant, bar. Outdoor pool, whirlpool. Fitness center. **$**

★
★★
★★
★

NEWBERG

Quakers settled here and established Pacific Academy in 1885. Herbert Hoover graduated in the school's first class.

Information: Chehalem Chamber of Commerce, 415 E. Sheridan, Newberg, 503-538-2014; www.chehalemvalley.org

WHAT TO SEE AND DO

CHAMPOEG STATE HERITAGE AREA

7679 Champoeg Road Northeast, 503-678-1251; www.oregonstateparks.org

A 615-acre park on site of an early Willamette River settlement, Champoeg State Heritage Area includes the site of the settlers' vote in 1843 for a provisional territorial government, which was swept away by the flood of 1861. The area features fishing, a boat dock on Willamette River, hiking and picnicking. French Prairie Loop 40-mile auto or bike tour begins and ends here.

CHAMPOEG STATE PARK VISITOR CENTER

8239 Champoeg Road N.E., Newberg, 503-678-1251;
www.oregonstateparks.org

Interpretive historical exhibits tell the story of "Champoeg: Birthplace of Oregon."
The center also offers films and tours. Daily.

HOOVER-MINTHORN HOUSE MUSEUM

115 S. River St., Newberg, 503-538-6629; www.nscda.org

Herbert hoover lived here with his uncle, Dr. Henry Minthorn. The quaker house
was built in 1881 and contains many original furnishings, photographs and souvenirs
of hoover's boyhood. March-November, Wednesday-Sunday 1-4 p.m. December and
February, Saturday and Sunday 1-4 p.m.; closed January, holidays.

NEWELL HOUSE MUSEUM

8089 Champoeg Road N.E., Newberg, 503-678-5537;
www.newellhouse.com

The reconstructed home of Robert Newell, one-time mountain man and friend of the
Native Americans, contains period furnishings, quilts, coverlets and examples of fine
handiwork. Other features include a collection of inaugural gowns worn by wives of
Oregon governors and Native American artifacts. March-October, Friday-Sunday and
major holidays 1-5 p.m. or by appointment.

PIONEER MOTHER'S MEMORIAL LOG CABIN

158

8035 Champoeg Road N.E., Newberg, 503-633-2237;
www.newellhouse.com

A replica, much enlarged, of the type of log cabin built by early pioneers, it was constructed of peeled hand-hewn logs and with a shake roof. it has a massive stone fireplace in the living room, a sleeping loft and two small bedrooms along with many
pioneer items including an old Hudson's Bay heating stove, a collection of guns and
muskets dating from 1777 to 1853, a fife played at Lincoln's funeral, china and glass-
ware and original furnishings from pioneer homes. March-October, Friday-Sunday and
holidays 1-5 p.m. or by appointment.

OREGON

HOTEL

★SHILO INN

501 Sitka Ave., Newberg, 503-537-0303, 800-222-2244; www.shiloinns.com

60 rooms. Complimentary continental breakfast. Fitness center. Outdoor pool, whirlpool. Business Center. Pets accepted, some restrictions; fee. **$**

NEWPORT

This fishing port at the mouth of the Yaquina River has been a resort for more than
100 years. Crabbing is a popular activity here.

Information: Chamber of Commerce, 555 S.W. Coast Highway, Newport,
541-265-8801, 800-262-7844; www.newportchamber.org

WHAT TO SEE AND DO

BEVERLY BEACH STATE PARK

198 N.E. 123rd St., Newport, 541-265-9278, 800-551-6949;
www.oregonstateparks.org

A 130-acre park with beach access, attractions include fishing, hiking and picnicking.

DEVILS PUNCH BOWL STATE NATURAL AREA

Eight miles north off Highway 101, 800-551-6949; www.oregonstateparks.org

An 8-acre park noted for its bowl-shaped rock formation that fills at high tide, Devils Punch Bowl features ocean-carved caves, marine gardens, a beach, trails and an observation point.

HATFIELD MARINE SCIENCE CENTER OF OREGON STATE UNIVERSITY

2030 S.E. Marine Science Drive, Newport, 541-867-0100; www.hmsc.oregonstate.edu

Hatfield Marine Science Center conducts research on oceanography, fisheries, water quality, marine science education and marine biology. The facility includes a nature trail, aquarium museum, films, special programs in the summer and gray whale programs in winter and spring.

LINCOLN COUNTY HISTORICAL SOCIETY MUSEUMS

Log Cabin Museum, 545 S.W. Ninth St., Newport, 541-265-7509;
www.oregoncoast.history.museum

The museums house Victorian-era household furnishings and clothing to teach the history of Lincoln County. Summer, Tuesday-Sunday 10 a.m.-5 p.m. Winter, Tuesday-Sunday 11 a.m.-4 p.m.; closed major holidays.

ONA BEACH STATE PARK

Eight miles south on Highway 101, 800-551-6949;
www.oregonstateparks.org

A 237-acre day-use park with ocean beach, Ona Beach offers swimming, fishing (boat ramp) and picnicking.

OREGON COAST AQUARIUM

2820 S.E. Ferry Slip Road, Newport, 541-867-3474; www.aquarium.org

The aquarium houses 15,000 animals representing 500 species in unique habitats. Winter, daily 10 a.m.-5 p.m. Memorial Day-Labor Day, daily 9 a.m.-6 p.m. Closed December 25.

RIPLEY'S BELIEVE IT OR NOT

250 S.W. Bay Blvd., Newport, 541-265-2206; www.marinersquare.com/ripleys

Exhibits include replicas of a backwards fountain, King Tut's tomb, the Titanic and the Fiji mermaid.

OREGON

★
★
★
★
★

SOUTH BEACH STATE PARK

5580 S. Coast Highway, South Beach, 541-867-4715, 800-551-6949;
www.oregonstateparks.org

More than 400 acres, South Beach State Park features a sandy beach, dunes, Fishing, hiking and picnicking.

UNDERSEA GARDENS

250 S.W. Bay Blvd., Newport, 541-265-2206;
www.marinersquare.com/undersea-gardens/

Visitors descend beneath the sea for an underwater show. Watch native sea life through viewing windows, including a giant octopus, while guides narrate as scuba divers perform.

WAX WORKS

250 S.W. Bay Blvd., Newport, 541-265-2206; www.marinersquare.com/wax-works
Events of the past and future are shown with animation and special effects.

YAQUINA HEAD

750 N.W. Lighthouse Drive (at Highway 101), Newport, 541-574-3100;
www.blm.gov/or/resources/recreation/yaquina/

The lighthouse here is a popular spot for whale-watching and fully accessible tidal pool viewing. Daily.

SPECIAL EVENT
LOYALTY DAYS AND SEA FAIR FESTIVAL

Newport, 541-961-1466; www.loyaltydays.com
Festival features military ships, parade, sailboat races and entertainment. First weekend in May.

HOTELS
★★EMBARCADERO RESORT HOTEL

1000 S.E. Bay Blvd., Newport, 541-265-8521, 800-547-4779;
www.embarcadero-resort.com

70 rooms. Restaurant, bar. Indoor pool, whirlpool. Airport transportation available. **$**

★★SHILO INN

536 S.W. Elizabeth St., Newport, 541-265-7701, 800-222-2244; www.shiloinns.com
179 rooms. Pets accepted, some restrictions; fee. Restaurant, bar. Indoor pool. High-speed Internet access. Business Center. **$**

NORTH PLAINS
SPECIAL EVENT
ELEPHANT GARLIC FESTIVAL

Jessie Mayes Community Center, 30955 N.W. Hillcrest, North Plains,
503-647-2619; www.funstinks.com

How can you go wrong with a festival whose motto is "Where fun stinks?" Garlic ice cream, garlic beer and other delicacies dominate this yearly extravaganza. Elephant garlic has been the theme only since 1998, when it was made the focus after almost

10 years of lackluster attendance at North Plains Days. Since then, the festival has blossomed, and attendance has increased almost every year. Early August. Free admission.

OREGON CAVES NATIONAL MONUMENT
WHAT TO SEE AND DO
OREGON CAVES NATIONAL MONUMENT
20 miles east of Cave Junction on Highway 46, 541-592-2100; www.nps.gov/orca
This area was discovered in 1874, when hunter Elijah Davidson's dog followed a bear into the cave. After a visit in 1907, frontier poet Joaquin Miller called this "The Marble Halls of Oregon." In 1909, the cave and 480 acres of the Siskiyou Mountains were made a national monument. The cave has many chambers including Paradise Lost, Joaquin Miller's Chapel and Ghost Room. Guide service is required. The average temperature is 42 degrees Fahrenheit. Evening talks are given by National Park Service naturalists in summer. On the surface, the area is covered with a beautiful old-growth forest with abundant wildlife, birds, wildflowers and an interesting variety of trees and shrubs. A maintained and marked system of trails provides access to these areas.

OREGON CITY
Below Willamette Falls, where the river spills over a 42-foot drop, is historic Oregon City. Salmon fishing in the Willamette and Clackamas rivers is from early March until mid-May. The city is built on terraces, and there is an enclosed elevator to an observation platform.
Information: Oregon City Chamber of Commerce and Visitors Center, 503-656-1619; www.oregoncity.org

WHAT TO SEE AND DO
END OF THE OREGON TRAIL INTERPRETIVE CENTER
1726 Washington St., Oregon City, 503-657-9336; www.endoftheoregontrail.org
The mueum features exhibits on the journey made by early settlers over the Oregon Trail. Tuesday-Saturday 11 a.m.-4 p.m., Sunday, noon-4 p.m.; winter, closed Sunday-Monday, holidays.

JOHN INSKEEP ENVIRONMENTAL LEARNING CENTER
19600 S. Molalla Ave., Oregon City, 503-657-6958; depts.clackamas.cc.or.us/elc
With 8 acres developed on a former industrial site to demonstrate wildlife habitat in an urban setting, John Inskeep Environmental Learning Center includes extensive birds of prey exhibits, various plant and wildlife displays, a plant nursery and Haggart Astronomical Observatory. Daily dawn to dusk.

MCLOUGHLIN HOUSE NATIONAL HISTORIC SITE
713 Center St., Oregon City, 503-656-5146; www.mcloughlinhouse.org
The Georgian frame building was built in 1845-1846 by Dr. John McLoughlin, chief factor of the Hudson's Bay Company, who ruled the Columbia River region from 1824 to 1846. It includes period furnishings and many are original pieces, most having

★
★
★
★
☆

come around Cape Horn on sailing ships. Wednesday-Saturday 10 a.m.-4 p.m., Sunday 1-4 p.m.; closed January.

MILO MCIVER STATE PARK
24101 S. Entrance Road, Estacada, 503-630-7150,
800-551-6949; www.oregonstateparks.org
On the Clackamas River, this 937-acre park offers a panoramic view of Mount Hood and includes fishing, boating, hiking, horseback trails, a Disc golf course and interpretive programs. Mid March-October.

OLD AURORA COLONY MUSEUM
212 Second St. N.E., Aurora, 503-678-5754;
www.auroracolonymuseum.com
A complex of buildings forms the historical museum of the Aurora Colony, a German religious communal society, founded by Dr. William Keil. This museum includes Kraus House, a colony house with original artifacts; Steinbach Cabin; a house used by colony women for washing, soap making and canning and a herb garden divided into various uses including teas, cooking, medicinal and fragrances. Exhibits show off furniture, musical instruments, quilts and tools. Admission: adults $6, seniors $5, students $2, children 5 and under free. Tours. Tuesday-Saturday 11 a.m.-4 p.m., Sunday noon-4 p.m.; closed January, major holidays.

WILLIAM HOLMES HOUSE (ROSE FARM)
Holmes Lane and Rilance streets, Oregon City, 503-656-5146;
www.mcloughlinhouse.org
The oldest standing American home in Oregon City was built in 1847. The first territorial governor gave his original address here in 1849 and the upstairs ballroom was the scene of many social events. April-October, Sunday; closed holidays.

HOTEL
★★BEST WESTERN RIVERSHORE HOTEL
1900 Clackamette Drive, Oregon City, 503-655-7141,
877-780-7234; www.bestwestern.com
114 rooms. Restaurant, bar. High-speed Internet access. Outdoor pool, whirlpool. Pets accepted, some restrictions; fee. **$**

PENDLETON
Located on the old Oregon Trail, Pendleton is a trading center for the extensive cattle, wheat and green pea production in the area.
Information: Chamber of Commerce, 501 S. Main St., Pendleton,
541-276-7411, 800-547-8911; www.pendletonchamber.com

WHAT TO SEE AND DO
EMIGRANT SPRINGS STATE HERITAGE AREA
26 miles southeast off Interstate 84, 541-983-2277,
800-551-6949; www.oregonstateparks.org
A 23-acre park near summit of Blue Mountains features a ponderosa pine forest and Oregon Trail display.

UKIAH-DALE FOREST STATE SCENIC CORRIDOR

50 miles south on Highway 395, three miles southwest of Ukiah,
800-551-6949; www.oregonstateparks.org

A 3,000-acre scenic forest canyon extending along Camas Creek and the north fork of the John Day River Ukiah-Dale offers fishing for trout, steelhead and salmon.

UMATILLA INDIAN RESERVATION

73239 Confederated Way, five miles east via Mission Highway, Pendleton,
(Highway 30), 541-276-3165; www.umatilla.nsn.us

Visitors to the reservation, which was created by the Walla Walla Valley Treaty of 1855, can get a firsthand view of a Native American community in transition with historical and contemporary perspectives. One of the first Catholic missions in the United States is here. Indian Lake has good fishing and camping and beautiful scenery. The foothills and lowlands of the Blue Mountains provide excellent upland game and waterfowl hunting. In addition, the Umatilla Tribes have re-established runs of chinook salmon and steelhead within the Umatilla River.

UMATILLA NATIONAL FOREST

2517 S.W. Hailey Ave., northeast and south of Pendleton, reached by I-84,
Highways 395, 11, 204, 82, 244, 207 and 12, 541-278-3716; www.fs.fed.us/r6/uma

Located on more than one million acres, partly in Washington, Lewis and Clark passed through this region on the Columbia River in 1805. Umatilla includes spectacular views of the Tucannon, Umatilla, Grande Ronde, North Fork John Day and Wenaha River canyons. Remnants of historic gold mining can be found in the Granite area in sight of the Greenhorn Mountain Range. North Fork John Day, North Fork Umatilla and the Wenaha-Tucannon wilderness areas may be reached on horseback or on foot. In forest is:

SPECIAL EVENT
PENDLETON ROUND-UP

1114 S.W. Court Ave., Pendleton, 541-276-2553,
800-457-6336; www.pendletonroundup.com

This Old West rodeo and pageantry has been held annually since 1910. It brings in a gathering of Native Americans, Professional Rodeo Cowboys Association working cowboys and thousands of visitors. Mid-September.

HOTEL
★★RED LION

304 S.E. Nye Ave., Pendleton, 541-276-6111, 800-733-5466; www.redlion.com

170 rooms. Wireless Internet access. Restaurant, bar. Outdoor pool, whirlpool. Airport transportation available. Business Center. Pets accepted. $

PORT ORFORD

The westernmost incorporated city in the contiguous United States, Port Orford overlooks the Pacific Ocean with spectacular views. Captain George Vancouver spotted this area in 1792 and named it for the Earl of Orford. The cedar trees that grow in the area, sometimes called Lawson cypress and later named for the earl, are favored for boat construction.

Information: Chamber of Commerce, 502 Battle Rock City Park, 541-332-8055;
www.portorfordoregon.com

OREGON

★
★
★
★
★

WHAT TO SEE AND DO
HUMBUG MOUNTAIN STATE PARK
Six miles south on Highway 101, 541-332-6774, 800-551-6949;
www.oregonstateparks.org
A 1,842-acre park with a winding trail leading to the summit of Humbug Mountain, the peak looks out on virgin forest, trout streams and a sand beach. Windsurfing, scuba diving, fishing and hiking can be found here.

HOTEL
★★WILDSPRING GUEST HABITAT
92978 Cemetery Loop, Port Orford, 866-333-9453; www.wildspring.com
Five rooms. Complimentary continental breakfast. High-speed Internet access. Spa. Pets not allowed. $$

PORTLAND
Oregon's largest city sprawls across both banks of the Willamette River just south of its confluence with the Columbia. Portland's freshwater harbor is visited by more than 1,400 vessels annually.

Portland is surrounded by spectacular scenery. The Columbia River Gorge, Mount Hood, waterfalls, forests, ski slopes, fishing streams and hunting and camping areas are within easy access. The city has a number of major convention venues: the Memorial Coliseum complex, the Metropolitan Exposition Center and the Oregon convention center.

Portland justifies its reputation as the "city of roses" through its international rose test garden and the annual portland rose festival. Mount St. Helens, in Washington's gifford pinchot national forest, can be seen from numerous vantage points in the city. Portland is also an educational center, with Portland State University, the University of Portland, Lewis & Clark College and Reed College.

Information: Portland Oregon Visitors Association, 26 S.W. Broadway, Portland,
503-275-9750, 800-962-3700; www.pova.com

WHAT TO SEE AND DO
BENSON STATE RECREATION AREA
30 miles east on I-84, 800-551-6949; www.oregonstateparks.org
Thirty miles east of Portland, near Multnomah Falls, the Benson State Recreation Area has a lake that's perfect for fishing, swimming and boating (non-motorized boats only). Picnicking is also popular here, and the park even has a disc golf course. Daily.

COUNCIL CREST PARK
Southwest Council Crest Drive, S.W. Greenway Avenue
(follow the blue and white scenic tour signs), Portland, 503-823-7529;
www.portlandonline.com/parks
Council Crest Park is not just the city's highest park, it's the site of Portland's highest point, topping off at 1,073 feet above sea level. That may not sound all that high, but it's high enough to afford wonderful views of the Tualatin Valley, the Willamette River, Mount St. Helens and the truly high and mighty Mount Hood.

★
★
★
★
★

PORTLAND'S PASSION FOR MICROBREWS

San Francisco has wine and Seattle has coffee, but in unpretentious and easygoing Portland, the beverage of choice is beer. If you appreciate fresh, handcrafted beer, you're certain to enjoy your stay here. Portland has been dubbed America's Microbrew Capital, an appropriate moniker given the city's numerous thriving microbreweries. Beer drinkers flock daily to brewpubs such as the **Laurelwood Public House** (*1728 N.E. 40th Ave.*) and **BridgePort Brewpub** (*1313 N.W. Marshall St.*), where they enjoy a variety of ales crafted in the old-world tradition, often using locally grown barley and hops.

Portland's beer history dates to 1852, when German brewer Henry Saxer moved to the Oregon Territory, opening Liberty Brewery near First and Davis streets. Saxer's brewery experienced immediate success, and other breweries opened soon after to tap into locals' seemingly insatiable thirst for beer.

In the mid-1980s, Portland's brew tastes focused on European-style microbrews, a trend driven by a law passed by the Oregon state legislature that enabled brewers to sell beer directly to the public. Suddenly, microbreweries and brewpubs were popping up all over the state. Nobody took better advantage of the new law than Mike and Brian McMenamin, who in 1984 opened the Hillsdale Brewery and Public House (www.mcmenamins.com), the state's first brewpub since Prohibition. The McMenamins admit that their first brew, Hillsdale Ale, needed improvement, but after experimenting with different recipes, they were able to concoct colorfully named beers (Hammerhead, Terminator) that quickly became popular. The McMenamin brothers parlayed these early successes into a brewing empire, opening more than 50 breweries and brewpubs in the Northwest, as well as seven theater pubs and six hotels.

A fun and safe way to experience the city's many microbrews is to book a trip on the **Portland Brew** Bus (*www.brewbus.com*). The five-hour tour aboard the Brew Bus takes you to three or four local brewers, where you'll sample 15 to 25 beers, recording your impressions of each on a complimentary sampling scorecard. The bus often stops at Widmer **Brothers Gasthaus Restaurant & Pub** (*955 N. Russell St.*), founded by siblings Kurt and Rob in 1984. Widmer Brothers Brewing Company has emerged as one of the most successful brewers in the northwest, thanks largely to the popularity of its Hefeweizen, a strongly aromatic beer that goes unfiltered from the lagering tank to the bottle.

Another way to enjoy beer in Portland is to attend the **Oregon Brewers Festival**. Since 1987, OBF (*www.oregonbrewfest.com*) has been attracting tens of thousands of beer drinkers to Tom McCall Waterfront Park in downtown Portland.

OREGON

★
★★
★★
★

CROWN POINT STATE SCENIC CORRIDOR

40700 Historic Columbia River Highway, Corbett, 503-695-2261, 800-551-6949;
www.oregonstateparks.org

This 307-acre park possesses a 725-foot-high vantage point alongside the Columbia River Gorge, allowing for spectacular views of the gorge's rock walls, which rise 2,000 feet above the river. The historic Vista House, an octagonal building with a copper dome, was recently restored.

CRYSTAL SPRINGS RHODODENDRON GARDEN

Southeast 28th Ave., Portland, 503-771-8386; www.portlandonline.com

The pathways at Crystal Springs wind through a woodland setting, passing some 2,500 rhododendrons, azaleas and companion plants. A spring-fed lake attracts many species of birds and waterfowl. Admission: Labor Day-February, free; March-Labor Day, $3. Garden hours: April 1-September 30, daily 6 a.m.-10 p.m., October 1-March 31, daily 6 a.m.-6 p.m.

DABNEY STATE RECREATION AREA

19 miles east off Interstate 84, at Stark St., Bridge on
Highway 30, 800-551-6949; www.oregonstateparks.org

East of Portland, this 135-acre park is a popular summertime destination thanks to its idyllic swimming hole and picnic area. The park even offers electric cooking stations to fry up those hamburgers and tofu dogs. Other amenities include a group shelter, walking trails, beach, boat ramp and disc golf course. Many visitors enjoy fishing for salmon and steelhead in the Sandy River.

166

FOREST PARK

N.W. 29th Avenue and Upshur Street to Newberry Road, Portland,
503-823-7529; www.portlandonline.com

The park encompasses over 5,000 wooded acres, making it the largest wilderness park within city limits in the United States. Visitors can take advantage of 74 miles of hiking, bicycling and equestrian trails. Wildwood Trail begins at the Vietnam Veterans Living Memorial in Hoyt Arboretum and extends 27 miles, ending deep in the park beyond Germantown Road. Some 100 bird species and 60 mammal species inhabit the park. Daily 5 a.m.-10 p.m.

GRAY LINE BUS TOURS

Pioneer Courthouse Square, S.W. Morrison and S.W. Broadway,
Portland; www.grayline.com

Gray Line offers various tours that originate in Portland, including a three-hour tour of the city and a nine-hour tour that retraces Lewis and Clark's journey along the Columbia River.

THE GROTTO

Sandy Boulevard, (Highway 30) at N.E. 85th Avenue,
Portland, 503-254-7371; www.thegrotto.org

The National Sanctuary of Our Sorrowful Mother—commonly called The Grotto—is a 62-acre Catholic shrine and botanical garden. Created in 1924, The Grotto cuts into the side of a 110-foot cliff and is surrounded by beautiful plants and flowers.

An elevator takes visitors to the Natural Gallery in the woods, where you'll find more than 100 statues. The landscaped upper level has a meditation chapel overlooking the Columbia River with Mount St. Helens visible in the distance. Daily.

GUY W. TALBOT STATE PARK
Columbia River Highway, Troutdale, 800-551-6949; www.oregonstateparks.org
These 371-lush acres served as the estate of Guy Webster Talbot and his family until the property was donated to the state in 1929. The park is regarded as a wonderful picnicking destination, as it is rarely crowded and features beautiful surroundings, including 250-foot-high Latourell Falls, the second-highest falls along the Columbia River Gorge.

HOWELL TERRITORIAL PARK AND THE BYBEE HOUSE
13901 N.W. Howell Park Road, Portland, 503-797-1700; www.metro-region.org
The Howell Territorial Park, occupying 93 pastoral acres on Sauvie Island, is home to the Bybee House, an impressive example of Greek Revival architecture. Originally a private home, the Bybee House was purchased in 1961 by Multnomah County and soon after restored to appear as it would have at the time of its construction in 1858. Daily.

HOYT ARBORETUM
4000 S.W. Fairview Blvd., Portland, 503-865-8733; www.hoytarboretum.org
Within its 175 acres, the Hoyt Arboretum boasts more than 900 species of trees and shrubs, including one of the largest collections of conifers in the United States. The arboretum sits upon a ridge overlooking the Oregon Zoo. Daily. Guided tours: April-October, 2 p.m. Saturday-Sunday.

★
★
★
★
★

JAPANESE GARDEN
611 S.W. Kingston Ave., Portland, 503-223-1321
This five-acre enclave of tranquility is considered one of the most authentic Japanese gardens outside of Japan. Masterfully designed by Professor Takuma Tono, the garden opened in 1967 as a place for reflection and serenity within an environment of natural beauty. The Japanese Garden possesses five formal garden styles: Natural Garden, Sand and Stone Garden, Tea Garden, Strolling Pond Garden and Flat Garden. The Japanese Garden Gift Store offers an eclectic array of arts and crafts merchandise, most from Japan.

LEWIS AND CLARK COLLEGE
615 S.W. Palatine Hill Road, Portland, 503-768-7000; www.lclark.edu
The campus at Lewis and Clark College is highlighted by the floral display at the Memorial Rose Garden. Two campus buildings, the Manor House and Gatehouse, are listed in the National Register of Historic Places.

LEWIS AND CLARK STATE RECREATION SITE
16 miles east on I-84, 800-551-6949; www.oregonstateparks.org
Situated near the confluence of the Columbia and Sandy rivers, this park offers picnic tables, a beach and a boat ramp. Anglers and swimmers are a common sight in the cool waters of the Sandy River. Hiking also is popular here, particularly along a trail

that leads to Broughton's Bluff. The park's namesakes camped and explored the area in November 1805.

LLOYD CENTER

2201 Lloyd Center, Portland, 503-282-2511; www.lloydcentermall.com

Billing itself as the biggest mall in Oregon, the tri-level Lloyd Center features anchor stores such as Nordstrom and Meier & Frank, discount stores like Marshall's, numerous eateries and an 18-screen movie theater.

MOUNT TABOR PARK

S.E. 60th Avenue and Salmon Street, Portland, 503-823-2223;
www.portlandonline.com

This 195-acre park has something for everyone with a basketball court, volleyball court, horseshoe pit, playground, picnic shelter and tennis courts, as well as an off-leash area for dogs. The park contains an extinct volcano, making Portland one of only two U.S. cities to have an extinct volcano within its city limits. Daily 5 a.m.-midnight.

MULTNOMAH FALLS

I-84 to Multnomah Falls turnoff, Bridal Veil,
503-695-2372; www.fs.fed.us

Multnomah Falls is chief among the 11 waterfalls along 11 miles of this highway. It is the fourth highest in the United States.

★
★
★
★
★

OAKS AMUSEMENT PARK

7805 S.E. Oaks Park Way, Portland, 503-233-5777; www.oakspark.com

Opened in 1905, Oaks Park is one of the oldest continuously operating amusement parks in the United States. It features thrill rides, a children's area and roller rink. Spring and fall, weekends; summer daily.

OREGON CONVENTION CENTER

777 N.E. Martin Luther King, Jr. Blvd., Portland,
503-235-7575, 800-791-2250; www.oregoncc.org

Located within Portland's city center, the Oregon Convention Center hosts conferences, exhibitions and parties year round within its 255,000-square-foot facility. OCC provides Wi-Fi access throughout the property, a big plus for visitors seeking a high-speed connection to the Internet. The MAX light rail stops at OCC's front door.

OREGON HISTORICAL SOCIETY

1200 S.W. Park Ave., Portland, 503-222-1741; www.ohs.org

The Oregon Historical Society features a broad range of exhibits and collections within its museum and research library. The history of Oregon and the Pacific Northwest is documented through photographs, audio recordings, artifacts and books. The library houses a book collection exceeding 35,000 titles. Tuesday-Sunday; closed holidays.

OREGON MUSEUM OF SCIENCE AND INDUSTRY

1945 S.E. Water Ave., Portland, 503-797-6674, 800-955-6674; www.omsi.edu

The museum has six exhibit halls and labs featuring fun exhibits on astronomy, electronics, Earth science, biology and dinosaurs. The museum is also home to a planetarium and OMNIMAX Theater, as well as the U.S.S. *Blueback*, the Navy's last non-nuclear, fast-attack submarine. Labor Day-Memorial Day, Tuesday-Sunday; October-May, daily.

OREGON ZOO

4001 S.W. Canyon Road, Portland, 503-226-1561; www.oregonzoo.org

Specializing in breeding and protecting rare and endangered species, the Oregon Zoo has about 1,029 living specimens, 54 of which are considered either endangered or threatened. Opened as the Washington Park Zoo in 1887, the Oregon Zoo houses large and small creatures, ranging from elephants and giraffes to millipedes and scorpions. The botanical gardens have more than 1,000 species of exotic plants. The zoo is a five-minute ride from downtown Portland on the MAX light rail. A separate zoo railway links to the popular Washington Park. Daily.

PENINSULA PARK AND COMMUNITY CENTER

700 N. Rosa Parks Way, Portland, 503-823-7529; www.portlandonline.com

Home to Portland's first public rose garden and community center, Peninsula Park has extensive facilities, including softball, football and soccer fields; a basketball court; an outdoor swimming pool; tennis courts; a horseshoe pit; a playground and a picnic shelter. An amazing 8,900 plantings grow in the two-acre rose garden. Community center: Monday-Friday, closed most holidays.

PITTOCK MANSION

3229 N.W. Pittock Drive, Portland, 503-823-3623; www.pittockmansion.com

This restored and furnished French châteauesque mansion, dating to 1914, is surrounded by 46 forested and landscaped acres. Spectacular views of rivers, the city and snowcapped mountains, including Mount St. Helens and Mount Hood, are an added bonus. Summer, daily 11 a.m.-4 p.m.; fall-spring, noon-4 p.m.; closed holidays.

PORTLAND ART MUSEUM

1219 S.W. Park Ave., Portland, 503-226-2811; www.pam.org

Founded in 1892, the Portland Art Museum holds a collection of more than 32,000 works of art, including European paintings and sculptures from the Renaissance to the present, 19th- and 20th-century American works, a noted collection of Northwest Coast Native American art, Asian, pre-Columbian, West African, classical Greek and Roman art, British silver and creative photography. The museum hosts lectures, films, concerts and other art-related special events. Tuesday-Sunday; closed holidays.

PORTLAND CHILDREN'S MUSEUM

4015 S.W. Canyon Road, Portland, 503-223-6500; www.portlandcm2.org

This museum offers plenty of hands-on play spaces, including the Clay Studio and Grasshopper Grocery, a children-sized grocery store with miniature carts and aisles

169

OREGON

★
★
★
☆
☆

of fake food. Sunday 11 a.m.-5 p.m., Monday-Thursday and Saturday 9 a.m.-5 p.m.; Friday 9 a.m.-8 p.m.

PORTLAND SATURDAY MARKET

108 W. Burnside, Portland, 503-222-6072; www.portlandsaturdaymarket.com

This is one of largest, oldest open-air community markets in the United States. It features 350 vendor booths with arts and crafts made by Pacific Northwest artisans and a wide variety of foods. Street entertainers, face painters and the like enliven the atmosphere. March-December 24: Saturday 10 a.m.-5 p.m., Sunday 11 a.m.-4:30 p.m.

PORTLAND STATE UNIVERSITY

Student Union, 1825 S.W. Broadway St., Portland, 503-725-3000; www.pdx.edu

Located in the woodsy South Park Blocks area, the university enrolls more than 21,000 students in its undergraduate and graduate programs. Art exhibits are often featured in the Smith Memorial Center and Neuberger Hall.

POWELL'S CITY OF BOOKS

1005 W. Burnside, Portland, 503-228-4651, 800-291-9676; www.powells.com

A must-stop for bibliophiles, Powell's City of Books stocks more than one million new and used titles within a sprawling 68,000-square-foot facility that occupies an entire city block in downtown Portland. First-time visitors should pick up a complimentary store map to help them navigate through nine color-coded rooms, perusing an inventory that's divided into 122 major subject areas and approximately 3,500 subsections. If you're a collector looking for, say, a signed first edition of *The Hobbit*, be sure to check out the Rare Book Room, which houses autographed first editions and other collectible volumes. Daily 9 a.m.-11 p.m.

ROOSTER ROCK STATE PARK

East on I-84, 503-695-2261, 800-551-6949; www.oregonstateparks.org

A short drive east of Portland, Rooster Rock offers three miles of sandy beaches along the Columbia River. The park is a popular destination for windsurfing, boating, fishing, swimming, hiking and picnicking. One of Oregon's two designated nude beaches is located at the park's eastern edge. The nude beach is secluded and cannot be seen from the clothing-required area.

STERNWHEELER "COLUMBIA GORGE"

110 S.E. Caruthers St., Portland, cruises leave from Marine Park in Cascade Locks, east on I-84, 503-224-3900, 800-224-3901; www.portlandspirit.com

Climb aboard the Columbia Gorge, an authentic triple-deck paddle wheeler, and enjoy spectacular views as you journey along the Columbia River. A variety of excursions are offered, including champagne brunch cruises and dinner cruises.

WASHINGTON PARK

400 S.W. Kingston, Portland, 503-823-7529; www.portlandonline.com

Washington Park encompasses 129 scenic acres on a hill overlooking the city. On a clear day, the views are simply spectacular, with Mount Hood towering majestically in the east and Mount St. Helens visible on the northern horizon. The Shakespeare Garden, Lewis and Clark Memorial Holocaust Memorial and Sacajawea Statue can be found in the park, as well as the International Rose Test Garden and Japanese Garden.

★
★
★
★
★

Washington Park facilities include softball and soccer fields, lighted tennis courts, covered picnic areas, a playground and hiking trails. 5 a.m.-10 p.m.

WATER TOWER AT JOHNS LANDING
5331 S.W. Macadam Ave., Portland, 503-275-8355
Once a three-story furniture factory with a water tower used for fighting fires, this structure now houses specialty shops and restaurants. A cobblestone courtyard and rustic beamed ceilings make for a unique shopping experience. Daily; closed holidays.

WILLAMETTE STONE STATE HERITAGE SITE
Skyline Boulevard and West Burnside, Portland, 800-551-6949;
www.oregonstateparks.org
Willamette Stone serves as the zero point for the Willamette Meridian region, encompassing all of the land west of the Cascade Mountains in Oregon and Washington. A 500-foot trail cuts through dense forest as it leads to the actual marker and a plaque describing its relevance.

WORLD FORESTRY CENTER
4033 S.W. Canyon Road, Portland, 503-228-1367; www.worldforestry.org
The World Forestry Center is highlighted by the Forest Discovery Center, a museum celebrating the importance and diversity of tree life. Opened in 1971, the museum features educational programs, gallery shows and exhibits. The museum's most popular exhibit is a 70-foot-high talking tree, a replica Douglas fir that teaches tree biology in five different languages: English, French, Japanese, Spanish and German. Daily 10 a.m.-5 p.m.; closed Thanksgiving, Christmas Eve, Christmas Day.

171

SPECIAL EVENTS
CHAMBER MUSIC NORTHWEST
522 S.W. Fifth Ave., Portland, 503-294-6400; www.cmnw.org
The nationally acclaimed chamber music festival offers 25 concerts featuring 40-50 artists each summer. A catered picnic precedes each concert. Children below seven are only permitted at Family Concert. Mid-June-late July.

PORTLAND MARATHON
Portland, 503-226-1111; www.portlandmarathon.org
The world-class running event features international competition. Early October.

PORTLAND ROSE FESTIVAL
5603 S.W. Hood Ave., Portland, 503-227-2681; www.rosefestival.org
Held for more than 90 years, this festival includes the Grand Floral Parade and two other parades, a band competition, rose show, championship auto racing, hot air balloons, air show, carnival and Navy ships. Late May-June.

ST. PATRICK'S IRISH FESTIVAL
112 S.W. Second Ave., Portland, 503-227-4057; www.kellsirish.com/portland
Portland hosts one of the largest Irish festivals in the Pacific Northwest. Three days in March.

OREGON

HOTELS

★★★AVALON HOTEL & SPA

0455 S.W. Hamilton Court, Portland, 503-802-5800; www.avalonhotelandspa.com

Carefree yet sophisticated, Portland's Avalon Hotel & Spa is a unique destination. On the edge of downtown, this boutique hotel offers rooms with marble baths, CD players and private balconies; suites add fireplaces and double vanities. The Avalon Spa captures the essence of the region while paying tribute to Asian and European traditions. The excellent Avalon Fitness Club offers classes like Pilates and kickboxing. 99 rooms. Wireless Internet access. Restaurant, bar. Fitness center. Spa. Whirlpool. $$

★COMFORT SUITES

1477 N.E. 183rd St., Portland, 503-661-2200, 877-424-6423; www.comfortsuites.com

82 rooms, all suites. Complimentary continental breakfast. High-speed Internet access. $

★★★CROWNE PLAZA

14811 Kruse Oaks Blvd., Lake Oswego, 503-624-8400, 877-227-6963; www.crowneplaza.com

Located just minutes from the downtown area, this hotel is convenient to the convention center and many area universities. 161 rooms. Pets accepted; fee. High-speed Internet access. Restaurant, bar. Indoor pool, outdoor pool, whirlpool. $$

★DAYS INN PORTLAND SOUTH

9717 S.E. Sunnyside Road, Clackamas, 503-654-1699, 800-329-7466; www.daysinn.com

110 rooms. Complimentary continental breakfast Restaurant, bar. Outdoor pool, whirlpool. Fitness center. $

★DOUBLETREE HOTEL PORTLAND-LLOYD CENTER

1000 N.E. Multnomah St., Portland, 503-281-6111, 800-222-8733; www.doubletree.com

476 rooms. High-speed Internet access. Outdoor pool. Fitness center. Restaurant, bar. $$

★★★EMBASSY SUITES PORTLAND DOWNTOWN

319 S.W. Pine St., Portland, 503-279-9000, 800-362-2779; www.embassyportland.com

The downtown Portland location is a historic hotel, opened originally in 1912. The restored lobby remains true to its origins, adorned with gold-leafed columns, marble stairways and crystal chandeliers. Guests dine at Portland Steak and Chophouse, which offers more than 100 scotches and whiskies. 276 rooms. Complimentary full breakfast. Wireless Internet access. Restaurant, bar. Indoor pool, whirlpool. Fitness center. $$

★★★GOVERNOR HOTEL

614 S.W. 11th Ave., Portland, 503-224-3400, 800-554-3456; www.govhotel.com

The historic building sports a unique Lewis and Clark theme. The lobby features a totem pole, wood-burning fireplace, panoramic murals retracing Lewis and Clark's expedition and turn-of-the-century frescoes. Some guest rooms have fireplaces, wet bars and balconies. 100 rooms. Wireless Internet access. Restaurant, bar. Fitness center. Indoor pool, whirlpool. $$

★★★THE HEATHMAN HOTEL
1001 S.W. Broadway, Portland, 503-241-4100, 800-551-0011;
www.heathmanhotel.com
Dating to 1927, this hotel features a mix of artwork from Art Deco mirrors to 18th-century French canvases and Andy Warhol silk screens. The guest rooms also have varied pieces of art. Distinguishing touches include a 400-film library, afternoon tea and nightly jazz in the Tea Court. 150 rooms. Pets accepted, some restrictions; fee. High-speed Internet access. Restaurant, bar. $$

★★★HILTON PORTLAND & EXECUTIVE TOWER
921 S.W. Sixth Ave., Portland, 503-226-1611, 800-445-8667; www.portland.hilton.com
Located in Portland's entertainment and cultural district, this hotel features fine dining and an athletic club. It is near the Performing Arts Center, shopping and more than 60 restaurants. 782 rooms. Pets accepted, some restrictions; fee. High-speed Internet access. Restaurants, bar. Indoor pool, whirlpool. Fitness center. $$

★★HOLIDAY INN-DOWNTOWN CONVENTION CENTER
1441 N.E. Second Ave., Portland, 503-233-2401, 888-465-4329; www.holiday-inn.com
239 rooms. Wireless Internet access. Restaurant, bar. Indoor pool, whirlpool. Airport transportation available. Fitness center. $

★HOLIDAY INN EXPRESS TROUTDALE
1000 N.W. Graham Road, Troutdale, 503-492-2900, 888-465-4329;
www.holiday-inn.com
77 rooms. Pets accepted; fee. Complimentary full breakfast. Wireless Internet access. Fitness center. $

★★HOLIDAY INN GRESHAM
2752 N.E. Hogan Drive, Gresham, 503-907-1777, 888-465-4329; www.holiday-inn.com
168 rooms. Pets accepted, some restrictions. Wireless Internet access. Restaurant, bar. Children's indoor pool. Fitness center. $

★★★HOTEL DELUXE
729 S.W. 15th Ave., Portland, 503-219-2094; www.hoteldeluxeportland.com
This is a boutique hotel that pays homage to Hollywood's golden era. Located in downtown Portland, this historic building is steps away from the Pearl District, upscale shopping, fabulous restaurants and much more. The room décor is contemporary, providing warm and comfortable atmosphere; a pillow menu further enhances your comfort. Also featured is a screening room, where guest may view recent films by local filmmakers. 130 rooms. Pets accepted; fee. Wireless Internet access. Restaurant, bar. Fitness room. Business center. $$

★★★HOTEL LUCIA
400 S.W. Broadway at Stark, Portland, 503-225-1717, 877-225-1717;
www.hotellucia.com
This hotel in the downtown area offers guests a memorable stay. The décor is unique, with rich chocolate brown furniture, black-and-white photographs by David Kennerly,

and an interesting collection of artwork and sculptures. 127 rooms. Wireless Internet access. Restaurant, bar. $$

★★★HOTEL MONACO PORTLAND

506 S.W. Washington St., Portland, 503-222-0001, 888-207-2201;
www.monaco-portland.com

This centrally located, full-service historic hotel has been renovated. The accommodations are decorated in soft colors, with subtle lighting and comfortable furniture adding to the cozy feel. The elegant lobby features soaring ceilings of molded plaster and wood, floor-to-ceiling windows and a large corner fireplace surrounded by marble and topped with an antique mirror. Dine on Pacific Northwest cuisine at the Red Star Tavern & Roast House. 221 rooms. Pets accepted; fee. Wireless Internet access. Restaurant, bar. $$

★★★HOTEL VINTAGE PLAZA

422 S.W. Broadway, Portland, 503-228-1212, 800-263-2305; www.vintageplaza.com

Listed on the National Register of Historic Places, the hotel celebrates local wine-making by offering tasting of Oregon vintage wines in the evenings. Guest accommodations feature Tuscan wine country décor with Italian tapestries and bright colors. Pazzo Ristorante offers fine Italian cuisine and wines. 117 rooms. Wireless Internet access. Restaurant, bar. Pets accepted. $$

★★★MARRIOTT PORTLAND CITY CENTER

520 S.W. Broadway, Portland, 503-226-6300, 888-236-2427; www.marriott.com

249 rooms. Pets accepted; fee. High-speed Internet access. Restaurant, bar. Whirlpool. $$

★★★MARRIOTT PORTLAND DOWNTOWN WATERFRONT

1401 S.W. Naito Parkway, Portland, 503-226-7600, 888-236-2427; www.marriott.com

The Marriott Portland Downtown is conveniently located within the city's business and financial district. Guest rooms are decorated in warm tones and some overlook a city park. 503 rooms. Pets accepted, some restrictions. High-speed Internet access. Restaurant, bar. Indoor pool, whirlpool. $$

★★★PARAMOUNT HOTEL

808 S.W. Taylor St., Portland, 503-223-9900; www.portlandparamount.com

This 15-story boutique hotel is located in downtown Portland within walking distance of Pioneer Square and the Center for the Performing Arts. The hotel's marble-tiled lobby has soaring ceilings, hand-loomed Persian rugs and original artwork. Rooms feature warm tones and black-and-white photography. The hotel's Dragonfish Asian Café offers eclectic pan-Asian cuisine. 154 rooms. Pets accepted; fee. Wireless Internet access. Restaurant, bar. $

★★RED LION HOTEL ON THE RIVER - JANTZEN BEACH

909 N. Hayden Island Drive, Portland, 503-283-4466, 800-733-5466;
www.redlion.rdln.com

318 rooms. Pets accepted, some restrictions; fee. Wireless Internet access. Restaurant, bar. Outdoor pool, whirlpool. Airport transportation available. $

★★★RIVERPLACE HOTEL

1510 S.W. Harbor Way, Portland, 503-228-3233, 800-227-1333;
www.riverplacehotel.com

Situated on the Willamette River, the RiverPlace Hotel is only a few blocks from downtown. Guests can relax on patio rocking chairs while enjoying the views. Kayaks and bikes are available for rental. 84 rooms. Pets accepted; fee. Wireless Internet access. Restaurant, bar. Whirlpool. $$

★★★SHERATON PORTLAND AIRPORT HOTEL

8235 N.E. Airport Way, Portland, 503-281-2500, 800-325-3525;
www.starwoodhotels.com/sheraton

This hotel is located conveniently on the grounds of the airport and offers many services and amenities. 218 rooms. Pets accepted; fee. Wireless Internet access. Restaurant, bar. Indoor pool, whirlpool. Airport transportation available. $

SPECIALTY LODGINGS

HERON HAUS

2545 N.W. Westover Road, Portland, 503-274-1846; www.heronhaus.com

This charming restored 1904 Tudor-style house features a TV room, enclosed sunroom and library. Guests can take in the view of a small apple and pear orchard. Located in a historic area, the Heron Haus is about 10 minutes from the city center. Six rooms. Complimentary continental breakfast. High-speed Internet access. $$

MCMENAMINS EDGEFIELD MANOR

2126 S.W. Halsey St., Troutdale, 503-669-8610, 800-669-8610;
www.mcmenamins.com/edge

103 rooms. Complimentary full breakfast. Restaurant, bar. Renovated in the style of a European village complete with theater, winery, distillery and brewery. Golf, spa. $

PORTLAND'S WHITE HOUSE BED AND BREAKFAST

1914 N.E. 22nd Ave., Portland, 503-287-7131, 800-272-7131;
www.portlandswhitehouse.com

Located in a historic neighborhood within walking distance to shopping, dining, fitness facilities and local attractions, this bed and breakfast offers finely furnished rooms, each with a full bath. The colonial mansion bears a striking resemblance to the White House. Nine rooms. Complimentary full breakfast. Wireless Internet access. $$

RESTAURANTS

★★AL-AMIR LEBANESE RESTAURANT

223 S.W. Stark St., Portland, 503-274-0010; www.alamirportland.com

Lebanese menu. Lunch, dinner, late-night. Bar. Children's menu. Casual attire. Reservations recommended. $$

★ALESSANDRO'S

301 S.W. Morrison St., Portland, 503-222-3900; www.alessandros.ypguides.net

Italian menu. Lunch, dinner. Bar. Children's menu. Casual attire. Reservations recommended. Outdoor seating. $$

★
★
★
★
★

★ALEXIS

215 W. Burnside, Portland, 503-224-8577; www.alexisfoods.com

Greek menu. Lunch, dinner. Closed Sunday; holidays. Bar. Casual attire. Reservations recommended. $$

★★BUGATTI'S RISTORANTE

18740 Willamette Drive, West Linn, 503-636-9555; www.bugattisrestaurant.com

Italian menu. Dinner. Closed holidays. Children's menu. Outdoor seating. $$

★★BUSH GARDEN

900 S.W. Morrison St., Portland, 503-226-7181; www.bush-garden.com

Japanese menu. Lunch, dinner. Closed holidays. Bar. Casual attire. Reservations recommended. $$

★★★CAPRIAL'S BISTRO

7015 S.E. Milwaukie Ave., Portland, 503-236-6457; www.caprialandjohnskitchen.com

Located in the Westmoreland section of Portland, Caprial's Bistro features a seasonal Northwest menu that changes monthly. Cooking classes and wine tasting are also offered. American menu. Lunch, dinner. Closed Sunday-Monday. Bar. Casual attire. Reservations recommended. $$$

★★CHART HOUSE RESTAURANT

5700 S.W. Terwilliger Blvd., Portland, 503-246-6963; www.chart-house.com

Seafood, steak menu. Lunch, dinner. Bar. Children's menu. Casual attire. Reservations recommended. Valet parking. $$$

176

★CORBETT FISH HOUSE

5901 S.W. Corbett Ave., Portland, 503-246-4434; www.corbettfishhouse.com

Seafood menu. Lunch, dinner. Bar. Children's menu. Casual attire. Outdoor seating. $$

★DAN & LOUIS OYSTER BAR

208 S.W. Ankeny St., Portland, 503-227-5906; www.danandlouis.com

Seafood menu. Lunch, dinner. Closed holidays. Bar. Children's menu. Casual attire $$

★★★GENOA

2832 S.E. Belmont St., Portland, 503-238-1464; www.genoarestaurant.com

Genoa is a hidden gem where glorious Italian feasts are served nightly. If you require predictability and control in your life, this restaurant may not be the place for you. There is no printed menu at Genoa. Your gracious waiter will offer you a choice of three entrées but all other decisions rest with the chef. The prix fixe menu includes seven courses: antipasto, soup, pasta, fish or salad, your chosen entrée, dessert and then fruit. With this much food to consume, dinner at Genoa is a lengthy, leisurely affair. Italian menu. Dinner. Closed Monday. Bar. Casual attire. Reservations recommended. $$$

OREGON

★
★ ★
★ ★
★

★★★HEATHMAN

1001 S.W. Broadway, Portland, 503-241-4100, 800-551-0011;
www.portland.heathmanhotel.com

Executive chef Philippe Boulot offers classic French cooking in a tri-level dining room. American, French menu. Breakfast, lunch, dinner, late-night. Bar. Children's menu. Casual attire. Reservations recommended. Valet parking. Outdoor seating. $$$

★★★HIGGINS RESTAURANT AND BAR

1239 S.W. Broadway, Portland, 503-222-9070; www.higgins.ypguides.net

Designed like a French bistro, the restaurant uses local, organic ingredients. American menu. Lunch, dinner, late-night. Closed holidays. Bar. Children's menu. Casual attire. Reservations recommended. $$$

★★HUBER'S CAFÉ

411 S.W. Third Ave., Portland, 503-228-5686; www.hubers.com

American, seafood menu. Breakfast, lunch, dinner, late-night. Bar. Children's menu. Casual attire. Reservations recommended. Outdoor seating. $$

★★JAKE'S FAMOUS CRAWFISH

401 S.W. 12th Ave., Portland, 503-226-1419, 888-344-6861;
www.jakesfamouscrawfish.com

Seafood menu. Breakfast, lunch, dinner, late-night. Bar. Children's menu. Casual attire. Valet parking. Outdoor seating. $$

★★★JAKE'S GRILL

611 S.W. 10th Ave., Portland, 503-220-1850, 888-344-6861;
www.mccormickandschmicks.com

A favorite in downtown Portland, the restaurant is decorated with dark woods and exudes an old-fashioned steakhouse atmosphere. American menu. Breakfast, lunch, dinner, late-night, brunch. Bar. Children's menu. Casual attire. Reservations recommended. Valet parking. Outdoor seating. $$$

★★MARRAKESH AUTHENTIC MOROCCAN RESTAURANT

1201 N.W. 21st Ave., Portland, 503-248-9442; www.marrakesh.us

Moroccan menu. Dinner. Children's menu. Casual attire. $$

★★NOHO'S HAWAIIAN CAFÉ

2525 S.E. Clinton St., Portland, 503-233-5301; www.nohos.com

Hawaiian menu. Lunch, dinner. Casual attire. Outdoor seating. $$

★★★PALEY'S PLACE

1204 N.W. 21st Ave., Portland, 503-243-2403; www.paleysplace.net

The bistro fare at Paley's Place uses fresh, local ingredients and features imaginative and beautifully presented entrées. Homemade chocolates arrive with the bill, in keeping with the warm service. French bistro menu. Dinner. Bar. Casual attire. Reservations recommended. Outdoor seating. $$$

OREGON

★
★
★
★
★

★★★PAZZO RISTORANTE

627 S.W. Washington, Portland, 503-228-1515; www.pazzo.com

This authentic northern Italian restaurant is a favorite among the locals, thanks to its cozy, friendly atmosphere. Guests can sample handmade pastas and hearty dishes such as leg of lamb with goat cheese. Italian menu. Breakfast, lunch, dinner, brunch. Bar. Children's menu. Casual attire. Reservations recommended. Valet parking. Outdoor seating. $$

★★PERRY'S ON FREMONT

2401 N.E. Fremont St., Portland, 503-287-3655; www.perrysonfremont.com

American menu. Dinner. Closed Sunday. Bar. Children's menu. Casual attire. Valet parking. Outdoor seating $$

★★★PLAINFIELDS' MAYUR

852 S.W. 21st Ave., Portland, 503-223-2995; www.plainfields.com

Plainfields' Mayur is located downtown in a historic Victorian house near the Civic Stadium. The restaurant serves East Indian cuisine, including vegan and vegetarian entrées. An extensive wine list is also offered. Indian menu. Dinner. Casual attire. Reservations recommended. Outdoor seating. $$

★POOR RICHARD'S

39th N.E. Broadway, Portland, 503-288-5285; www.poorrichardstwofer.com

Steak menu. Lunch, dinner. Bar. Children's menu. Casual attire. Reservations recommended. Outdoor seating. $$

★★★RINGSIDE DOWNTOWN

2165 W. Burnside St., Portland, 503-223-1513; www.ringsidesteakhouse.com

Established in the 1940s, RingSide is a classic steakhouse located on top of Nob Hill, just a few minutes from the city center. Pictures of famous patrons and various awards decorate the walls. Seafood, steak menu. Dinner, late-night. Bar. Casual attire. Reservations recommended. Valet parking. $$$

★★RINGSIDE EAST AT GLENDOVEER

14021 N.E. Glisan, Portland, 503-255-0750; www.ringsidesteakhouse.com

Seafood, steak menu. Lunch, dinner. Bar. Casual attire. Reservations recommended. $$

★★SALTY'S ON THE COLUMBIA RIVER

3839 N.E. Marine Drive, Portland, 503-288-4444; www.saltys.com

Seafood menu. Lunch, dinner, Sunday brunch. Bar. Children's menu. Casual attire. Reservations recommended. Outdoor seating. $$$

★★SAUCEBOX

214 S.W. Broadway, Portland, 503-241-3393; www.saucebox.com

Pan-Asian menu. Dinner. Closed Sunday, Monday. Bar. Casual attire. Reservations recommended. Outdoor seating. $$

★SAYLER'S OLD COUNTRY KITCHEN

10519 S.E. Stark St., Portland, 503-252-4171; www.saylers.com

American, steak menu. Dinner, Sunday brunch. Closed holidays. Bar. Children's menu. Casual attire. **$$**

★★TYPHOON! ON BROADWAY

410 S.W. Broadway, Portland, 503-224-8285; www.typhoonrestaurants.com

Thai menu. Lunch, dinner. Casual attire. Reservations recommended. Outdoor seating. **$$**

★★TYPHOON! ON EVERETT STREET

2310 N.W. Everett St., Portland, 503-243-7557; www.typhoonrestaurants.com

Thai menu. Lunch, dinner. Closed holidays. Outdoor seating. **$$**

★★WIDMER GASTHAUS PUB

929 N. Russell St., Portland, 503-281-3333; www.widmer.com

German menu. Lunch, dinner. Bar. Outdoor seating. **$$**

★★★WILDWOOD RESTAURANT AND BAR

1221 N.W. 21st Ave., Portland, 503-248-9663; www.wildwoodrestaurant.com

This acclaimed Oregon restaurant serves fresh seafood and seasonal Northwest ingredients in elegant combinations. A wood-burning oven turns out crisp pizzas and adds warmth to the dining room. American menu. Lunch, dinner, Sunday brunch. Bar. Casual attire. Reservations recommended. Outdoor seating. **$$$**

SPA

★★★AVALON SPA

0455 S.W. Hamilton Court, Portland, 503-802-5900;
www.avalonhotelandspa.com

The Avalon Spa captures the essence of the Pacific N.W. while paying tribute to Asian and European traditions. Dedicated to well-being, the spa's carefully selected treatment menu utilizes natural ingredients and innovative therapies to relax you. Warm and attentive, the exceptional staff enhances the experience. Expectant mothers in their second or third trimesters enjoy customized massages designed for them. The spa also offers salon services, including hair care, manicures, pedicures, waxing and makeup instruction and applications.

PRINEVILLE

Two-thirds of the population of Crook County lives in or near Prineville. Livestock, alfalfa, wheat, mint, sugar beets and lumbering are important in this county. Hunting, fishing and rock hounding are popular activities. The City of Prineville's railroad, 19 miles of main line connecting the Union Pacific and Oregon Trunk Railway, is one of the few municipally owned railroads in the country. Two Ranger District offices and headquarters of the Ochoco National Forest are located in Prineville.

Information: Prineville-Crook County Chamber of Commerce, 390 N.E. Fairview,
Prineville, 541-447-6304; www.prineville-crookcounty.org

OREGON

★
★
★
★
★

WHAT TO SEE AND DO
OCHOCO LAKE CAMPGROUND
Seven miles east on Highway 26, 541-447-1209; www.ccprd.org
A 10-acre, juniper-covered promontory on the north shore of Ochoco Reservoir, the campground features fishing, boating, hiking and picnicking.

REDMOND
Popular with sports enthusiasts and tourists, Redmond is also the agricultural, lumbering and industrial heart of central Oregon. A Ranger District office of the Deschutes National Forest is located here. The U.S. Forest Service Redmond Regional Air Center is located at Roberts Field.
Information: Chamber of Commerce, 446 S.W. Seventh St., Redmond,
541-923-5191; www.redmondcofc.com

HOTELS
★COMFORT SUITES AIRPORT
2243 S.W. Yew Ave., Redmond, 541-504-8900, 877-424-6423; www.choicehotels.com
92 rooms. Complimentary continental breakfast. Indoor pool. High-speed Internet access. $

★★INN AT EAGLE CREST RESORT
1522 Cline Falls Road, Redmond, 541-923-2453, 800-682-4786; www.eagle-crest.com
100 rooms. Restaurant, bar. Outdoor pool, whirlpool. Airport transportation available. Golf. Tennis. Spa. Fitness center. $

REEDSPORT
Surrounded by rivers, lakes and the ocean, Reedsport has an abundance and variety of fish, particularly striped bass, steelhead and salmon. Two of the best bass fishing lakes in Oregon are nearby. Reedsport was originally marshland subject to flooding at high tides, so the earliest buildings and sidewalks were built 3 to 8 feet above ground. A dike was constructed after the destructive 1964 Christmas flood to shield the lower part of town.
Information: Reedsport/Winchester Bay Chamber of Commerce, 855 Highway Ave.,
Reedsport, 541-271-3495, 800-247-2155; www.reedsportcc.org

WHAT TO SEE AND DO
UMPQUA DISCOVERY CENTER
409 Riverfront Way, Reedsport, 541-271-4816; www.umpquadiscoverycenter.com
Interpretive displays center on the cultural and natural history of area. Summer, daily 9 a.m.-5 p.m.; winter, daily 10 a.m.-4 p.m.

UMPQUA LIGHTHOUSE STATE PARK
460 Lighthouse Road, Reedsport, 541-271-3611;
www.oregonstateparks.org
This 450-acre park touches the mouth of the Umpqua River, borders the Umpqua Lighthouse Reservation and skirts the ocean shore for more than two miles. Sand dunes rise 500 feet making them the highest in U.S. The park is noted for its marvelous,

seasonal display of rhododendrons and also features swimming, fishing, hiking and a whale-watching area.

ROCKAWAY BEACH

Once a popular resort town for Portland residents, Rockaway Beach is quieter now, though its seven-mile stretch of sandy beach still attracts a crowd on summer weekends. It's not uncommon to see a cluster of kites darting and diving in the sky as the town hosts a kite-flying festival each spring. Rockaway Beach is located on Highway 101, a short drive north of Tillamook.

Information: Rockaway Beach Chamber of Commerce, Little Red Caboose at the Wayside, Highway 101, Rockaway Beach, 503-355-8108; www.rockawaybeach.net

HOTEL

★SURFSIDE MOTEL

101 N.W. 11th Ave., Rockaway Beach, 503-355-2312, 800-243-7786; www.surfsideocean.com

79 rooms. Pets accepted, some restrictions; fee. Indoor pool. Wireless Internet access. **$**

SALEM

The state capital and third-largest city in Oregon, Salem's economy is based on state government, food processing, light manufacturing, agriculture and wood products. Salem shares Oregon's sports attractions with other cities of the Willamette Valley.

Information: Convention & Visitors Association, 1313 Mill St. S.E., 503-581-4325, 800-874-7012; www.travelsalem.com

WHAT TO SEE AND DO

BUSH BARN ART CENTER

600 Mission St. S.E., Salem, 503-581-2228; www.salemart.org

This remodeled barn houses two exhibit galleries, with monthly shows and a sales gallery featuring Northwest artists. Tuesday-Friday 10 a.m.-5 p.m., Saturday and Sunday noon-5 p.m.; closed Monday.

★
★
★
★
★

CLINE FALLS STATE SCENIC VIEWPOINT

725 Summer St. N.E., Salem, 800-551-6949; www.oregonstateparks.org

A 9-acre park on the banks of the Deschutes River, it offers fishing and picnicking.

HISTORIC DEEPWOOD ESTATE

1116 Mission St. S.E., Salem, 503-363-1825; www.historicdeepwoodestate.org

A Queen Anne-style house and carriage house designed by W. C. Knighton, the Deepwood Estate features Povey Brothers stained-glass windows, golden oak woodwork, a solarium, Lord and Schryver gardens with a wrought-iron gazebo from 1905, boxwood gardens, a perennial garden with English teahouse and a nature trail. May-September, Monday-Friday, Sunday; October-April, Tuesday-Saturday; closed holidays.

HONEYWOOD WINERY

1350 Hines St. S.E., Salem, 503-362-4111, 800-726-4101;
www.honeywoodwinery.com

Oregon's oldest producing winery offers tours, a tasting room and a gift shop. Monday-Friday 9 a.m.-5 p.m., Saturday 10 a.m.-5 p.m., Sunday 1-5 p.m.

MISSION MILL MUSEUM

1313 Mill St. S.E., Salem, 503-585-7012; www.missionmill.org

Thomas Kay Woolen Mill Museum shows the details of processing fleece into fabric. The Jason Lee House, John D. Boon House, Methodist Parsonage and Pleasant Grove-Presbyterian Church help interpret missionary family life. Monday-Saturday 10 a.m.-5 p.m.; closed Sunday and some holidays.

STATE CAPITOL

900 Court St. N.E., Salem, 503-986-1388; www.leg.state.or.us/capinfo/

Built with marble for a modern Greek design, the Capitol is topped with a fluted tower and a bronze, gold-leafed statue symbolic of the pioneers who carved Oregon out of the wilderness. Tours: June-August, daily; September-May, by appointment.

CAPITOL MALL

900 State St., Salem, 503-986-1388; www.leg.state.or.us/capinfo/

Flanked by four state buildings in Modern Greek style, Capitol Mall includes the Public Service, Transportation, Labor and Industries and State Library buildings. The grounds are an arboretum with an historical statuary and monuments.

HOTELS

★BEST WESTERN BLACK BEAR INN

1600 Motor Court N.E., Salem, 503-581-1559, 800-780-7234;
www.bestwestern.com

101 rooms. Pets accepted, some restrictions; fee. Indoor pool, whirlpool Tennis. Complimentary continental breakfast. Fitness center. High-speed Internet access. $

★★RED LION

3301 Market St. N.E., Salem, 503-370-7888, 800-733-5466; www.redlion.com

150 rooms. Pets accepted, fee. Restaurant, bar. Indoor pool, whirlpool. High-speed Internet access. $

SPECIALTY LODGING

A CREEKSIDE GARDEN INN

33 Wyatt Court N.E., Salem, 503-391-0837; www.salembandb.com

Five rooms. Children over 14 years only. Airport transportation available. Bar. $

RESTAURANTS

★★★ALESSANDRO'S RISTORANTE & GALLERIA

120 N.E. Commercial St., Salem, 503-370-9951, 866-225-7985; www.alessandros.net

This family-owned northern Italian restaurant and bar has been in business for more than 22 years, serving specialties such as baked salmon, various veal dishes and tiramisu. Italian menu. Lunch, dinner. Closed Sunday. Bar. Children's menu. Casual attire. $$

★★KWAN'S ORIGINAL CUISINE
835 Commercial St. S.E., Salem, 503-362-7711; www.kwanscuisine.com
Chinese menu. lunch, dinner. closed holidays. bar. children's menu. $$

SEASIDE
Seaside is the largest and oldest seashore town in Oregon. It has a concrete promenade two miles long, and its beaches provide clam digging, surfing, surf fishing and beachcombing.
Information: Chamber of Commerce, 7 N. Roosevelt, Seaside, 503-738-6391;
www.seasidechamber.com

HOTELS
★★BEST WESTERN OCEAN VIEW RESORT
414 N. Promenade, Seaside, 503-738-3334, 800-234-8439;
www.oceanviewresort.com,
107 rooms. Pets accepted, some restrictions, fee. Restaurant, bar. Indoor pool, whirlpool. High-speed Internet access. $

★★GEARHART BY THE SEA RESORT
1157 N. Marion Ave., Gearhart, 503-738-8331, 800-547-0115; www.gearhartresort.com
80 rooms. Pets accepted, some restrictions; fee. Restaurant, bar. Indoor pool. Golf. $

★★SHILO INN SEASIDE OCEANFRONT
30 N. Promenade, Seaside, 503-738-9571, 800-222-2244; www.shiloinns.com
112 rooms. Restaurant, bar. Indoor pool, whirlpool. Airport transportation available. High-speed Internet access. Fitness center. $

SPECIALTY LODGINGS
CUSTER HOUSE BED & BREAKFAST
811 First Ave., Seaside, 503-738-7825, 800-467-0201; www.custerhouse.com
Three rooms. Complimentary full breakfast. $

GILBERT INN BED & BREAKFAST
341 Beach Drive, Seaside, 503-738-9770, 800-410-9770; www.gilbertinn.com
This Queen Anne Victorian home, built in 1892, features a large fireplace in the parlor and a warm atmosphere. It is located near shops, restaurants, beaches and other attractions of the Northwest coast. 10 rooms. Closed January. Complimentary full breakfast. Airport transportation available. $

RESTAURANTS
★CAMP 18
42362 Highway 26, Seaside, 503-755-1818
American menu. Breakfast, lunch, dinner, Sunday brunch. Bar. Children's menu. $$

OREGON

★
★
★
★
★

★★DOOGER'S SEAFOOD & GRILL
505 Broadway St., Seaside, 503-738-3773
Seafood, steak menu. lunch, dinner. children's menu. **$$**

SWEET HOME

The gateway to Santiam Pass and the Cascades, the area around Sweet Home is popular for fishing, boating, skiing and hiking. A Ranger District office of Willamette National Forest is located in Sweet Home.

Information: Chamber of Commerce, 1575 Main St., Sweet Home,
541-367-6186; www.sweethomechamber.org

THE DALLES

At one time, The Dalles was the end of the wagon haul on the Oregon Trail. Pioneers loaded their goods on boats and made the rest of their westward journey on the Columbia River. The falls and rapids that once made the river above The Dalles unnavigable are now submerged under water backed up by the Columbia River dams. The Dalles Dam is part of a system of dams extending barge traffic inland as far as Lewiston in Idaho and Pasco in Washington. The chief source of income in the area is agriculture. The Dalles is noted for the cherry orchards and wheat fields located in the many canyons along the river.

Information: Chamber of Commerce, 404 W. Second St., The Dalles,
541-296-2231, 800-255-3385; www.thedalleschamber.com

WHAT TO SEE AND DO
COLUMBIA GORGE DISCOVERY CENTER
5000 Discovery Drive, The Dalles, three miles northwest at Crate's Point,
541-296-8600; www.gorgediscovery.org
Hands-on and electronic exhibits detail the volcanic upheavals and raging floods that created the Gorge, describe the history and importance of the river and look to the Gorge's future. Daily 9 a.m.-5 p.m.

MAYER STATE PARK
10 miles west off I-84, exit 77, 800-551-6949; www.oregonstateparks.org
A 613-acre park comprised of an undeveloped area with an overlook on Rowena Heights and a developed area on the shores of the Columbia River.

SOROSIS PARK
350 E. Scenic Drive; www.nwprd.org
This 15-acre park overlooks the city from the highest point on Scenic Drive, giving a view of the Columbia River, Mt. Adams and The Dalles. Bones of three types of camels, the ancient horse and mastodons were found near here.

HOTEL
★★COUSINS COUNTRY INN
2114 W. Sixth St., The Dalles, 541-298-5161, 800-848-9378;
www.cousinscountryinn.com
85 rooms. Pets accepted; fee. Restaurant. Outdoor pool, whirlpool. **$**

OREGON

RESTAURANTS
★COUSINS RESTAURANT
2114 W. Sixth St., The Dalles, 541-298-2771; www.cousins-restaurant.com
American menu. Breakfast, lunch, dinner. Bar. Children's menu. $$

★WINDSEEKER
1535 Bargeway Road, The Dalles, 541-298-7171; www.windseekerrestaurant.com
American menu. breakfast, lunch, dinner. $

TILLAMOOK
Located at the southern end of Tillamook Bay, Tillamook is the county seat. Dairy, timber and fishing are the main industries. There are many beaches for swimming, crabbing, clamming and beachcombing. Boat landings, camping, picnicking and fishing sites are also in the area.
Information: Tillamook Chamber of Commerce, 3705 Highway 101 N., Tillamook, 503-842-7525; www.tillamookchamber.org

WHAT TO SEE AND DO
CAPE LOOKOUT STATE PARK
13000 Whiskey Creek Road, 12 miles southwest off Highway 101, Tillamook, 503-842-4891, 800-551-6949; www.oregonstateparks.org
A 1,974-acre park with virgin spruce forest and an observation point, Cape Lookhout is one of most primitive ocean shore areas in the state.

HOTELS
★BEST WESTERN INN & SUITES
1722 N. Makinster Road, Tillamook, 503-842-7599, 800-780-7234; www.bestwestern.com
51 rooms. Complimentary continental breakfast. Free wireless Internet access. Business center. Fitness center. Indoor pool, whirlpool. $

★★SHILO INN SUITES
2515 N. Main St., Tillamook, 503-842-7971, 800-222-2244; www.shiloinns.com
101 rooms. Pets accepted; fee. Restaurant, bar. Fitness center. Indoor pool, whirlpool.

SPECIALTY LODGING
SANDLAKE COUNTRY INN
8505 Galloway Road, Cloverdale, 503-965-6745, 877-726-3525; www.sandlakecountryinn.com
Four rooms. Complimentary full breakfast. $

YACHATS
Yachats (YA-hots) is a resort area on the central Oregon coast west of Siuslaw National Forest. Derived from a Native American phrase meaning "waters at the foot of the mountain," Yachats is along a rocky shore with a fine sandy beach.
Information: Yachats Area Chamber of Commerce, 241 Highway 101, Yachats, 541-547-3530, 800-929-0477; www.yachats.org

WHAT TO SEE AND DO
NEPTUNE STATE SCENIC VIEWPOINT
Three miles south on Highway 101, 800-551-6949; www.oregonstateparks.org

This 302-acre park features Cook's Chasm (near the north end), a long, narrow, deep fissure where the sea falls in with a spectacular fury; wind-depressed forest trees (near the north end); and slopes covered with huckleberry shrubs. A community of harbor seals makes its home on the rocks below Strawberry Hill; whales are also spotted here.

HOTEL
★OVERLEAF LODGE
280 Overleaf Lodge Lane, Yachats, 541-547-4880, 800-338-0507; www.overleaflodge.com

39 rooms. Complimentary continental breakfast. Fitness center. Spa. **$$**

SPECIALTY LODGING
SEA QUEST BED & BREAKFAST
95354 Highway 101 S. Yachats, 541-547-3782, 800-341-4878; www.seaquestinn.com

Five rooms. Children over 14 years only. Complimentary full breakfast. **$$**

WASHINGTON

IN ADDITION TO DRAMATIC MOUNTAIN RANGES, EXPANSIVE FORESTS AND INVITING HARBORS, Washington State is a cornerstone of American hydroelectric technology. Here are the majestic spectacles of mighty Mount Rainier—revered as a god by the Native Americans—and the Olympic Peninsula, where one of the wettest and one of the driest parts of the country are separated by a single mountain; also here is Puget Sound, a giant inland sea where 2,000 miles of shoreline bend into jewel-like bays.

Although British and Spanish navigators were the first Europeans to explore Washington's serrated shoreline, the first major discoveries were made in 1792, when an American, Captain Robert Gray, gave his name to Gray's Harbor and the name of his ship, Columbia, to the great river. An Englishman, Captain George Vancouver, explored and named Puget Sound and christened Mount Baker and Mount Rainier, which he could see far inland. Fort Vancouver was the keystone of the British fur industry, dominating a Northwest empire. After conflicting U.S. and British claims were resolved, Americans surged into this area by ship and wagon train.

Civilization has not dissipated Washington's natural wealth. The state retains 24 million acres of superb forests, and miracles of modern engineering have almost completely erased the wastelands through which the wagon trains of the pioneers passed on their way to the sea.

The mighty Columbia River meanders through the heart of northeast and central Washington, then runs for 300 miles along the Oregon-Washington border. Through a series of dams and the Grand Coulee Reclamation Project, the energies of the Columbia have been harnessed and converted into what is presently one of the world's great sources of water power. Irrigation and a vast supply of inexpensive power gave a tremendous push to Washington's economy, sparking new industries and making possible the state's production of huge crops of grains, vegetables and fruit.

Central Washington is the nation's apple barrel; dairying is a big industry in the western valleys. Forestry and wood products, as well as the production of paper and allied products, are of major importance in the western and northern sections of the state; one-third of the state is covered by commercial forests. In recent years, Washington wines have enjoyed great popularity around the nation.

Since 1965, more than 25 percent of Washington's total manufacturing effort has been devoted to the production of transportation equipment, of which a large portion is involved in commercial jet aircraft. Along Puget Sound, industry means canning plants, lumber mills and pulp and paper plants, but even here there is a new economic dimension: petroleum refineries of four major companies have a daily capacity of 366,500 barrels of crude oil and gasoline; biotechnology and software development are growing industries. Tourism is the state's fourth-largest industry, amounting to more than $8.8 billion a year.

Information: www.tourism.wa.gov

★
★★
★★
★
★

FUN FACTS

Washington has more glaciers than the other 47 contiguous states combined.

More than half of all apples grown in the United States for fresh eating come from orchards in Washington.

ABERDEEN

Aberdeen and Hoquiam are twin cities on the eastern tip of Grays Harbor. Born as a cannery named for the city in Scotland, Aberdeen later blossomed as a lumber town, with one of the greatest stands of Douglas fir ever found in the Pacific Northwest at its back. Many Harbor residents are descendants of Midwestern Scandinavians who came here to fell the forests. Today, the town's commerce consists of wood processing, fishing and shipbuilding. The Port of Grays Harbor is located along the waterfront of the two towns.

Information: Grays Harbor Chamber of Commerce, 506 Duffy St.,
360-532-1924, 800-321-1924; www.graysharbor.org

WHAT TO SEE AND DO
LAKE SYLVIA STATE PARK
812 Lake Sylvia Road North, Montesano, 360-249-3611; www.parks.wa.gov
An old logging camp, this park contains approximately 233 acres of protected timber on the freshwater shoreline of Lake Sylvia. Activities include boating (non-motorized), swimming, fishing, hiking, mountain biking and bird-watching.

SCHAFER STATE PARK
13 miles east on Highway 12, then 10 miles north on an unnumbered road,
360-482-3852; www.parks.wa.gov
Approximately 120 acres on the Satsop River, activities at Schafer State Park include swimming, fishing for steelhead, cutthroat trout and salmon, hiking two miles of trails and bird-watching. Late April-October, daily 8 a.m.-dusk.

★
★★
★★★
★★★★

HOTEL
★RED LION HOTEL
521 W. Wishkah St., Aberdeen, 360-532-5210; www.redlion.com
67 rooms. Complimentary continental breakfast. Restaurant. High-speed Internet access. Business center. Pool, whirlpool. $

SPECIALTY LODGING
ABERDEEN MANSION BED AND BREAKFAST
807 N. M St., Aberdeen, 360-533-7079, 888-533-7079;
www.aberdeenmansionbb.com
This sunny Victorian home furnished with antiques was built in 1905 for a local lumber baron. Two libraries and a large wraparound porch encourage reading, conversation or quiet contemplation; the game room contains a pool table and board games for guest use. All five guest rooms have king-size beds and TVs, and the carriage house also has two twin beds and a small kitchen. Seven rooms. Children over 10 years only. Complimentary full breakfast. $

ANACORTES

Anacortes, at the northwest tip of Fidalgo Island, houses the San Juan Islands ferries. The town's name honors Anna Curtis, the wife of one of its founders.

Information: Visitor Information Center at the Chamber of Commerce,
819 Commercial Ave., 360-293-3832; www.anacortes.org

WHAT TO SEE AND DO
DECEPTION PASS STATE PARK
41229 Highway 20, Anacortes, 360-675-2417; www.parks.wa.gov

More than 4,100 acres of sheltered bays and deep old-growth forests with fjord-like shoreline, Deception Pass's four lakes provide ample opportunities for swimming, scuba diving, fishing, clamming and boating. More than 170 varieties of birds make this a popular bird-watching spot. You'll also find 38 miles of hiking trails, some accessible for the disabled. Summer, 6:30 a.m.-dusk; winter, 8 a.m.-dusk.

SAN JUAN ISLANDS TRIP
360-293-3832

Ferry boats leave several times daily for Lopez Island, Shaw Island, Orcas Island, Friday Harbor and Sidney, British Columbia. Leave your car at the dock in Anacortes, or take your vehicle with you and disembark at any point and explore from paved roads.

SWINOMISH NORTHERN LIGHTS CASINO
12885 Casino Drive, Anacortes, 360-293-2691; www.swinomishcasino.com

The largest Washington casino north of Seattle has tables, machines, off-track betting and a large poker room. Lower-key gamblers can hit the bingo hall or keno lounge. The Starlight Lounge features live comedy; you'll also find pro boxing, musical entertainment and a family-style restaurant with both buffets and table service. Daily.

WASHINGTON PARK
6300 Sunset Ave., 360-293-1927; www.anacortes.org

With more than 100 species of birds, this 220-acre park is popular with bird-watchers; it also draws whale-watchers in season.

SPECIAL EVENTS
SHIPWRECK DAY
819 Commercial Ave., Anacortes, 360-293-7911; www.anacortes.org

Shipwreck Day flea market is a fun annual event featuring eight city blocks in downtown Anacortes packed full of good junk, antiques, collectibles, tools and all kinds of treasures for today's bargain hunter or urban pirate. There are also food and merchant sidewalk sales to plunder. Mid-July.

WATERFRONT FESTIVAL
1019 Q Ave., Anacortes, 360-293-7911; www.anacortes.org

Fidalgo Island is the place to be for this traditional celebration of Anacortes' maritime heritage. It's a great family festival, with activities and entertainment, food and displays. Mid-May 10 a.m.-5 p.m.

HOTEL
★SHIP HARBOR INN
5316 Ferry Terminal Road, Anacortes, 360-293-5177, 800-852-8568; www.shipharborinn.com

28 rooms. Pets accepted, some restrictions; fee. Complimentary continental breakfast. Bar. $

★
★
★
★
★

AUBURN

Information: Auburn City Hall, 25 W. Main St., 253-931-3000;
www.ci.auburn.wa.us

WHAT TO SEE AND DO

AUBURN GOLF COURSE

29630 Green River Road, Auburn, 253-833-2350; www.auburngolf.org

This excellent 18-hole public course abuts the Green River in Auburn, about 25 miles southeast of downtown Seattle. Well known for its lush vegetation and challenging greens, the course is alternately flat (the front nine) and hilly (after the turn). It is widely regarded as one of the best golf values in the state and is accordingly crowded on weekends.

EMERALD DOWNS

2300 Emerald Downs Drive, Auburn, 253-288-7000;
www.emdowns.com

The only live thoroughbred horse racing venue in the Seattle area, Emerald Downs features a full slate of races from spring to late summer. The esteemed Longacre's Mile, an area tradition since the 1930s with an ever-growing purse ($300,000 in 2008), is the schedule's highlight, held in August. Built in 1996, the grandstand is thoroughly modern, with a wide range of seating on six levels and numerous food stands, restaurants and bars. The one-mile oval track hosts a number of special events and concerts (including an Independence Day celebration with fireworks). Sundays bring family fun days, with clowns, face painting, pony rides and other kid-friendly diversions.

★
★★
★★★
★★
☆

MUCKLESHOOT CASINO

2402 Auburn Way S., Auburn, 800-804-4944; www.muckleshootcasino.com

Located between Seattle and Tacoma, Muckleshoot Casino sports a tropical theme and more than 2,000 gaming machines, as well as the usual array of Vegas-style tables. The distinguishing features here are a piano lounge/cigar bar and a sushi bar. Entertainment includes a Legends show (with impersonators aping Elvis, Madonna and other stars) and pro boxing matches on Saturday nights. Saturday-Tuesday 24 hours, Wednesday-Friday 10 a.m.-5:45 p.m.

WHITE RIVER VALLEY MUSEUM

918 H St. S.E., Auburn, Auburn Community Campus,
253-288-7433; www.wrvmuseum.org

Situated in Les Gove Park, this historically rich museum celebrates the settlement of the White River Valley during the early part of the 20th century. Visitors can explore a Japanese-American farmhouse, climb aboard a Northern Pacific caboose and tour a replica of downtown Auburn complete with public market, drugstore and hat shop. Wednesday-Sunday noon-4 p.m.

BELLEVUE

Incorporated in 1953, Bellevue has rapidly become the state's fourth largest city. It is linked across Lake Washington to Seattle by the Evergreen Floating Bridge.
Information: Bellevue Chamber of Commerce, 10500 N.E. Eighth St.,
425-454-2464; www.bellevuechamber.org

WHAT TO SEE AND DO
BELLEVUE BOTANICAL GARDEN

12001 Main St., Bellevue, 425-452-2750;
www.bellevuebotanical.org

Bellevue Botanical Gardens features 36 acres of woodlands, meadows and display gardens including Waterwise Garden, Japanese Gardens and Fuchsia Display. Daily.

BELLEVUE SQUARE

575 Bellevue Square, Bellevue, 425-646-3660; www.bellevuesquare.com

One of the biggest and most posh shopping centers in metro Seattle, Bellevue Square is located eight miles east of the city in suburban Bellevue, on the eastern shore of Lake Washington. Well-heeled locals love the place for its eye-catching design, climate-controlled corridors and 200 high-end stores: anchors such as Nordstrom and the Bon March, specialty stores like Pottery Barn and Williams-Sonoma and upscale eateries including P.F. Chang's China Bistro and Ruth's Chris Steak House. This is not to mention the nonshopping facilities and services, which are head and shoulders above that of the typical mall, with a concierge, valet parking, a local shuttle bus and two kids play areas. An Eastside institution since the 1940s, Bellevue Square underwent a major redevelopment in the 1990s that transformed it into the shoppers' paradise it is today.

HOTELS
★★★BELLEVUE CLUB HOTEL

11200 S.E. 6th St., Bellevue, 425-454-4424, 800-579-1110; www.bellevueclub.com

You instantly feel the hush of the Bellevue Club Hotel when you walk through its vine-covered entrance. While the Bellevue Club feels very private and exclusive, hotel guests are greeted with thoughtful touches and deluxe amenities. Each room comes complete with luxurious bedding, as well as baths crafted of marble, limestone or granite. Stone fireplaces, oversized baths or private balconies are featured in some rooms. 67 rooms. Pets accepted, some restrictions. Wireless Internet access. Restaurant, bar. Children's activity center. Fitness room. Spa. Indoor pool, outdoor pool, whirlpool. Tennis. Business center. $$

★★★HYATT REGENCY BELLEVUE

900 Bellevue Way N.E., Bellevue, 425-462-1234,
800-233-1234, 425-646-7567; www.bellevue.hyatt.com

Located in the fashionable Eastside area and directly across from Bellevue Square Mall, this hotel is situated within Bellevue Place, a mixed-use development that includes retail stores, a fitness center and plenty of dining options. The hotel encourages guests to use the Bellevue Place Club (for a fee) and to dine at one of the many nearby restaurants (the hotel restaurant isn't open for dinner). 381 rooms. High-speed Internet access. Restaurant, bar. Fitness center. Outdoor pool, whirlpool. $$

★★RED LION BELLEVUE INN

11211 Main St., Bellevue, 425-455-5240, 800-421-8193; www.redlion.com

181 rooms. Pets accepted, some restrictions; fee. High-speed Internet access. Restaurant, bar. Outdoor pool. Fitness center. $

★SILVER CLOUD INN BELLEVUE

10621 N.E. 12th Street, Bellevue, 425-637-7000, 800-205-6937; www.scinns.com

97 rooms. Complimentary continental breakfast. High-speed Internet access. Outdoor pool, whirlpool. $$

RESTAURANT

★★SEASTAR RESTAURANT AND RAW BAR

205 108th Ave. N.E., Bellevue, 425-456-0010; www.seastarrestaurant.com

American menu. Lunch, dinner. Bar. Casual attire. Reservations recommended. Valet parking. $$$

BELLINGHAM

This small city, located on Bellingham Bay, has the impressive Mount Baker as its backdrop and is the last major city before the Washington coastline meets the Canadian border. The broad curve of the bay was charted in 1792 by Captain George Vancouver, who named it in honor of Sir William Bellingham. When the first settlers arrived here, forests stretched to the edge of the high bluffs along the shoreline. Timber and coal played major roles in the town's early economy. Today, Bellingham has an active waterfront port supporting fishing, cold storage, boat building, shipping, paper processing and marina operations. Squalicum Harbor's commercial and pleasure boat marina accommodates more than 1,800 vessels, making it the second-largest marina on Puget Sound. The marina is a pleasant area to dine, picnic and watch the fishermen at work. Fairhaven, the downtown area, contains a mix of restaurants, art galleries and specialty shops. Bellingham is also home to Western Washington University, located on Sehome Hill, which affords a scenic view of the city and bay.

Information: Bellingham/Whatcom County Convention & Visitors Bureau,

904 Potter St., 360-671-3990, 800-487-2032; www.bellingham.org

WHAT TO SEE AND DO

MOUNT BAKER-SNOQUALMIE NATIONAL FOREST

2930 Wetmore Ave. Everett, 425-783-6000, 800-627-0062;
www.fs.fed.us/r6/mbs

The Mount Baker and Snoqualmie national forests were combined under a single forest supervisor in July 1974. Divided into five ranger districts, the combined forest encompasses nearly two million acres. The Snoqualmie section lies east and southeast of Seattle; the Mount Baker section lies east on Highway 542 and includes the Mount Baker Ski Area. The forest extends from the Canadian border south to Mount Rainier National Park and includes rugged mountains and woodlands on the western slopes of the Cascades, the western portions of the Glacier Peak and Alpine Lakes, Henry M. Jackson. Noisy-Diobsud, Boulder River, Jackson, Clearwater and Norse Peak wildernesses. Attractions include seven commercial ski areas; 1,440 miles of hiking trails; and picnic areas and campsites. Mount Baker rises 10,778 feet in the north, forming a center for recreation all year, famous for deep-powder snow skiing and snowboarding. Snoqualmie Pass (via Interstate 90) and Stevens Pass (via Highway 2) provide year-round access to popular scenic destinations; Baker Lake provides excellent boating and fishing.

SEHOME HILL ARBORETUM

25th Street and McDonald Parkway, Bellingham, 360-676-6985;
www.ac.wwu.edu/~sha

The 180-acre native plant preserve contains hiking and interpretive trails and scenic views of the city, Puget Sound, San Juan Islands and mountains from an observation tower.

HOTELS

★★BEST WESTERN HERITAGE INN

151 E. McLeod Road, Bellingham, 360-647-1912, 800-780-7234;
www.bestwestern.com

91 rooms. Complimentary continental breakfast. Restaurant. High-speed Internet access. Fitness center, pets accepted. Outdoor pool, whirlpool. Airport transportation available. **$**

★★BEST WESTERN LAKEWAY INN

714 Lakeway Drive, Bellingham, 360-671-1011, 888-671-1011;
www.bellingham-hotel.com

132 rooms. Pets accepted, some restrictions; fee. Restaurant, bar. Indoor pool, whirlpool. Business Center. **$**

★★★THE CHRYSALIS INN & SPA

804 10th St., Bellingham, 360-756-1005, 888-808-0005; www.thechrysalisinn.com
Relax at the spa or enjoy sophisticated European-style meals with a bottle of red from the Fino Wine Bar's extensive list. 43 rooms. Spa. Restaurant, bar. **$$**

★HAMPTON INN BELLINGHAM AIRPORT

3985 Bennett Drive, Bellingham, 360-676-7700, 800-426-7866; www.hamptoninn.com
132 rooms. Complimentary full breakfast. Outdoor pool. High-speed Internet access. **$**

★★★HOTEL BELLWETHER

1 Bellwether Way, Bellingham, 877-411-1200, 877-411-1200;
www.hotelbellwether.com

This waterfront hotel features an onsite spa, the Harborside Bistro and access to the Coast Guard-operated Pacific Sea Taxi. 66 rooms. Pets accepted; fee. High-speed Internet access. Restaurant, bar. Airport transportation available. **$$**

★QUALITY INN

100 E. Kellogg Road, Bellingham, 360-647-8000, 800-900-4661;
www.qualityinn.com

86 rooms. Pets accepted; fee. Complimentary continental breakfast. Outdoor pool, whirlpool. **$**

SPECIALTY LODGING

FAIRHAVEN VILLAGE INN

1200 10th St., Bellingham, 360-733-1311, 877-733-1100; www.fairhavenvillageinn.com
22 rooms. Complimentary continental breakfast. High-speed Internet access. **$$**

BLAINE

Blaine sits just south of the Canadian border on Interstate 5.

Information: Visitor Information Center, 215 Marine Drive,
360-332-4544, 800-487-2032; www.blaine.net

WHAT TO SEE AND DO

BIRCH BAY STATE PARK

5105 Helwig Road, Blaine, 360-371-2800; www.parks.wa.gov

Ten miles southwest via Interstate 5, exit 266, then seven miles west via Grandview Road, north via Jackson Road to Helwig Road. Approximately 190 acres, Birch Bay features swimming, scuba diving, fishing, crabbing, clamming, picnicking and camping. Daily, reservations advised Memorial Day-Labor Day.

SEMIAHMOO PARK

9261 Semiahmoo Parkway, Blaine, 360-733-2900; www.co.whatcom.wa.us

A cannery once located on this 1.5-mile-long spit was the last port of call for Alaskan fishing boats on Puget Sound. Restored buildings now house a museum, gallery and gift shop. June-mid-September, Saturday and Sunday afternoons. The park offers clam digging, picnicking and bird-watching.

HOTEL

★★★RESORT SEMIAHMOO

9565 Semiahmoo Parkway, Blaine, 360-318-2000, 800-770-7992;
www.semiahmoo.com

Spellbinding views are the calling card of Resort Semiahmoo. This cottage-style resort, located on a wildlife preserve at the tip of a peninsula stretching into Puget Sound, enjoys one of the most scenic spots in the state. Views of snow-capped peaks, the Gulf Islands, Drayton Harbor or Semiahmoo Bay captivate and enchant. Blond woods and clean lines create an uncluttered look throughout the resort, while fireplaces, patios and balconies enhance the exceedingly comfortable guest rooms and suites. Golf, water activities and a terrific spa compete for attention, and dining is especially memorable, with creative and artfully presented cuisine. 198 rooms. Pets accepted, some restrictions; fee. Restaurant, bar. Spa. Indoor pool, outdoor pool, whirlpool. Golf. Tennis. $

BREMERTON

The tempo of the Puget Sound Naval Shipyard is the heartbeat of Bremerton, a community surrounded on three sides by water. The six dry docks of the Naval Shipyard make Bremerton a home port for the Pacific fleet.

Information: Bremerton Chamber of Commerce, 301 Pacific Ave.,
Port Gamble, 360-479-3579; www.bremertonwa.com

SPECIAL EVENTS

ARMED FORCES DAY PARADE

301 Pacific, Bremerton, 360-479-3579; www.bremertonchamber.org

Bremerton's Armed Forces Day parade is the longest continually running Armed Forces Day event in the nation. It is one of only seven Armed Forces Day events to be officially recognized by the Department of Defense. Over a hundred floats, bands and dance teams from military and nonmilitary organizations participate in the parade. Mid-May.

★
★
★
★
★

BLACKBERRY FESTIVAL

Second and Washington, Bremerton, 360-479-3579; www.blackberryfestival.org

One can stop and sample the best blackberry jams, jellies, pies and cobblers as they walk down Main Street. The beer garden has blackberry cider, blackberry wine and over 100 vendors offer a vast array of foods, drinks and art. Early September.

MOUNTAINEERS' FOREST THEATER

3000 Seabeck Highway, Bremerton, 206-284-6310; www.foresttheater.com

The oldest outdoor theater in the Pacific Northwest, Mountaineers' Forest Theater is a natural amphitheater surrounded by hundreds of rhododendrons beneath old-growth Douglas fir and hemlock and shows family oriented plays Late May-early June.

HOTELS

★BEST WESTERN BREMERTON INN

4303 Kitsap Way, Bremerton, 360-405-1111, 800-780-7234;
www.bestwestern.worldexecutive.com

103 rooms. Complimentary continental breakfast. Outdoor pool, whirlpool. $

★★RED LION

3073 N.W. Bucklin Hill Road, Silverdale, 360-698-1000;
www.silverdalebeachhotel.com

151 rooms. Restaurant, bar. Indoor pool, whirlpool. Tennis. $

CASHMERE

Cashmere's history dates to the 1860s, when a Catholic missionary came to the area to set up a school for Native Americans. The town is located in the Wenatchee Valley in the center of the state on the North Cascade Loop. It has strong timber and fruit industries.

Information: Chamber of Commerce, 509-782-7404; www.visitcashmere.com

SPECIAL EVENT
FOUNDERS' DAY

Chelan County Historical Museum, 600 Cotlets Way, Cashmere,
509-782-3230; www.visitcashmere.com

Everyone's eyes will be on the sky as they wait in anxious anticipation for 5,000 ping-pong balls to be dropped from a hovering helicopter on to the fields at Riverside Park. The ping-pong ball drop is one of the most popular events during Cashmere's Founders' Days celebration. Last weekend in June.

CHEHALIS

First called Saundersville, this city takes its present name, Native American for "shifting sands," from its position at the point where the Newaukum and Chehalis rivers meet. Farms and an industrial park give economic sustenance to Chehalis and neighboring Centralia.

Information: The Centralia, Chehalis and Greater Lewis County Chamber of Commerce, 500 N.W. Chamber of Commerce Way,
360-748-8885, 800-525-3323; www.chamberway.com

WASHINGTON

★
★
★
★
★

SPECIAL EVENT
SOUTHWEST WASHINGTON FAIR
2555 N. National Ave., Chehalis, 360-736-6072; www.southwestwashingtonfair.net
First held in 1909, this is the state's second-oldest fair and one of the largest. Third week in August.

RESTAURANT
★MARY MCCRANK'S DINNER HOUSE
2923 Jackson Highway, Chehalis, 360-748-3662; www.marymccranks.com
American menu. Lunch, dinner. Closed Monday. Children's menu. $$

CHELAN
Located in an apple-growing region, Chelan is a gateway to Lake Chelan and the spectacular northern Cascade Mountains. A Ranger District office of the Wenatchee National Forest is located here.
Information: Lake Chelan Chamber of Commerce, 102 E. Johnson,
509-682-3503, 800-424-3526; www.lakechelan.com

WHAT TO SEE AND DO
LAKE CHELAN
7544 S. Lakeshore Drive, Chelan, 360-902-8844; www.parks.wa.gov
This fjord-like lake, the largest and deepest in the state, stretches northwest for approximately 55 miles through the Cascade Mountains to the community of Stehekin in the North Cascades National Park; the lake is nearly 1,500 feet deep in some areas. There are two state parks and several recreation areas along the lake.

LAKE CRUISES
1418 W. Woodin Ave., Chelan, 509-682-4584, 888-424-3526; www.ladyofthelake.com
The passenger boats Lady of the Lake II and Lady Express and the High-speed Lady Cat make daily cruises on Lake Chelan to Stehekin, Holden Village and North Cascades National Park.

HOTELS
★BEST WESTERN LAKESIDE LODGE AND SUITES
2312 W. Woodin Ave., Chelan, 509-682-4396, 800-468-2781; www.bestwestern.com
67 rooms. Pets accepted, some restrictions; fee. Complimentary continental breakfast. Indoor pool, outdoor pool, whirlpool. $

★★CAMPBELL'S RESORT AND CONFERENCE CENTER
104 W. Woodin Ave., Chelan, 509-682-2561, 800-553-8225; www.campbellsresort.com
170 rooms. High-speed Internet access. Restaurant, bar. Spa. Outdoor pool, whirlpool. $$

CHENEY
Cheney, on a rise of land that gives it one of the highest elevations of any municipality in the state, has been a university town since 1882. It is also a farm distribution and servicing center.
Information: Chamber of Commerce, 201 First St., 509-235-8480;
www.westplainschamber.org

WHAT TO SEE AND DO
CHENEY HISTORICAL MUSEUM
614 Third St., Cheney, 509-235-9015; www.cheneymuseum.org
The Cheney Historical Museum is a local history museum dedicated to gathering and preserving information and artifacts concerning the history of the Four Lakes, Marshall, Cheney, Tyler and Amber districts of Spokane County in eastern Washington. This museum tells the story of communities born from agriculture and railroads, committed to education, and tied together by families. May-September, Tuesday and Saturday 1-4 p.m.

TURNBULL NATIONAL WILDLIFE REFUGE
Four miles south on Cheney-Plaza Road, then two miles east,
509-235-4723; www.fws.gov/turnbull
Located on the Pacific Flyway, the area boasts more than 200 species of birds as well as deer, elk, coyotes, beaver, mink, chipmunks, red squirrels and Columbia ground squirrels. Daily.

CLARKSTON
Clarkston is located on the Washington-Idaho boundary at the confluence of the Clearwater and Snake rivers. The town became a shipping center when the construction of four dams on the lower Snake River brought barge transportation here. Many recreation areas are located near Clarkston, especially along the Snake River and in the Umatilla National Forest. River trips are available into Hell's Canyon.
Information: Chamber of Commerce, 502 Bridge St., 509-758-7712, 800-933-2128; www.clarkstonchamber.org

HOTELS
★BEST WESTERN RIVERTREE INN
1257 Bridge St., Clarkston, 509-758-9551, 800-597-3621; www.bestwestern.com
62 rooms. Complimentary continental breakfast. Outdoor pool, whirlpool. Business Center. High-speed Internet access. Pets accepted.

★★QUALITY INN
700 Port Drive, Clarkston, 509-758-9500, 800-228-5151; www.qualityinn.com
97 rooms. Complimentary breakfast. Restaurant, bar. High-speed Internet access. Pets accepted. Outdoor pool. $

RESTAURANT
★ROOSTER'S LANDING
1550 Port Drive, Clarkston, 509-751-0155; www.roosterslanding.com
American menu. Lunch, dinner. Bar. Children's menu. Outdoor seating. $$

COLVILLE
Once a brawling frontier town, Colville, the seat of Stevens County, has quieted down and now reflects the peacefulness of the surrounding hills and mountains. Many towns flourished and died in this area: Orchards, mills and mines all had their day. The portage at Kettle Falls, a fort and the crossing of several trails made Colville a thriving center.
Information: Chamber of Commerce, 121 E. Astor, 509-684-5973; www.colville.com

WASHINGTON

★
★
★
★
★

WHAT TO SEE AND DO
COLVILLE NATIONAL FOREST
765 S. Main St., Colville, 509-684-7000; www.fs.fed.us/r6/colville

This million-acre forest is located in the northeast corner of Washington, bordering Canada. The forest extends along its western boundary from the Canadian border south to the Colville Reservation and east across the Columbia River to Idaho. Comprising conifer forest types, small lakes and winding valleys bounded by slopes leading to higher mountainous areas, the forest offers good hunting and fishing and full-service camping. Also here is Sullivan Lake, offering such recreational opportunities as boating, fishing, swimming and hiking trails and developed and dispersed campground settings. The bighorn sheep that inhabit adjacent Hall Mountain can be viewed at a feeding station near the lake, which is cooperatively managed by the forest and the Washington Department of Wildlife.

ST. PAUL'S MISSION
12 miles northwest, near intersection of Columbia River and Highway 395, 509-738-6266; www.nps.gov/laro

A chapel was built by Jesuit Priests assisted by Native Americans near here in 1845, followed by the hand-hewn log church in 1847. It fell into disuse in the 1870s and in 1939 was restored to its original state.

COULEE DAM

Established as a construction community for workers on the Grand Coulee Dam project, this town is now the home of service and maintenance employees of the dam and the headquarters for the Lake Roosevelt National Recreation Area.

Information: Grand Coulee Dam Area Chamber of Commerce, 306 Midway Ave., Grand Coulee, 99133-0760, 509-633-3074, 800-268-5332; www.grandcouleedam.org

WHAT TO SEE AND DO
FORT SPOKANE
21 miles north of Davenport on State Highway 25, 509-725-2715; www.nps.gov/laro/historyculture/fort-spokane.htm

One of the last frontier military outposts of the 1880s, four of 45 buildings remain including a brick guardhouse which now serves as a visitor center and small museum. Built to maintain peace between the settlers and Native Americans, no shot was ever fired.

GRAND COULEE DAM
306 Midway Ave., Grand Coulee, 509-633-9265, 800-268-5332; www.grandcouleedam.org

This is the major structure of the multipurpose Columbia Basin Project, built by the Bureau of Reclamation to bring water to the dry farms in central Washington. Water is diverted from the Columbia River to what in prehistoric days was its temporary course down the Grand Coulee (a deep water-carved ravine). The project will reclaim more than a million acres through irrigation and already provides a vast reservoir of electric power. One of the largest concrete structures in the world, the dam towers 550 feet high and has a 500-foot-wide base and a 5,223-foot-long crest. Power plants contain some of world's largest hydro-generators. In summer, a nightly laser light show tells the story of the dam using the concrete spillway as a backdrop.

HOTEL
★COLUMBIA RIVER INN

10 Lincoln Ave., Coulee Dam, 509-633-2100, 800-633-6421;
www.columbiariverinn.com

34 rooms. Outdoor pool, whirlpool. **$**

COUPEVILLE

One of the oldest towns in the state, Coupeville was named for Thomas Coupe, a sea captain and early settler, the only man ever to sail a full-rigged ship through Deception Pass. Fortified to protect the settlers and for the defense of Puget Sound, Coupeville was once the home of the only seat of higher education north of Seattle, the Puget Sound Academy. Today it is near Whidbey Island Naval Air Station, home of naval aviation for the Pacific Northwest.

Information: Visitor Information Center, 107 S. Main St.,
360-678-5434; www.cometocoupeville.com

SPECIALTY LODGINGS
CAPTAIN WHIDBEY INN

2072 W. Captain Whidbey Inn Road, Coupeville, 360-678-4097, 800-366-4097;
www.captainwhidbey.com

This turn-of-the-century log inn is situated on a sheltered cove. 32 rooms. Complimentary full breakfast. Bar. **$**

GUEST HOUSE BED AND BREAKFAST COTTAGES

24371 Highway 525, Greenbank, 360-678-3115, 800-997-3115;
www.guesthouselogcottages.com

This inn is located on 25 acres of forest and features a scenic wildlife pond and marine and mountain views. Six rooms. No children allowed. Complimentary full breakfast. Outdoor pool. **$$**

ELLENSBURG

Although this community has long abandoned its first name, Robber's Roost, it cherishes the tradition and style of the west, both as a center for dude ranches and as the scene of one of the country's best annual rodeos. At the geographic center of the state, Ellensburg processes beef and dairy products. The county ranges from lakes and crags in the west through irrigated farmlands to sagebrush prairie along the Columbia River to the east. A Ranger District office of the Wenatchee National Forest is located here.

Information: Chamber of Commerce, 609 N. Main St., Ellensburg,
509-925-2002, 888-925-2204; www.ellensburg-chamber.com

WHAT TO SEE AND DO
GINKGO PETRIFIED FOREST/WANAPUM RECREATIONAL AREA

30 miles east from I-90 north to Ginkgo, south to Wanapum,
360-902-8844; www.parks.wa.gov

One of world's largest petrified forests (7,600 acres), it features more than 200 species of petrified wood, including a prehistoric ginkgo tree. Other activities include waterskiing, fishing, boating, hiking, picnicking and camping.

WASHINGTON

★
★
★
★
★

OLMSTEAD PLACE STATE PARK-HERITAGE SITE
Four miles east from I-90, 509-925-1943; www.parks.wa.gov
This turn-of-the-century Kittitas Valley farm, originally homesteaded in 1875, has been converted to a living historical farm.

THORP GRIST MILL
From Interstate 90, take exit 101, 509-964-9640; www.thorp.org
This flour mill, built in 1883, is the only one in the country with its machinery completely intact.

HOTEL
★★QUALITY INN & CONFERENCE CENTER
1700 Canyon Road, Ellensburg, 509-925-9800, 800-321-8791;
www.ellensburginn.com
106 rooms. Pets accepted, some restrictions; fee. Restaurant, bar. Indoor pool, whirlpool, children's pool. Fitness center. $

EPHRATA
The growth of this area is the result of the development of surrounding farmland, originally irrigated by wells and now supplied by the Columbia Basin irrigation project. Ephrata is the center of an area containing a series of lakes that offer fishing and water sports. There is excellent upland game bird hunting as well.
Information: Chamber of Commerce, 1 Basin St. Southwest,
Ephrata, 509-754-4656; www.ephratawachamber.com

★
★
★
★
★

HOTEL
★BEST WESTERN RAMA INN
1818 Basin St. S.W., Ephrata, 509-754-7111, 800-780-7234;
www.bestwestern.com
45 rooms. Complimentary continental breakfast. High-speed Internet access. Indoor pool, whirlpool. $

SPECIALTY LODGING
IVY CHAPEL INN BED AND BREAKFAST
164 D St. S.W., Ephrata, 509-754-0629;
www.theivychapelinn.com
Six rooms. Children over 10 years only. Complimentary full breakfast. $

EVERETT
This lumber, aircraft, electronics and shipping city is on a sheltered harbor where the Snohomish River empties into Port Gardner Bay. To the east is the snowcapped Cascade Mountain Range; to the west are the Olympic Mountains. Developed by eastern industrial and railroad money, Everett serves as a major commercial fishing port and receives and dispatches a steady stream of cargo vessels. The Boeing 747 and 767 are assembled here. Along the waterfront is a 1890s-style seaside marketplace, the Everett Marina Village.
Information: Everett Area Convention and Visitor Bureau, 2000 Hewitt Ave.,
Everett, 425-257-3222; www.everettchamber.com

MUKILTEO

Chamber of Commerce, 304 Lincoln Ave., Mukilteo, 425-347-1456;
www.mukilteo.org

This town, just west of Everett, is the major ferry point from the mainland to the southern tip of Whidbey Island. Its name means "good camping ground." A lighthouse built in 1905 is open for tours on Saturday.

WHAT TO SEE AND DO
HARBOUR POINTE GOLF CLUB

11817 Harbour Pointe Blvd., Mukilteo, 425-355-6060, 800-233-3128;
www.harbourpointegolf.com

Harbour Pointe is really a tale of two nines, with the front a very flat, target-oriented layout and the back lined with tall evergreen trees and narrower fairways, which force players to work their way around each hole for the best approach to each green. Opened in 1991, Harbour Pointe has won awards as one of America's best public courses. It is better to play on a day when it hasn't rained for at least a week; otherwise, the course plays considerably longer due to the moisture.

HOTEL
★BEST WESTERN CASCADIA INN

2800 Pacific Ave., Everett, 425-258-4141, 800-780-7234;
www.bestwestern.com

134 rooms. Complimentary continental breakfast. Fitness center. Pool. High-speed Internet access. Outdoor pool, whirlpool. **$**

FORKS

The major town in the northwest section of the Olympic Peninsula, Forks takes its name from the nearby junction of the Soleduck, Bogachiel and Dickey rivers. Timber processing is the major industry. A Ranger District office of the Olympic National Forest is located here.

Information: Chamber of Commerce, 1411 S. Forks Ave., Forks,
98331, 360-374-2531, 800-443-6757; www.forkswa.com

HOTEL
★FORKS MOTEL

351 S. Forks Ave., Forks, 360-374-6243, 800-544-3416; www.forksmotel.com

73 rooms. Wireless Internet access. Restaurant. Outdoor pool, children's pool. **$**

HOQUIAM

Twin city to Aberdeen, Hoquiam is the senior community of the two and the pioneer town of the Grays Harbor region. A deepwater port 12 miles from the Pacific, it docks cargo and fishing vessels, manufactures wood products and machine tools and cans the harvest of the sea.

Information: Grays Harbor Chamber of Commerce, 506 Duffy St.,
Aberdeen, 98520, 360-532-1924; www.graysharbor.org

WASHINGTON

★
★
★
★
★

WHAT TO SEE AND DO
HOQUIAM'S CASTLE
515 Chenault Ave., Hoquiam, 360-533-2005; www.hoquiamcastle.com
A 20-room mansion built in 1897 by lumber tycoon Robert Lytle, Hoquaim's Castile features antique furnishings, an oak-columned entry hall and authentic Victorian atmosphere. Summer, Wednesday-Saturday.

ISSAQUAH
Historic buildings and homes of Issaquah have been renovated and moved to a 7-acre farm site, called Gilman Village, where they now serve as specialty shops.
Information: Chamber of Commerce, 155 N.W. Gilman Blvd.,
Issaquah, 425-392-7024; www.issaquahchamber.com

WHAT TO SEE AND DO
BOEHM'S CHOCOLATE FACTORY
255 N.E. Gilman Blvd., Issaquah, 425-392-6652; www.boehmscandies.com
The home of Boehm's Candies was built here in 1956 by Julius Boehm. The candy-making process and the Edelweiss Chalet, filled with artifacts, paintings and statues, can be toured. The Luis Trenker Kirch'l, a replica of a 12th-century Swiss chapel, was also built by Boehm. Tours by appointment. July-August.

HOTEL
★★HOLIDAY INN
1801 12th Ave. N.W., Issaquah, 425-392-6421, 888-465-4329;
www.holiday-inn.com/sea-issaquah
100 rooms. Restaurant, bar. Outdoor pool. High-speed Internet access. Whirlpool. **$**

KELSO
Kelso straddles the Cowlitz River and is an artery for the lumber industry. The river also yields a variety of fish from giant salmon to tiny smelt.
Information: Kelso Longview Chamber of Commerce, 1563 Olympia Way,
Longview, 98632, 360-423-8400; www.kelsolongviewchamber.org

HOTELS
★COMFORT INN
440 Three Rivers Drive, Kelso, 360-425-4600, 877-424-6423;
www.choicehotels.com
57 rooms. Complimentary continental breakfast. Indoor pool, whirlpool. **$**

★MT. ST. HELENS MOTEL
1340 Mt. Saint Helens Way N.E., Castle Rock, 360-274-7721;
www.mountsthelens.com
32 rooms. **$**

★★RED LION
510 Kelso Drive, Kelso, 360-636-4400, 800-733-5466; www.redlion.com
161 rooms. Pets accepted; fee. Restaurant, bar. Outdoor pool, children's pool, whirlpool. Wireless Internet access. **$**

KENNEWICK

Huge hydroelectric dams harnessing the lower stem of the Columbia River have brought economic vitality to the "Tri-Cities" of Kennewick, Pasco and Richland. On the south bank of Lake Wallula and near the confluence of the Columbia, Snake and Yakima rivers, Kennewick has chemical and agricultural processing plants. Irrigation of the 20,500-acre Kennewick Highland project has converted sagebrush into thousands of farms, producing three cuttings of alfalfa annually plus corn and beans. Appropriately enough, this city with the Native American name meaning "winter paradise" enjoys a brief winter and is the center of the state's grape industry.

Information: Tri-City Area Chamber of Commerce, 3180 W. Clearwater Ave.,
509-736-0510; www.tricityregionalchamber.com

HOTELS
★QUALITY INN

7901 W. Quinault Ave., Kennewick, 509-735-6100, 877-424-6423; www.qualityinn.com
124 rooms. Complimentary continental breakfast. High-speed Internet access. Indoor pool, outdoor pool, whirlpool. $

★★RED LION

1101 N. Columbia Center Blvd., Kennewick, 509-783-0611, 800-733-5466;
www.redlion.com
162 rooms. Pets accepted. Wireless Internet access. Restaurant, bar. Outdoor pool. Airport transportation available. $

KIRKLAND

This Seattle suburb has a picturesque, waterfront downtown filled with charming shops, restaurants and more.

Information: Kirkland Chamber of Commerce, 401 Park Place, Kirkland,
425-822-7066; www.kirklandchamber.org

HOTEL
★★★THE WOODMARK HOTEL ON LAKE WASHINGTON

1200 Carillon Point, Kirkland, 425-822-3700, 800-822-3700;
www.thewoodmark.com
With the blinking lights of Seattle's skyline only seven miles in the distance, the Woodmark Hotel rests on the shores of scenic Lake Washington. Convenient to Bellevue and Redmond, the Woodmark is an ideal stop for travelers. From the friendly staff to the cozy furnishings, a relaxed, residential style pervades the hotel. Guest rooms feature lake, marina or creek views. The region's fresh, delicious cuisine is the highlight at Waters Lakeside Bistro, and the Library Bar serves a wonderful afternoon tea, complete with a special menu and china service for children. 100 rooms. Pets accepted, some restrictions; fee. Wireless Internet access. Restaurant, bar. Spa. $$

RESTAURANTS
★★★CAFÉ JUANITA

9702 120th Place N.E., Kirkland, 425-823-1505; www.cafejuanita.com
The dining destination for the Puget Sound region since 1979, Café Juanita serves some of the best northern Italian food around and local northwest fare. The wine list

★
★
★
★
★

complements the Café's chalkboard menu of well-executed cuisine by chef Holly Smith. Italian menu. Dinner. Closed Monday. Casual attire. $$$

★★THIRD FLOOR FISH CAFÉ
205 Lake St. South, Kirkland, 425-822-3553; www.fishcafe.com
Seafood menu. Dinner. Bar. Children's menu. Casual attire. $$$

LA CONNER
A picturesque town along the Swinomish Channel, La Conner is a popular destination for weekend travelers. Many of the town's homes and businesses are housed in the clapboard structures built by its founders around the turn of the century. Numerous boutiques, galleries and antique shops, some containing the works of local artists and craftspeople, line its streets.
Information: Chamber of Commerce, 606 Morris St., La Conner,
360-466-4778, 888-642-9284; www.laconnerchamber.com

SPECIALTY LODGINGS
LA CONNER COUNTRY INN
107 S. Second St., La Conner, 360-466-3101, 888-466-4113;
www.laconnerlodging.com
28 rooms. Pets accepted; fee. Complimentary continental breakfast. High-speed Internet access. Spa. Restaurant, bar. $

THE HERON
117 Maple Ave., La Conner, 360-466-4626, 877-883-8899; www.theheron.com
12 rooms. Children over 12 years only. Complimentary full breakfast. Spa. $

LANGLEY
This small community on Whidbey Island is a popular tourist destination for Seattle residents on daytrips.
Information: Langley Chamber of Commerce, 208 Anthes Ave., Langley,
360-221-6765, 888-232-2080; www.langleychamb.whidbey.com

RESTAURANT
★★CAFÉ LANGLEY
113 First St., Langley, 360-221-3090; www.cafelangley.com
Mediterranean menu. Lunch, dinner. Closed Tuesday. Bar. Children's menu. Casual attire. Reservations recommended. $$

LEAVENWORTH
Surrounded by the Cascade Mountains, Leavenworth has an old-world charm enhanced by authentic Bavarian architecture. Less than three hours from Seattle, the village is a favorite stop for people who enjoy river rafting, hiking, bicycling, fishing, golf and skiing. Two Ranger District offices of the Wenatchee National Forest are located here.
Information: Chamber of Commerce, 940 Highway 2, Leavenworth,
509-548-5807; www.leavenworth.org

★
★
★
★
★

WHAT TO SEE AND DO
LEAVENWORTH NUTCRACKER MUSEUM
735 Front St., Leavenworth, 509-548-4573, 800-892-3989;
www.nutcrackermuseum.com

Spanning the wall and floor space of a beautiful Bavarian-style house is the Nutcracker Museum, born out of Arlene Wagner's love of the Tchaikovsky ballet of the same name. Wagner now has more than 4,000 nutcrackers in her museum, having traveled the world over in search of the most exotic specimens. Some of the examples housed in the museum date as far back as the 15th century and detail the history of these very functional, yet ornamental, items. May-October, daily 2-5 p.m.; November-April, weekends or by appointment.

HOTELS
★★BEST WESTERN ICICLE INN
505 Highway 2, Leavenworth, 509-548-7000, 800-780-7234; www.bestwestern.com
92 rooms. Pets accepted, some restrictions; fee. Complimentary full breakfast. High-speed Internet access. Restaurant. Outdoor pool, whirlpool. $

★★★MOUNTAIN HOME LODGE
8201 Mountain Home Road, Leavenworth, 509-548-7077, 800-414-2378;
www.mthome.com

In a picturesque, serene setting, this great escape is a wonderful mix of luxury, comfort and style. Some guests come for relaxation and seclusion while others enjoy the activities. 12 rooms. No children allowed. Complimentary full breakfast. Restaurant. Outdoor pool, whirlpool. Tennis. $$$

SPECIALTY LODGINGS
ALL SEASONS RIVER INN
8751 Icicle Road, Leavenworth, 509-548-1425, 800-254-0555;
www.allseasonsriverinn.com

Located 80 feet above the Wenatchee River, this serene bed and breakfast feels more like a private home than a hotel. Guest rooms lack TVs and telephones, but lovely water views and Jacuzzi tubs provide their own form of entertainment. Passionate about antiques, the innkeeper has meticulously furnished each room with unique pieces. The inn makes bicycles available for the half-mile ride to downtown Leavenworth. six rooms. No children allowed. Complimentary full breakfast. $$

BOSCH GARTEN
9846 Dye Road, Leavenworth, 509-548-6900, 800-535-0069; www.boschgarten.com
Three rooms. Children over 12 years only. Complimentary full breakfast. Whirlpool. $

RUN OF THE RIVER BED & BREAKFAST
9308 E. Leavenworth Road, Leavenworth, 509-548-7171, 800-288-6491;
www.runoftheriver.com

This small, quiet inn on the Icicle River is tucked among the towering Cascade Mountains. Visitors will enjoy hiking, walking or mountain biking through forest trails. Six rooms. No children allowed. Complimentary full breakfast. Whirlpool. $$

WASHINGTON

★
★
★
★
★

LONG BEACH

This seashore resort is on one of the longest hard-sand beaches in the world, stretching 28 miles along a narrow peninsula just north of where the Columbia River empties into the Pacific Ocean.

Information: Peninsula Visitors Bureau, 3914 Pacific Way (Highway 101 at Highway 103), Seaview, 360-642-2400, 800-451-2542; www.funbeach.com

HOTELS

★CHAUTAUQUA LODGE

304 14th St. North, Long Beach, 360-642-4401, 800-869-8401; www.chautauqualodge.com

120 rooms. Pets accepted; fee. Bar. Indoor pool, whirlpool. **$**

★★EDGEWATER INN

409 10th St., Long Beach, 360-642-2311, 800-800-8000

84 rooms. Pets accepted, some restrictions; fee. Restaurant, bar. **$**

★SUPER 8

500 Ocean Beach Blvd., Long Beach, 360-642-8988, 800-800-8000; www.longbeachsuper8.com

50 rooms. Complimentary continental breakfast. **$**

SPECIALTY LODGINGS

BOREAS BED AND BREAKFAST

607 Ocean Beach Blvd. N., Long Beach, 360-642-8069, 888-642-8069; www.boreasinn.com

This scenic oceanfront bed and breakfast comes well equipped with many personal touches. Each of the suites is designed to reflect the style and fun-loving personalities at the inn. Five rooms. Complimentary full breakfast. **$**

A RENDEZVOUS PLACE BED AND BREAKFAST

1610 California Ave. S., Long Beach, 360-642-8877, 866-642-8877; www.rendezvousplace.com

Five rooms. Children over two years only. Complimentary full breakfast. **$**

RESTAURANTS

★★SANCTUARY

794 Highway 101, Chinook, 360-777-8380; www.sanctuaryrestaurant.com

Seafood menu. Dinner. Closed Monday-Thursday. Children's menu. Outdoor seating. **$$**

★★SHOALWATER

4503 Pacific Highway, Seaview, 360-642-4142; www.shoalwater.com

Seafood menu. Lunch, dinner. Bar. Children's menu. Outdoor seating. **$$**

★
★★
★★
★

MARYSVILLE

Natural surroundings, including lakes, rivers and wooded countryside, make Marysville a popular spot for outdoor recreation.

Information: The Greater Marysville Tulalip Chamber of Commerce, 8825 34th Ave. N.E., Tulalip, 360-659-7700; www.marysvilletulalipchamber.com

WHAT TO SEE AND DO
TULALIP CASINO

10200 Quil Ceda Blvd., Tulalip, 360-651-1111, 888-272-1111; www.tulalipcasino.com
About 35 miles north of downtown Seattle is the Tulalip Casino, which features an array of Vegas-style tables, a bingo parlor and more than 1,000 gaming machines. Hunger is sated at three eateries (a steak-and-seafood restaurant and two delis), and the waters of Puget Sound, just a stone's throw away, beckon nongamblers outdoors. Monday-Tuesday 10-6 a.m., Wednesday-Sunday 24 hours.

HOTEL
★★BEST WESTERN TULALIP INN

3228 Marine Drive N.E., Marysville, 360-659-4488, 800-780-7234; www.bestwestern.com
69 rooms. Complimentary full breakfast. High-speed Internet access. Restaurant, bar. Indoor pool, whirlpool. $

MOSES LAKE

Because of the water impounded by Grand Coulee Dam, the recreational and agricultural resources of this area have blossomed. Swimming, fishing and hunting abound within a 25-mile radius. The city is also an important shipping and processing point for agricultural products.

Information: Chamber of Commerce, 324 S. Pioneer Way, Moses Lake, 509-765-7888; www.moseslake.com

HOTELS
★BEST VALUE INN

1214 S. Pioneer Way, Moses Lake, 509-765-9173, 888-315-2378; www.bestvalueinn.com
20 rooms. Pets accepted, some restrictions. Outdoor pool. $

★★BEST WESTERN LAKE FRONT HOTEL

3000 Marina Drive, Moses Lake, 509-765-9211, 800-780-7234; www.bestwestern.com
171 rooms. Pets accepted, some restrictions; fee. Restaurant, bar. Fitness center. Outdoor pool, whirlpool. High-speed Internet access. Airport transportation available. $

★SHILO INN

1819 E. Kittleson, Moses Lake, 509-765-9317, 888-222-2244; www.shiloinns.com
100 rooms. Pets accepted, some restrictions; fee. Indoor pool, whirlpool. Airport transportation available. $

WASHINGTON

★
★
★
★
★

MOUNT RAINIER NATIONAL PARK

Majestic Mount Rainier, towering 14,411 feet above sea level and 8,000 feet above the Cascade Range of Western Washington, is one of America's outstanding tourist attractions. More than 2 million people visit this 378-square-mile park each year to picnic, hike, camp, climb mountains or simply admire the spectacular scenery along the many miles of roads.

The park's various "life zones," which change at different elevations, support a wide array of plant and animal life. Douglas fir, red cedar and western hemlock, some rising 200 feet into the air, thrive in the old-growth forests. In the summer, the sub-alpine meadows come alive with brilliant wildflowers. These areas are home to more than 130 species of birds and 50 species of mammals. Mountain goats, chipmunks and marmots are favorites among visitors, but deer, elk, bears, mountain lions and other animals can also be seen here.

Mount Rainier is the largest volcano in the Cascade Range, which extends from Mount Garibaldi in Southwestern British Columbia to Lassen Peak in northern California. The eruption of Mount St. Helens in 1980 gives a clue to the violent history of these volcanoes. Eruptions occurred at Mount Rainier as recently as the mid-1800s. Even today, steam emissions often form caves in the summit's ice cap and usually melt the snow along the rims of the twin craters.

A young volcano by geologic standards, Mount Rainier was once a fairly symmetrical mountain rising about 16,000 feet above sea level. But glaciers and further volcanic activity shaped the mountain into an irregular mass of rock. The sculpting action of the ice gave each face of the mountain its own distinctive profile. The glaciation continues today, as Mount Rainier supports the largest glacier system in the contiguous United States, with 35 square miles of ice and 26 named glaciers. Much of the park's beauty can be attributed to the glaciers, which at one time extended far beyond the park's boundaries. The moving masses of ice carved deep valleys separated by high, sharp ridges or broad plateaus. From certain vantages, the valleys accentuate the mountain's height. The glaciers are the source of the many streams in the park, as well as several rivers in the Pacific Northwest. The meltwaters also support the various plants and animals throughout the region.

Winters at Mount Rainier are legendary. Moist air masses moving eastward across the Pacific Ocean are intercepted by the mountain. As a result, some areas commonly receive 50 or more feet of snow each winter. At 5,400 feet in elevation, Paradise made history in 1971-1972, when it received 93 feet of snow, the heaviest snowfall ever recorded in this country. The three-story Paradise Inn is often buried up to its roof in snow. Because the mountain's summit is usually above the storm clouds, the snowfall there is not as great.

The park's transformation from winter wonderland to summer playground is almost magical. Beginning in June or July, the weather becomes warm and clear, although the mountain is occasionally shrouded in clouds. The snow at the lower elevations disappears, meltwaters fill stream valleys and cascade over cliffs, wildflowers blanket the meadows and visitors converge on the park for its many recreational activities.

There are several entrances to the park. The roads from the Nisqually entrance to Paradise and from the southeast boundary to Ohanapecosh are usually open year-round but may be closed temporarily during the winter. Following the first heavy snow, around November 1, all other roads are closed until May or June. The entrance fee is $10 per vehicle.

Information: 55210 238th Ave. East, Ashford, 360-569-2211; www.nps.gov/mora

★
★★
★★
★
☆

WHAT TO SEE AND DO

CARBON RIVER

Located on the Pacific side of Mount Rainier, the Carbon River area receives the most rainfall and contains the most luxurious forests in Washington. In fact, much of the woodland here is considered temperate rain forest.

www.nps.gov/mora

CRYSTAL MOUNTAIN RESORT

33914 Crystal Mountain Blvd., Crystal Mountain, 360-663-2265,
888-754-6199 (snow conditions); www.skicrystal.com

Located 75 miles south of Seattle in the shadows of Mount Rainier, Crystal Mountain is a ski resort with an impressive 3,100-foot vertical drop and equally impressive 340 inches of average annual snowfall. During the December-to-April ski season, 10 lifts service 1,300 acres of skiable terrain on Silver King Mountain with a nice balance of beginner, intermediate and advanced trails; an additional 1,000 acres of backcountry terrain is available for diehards. The place is known for its family-friendly perks, such as free children's passes with an adult purchase and a Kids Club that offers supervision, skiing classes and lunch while parents enjoy the slopes. The resort also encompasses several hotels and restaurants, as well as a rental shop, skiing and snowboarding school and day spa.

MOUNTAIN CLIMBING

360-569-2211; www.nps.gov/mora

The park has many opportunities for climbers; one of the most popular climbs is the two-day trek to the summit of Mount Rainier. The guide service at Paradise conducts various programs for new and experienced climbers. Climbs should be attempted only by persons who are in good physical condition and have the proper equipment; deep crevasses and unstable ridges of lava are dangerous. All climbers must register with a park ranger.

OHANAPECOSH

Mount Rainier National Park, southeast corner of park, 360-569-2211;
www.nps.gov/mora/planyourvisit/ohanapecosh.htm

A preserve of rushing waters and dense, old-growth forest, some of the largest trees in the park—many over 1,000 years old—are here. The Grove of the Patriarchs, a cluster of massive conifers on an island in the Ohanapecosh River, is reached by bridge along a popular trail that starts near the Steven's Canyon Entrance Station. At the Ohanapecosh Visitor Center exhibits tell the story of the lowland forest ecosystem, where Douglas fir, western hemlock and red cedar trees reign supreme.

WASHINGTON

★
★
★
★
☆

HOTELS

★★THE NISQUALLY LODGE

31609 Highway 706, Ashford, 360-569-8804, 888-674-3554;
www.escapetothemountains.com

24 rooms. Complimentary continental breakfast. Restaurant. Whirlpool. **$**

★★PARADISE INN/NATIONAL PARK INN

55106 Kernahan Road East, Ashford, 360-569-2275; www.rainier.guestservices.com
121 rooms. Closed mid-October-mid-May. Restaurant, bar. **$**

SPECIALTY LODGING
ALEXANDER'S COUNTRY INN

37515 Highway 706 E., Ashford, 360-569-2300, 800-654-7615;
www.alexanderscountryinn.com
14 rooms. Complimentary full breakfast. Restaurant. Spa. **$**

MOUNT ST. HELENS NATIONAL VOLCANIC MONUMENT

In 1978, two geologists who had been studying Mount St. Helens warned that the youngest volcano in the Cascade Range could erupt again by the end of the century. On March 27, 1980, the volcano did just that, ending 123 years of inactivity. Less than two months later, on May 18, a massive eruption transformed this beautiful snow-capped mountain and the surrounding forest into an eerie, desolate landscape with few signs of life.

The eruption sent a lateral blast of hot ash and gases out across the land at speeds up to 670 miles per hour, flattening 150 square miles of forest north of the volcano. An ash plume rising 13 miles into the atmosphere was spread eastward by the wind, coating many cities in Washington, Idaho and Montana with a fine grit. Rivers were choked with logs and mud; huge logging trucks were toppled like small toys and the mountain, having lost 1,300 feet of its summit, was left with a gaping crater 2,000 feet deep, half a mile wide and a mile long.

Among the 57 people missing or killed by the eruption was 83-year-old Harry Truman, who for many years owned a lodge on Spirit Lake just north of the mountain. Truman refused to heed evacuation warnings, believing his "beloved mountain" would not harm him; he and his lodge are now beneath hundreds of feet of mud and water.

The Monument, established in 1982, covers 110,000 acres within the Gifford Pinchot National Forest and provides a rare natural laboratory in which scientists and visitors can view the effects of a volcanic eruption. Despite the destruction, the return of vegetation and wildlife to the blast zone has been relatively rapid. Within just weeks of the eruption, small plants and insects had begun to make their way through the ash. Today, herds of elk and other animals, as well as fir trees and wildflowers, have taken a strong foothold here.

Forest Service Road 25, which runs north-south near the eastern boundary, provides access to views of the volcano. The roads are usually closed from approximately November-May because of snow; some roads are narrow and winding.

Visitors are advised to phone ahead for current road conditions. Although volcanic activity at Mount St. Helens has decreased greatly in the last few years, some roads into the Monument could be closed if weather conditions dictate.

From Interstate 5 exit 68: 48 miles east on Highway 12 to Randle, then south on Forest Service Road 25, from I-5 exit 21: approximately 35 miles northeast on Highway 503, Forest Service Roads 90, 25, 42218 Northeast Yale Bridge Road, Amboy, 360-449-7800; Information: www.fs.fed.us/gpnf/mshnvm/

WASHINGTON

WHAT TO SEE AND DO
APE CAVE
Forest Service Road in southern part of monument, Amboy,
360-247-3900; www.fs.fed.us/gpnf/04mshnvm
At 12,810 feet in length, the cave is said to be one of the longest intact lava tubes in the continental United States. The downslope portion of cave, extending approximately 4,000 feet, is the most easily traveled. The upslope portion, extending nearly 7,000 feet, is recommended only for visitors carrying the proper equipment. All visitors are advised to carry three sources of light and wear sturdy shoes or boots and warm clothing. The cave is a constant 42 F.

JOHNSTON RIDGE OBSERVATORY
24000 Spirit Lake Highway, Mount St. Helens National Volcanic Monument,
360-274-2140; www.fs.fed.us/gpnf/04mshnvm
At 4,200 feet, state-of-the-art interpretive displays focus on the sequence of geological events that drastically altered the landscape and opened up a new era in the science of monitoring an active volcano and forecasting eruptions.

MOUNT ST. HELENS VISITOR CENTER
3029 Spirit Lake Highway, Castle Rock, 360-274-0962;
www.parks.wa.gov/mountsthelens.asp
Outside the monument, the center houses exhibits that include a walk-through model of the volcano, displays on the history of the mountain and the 1980 eruption, and volcano monitoring equipment. A 10-minute slide program and a 22-minute movie are shown several times daily, and special programs are held throughout the year. Also here are volcano viewpoints and a nature trail along Silver Lake. Daily; closed holidays.

MOUNT VERNON
Developed by farmers and loggers, Mount Vernon is a major commercial center. Centrally located between Puget Sound and the North Cascades, the Skagit Delta's deep alluvial soil grows 125 varieties of produce, including flowers, bulbs, fruits and vegetables. Spring brings fields of daffodils, tulips and irises to the country. The city is named for George Washington's plantation in Virginia.
Information: Chamber of Commerce, 105 E. Kincaid St., Mount Vernon,
360-428-8547; www.mountvernonchamber.com

WHAT TO SEE AND DO
PRIME OUTLETS AT BURLINGTON
448 Fashion Way, Burlington, 360-757-3549;
www.theoutletshoppesatburlington.com
If you're a bargain hunter who wants to take a drive out of the city, the Prime Outlets at Burlington is your place. Just about 65 miles north of Seattle, this shoppers' paradise houses nearly 50 stores, such as Tommy Hilfiger, Gap, Reebok, Farberware and Samsonite. On the drive here, you'll be able to enjoy some of the northwest's breathtaking scenery.

SPECIAL EVENT
SKAGIT VALLEY TULIP FESTIVAL
Tulip Office and Museum, 100 E. Montgomery St., Mount Vernon,
360-428-5959; www.tulipfestival.org
This annual festival gives the county's two primary tulip growers, the Skagit Valley
Bulb Farm and the Washington Bulb Company, a chance to display their beautiful
blooms at sites throughout the county. Each grower invites visitors to tour its gardens, which feature hundreds of thousands of bulbs and more than 60 varieties of the
famous Dutch export. But this month-long festival is about more than just flowers: the
many events include the Anacortes Quilt Walk, Art in a Pickle Barn, and a bald eagle
and birding float trip. April.

HOTEL
★★BEST WESTERN COTTONTREE INN
2300 Market St., Mount Vernon, 360-428-5678, 800-662-6886;
www.bestwesterncottontreeinn.com
120 rooms. Pets accepted, some restrictions; fee. Complimentary full breakfast. Wireless Internet access. Restaurant, bar. Outdoor pool. $

SPECIALTY LODGING
THE WHITE SWAN GUEST HOUSE
15872 Moore Road, Mount Vernon, 360-445-6805; www.thewhiteswan.com
Three rooms. Complimentary continental breakfast. $$

NEWPORT
A shopping, distribution and lumbering center, Newport was born in Idaho. For a
while, there was a Newport on both sides of the state line, but the U.S. Post Office
interceded on behalf of the Washington community, which was the county seat of
Pend Oreille County. Newport is known as "the city of flags" and flags from around
the world are displayed on the main streets. A Ranger District office of the Colville
National Forest is located here.
Information: Newport-Oldtown Chamber of Commerce, 325 W. Fourth St., Newport,
509-447-5812, 877-818-1008; www.newportoldtownchamber.org

WHAT TO SEE AND DO
PEND OREILLE COUNTY MUSEUM
402 S. Washington Ave., Newport, 509-447-5388; www.pocmuseum.org
Located in and old railroad depot, the musuem houses historical artifacts of Pend
Oreille County and two reconstructed log cabins. Mid-May-September, daily.

NORTH BEND
A gateway to Mount Baker-Snoqualmie National Forest (Snoqualmie section) and a
popular winter sports area, North Bend also serves as a shipping town for this logging,
farming and dairy region. A Ranger District office of the Mount Baker-Snoqualmie
National Forest is located here.
Information: The Upper Snoqualmie Valley Chamber of Commerce,
425-888-4440; www.snovalley.org

WASHINGTON

WHAT TO SEE AND DO
FACTORY STORES AT NORTH BEND

461 South Fork Ave. Southwest, North Bend, 425-888-4505;
www.premiumoutlets.com

Located just 40 minutes from Seattle, this complex of outlet stores offers amazing bargains from names such as Eddie Bauer, Gap, Naturalizer, KB Toys and many more. The mall itself doesn't have many choices for satiating the appetite you're sure to work up after power shopping, but there are many options across the street.

MEADOWBROOK FARM

1711 Boalch Ave., North Bend, 425-831-1900; www.meadowbrookfarmpreserve.org

This preserved farm on 450 acres in the heart of Snoqualmie Valley was the site of a Native American village and, later, the world's largest hop ranch.

MOUNT SI GOLF COURSE

9010 Boalch Ave. Southeast, Snoqualmie, 425-391-4926; www.mtsigolf.com

Mount Si used to be the world's largest field for growing hops for beer before being turned into an 18-hole course in the 1930s. Since then, it has undergone several renovations, most recently in 1994, when eight of the holes were completely changed. The change upped the length of the course to more than 6,300 yards, as well moving or adding more than 100 trees. The course has several leagues and sessions for younger golfers to learn the game, making it one of the better organized courses in the Seattle area.

HOTEL
★★★SALISH LODGE & SPA

6501 Railroad Ave., Snoqualmie, 425-888-2556, 800-272-5474;
www.salishlodge.com

Just 30 miles east of Seattle, the Salish Lodge & Spa is a celebration of the rugged beauty of the Pacific Northwest. Nestled in the foothills of the Cascade Mountains, this rustic, understated lodge enjoys a majestic setting amid lush evergreen forests and the Snoqualmie Falls. World-weary travelers quickly adopt a gentle pace here, whether hiking the serene mountain trails or enjoying a hot rock massage in the Asian-inspired spa. Luxurious details such as wood-burning fireplaces, whirlpool tubs and pillow menus ensure maximum comfort, and large windows reveal serene views. Three exceptional restaurants highlight fresh, regional cuisine. 91 rooms. Restaurant, bar. Fitness center. Spa. Whirlpool. $$$

RESTAURANT
★★★SALISH LODGE & SPA DINING ROOM

6501 Railroad Ave., Snoqualmie, 425-888-2556, 800-272-5474;
www.salishlodge.com

With views overlooking the magnificent Snoqualmie Falls, the ambience is one of casual elegance at this rustic lodge restaurant. The menu features dishes such as a tasting quince platter, local seafood and vegetables and regional game like pheasant and elk. Northwestern menu. Breakfast, lunch, dinner, brunch. Closed Monday. Bar. Casual attire. Valet parking. $$$

WASHINGTON

★
★
★
★
★

OAK HARBOR

This trading center on Whidbey Island was first settled by sea captains and adventurers and then in the 1890s by immigrants from the Netherlands, who developed the rich countryside. The town's name was inspired by the oak trees that cloaked the area when the first settlers arrived and have been preserved. Side roads lead to secluded beaches and excellent boating and fishing with marinas nearby.

Information: Chamber of Commerce Visitor Information Center, 32630 Highway 20, Oak Harbor, 360-675-3535; www.oakharborchamber.org

HOTEL

★★BEST WESTERN HARBOR PLAZA

33175 Highway 20, Oak Harbor, 360-679-4567, 800-927-5478, 800-780-7234; www.bestwestern.com/harborplaza

80 rooms. Pets accepted; fee. Complimentary continental breakfast. Restaurant, bar. Outdoor pool. $

OCEAN SHORES

This 6,000-acre area at the southern end of the Olympic Peninsula is a seaside resort community with six miles of ocean beaches, 23 miles of lakes and canals and 12 miles of bay front. Clamming, crabbing, trout and bass fishing are popular.

Information: Chamber of Commerce, Ocean Shores, 360-289-2451, 800-762-3224; www.oceanshores.org

HOTELS

★CANTERBURY INN

643 Ocean Shores Blvd., Ocean Shores, 360-289-3317, 800-562-6678; www.canterburyinn.com

45 rooms. Indoor pool, whirlpool. $

★★SHILO INN

707 Ocean Shores Blvd. Northwest, Ocean Shores, 360-289-4600, 800-222-2244; www.shiloinns.com

113 rooms. Restaurant, bar. Indoor pool, whirlpool. $

OLYMPIA

As though inspired by the natural beauty that surrounds it—Mount Rainier and the Olympic Mountains on the skyline and Puget Sound at its doorstep—Washington's capital city is a carefully groomed, parklike community. Although concentrating on the business of government, Olympia also serves tourists and the needs of nearby military installations. It is a deep-sea port and a manufacturer of wood products, plastics and mobile homes. The tiny village of Smithfield was chosen in 1851 as the site for a customhouse. The U.S. Collector of Customs prevailed on the citizens to rename the community for the Olympic Mountains. Shortly afterward, agitation to separate the land north of the Columbia from Oregon began. In 1853 the new territory was proclaimed with Olympia as territorial capital. The first legislature convened here in 1854, despite conflicts with Native Americans that forced construction of a stockade ringing the town. (The 15-foot wall was later dismantled and used to plank the capital's streets.) The Olympia metropolitan area also includes the communities of Lacey and Tumwater, the oldest settlement in the state north of the Columbia River. The city today has a compact, 20-square-block business section and a variety of stores that attract shoppers from a wide area.

Information: Thurston County Chamber of Commerce, 809 Legion Way Southeast, Olympia, 360-357-3362; www.thurstonchamber.com

WHAT TO SEE AND DO

MIMA MOUNDS NATURAL AREA PRESERVE

I-5 South to exit 95, west on Maytown Road (Highway 121), then 128th Avenue S.W., then North on Waddell Creek Road, Olympia, 360-902-1004; www.dnr.wa.gov

Mounds 8 to 10 feet high and 20 to 30 feet in diameter spread across miles of meadows west of Olympia. Once thought to be ancient burial chambers, they are now believed to be the result of Ice Age freeze-thaw patterns. Trails wind through 500-acre site.

WOLF HAVEN INTERNATIONAL

3111 Offut Lake Road, Tenino, exit 94 off I-90, 1.5 miles east on 93rd Avenue, 1/2 mile south on Old Highway 99, left on Offut Lake Road, 360-264-4695, 800-448-9653; www.wolfhaven.org

The 75-acre sanctuary is home to 40 wolves no longer able to live in the wild. May-September, daily; October-April, Wednesday-Sunday; closed January-February.

YASHIRO JAPANESE GARDENS

Plum Street and Union Avenue, Olympia, 360-753-8380; www.ci.olympia.wa.us

A cooperative project between Olympia and its sister city, Yashiro, Japan, the gardens include a pagoda, bamboo grove, pond and waterfall. Daily during daylight hours.

HOTELS

★BEST WESTERN TUMWATER INN

5188 Capitol Blvd. S.E., Tumwater, 360-956-1235, 800-780-7234; www.bestwestern.com

89 rooms. Pets accepted; fee. Complimentary continental breakfast. Fitness center. High-speed Internet access. **$**

★★GOVERNOR HOTEL

621 S. Capitol Way, Olympia, 360-352-7700, 877-352-7701; www.olywagov.com

125 rooms. Pets accepted; fee. Complimentary full breakfast. Restaurant, bar. Outdoor pool, whirlpool. High-speed Internet access. **$**

★★RED LION

2300 Evergreen Park Drive, Olympia, 360-943-4000, 800-733-5466; www.redlion.com

192 rooms. Pets accepted; fee. Complimentary continental breakfast. High-speed Internet access. Restaurant, bar. Outdoor pool, whirlpool. Fitness center. **$**

RESTAURANT

★★BUDD BAY CAFÉ

525 N.W. Columbia St., Olympia, 360-357-6963; www.buddbaycafe.com

Seafood menu. Lunch, dinner, Sunday brunch. Bar. Children's menu. Casual attire. Reservations recommended. Outdoor seating. **$$**

★
★
★
★
★

OLYMPIC NATIONAL PARK

In these 1,442 square miles of rugged wilderness are such contrasts as the wettest climate in the contiguous United States (averaging 140-167 inches of precipitation a year) and one of the driest; seascapes and snow-cloaked peaks; glaciers and rain forests; elk and seals. With Olympic National Forest, State Sustained Yield Forest No. 1, much private land and several American Indian reservations, the national park occupies the Olympic Peninsula due west of Seattle and Puget Sound.

In 1774, the Spanish explorer Juan Perez was the first European to spot the Olympic Mountains. However, the first major western land exploration did not take place until more than a century later. Since then, generations of adventurous tourists have rediscovered Mount Olympus, the highest peak (7,965 feet), several other 7,000-foot peaks and hundreds of ridges and crests between 5,000 and 6,000 feet high. The architects of these ruggedly contoured mountains are glaciers, which have etched these heights for thousands of years. About 60 glaciers are still actively eroding these mountains; the largest three are on Mount Olympus.

From approximately November-March, the west side of the park is soaked with rain and mist, while the northeast side is the driest area on the West Coast except southern California. The yearly deluge creates a rain forest in the western valleys of the park. Here Sitka spruce, western hemlock, Douglas fir and western red cedar grow to heights of 250 feet with 8-foot diameters. Mosses carpet the forest floor and climb tree trunks. Club moss drips from the branches.

Some 50 species of mammals inhabit this wilderness, including several thousand elk, Olympic marmots, black-tailed deer and black bears. On the park's 60-mile strip of Pacific coastline wilderness, deer, bears, raccoons and skunks can be seen; seals sun on the offshore rocks or plow through the water beyond the breakers. Mountain and lowland lakes sparkle everywhere; Lake Crescent is among the largest. Some roads are closed in winter.

Information: Heart o' the Hills Road, Port Angeles, 119 miles northwest of Olympia on Highway 101, then south on Hurricane Ridge Road, northeast corner of Park, 360-565-3130; www.nps.gov/olym

HOTELS

★★KALALOCH LODGE
157151 Highway 101, Forks, 360-962-2271, 866-525-2562, 888-896-3826; www.visitkalaloch.com
65 rooms. Pets accepted, some restrictions; fee. Restaurant. $

★★SOL DUC HOT SPRINGS RESORT
12076 Sol Duc Hot Springs Road at Highway 101, Port Angeles, 360-327-3583, 866-476-5382, 888-896-3828; www.visitsolduc.com
32 rooms. Closed October-late March. Restaurant. Outdoor pool, mineral pools, children's pool. $

OMAK

This lumber town, the largest in north-central Washington, is also known for its production of apples and its many orchards. The name of the town and nearby lake and

★
★
★
★
★

mountain is derived from a Native American word meaning "good medicine." Omak is the "baby's breath capital of the world" to florists.

Information: Chamber of Commerce, 401 Omak Ave., Omak, 509-826-1880; www.omakchamber.com

HOTEL

★★OKANOGAN INN & SUITES

1 Apple Way, Okanogan, 509-422-6431, 877-422-7070; www.okanoganinn.com

77 rooms. Pets accepted; fee. Restaurant, bar. Outdoor pool, complimentary continental breakfast. High-speed Internet access. Fitness center. **$**

OTHELLO

A beneficiary of the Grand Coulee project, Othello had a population of only 526 in 1950 and today has 10,000 people living in the environs. The Potholes Canal runs by the town, linking the Potholes Reservoir and the smaller Scooteney Reservoir.

Information: Chamber of Commerce, 33 E. Larch, Othello, 866-684-3556; www.othellochamber.com

HOTEL

★★BEST WESTERN LINCOLN INN

1020 E. Cedar St., Othello, 509-488-5671, 800-780-7234; www.bestwestern.com

50 rooms. Pets accepted; fee. Complimentary continental breakfast. Restaurant. Outdoor pool. High-speed Internet access. **$**

PACKWOOD

Named for William Packwood, a colorful explorer who helped open this region, this town is a provisioning point for modern-day explorers of Mount Rainier National Park and Snoqualmie and Gifford Pinchot national forests. A Ranger District office of the Gifford Pinchot National Forest is located here. The area abounds in edible wild berries and mushrooms and no permit is needed for picking. Winter and spring are popular with game watchers and elk, deer, bears and goats can be spotted in the local cemetery as well as in nearby parks.

HOTELS

★COWLITZ RIVER LODGE

13069 Highway 12, Packwood, 360-494-4444, 888-305-2185; www.escapetothemountains.com

32 rooms. Complimentary continental breakfast. Whirlpool. **$**

★CREST TRAIL LODGE

12729 Highway 12, Packwood, 360-494-4944, 800-477-5339; www.cresttraillodge.com

27 rooms. Complimentary continental breakfast. Airport transportation available. **$**

WASHINGTON

★
★
★
★
★

PASCO

One of the "Tri-Cities," Pasco has been nurtured by transportation throughout its history. Still a rail, air, highway and waterway crossroads, Pasco is enjoying increased farm and industrial commerce thanks to the Columbia Basin project.

Information: Greater Pasco Area Chamber of Commerce, 1925 N. 20th St.,
Pasco, 509-547-9755; www.pascochamber.org

SPECIAL EVENT
FIERY FOOD FESTIVAL

509-545-0738; www.pascofieryfoods.com
The Festival provides two fun-filled days with wonderful food, great arts and crafts, fresh fruits and vegetables and entertainment on two stages. Weekend after Labor Day.

HOTEL
★★RED LION

2525 N. 20th Ave., Pasco, 509-547-0701, 800-733-5466; www.redlion.com
279 rooms. Pets accepted. Wireless Internet access. Restaurant, bar. Outdoor pool, whirlpool. Fitness center. Airport transportation available. $

PORT ANGELES

Sitting atop the Olympic Peninsula, Port Angeles has the Olympic Mountains at its back and the Juan de Fuca Strait at its shoreline; just 17 miles across the strait is Victoria, British Columbia. Ediz Hook, a sandspit, protects the harbor and helps make it the first American port of entry for ships coming to Puget Sound from all parts of the Pacific; there is a U.S. Coast Guard Air Rescue Station here. A Spanish captain who entered the harbor in 1791 named the village he found here Port of Our Lady of the Angels, a name that has survived in abbreviated form. The fishing fleet; pulp, paper and lumber mills and tourism are its economic mainstays today.

Port Angeles is the headquarters for Olympic National Park. It is an excellent starting point for expeditions to explore the many faces of the peninsula.

Information: Chamber of Commerce, 121 E. Railroad Ave.,
Port Angeles, 360-452-2363; www.portangeles.org

WHAT TO SEE AND DO
JOYCE DEPOT MUSEUM

16 miles west of Port Angeles on Highway 112, 360-928-3568; www.joycewa.com
The museum is located in a former railroad station. Visitors can browse through general store items from the 1920s through the 1940s, logging equipment and historical railroad equipment. Old photos of the area have been preserved, as well as articles from the former City of Port Crescent newspaper. Stop for a short trip back to the early days of this area.

JOYCE GENERAL STORE

16 miles west of Port Angeles on Highway 112, 360-928-3568; www.joycewa.com
Built in the early 1900s, the Joyce General Store still has the original false front, beaded ceiling, oiled wood floors and fixtures. Much of the interior came from the

Markham House Hotel, which stood in the now-extinct town of Port Crescent. Joyce's namesake, Joe Joyce, transported much of what was used to build the store from Port Crescent (now Crescent Bay) to its present location. The store has been in the same family for more than 48 years.

MERRILL AND RING TREE FARM INTERPRETIVE TOUR
Highway 112, Port Angeles, 800-998-2382;
www.nps.gov/olym
Merrill and Ring Tree Farm and Forestry Trail offers self-guided tours. Along the trail are interpretive resources explaining resource management and reforestation, providing an opportunity to educate visitors about the clear-cuts along the SR 112 corridor. The Merrill and Ring Tree Farm also offers a bit of history, as the site still has the original cabins built by Merrill and Ring to house its loggers in the early 1900s.

SPECIAL EVENT
DUNGENESS CRAB & SEAFOOD FESTIVAL
Festival at various locations, 360-452-6300;
www.crabfestival.org
The annual festival celebrates the region's diverse bounty of seafood, agriculture and maritime traditions. Mid-October.

HOTELS
★PORT ANGELES INN
111 E. Second St., Port Angeles, 360-452-9285, 800-421-0706;
www.portangelesinn.com
24 rooms. High-speed Internet access. Complimentary continental breakfast. $

★★RED LION HOTEL
221 N. Lincoln, Port Angeles, 360-452-9215, 877-333-2733;
www.redlion.com
187 rooms. Pets accepted, some restrictions; fee. Restaurant. Outdoor pool, whirlpool. Wireless Internet access. Fitness center. $

SPECIALTY LODGINGS
DOMAINE MADELEINE
146 Wildflower Lane, Port Angeles, 360-457-4174, 888-811-8376;
www.domainemadeleine.com
The guest rooms at this intimate bed and breakfast are individually decorated. The views of Victoria, British Columbia and the San Juan Islands are magnificent. Five rooms. Children over 12 only. Complimentary full breakfast. Airport transportation available. $$

FIVE SEASUNS BED & BREAKFAST
1006 S. Lincoln St., Port Angeles, 360-452-8248, 800-708-0777;
www.seasuns.com
A restored Dutch Colonial inn built in 1920s, it features a pond and waterfall. Five rooms. Children over 12 years only. Complimentary full breakfast. Whirlpool. $

★
★
★
★
★

TUDOR INN BED & BREAKFAST

1108 S. Oak St., Port Angeles, 360-452-3138, 866-286-2224;
www.tudorinn.com

This Tudor-style bed and breakfast offers guests a historical location from which to enjoy the Pacific Northwest. Visitors can relax in the living room, the library or the inn's natural surroundings while enjoying the view of the Strait of Juan de Fuca. Five rooms. Children over 12 only. Complimentary full breakfast. $

RESTAURANTS

★★BELLA ITALIA

118 E. First St., Port Angeles, 360-457-5442; www.bellaitaliapa.com

Italian menu. Dinner. Bar. Children's menu. Casual attire. Reservations recommended. $$

★★BUSHWHACKER

1527 E. First St., Port Angeles, 360-457-4113; www.bushwhackerpa.com

Seafood menu. Dinner. Bar. Children's menu. Casual attire. $$

★★★C'EST SI BON

23 Cedar Park Road, Port Angeles, 360-452-8888;
www.cestsibon-frenchcuisine.com

French menu. Dinner. Closed Monday. Bar. Casual attire. Reservations recommended. Outdoor seating. $$$

★LANDINGS

115 E. Railroad Ave., Port Angeles, 360-457-6768

Seafood menu. Breakfast, lunch, dinner. Children's menu. Casual attire. Outdoor seating. $

WASHINGTON

★
★
★
★
★

PORT GAMBLE

Captain William Talbot, a native of Maine, discovered the vast Puget Sound timberlands and built what has become the oldest continuously operating sawmill in North America here. Spars for the ships of the world were a specialty. The community, built by the company and still owned by it, gradually developed a distinctive appearance because of its unusual (to this part of the country) New England-style architecture.

The company, realizing an opportunity to preserve a bit of the past, has rebuilt and restored more than 30 homes, commercial buildings and St. Paul's Episcopal Church. Replicas of gas lamps and underground wiring have replaced modern-looking street lighting. The entire town has been declared a historic district.

Information: Kitsap Peninsula Visitor & Convention Bureau, 32220 Rainier Ave.
N.E., Port Gamble, 360-297-8200, 800-416-5615; www.visitkitsap.com

WHAT TO SEE AND DO

OF SEA AND SHORE MUSEUM

General Store Building, 3 Rainier Ave., Port Gamble,
360-297-2426; www.ofseaandshore.com

Of Sea and Shore Museum features one of the largest shell collections in the country along with a gift and book shop. Daily 9 a.m.-5 p.m.

PORT GAMBLE HISTORIC MUSEUM

3 Rainier Ave., Port Gamble, downhill from the General Store,
360-297-8074; www.portgamble.com

Exhibits trace the history of the area and the timber company with displays arranged in order of time including a replica of an old saw filing room and Forest of the Future exhibit. May-October, daily.

PORT LUDLOW

Information: Port Ludlow Olympic Peninsula Gateway Visitor Center,
93 Beaver Valley Road (Highways 104 & 19) Porrt Ludlow,
360-437-0120; www.portludlowchamber.org

HOTEL

★★★INN AT PORT LUDLOW

1 Heron Road, Port Ludlow, 360-437-7000, 877-805-0868;
www.portludlowresort.com

This inn, resting on the shores of the Olympic Peninsula, offers a distinctive charm. Built to resemble an estate in Maine, the inn features rooms with exquisite views, comfortable amenities and tasteful touches. 39 rooms. Complimentary continental breakfast. Restaurant. **$$**

RESTAURANT

★★★THE FIRESIDE

1 Heron Road, Port Ludlow, 360-437-7000, 877-805-0868;
www.portludlowresort.com

Reminiscent of the East Coast's charming summer homes, this veranda-wrapped inn provides a serene setting for waterfront dining at its best. Seafood menu. Dinner. Bar. Children's menu. Casual attire. Reservations recommended. Outdoor seating. **$$**

PORT TOWNSEND

Located on the Quimper Peninsula at the northeast corner of the Olympic Peninsula, this was once a busy port city served by sailing vessels and sternwheelers. Captain George Vancouver came ashore in 1792 and named the spot Port Townsend after an English nobleman. Today Port Townsend is a paper mill town with boat building and farming.

Information: Tourist Information Center, 2437 E. Sims Way, Port Townsend,
360-385-2722, 888-365-6978; www.ptchamber.org

HOTEL

★★INN AT PORT HADLOCK

310 Hadlock Bay Road, Port Hadlock, 360-385-7030, 800-785-7030;
www.innatporthadlock.com

47 rooms. Pets accepted, some restrictions; fee. Wireless Internet access. Restaurant, bar. **$**

WASHINGTON

★
★
★
★
★

SPECIALTY LODGINGS

ANN STARRETT MANSION VICTORIAN BED & BREAKFAST

744 Clay St. at Adams Street, Port Townsend, 360-385-3205, 800-321-0644;
www.starrettmansion.com

Overlooking the mountains and waters of Puget Sound, this bed and breakfast was built in 1889 using Victorian architecture. It is furnished with antiques and decorated with carvings and fine art work, and features a winding staircase and frescoed ceilings. 11 rooms. Complimentary full breakfast. $$

BISHOP VICTORIAN GUEST SUITES

714 Washington St., Port Townsend, 360-385-6122, 800-824-4738;
www.bishopvictorian.com

16 rooms, all suites. Pets accepted, some restrictions; fee. Complimentary continental breakfast. Wireless Internet access. $

F. W. HASTINGS HOUSE OLD CONSULATE INN

313 Walker St., Port Townsend, 360-385-6753, 800-300-6753;
www.oldconsulateinn.com

This elegant and tastefully stylish inn has the feel of an old Victorian manor home. The staff tends to all the details. Eight rooms. Children over 12 only. Complimentary full breakfast. Airport transportation available. $$

HOLLY HILL HOUSE BED&BREAKFAST

611 Polk St., Port Townsend, 360-385-5619, 800-435-1454; www.hollyhillhouse.com

This guest house is located only a short walk from downtown, antique shops, museums, art galleries and restaurants. Some rooms offer a view of the water. Five rooms. Children over 12 only. Complimentary full breakfast. $

JAMES HOUSE

1238 Washington St., Port Townsend, 800-385-1238; www.jameshouse.com

Built in 1889, this grand Victorian mansion sits on a bluff overlooking Puget Sound and mountains. Featuring fine woodwork, furnishings and well-kept gardens, this bed and breakfast is a perfect place for a getaway. 12 rooms. Children over 12 only. Complimentary full breakfast. $

PALACE

1004 Water St., Port Townsend, 360-385-0773, 800-962-0741;
www.palacehotelpt.com

19 rooms. Pets accepted; fee. Complimentary continental breakfast. $$

RESTAURANTS

★★★CASTLE KEY

Seventh and Sheridan streets, Port Townsend, 360-385-5750, 800-732-1281;
www.manresacastle.com

This century-old, European-inspired castle is the home of an elegant yet casual dining room with spectacular views of the Olympic and Cascade Mountains. American menu. Dinner, Sunday brunch. Closed Monday. Bar. Casual attire. Reservation recommended. $$

★★SILVERWATER CAFÉ

237 Taylor St., Port Townsend, 360-385-6448; www.silverwatercafe.com

Seafood menu. Lunch, dinner. Bar. Children's menu. Casual attire. Reservations recommended. **$$**

PULLMAN

A university town and an agricultural storage and shipping center in the fertile Palouse Hills, this community is named for George M. Pullman, the inventor/tycoon who gave his name to the railroad sleeping car.

Information: Chamber of Commerce, 415 N. Grand Ave., Pullman,
509-334-3565, 800-365-6948; www.pullmanchamber.com

HOTELS

★HOLIDAY INN EXPRESS HOTEL & SUITES PULLMAN

S.E. 1190 Bishop Blvd., Pullman, 509-334-4437, 800-465-4329;
www.hiexpress.com/pullmanwa

130 rooms. Complimentary continental breakfast. Restaurant, bar. Business center. Fitness center.

★QUALITY INN PARADISE CREEK

S.E. 1400 Bishop Blvd., Pullman, 509-332-0500, 877-424-6423;
www.qualityinn.com

66 rooms. Complimentary continental breakfast. Pets accepted, some restrictions; fee. Outdoor pool, whirlpool. Airport transportation available. **$**

PUYALLUP

Puyallup freezes the farm produce from the fertile soil and mild climate of the valley between Mount Rainier and Tacoma. A $2 million bulb industry (irises, daffodils and tulips) was born in 1923, when it was discovered that the valley was ideal for growing them. Ezra Meeker crossed the plains by covered wagon and named this city Puyallup (meaning "generous people") after a tribe that lived in the valley; Puyallups still live in the area.

Information: Puyallup/Sumner Chamber of Commerce, 417 E. Pioneer St.,
Puyallup, 253-845-6755; www.puyallupchamber.com

SPECIAL EVENT

PUYALLUP FAIR

Puyallup Fair & Events Center, 110 Ninth Ave. S.W., Puyallup,
253-841-5045, 253-845-1771; www.thefair.com

An annual tradition every September since 1900, the Puyallup Fair is held on fairgrounds about 40 miles south of downtown Seattle for a period of nearly three weeks. The event includes all sorts of entertainment (including racing pigs, hypnotists and local and national musical acts), as well as rodeo competitions, a full carnival with thrill rides and a midway, and a petting farm. There is also a three-day Spring Fair held here in April. Seventeen days in September.

QUINAULT

Quinault, on the shore of Lake Quinault, is the south entrance to Olympic National Park. In the heart of the Olympic National Forest, it is the gateway to any of three valleys—the Hoh, Queets and Quinault—that make up the rain forest, a lushly green ecological phenomenon. It also provides an entrance to the Enchanted Valley area of the park. The Quinault Reservation is two miles west. A Ranger District office of the Olympic National Forest is located here.

Information: Grays Harbor Chamber of Commerce, 506 Duffy St.,
Aberdeen, 360-532-1924; www.graysharbor.org

HOTEL
★★LAKE QUINAULT LODGE

345 South Shore Road, Quinault, 360-288-2900, 800-562-6672,
888-896-3827; www.visitlakequinault.com
92 rooms. Restaurant, bar. Indoor pool. $

QUINCY

Although this area gets only about 8 inches of rain a year, irrigation has turned the surrounding countryside green. Quincy processes and markets farm produce; more than 80 crops are grown in the area. Deposits of diatomaceous earth (soft, chalky material used for fertilizers, mineral aids and filters) are mined in the area and refined in Quincy. Fishing and game bird hunting are good in the surrounding area.

Information: Quincy Valley Chamber of Commerce, 119 F St. S.E.,
509-787-2140; www.quincyvalley.org

HOTEL
★TRADITIONAL INNS

500 F St. S.W., Quincy, 509-787-3525;
www.traditionalinns.com
24 rooms. Pets accepted, some restrictions; fee. $

REDMOND

Redmond experienced dramatic change over the course of the 20th century, evolving from a sleepy logging town to a high-tech hub, a transformation driven by the exponential growth of Microsoft, which is headquartered here. Situated at the northern tip of Lake Sammamish, Redmond boasts safe neighborhoods, excellent schools and a public park system that covers 1,350 acres and more than 25 miles of trails. A wide variety of shops and restaurants can be found at Redmond Town Center. The city is a short drive east of Seattle on Highway 520.

Information: Greater Redmond Chamber of Commerce, 16210 N.E. 80th St.,
Redmond, 425-885-4014; www.redmondchamber.org

WHAT TO SEE AND DO
CELTIC BAYOU IRISH PUB & CAJUN CAFÉ

7281 W. Lake Sammamish Parkway N.E., Redmond,
425-869-5933; www.celticbayou.com
An Irish pub with a laid-back vibe, a Cajun menu and an in-house brewery, Celtic Bayou is a pleasant place to unwind with walls clad in mellow-toned wood, booths

and tables and an outdoor beer garden. The place attracts its fair share of Microsoft employees and other high-tech types. Live music is featured on Saturday nights. Sunday-Monday 11:30 a.m.-10 p.m., Tuesday-Thursday 11:30 a.m.-midnight, Friday-Saturday 11:30-1 a.m.

MARYMOOR PARK

6046 W. Lake Sammamish Parkway, Redmond, 206-205-3661;
www.metrokc.gov

Marymoor Park is the largest, and likely the busiest, park in metro Seattle. With 640 acres of parkland around a historic farmhouse, it is home to the area's only velodrome, as well as a climbing rock, a model airplane field and numerous sports fields. Marymoor is also home to a very popular off-leash dog park, about 40 acres of forest and meadow on the shores of a slow-moving river.

REDMOND TOWN CENTER

76th Street and 166th Avenue, Redmond, 425-867-0808;
www.shopredmondtowncenter.com

This 120-acre, open-air shopping and entertainment hub includes national chains such as Gap, REI, Borders and Eddie Bauer. There are also a number of restaurants (including national chains) and an eight-screen movie theater. Every Saturday from May-October, a farmers' market offers fresh produce and flowers, and on Tuesday evenings in summer, live music can be enjoyed. There are also a number of events for children on the Redmond Town Center calendar. Monday-Saturday 10 a.m.-8 p.m., Sunday 11 a.m.-6 p.m.

225

SAMMAMISH RIVER TRAIL

www.metrokc.gov

An 11-mile paved trail running southeast from Bothell to Redmond, the Sammamish River Trail connects with the Burke-Gilman Trail, forming a 27-mile route that leads to Gas Works Park in Seattle. This peaceful, mostly level trail follows alongside the gentle current of the Sammamish River, passing through Woodinville, its two wineries and the Redhook Ale Brewery a short jaunt off the trail. The trail is popular with joggers, walkers, cyclists and in-line skaters. At the north end of the trail, start your journey at **Bothell Landing Park** (*9919 N.E. 180th St.*). Down south in Redmond, begin your trek at **Marymoor Park** (*6046 W. Lake Sammamish Parkway N.E.*).

WILLOWS RUN GOLF CLUB

10402 Willows Road N.E., Redmond, 425-883-1200; www.willowsrun.com

Willows Run offers an intriguing mix of golf getaway and closeness to civilization during your round. Much of the back nine is built next to an industrial park, but the course has few trees and resembles British Open layouts. There are two 18-hole tracks and a 9-hole par-three course as well. The holes are closely packed, but they are challenging, with plenty of water along either 18. The facility's signature hole is the 17th on the Eagle's Talon course, a long hole with a nearly island green that slopes to the front, assuring that those who do not hit the ball far enough will go fishing.

WASHINGTON

★
★
★
★
★

RICHLAND

Although it's one of the "Tri-Cities," Richland has an entirely different personality due to the 560-square-mile Hanford Works of the Department of Energy, formerly the U.S. Atomic Energy Commission. In 1943, Richland was a village of 250 dedicated to fruit cultivation. A year later, the government established Hanford as one of four main development points for the atomic bomb, along with Oak Ridge, Tennessee; Los Alamos, New Mexico; and the Argonne Laboratory, near Chicago. Hanford no longer is involved in the production of plutonium, and the more than 16,000 employees are now dedicated to environmental cleanup and safe disposal of nuclear and hazardous wastes. Once largely desert, Richland today is surrounded by vineyards and orchards, thanks to irrigation from the Grand Coulee Dam and the Yakima River Irrigation Projects. The city is at the hub of an area of spectacular scenery and outdoor activities within a short drive in any direction.

Information: City of Richland, 505 Swift Blvd., Richland,
509-942-7390; www.ci.richland.wa.us

HOTELS

★HAMPTON INN RICHLAND-TRI CITIES

486 Bradley Blvd., Richland, 509-943-4400, 800-426-7866; www.hamptoninn.com
100 rooms. Pets accepted, some restrictions. Complimentary continental breakfast. Wireless Internet access. Fitness center. Business center. Indoor pool, whirlpool. Airport transportation available. $

★★RED LION

802 George Washington Way, Richland, 509-946-7611, 800-733-5466;
www.redlion.com
149 rooms. Pets accepted; fee. Wireless Internet access. Restaurant, bar. Outdoor pool, whirlpool. Business center. Airport transportation available. $

SAN JUAN ISLANDS

Information: San Juan Islands Visitors Bureau, Friday Harbor,
888-468-3701; www.guidetosanjuans.com

WHAT TO SEE AND DO

SAN JUAN ISLAND

www.sanjuanisland.org
San Juan Island gave birth in 1845 to the expansionist slogan "fifty-four forty or fight" and was the setting for the "pig war" of 1859, in which a British pig uprooted an American potato patch. The subsequent hostilities between the islands' 7 British and 14 American inhabitants reached such proportions that eventually Kaiser Wilhelm I of Germany was called in to act as arbiter and settle the boundaries. During the 13 years of controversy, the pig was the only casualty. This island was the last place the British flag flew within the territorial United States.

On the eastern shore, Friday Harbor, the most westerly stop in the United States on San Juan Islands ferry tour, is the county seat of San Juan. It serves as a base for the salmon fleet and is the major commercial center of the islands.

SAN JUAN ISLANDS

www.guidetosanjuans.com

These 172 islands nestled between the northwest corner of Washington and Vancouver Island, compose a beautiful and historic area. Secluded coves, giant trees, freshwater lakes, fishing camps, modest motels, numerous bed and breakfasts and plush resorts characterize the four major islands. More than 500 miles of paved or gravel roads swing through virgin woodlands and along lovely shorelines. The islands are accessible by ferry from Anacortes.

WHALE MUSEUM

62 First St. N., Friday Harbor, 360-378-4710; www.whale-museum.org

Art and science exhibits document the lives of whales and porpoises in this area. Daily; closed holidays.

HOTELS

★HOTEL DE HARO AT ROCHE HARBOR SEASIDE VILLAGE

248 Reuben Memorial Drive, Roche Harbor, 360-378-2155,
800-451-8910; www.rocheharbor.com

29 rooms. Bar. Outdoor pool. Tennis. $

★★★ROSARIO RESORT

1400 Rosario Road, Eastsound, 360-376-2222, 800-562-8820;
www.rosarioresort.com

Visitors land directly in front of the resort, located at the tip of Orcas Island in Washington's picturesque San Juan Islands, via a thrilling and scenic seaplane ride (less adventurous types may opt for the ferry). This resort is a veritable eden for outdoor enthusiasts; from whale-watching and sea kayaking to nature hikes in Moran State Park, Rosario's backdrop is a playground for visitors. Back at the resort, the Avanyu Spa soothes frayed nerves, and four restaurants satisfy hearty appetites. Fanning out across Cascade Bay, the welcoming guest accommodations reflect the resort's dedication to casual elegance. Rosario Resort is currently closed for renovations. 116 rooms. Restaurant, bar. Fitness center. Spa. Indoor pool, two outdoor pools, children's pool, whirlpool. Airport transportation available. $$

SPECIALTY LODGINGS

ARGYLE HOUSE BED & BREAKFAST

685 Argyle Ave., Friday Harbor, 360-378-4084, 800-624-3459; www.argylehouse.net

Four rooms. Children over 10 only. Complimentary full breakfast. $

FRIDAY'S HISTORIC INN

35 First St., Friday Harbor, 360-378-5848, 800-352-2632; www.friday-harbor.com

Only a short walk from this bed and breakfast are Friday Harbor's waterfront, town shops and restaurants. The property features limited-edition wildlife art, soundproof rooms and a large parlor. 15 rooms. Complimentary continental breakfast. $$

★
★
★
★
★

HILLSIDE HOUSE BED AND BREAKFAST

365 Carter Ave., Friday Harbor, 360-378-4730, 800-232-4730; www.hillsidehouse.com

A contemporary home among acres of fir and pine trees, some rooms overlook the atrium and others have a view of the harbor. Seven rooms. Complimentary full breakfast. **$**

INN AT SWIFTS BAY

856 Port Stanley Road, Lopez Island, 360-468-3636, 888-903-9536;
www.swiftsbay.com

Incredible comfort and unsurpassed amenities are on the top of the list at this Tudor-style bed and breakfast. It lies in the San Juan Islands away from busy city life and offers amazing bedrooms and a great living area, dining room and library. Five rooms. Complimentary full breakfast. **$$**

TUCKER HOUSE BED & BREAKFAST

260 B St., Friday Harbor, 360-378-2783, 800-965-0123; www.tuckerhouse.com

Six rooms. Pets accepted; fee. Complimentary full breakfast. **$**

TURTLEBACK FARM INN

1981 Crow Valley Road, Eastsound, 360-376-4914, 800-376-4914;
www.turtlebackinn.com

The inn is a country farmhouse located on Orcas Island overlooking the clear waters of the Puget Sound. It features spacious guest rooms decorated with antiques and contemporary pieces. Fine dining and unique shopping are nearby. 11 rooms. Complimentary full breakfast. **$$**

RESTAURANTS

★★★CHRISTINA'S

310 Main St., Eastsound, 360-376-4904; www.christinas.net

Christina's is one of the most highly regarded establishments in the northwest. Photos of the owners' Hollywood connections adorn the wall of the small bar. The innovative treatments of meat, fresh northwestern seafood and fowl keep devotees returning. Seafood menu. Dinner. Closed first three weeks in November. Bar. Children's menu. Casual attire. Reservations recommended. Outdoor seating. **$$$**

★★DOWNRIGGERS

10 Front St., Friday Harbor, 360-378-2700; www.downriggerssanjuan.com

Seafood, steak menu. Breakfast, lunch, dinner. Closed on Thanksgiving and Christmas. Bar. Outdoor seating. **$$**

★★MANSION DINING

1400 Rosario Road, Eastsound, 360-376-2152, 800-562-8820;
www.rosarioresort.com

Seafood menu. Breakfast, lunch, dinner. Bar. Children's menu. Casual attire. Reservations recommended. Outdoor seating. **$$$**

SEATTLE

Seattle has prospered from the products of its surrounding forests, farms and waterways, serving as a provisioner to Alaska and Asia. Since the 1950s, it has acquired a new dimension from the manufacture of jet airplanes, missiles and space vehicles, which, along with tourism, comprise the city's most important industries.

The Space Needle, which dominated Seattle's boldly futuristic 1962 World's Fair, still stands, symbolic of the city's forward-looking character. The site of the fair is now the Seattle Center. Many features of the fair have been made permanent. Seattle is on Elliott Bay, nestled between Puget Sound, an inland-probing arm of the Pacific Ocean, and Lake Washington, a 24-mile stretch of fresh water. The city sprawls across hills and ridges, some of them 500 feet high, but all are dwarfed by the Olympic Mountains to the west and the Cascades to the east. Elliott Bay, Seattle's natural harbor, welcomes about 2,000 commercial deep-sea cargo vessels a year. From Seattle's piers, ships wind their way 125 nautical miles through Puget Sound and the Strait of Juan de Fuca, two-thirds of them Asia-bound, the others destined for European, Alaskan and East Coast ports.

On the same latitude as Newfoundland, Seattle is warmed by the Japan Current, shielded by the Olympics from excessive winter rains and protected by the Cascades from midcontinent winter blasts. Only twice has the temperature been recorded at 100 F; there isn't a zero on record.

Five families pioneered this place and named the town for a friendly Native American chief. The great harbor and the timber surrounding it made an inviting combination;

UNDER AND ABOVE GROUND IN DOWNTOWN SEATTLE

Begin in Seattle's Pioneer Square district, the city's original downtown, which was built in the 1890s (after a disastrous fire) as money from the Yukon Gold Rush started pouring in. The architecture is amazingly harmonious (one architect was responsible for nearly 60 major buildings in a 10-block radius) and graciously restored. The area also features the underground tour and many galleries, cafés and antique shops. A collection of totem poles can be found in tree-lined Occidental Park and in Pioneer Square itself.

Continue across Alaskan Way (or take Waterfront Trolley, a vintage streetcar that runs from Pioneer Square to the waterfront to Pike Place Market) to the waterfront. Walk along the harbor, watching ferries dart to and fro, or take a boat tour. Stop at the Seattle Aquarium, located in Waterfront Park at Pier 59, then stop for clam chowder at Ivars, located at Pier 54.

Continue north, recrossing Alaskan Way, and climb to Pike Place Market, eight stories above the harbor on a bluff. There are two ways to do this: there's an elevator hidden at the base of the market, or you can take the Harbor Stairs, a new cascade of steps flanked by shops and gardens. The Pike Place Market is one of Seattle's most interesting destinations, an old-fashioned public market (built around 1910) in a warren-like building with three floors of food, baked goods, ethnic shops, fresh fish and crafts. You could spend hours here. Also in the Market are some of Seattle's best-loved restaurants; many of them have great views over the harbor to the islands and Olympic Mountains to the west. Just down the street is the new Seattle Art Museum with its excellent collection of Northwest Native Art.

WASHINGTON

★
★★
★★
★

shortly thereafter, a sawmill and a salmon-canning plant were in operation. Soon wagon trains were rolling to Seattle through Snoqualmie Pass, a tempting 3,022 feet, lower than any other pass in the northwest.

Isolated at the fringe of the continent by the vast expanse of America, Seattle enjoyed great expectations but few women, an obvious threat to the community's growth and serenity. Asa Mercer, a civic leader and the first president of the Territorial University, went east and persuaded 11 proper young women from New England to sail with him around the Horn to Seattle to take husbands among the pioneers. This venture in long-distance matchmaking proved so successful that Mercer returned east and recruited 100 Civil War widows. Today, many of Seattle's families proudly trace their lineage to these women.

When a ship arrived from Alaska with a "ton of gold" in 1897, the great Klondike Gold Rush was on, converting Seattle into a boomtown. Since then, Seattle has been the natural gateway to Alaska because of the protected Inside Passage; the commercial interests of the two remain tightly knit. Another major event for Seattle was the opening of the Panama Canal in 1914, a tremendous stimulant for the city's commerce.

Information: Seattle-King County Convention & Visitors Bureau, Washington State Convention & Trade Center, Seventh and Pike streets, 206-461-5840; www.seeseattle.org

THE BUZZ ON SEATTLE'S CAFFEINE CULTURE

For most of the 20th century, Seattle was regarded as a great place to partake in fresh fish, not fresh coffee. The emergence of Seattle's coffee scene corresponded with the spectacular success of a local company bearing a now familiar name, Starbucks. Founded in 1971, Starbucks' first coffeehouse opened in the city's Pike Place Market. Not until the mid-1980s, when Starbucks employee Howard Schultz convinced the company's founders to develop a coffee bar culture similar to that found in Milan's espresso bars, did Starbucks' fortunes take off. It soon became a cultural and commercial phenomenon in Seattle and around the globe. Attempting to take advantage of the coffee craze, the likes of Seattle's Best Coffee and Tully's opened numerous Seattle locations, and now it's almost impossible to walk a city block without passing a franchise coffeehouse.

To appreciate Seattle's coffee culture fully, you should visit a few of the city's many independent coffee shops, one of the best being **Espresso Vivace Roasteria** (*901 E. Denny Way; www.espressovivace.com*). Situated on Capitol Hill near the Seattle Center, Espresso Vivace has made espresso preparation an art form, having spent 15 years perfecting the roasting process for its signature beverage. Espresso Vivace even offers an intensive three-day espresso preparation course.

Artists like to gather downtown at the stylish and hip **Zeitgeist Coffee** (*171 S. Jackson St.; www.zeitgeistcoffee.com*). Zeitgeist is particularly crowded on the first Thursday of each month, when the art galleries in and around Pioneer Square stay open late and hundreds of art lovers congregate in the area. Coffee is not the only thing on the menu; Zeitgeist also serves fresh pastries and grilled sandwiches.

Visitors to the Queen Anne neighborhood should stop by **Uptown Espresso** (*525 Queen Anne Ave. N.; www.uptownespresso.net*). Weekends are particularly crowded at this casual coffeehouse situated at the bottom of Queen Anne Hill. Uptown Espresso's velvet foam lattes are a local favorite. The coffeehouse features vintage décor and the artwork of local painters.

WHAT TO SEE AND DO

5 AVENUE THEATER
1308 Fifth Ave., Seattle, 206-625-1900, 888-584-4849; www.5thavenue.org
This historic theater, which opened as a vaudeville house in 1926, now features musicals, concerts, films and lectures. Its ornate interior, modeled after some of China's architectural treasures, may well distract you from whatever's taking place onstage.

ACT THEATRE
700 Union St., Seattle, 206-292-7676; www.acttheatre.org
ACT Theatre presents contemporary (read: edgy and daring) pieces as well as classic plays and musicals. Performances are held in two main theaters in Kreielsheimer Place, a renovation of the historic Eagles Auditorium completed in 1996. The Allen, a theater in the round, was carved out of the old auditorium's floor; the top row of seats is actually at ground level. The Falls features a restored Joshua Green Foundation Vault, used by the Eagles as a bank vault.

ALDERWOOD MALL
3000 184th St. Southwest, Lynnwood, 425-771-1211; www.alderwoodmall.com
The largest shopping center in north Seattle, the Alderwood Mall is an upscale retail and entertainment destination with shops in an indoor village and on outdoor terraces, as well as a 16-screen movie theater. Of the 120-plus stores, Alderwood's anchors include Nordstrom. Monday-Thursday 10 a.m.-9:30 p.m., Friday-Saturday 10 a.m.-10 p.m., Sunday 11 a.m.-7 p.m.

ALKI BEACH
1702 Alki Ave. S.W., Seattle, 206-684-4075; www.seattle.gov/parks
Skirting the northwestern waterfront of the South Seattle neighborhood, the 2 1/2-mile Alki Beach is a mecca for outdoor types of all kinds—joggers, divers, bicyclists, beach volleyball players, sunbathers and rollerbladers. The beach, administered by the Seattle Parks Department, runs from Duwamish Head to Alki Point on Elliot Bay and offers stunning views of Puget Sound and the city skyline. Facilities are a notch above the norm with scads of picnic tables, a playground, small boat access and a wide, multiuse path. At Alki Point (the southern end of the beach), there is a bathhouse/art studio and a plaque commemorating the landing of the first settlers here in 1851. At Duwamish Head (the northern tip of the beach) are the sea-walled site of a former amusement park and a miniature version of the Statue of Liberty. April 15-October 1, 6 a.m.-11 p.m.; October 2-April 14, 4 a.m.-11:30 p.m.

★
★
★
★
★

ARGOSY HARBOR CRUISE
Pier 55 Alaskan Way, Seattle, 206-623-1445, 800-642-7816;
www.argosycruises.com
Boasting a 50-year history in Seattle's harbors, the family-owned Argosy Cruises is in proud possession of a fleet of nine cruise ships, ranging in size from the 36-foot *Queen's Launch* to the 180-foot *Royal Argosy*. The company operates from piers at the Seattle waterfront, Lake Union and suburban Kirkland (on the eastern shore of Lake Washington). The most basic Argosy outing is a one-hour Harbor Cruise, which

explores Seattle's downtown shoreline and offers some nice skyline views. Longer options include the Locks Cruise, which meanders from the salty waters of Puget Sound to Lake Union via the Ballard Locks, and a pair of lake cruises that explore Lake Union and Lake Washington. Snacks and beverages are offered on every Argosy cruise, but food is not included in the ticket price—the exceptions being ritzy lunch and dinner trips on the *Royal Argosy*. Daily.

BAINBRIDGE ISLAND

Chamber of Commerce, 590 Winslow Way East, Bainbridge Island, 206-842-3700; www.bainbridgechamber.com

Reached via a half-hour ferry trip from downtown Seattle (ferries depart regularly throughout the day), Bainbridge Island is the size of Manhattan but a world apart. In the late 1800s, the island boasted the world's largest sawmill and a substantial shipbuilding industry, but its economy stumbled. It has recently regained footing as a tourist destination. With about 20,000 residents, the city of Bainbridge Island is now known for its delightful Victorian architecture and abundant shops and galleries. Densely wooded and lush with greenery, the island also attracts outdoor enthusiasts of all stripes and boasts an active arts and entertainment scene. **The Bainbridge Island Historical Museum** (*215 Ericksen Ave., Northeast; www.bainbridgehistory.org*) is a great starting point, presenting displays on the island's geology, history and industry in a converted 1908 schoolhouse.

BALLARD LOCKS

2606 N.W. 58th St., Seattle, 206-783-7059; www.ci.seattle.wa.us

Popularly known as the Ballard Locks because of their location in Seattle's Ballard neighborhood, the Hiram M. Chittenden Locks are a marvel of engineering. Built in the early 20th century by the U.S. Army Corps of Engineers, the locks are part of the canal system that connects salty Puget Sound (and, by extension, the Pacific Ocean) to Seattle's freshwater, providing safe passage for watercraft. Salmon use a man-made fish ladder here to navigate their annual spawning migration past the locks. Underwater observation windows afford visitors a firsthand look at the migrating fish (and the seals and sea lions that feast on them, which workers struggle to keep out), but only at certain times of the year; the coho and chinook runs peak in midsummer. A visitor center presents exhibits that detail the lock's history and ecology, and an impressively vibrant botanical garden is also onsite. May-September, Daily 7 a.m.-9 p.m.; October-April, Thursday-Monday 7 a.m.-8 p.m.

CAPITOL HILL

12th Avenue to Boren Avenue and East Madison Street to Denny Way, Seattle; www.ci.seattle.wa.us

Melding metropolitan chic, Victorian elegance and urban grunge just east of downtown, Capitol Hill is one of Seattle's oldest and grandest neighborhoods and, today, is the nexus of the city's youth culture and gay scene. Broadway, the heart of Capitol Hill and one of the city's liveliest thoroughfares, has hip nightclubs, eateries and tattoo parlors to spare. The neighborhood also features an eclectic mix of stores that cater to fashion plates, tattooed punks, antique lovers and everyone in between. The primary shopping areas here are on Broadway (home to a bevy of youth fashion and resale shops, music retailers and unusual bookstores), 15th Street (plenty of home and garden stores with a more upscale slant than Broadway), and Pike and Pine streets (a mix of antique stores, florists, coffee shops and funky specialty retailers).

CENTER FOR WOODEN BOATS

1010 Valley St., Seattle, 206-382-2628; www.cwb.org

Located north of downtown on the southern tip of Lake Union, this is a hands-on maritime heritage museum with a focus on historic wooden sailboats, kayaks and canoes. Visitors can learn time-tested boat-building skills from master craftsmen, take sailing lessons or rent a classic sailboat for a spin around the lake. The center also provides the setting for numerous annual festivals and boat shows. Winter, daily 11 a.m.-5 p.m.; spring and fall, daily 10 a.m.-6 p.m.; summer, daily 10 a.m.-8 p.m.

CENTRAL LIBRARY

1000 Fourth Ave., Seattle, 206-386-4636; www.spl.org

The Central Library opened to much acclaim in 2004. The library was designed by famed Dutch architect Rem Koolhaas, winner of the 2000 Pritzker Prize, his profession's highest honor. With a transparent exterior of diamond-shaped panes of glass, the library stands as a marvel of contemporary architecture. The interior is equally amazing, highlighted by the Books Spiral, a series of tiers and ramps winding through four floors of book stacks. The library features more than 400 public computers and wireless Internet access is available throughout the facility. Built at a cost of $165.5 million, the 11-level library exemplifies Seattle's passion for books and learning. Monday-Thursday 10 a.m.-8 p.m., Friday-Saturday 10 a.m.-6 p.m., Sunday noon-6 p.m.

CENTURY BALLROOM

915 E. Pine, Seattle, 206-324-7263, 206-325-6500;
www.centuryballroom.com

Home to one of Seattle's largest dance floors (2,000 square feet of refinished wood), the stylishly restored Century Ballroom is the place to go for swing and salsa dancing in the Emerald City. Many nights are themed (tango night, salsa night, swing night). For those with two left feet, lessons are offered; while most are multiweek endeavors, there are occasional one-shot workshops. With a full bar, seating at comfortable tables and a cavernous downtown location, the venue also hosts a number of concerts every month, mostly jazz acts and singer/songwriters. A popular restaurant here serves lunch, dinner and Sunday brunch. The cuisine is eclectic with a menu that melds the Far East with the Deep South (e.g., potpies and Vietnamese noodle bowls). Daily.

WASHINGTON

★
★
★
★
★

CHINATOWN INTERNATIONAL DISTRICT

Fourth Avenue to Interstate 5 and Yesler to South Dearborn Street;
www.ci.seattle.wa.us

Southeast of downtown, the colorful International District is home to one of the largest and most vibrant Asian communities in the United States. It took root in the late 19th century, and the neighborhood is now home to one of the most diverse ethnic populations in the world. Asian markets and eateries of all kinds dot the streets. Top attractions include the Wing Luke Asian Museum, the Nippon Kan Theatre and Uwajimaya, a huge food market and cooking school.

DIMITRIOU'S JAZZ ALLEY
2033 Sixth Ave., Seattle, 206-441-9729; www.jazzalley.com
Widely considered the best jazz club in Seattle, the downtown venue originally opened in the University District in 1979, then moved downtown in 1985, and has seen performances by such big names as Taj Mahal and Eartha Kitt. The atmosphere is refined, with chairs and tables surrounding the circular stage and a mezzanine overlooking it. A renovation in 2002 expanded Jazz Alley's capacity and bolstered the sound system while retaining the heralded ambiance. A restaurant serves an international menu with many Italian and northwestern dishes. Tuesday-Sunday; doors open Tuesday-Saturday 5:30 p.m., Sunday 4:30 p.m.

DISCOVERY PARK
3801 W. Government Way, Seattle, 206-386-4236; www.cityofseattle.net
An in-city wildlife sanctuary and nature preserve, the 534-acre Discovery Park is the largest park in Seattle. Located on the western shores of the swanky Magnolia neighborhood, it is centered on a tall bluff that formerly served as a post for the U.S. Army, making for great views of the Olympic Mountains to the west and the Cascades to the east and granting waterfront access to the north and west. An extensive trail system lures joggers, bikers and other fitness buffs from all over the city, but the educational program is at the heart of the park's mission; hence the "Discovery" tag. School buses and day campers frequent the park year-round, but the events calendar has something for every age and interest. A diverse population of flora and fauna calls the park's dunes, thickets, forests and tide pools home. Tuesday-Sunday 8 a.m.-5 p.m.

DOWNTOWN SHOPPING DISTRICT
First to Seventh avenues and Madisonto and Pine streets, Seattle,
www.downtownseattle.com
Prime window-shopping corridors include First and Second Avenues, populated by fashionable boutiques, upscale galleries and a few quirky curiosities to boot and Fifth and Sixth Avenues, brimming with jewelers, kitchen stores and clothing stores ranging from small boutiques to mega sized versions of national staples. There are also two malls on Pine Street: Westlake (between Fourth and Fifth Avenues), a fairly typical enclosed shopping center, and the ritzy Pacific Place Mall, downtown Seattle's newest (and most stylish) retail destination. The centerpiece of the whole shopping district is Nordstrom (500 Pine St.), the flagship of the Seattle-based department store chain.

DRUIDS GLEN GOLF COURSE
29925 207th Ave. S.E., Covington, 253-638-1200; www.druidsglengolf.com
Completed in June 2003, Druids Glen offers affordable prices, the backdrop of Mount Rainier and a sparkling new course. The second hole offers a view of the majestic mountain from the tee box. Several holes require difficult shots over water right off

the tee or on the approach to the green. Four different pros are available for private lessons, and the practice facility is unblemished.

EXPERIENCE MUSIC PROJECT

325 Fifth Ave. N., Seattle, 206-770-2700, 877-367-7361; www.emplive.com

More than 30 years after his death, legendary rock guitarist Jimi Hendrix remains Seattle's favorite native son, and this thoroughly modern museum is a tribute to the huge impact of his short life. Financed by Microsoft cofounder and Hendrix fanatic Paul Allen, the $200 million museum opened in 2000. The striking architecture's sharp angles, contrasting textures and bright hues evoke the image of a smashed guitar and the rhythms of rock and roll. The facilities within are similarly cutting-edge, from the grand hall/musical venue dubbed the "Sky Church" to Crossroads, an exhibit space that meshes historical artifacts with multimedia to present the history of American music. Food and drink (and live music) are available at the contemporary Revolution Bar & Grill. Memorial Day-Labor Day, Daily 10 a.m.-8 p.m.

FREEWAY PARK

700 Seneca St., Seattle, 206-864-4075; www.seattle.gov/parks

This 5-acre park features dramatic water displays. Daily 6 a.m.-11:30 p.m.

FREMONT DISTRICT

Bounded by Fremont Avenue and 46th Street, Seattle;
www.ci.seattle.wa.us

Undoubtedly Seattle's funkiest neighborhood, Fremont wears its eccentricity like a badge: The self-proclaimed "Center of the Universe" went as far as to declare facetious independence from Seattle in 1994. North of downtown and the Lake Washington Ship Canal, the former lumber-mill center is now an artists' paradise, well known for such public sculptures as a towering statue of Vladimir Lenin, a post-Cold War import from the former Soviet Union; the Fremont Troll, gobbling a VW Beetle under Aurora Bridge; and Waiting for Interurban, six cast aluminum figures waiting for the bus. The area is also home to a high concentration of brewpubs, coffee shops, secondhand stores and galleries. Typical shopping strips line Fremont Avenue, Fremont Place, and 34th and 35th streets.

FRYE ART MUSEUM

704 Terry Ave., Seattle, 206-622-9250; www.fryeart.org

In a city where abstract and postmodern art are the norm, the conservative Frye Art Museum bucks the trend by focusing solely on representational art: contemporary and classic landscapes and portraits. The works are both dark and bright (in both tint and theme) and are all bathed in natural light in simple, classic settings. Among the artists represented here are Winslow Homer and Andrew Wyeth. The café and the bookstore here are both excellent and worth a visit. Tuesday-Wednesday, Friday-Saturday 10 a.m.-5 p.m., Thursday to 8 p.m., Sunday noon-5 p.m.; closed holidays.

★
★
★
★
★

GAS WORKS PARK

2101 N. Northlake Way, Seattle, 206-684-4075; www.seattle.gov/parks

A former gas-processing plant on the north side of Lake Union, the 20-acre Gas Works Park is a model for urban renewal and a magnet for kite flyers. The plant's facilities have been nicely converted for recreational use: the boiler house is now a picnic area and the exhauster-compressor building is now the Play Barn, a brightly painted playground for kids. The 12 1/2-mile Burke-Gilman trail begins here, offering a paved route north to suburban Kirkland for joggers and bikers. Daily 4 a.m.-11:30 p.m.

GOLDEN GARDEN PARK

8498 Seaview Place N.W., Seattle, 206-684-7254; www.seattle.gov/parks

Nestled on the bluffs that front Puget Sound in Seattle's Ballard neighborhood, Golden Gardens Park attracts sunbathers and fishermen to its beach and pier and all sorts of outdoor buffs to its myriad recreational opportunities. The park's trail system connects the beach with the forested bluffs above with a leash-optional dog park at the summit. A teen center on the beach called the Brick House features concerts and other events year-round.

GOLF CLUB AT NEWCASTLE

15500 Six Penny Lane, Newcastle, 425-793-4653; www.newcastlegolf.com

Some of the best views in the Seattle area can be found at Newcastle, which includes sightlines of the city's skyline and Mount Rainier. There are two courses, the Coal Creek and the China Creek, with the latter the more difficult of the two. There is a putting course and a practice facility for warming up before your round and an excellent restaurant and bar for afterwards.

★
★
★
★
★

GRAY LINE BUS TOURS

4500 W. Marginal Way S.W., Seattle, 206-624-5077, 800-426-7532;
www.graylineofseattle.com

Tours include the fast-paced City Sights tour of Seattle neighborhoods and the self-paced hop-on/hop-off Double Decker tour, as well as the day-long Boeing and Mount Rainier tours.

GREEN LAKE PARK

7201 E. Green Lake Drive N., Seattle, 206-684-4075; www.seattle.gov/parks/

Ground zero for jogging in fitness-crazy Seattle, Green Lake is the heart of a bustling 320-acre park of the same name. Two paved trails encircle the lake and see a good deal of use from a cross-section of ages and speeds. Each trail is about three miles around the lake and there are separate lanes for bikers, walkers and runners. Trails aside, the lake itself is a recreation destination: a private company provides boat rentals and the Green Lake Small Craft Center offers rowing, sailing and canoe classes and organizes several annual regattas. The lush park surrounding Green Lake is home to a pitch-and-putt golf course and an indoor pool, as well as a community center, tennis courts, picnic tables and a children's playground.

JEFFERSON PARK GOLF CLUB

4101 Beacon Ave. S., Seattle, 206-762-4513;
www.seattlegolf.com

Seattle's Jefferson Park is a short, par-70 layout, but it doesn't cost quite as much as other courses in the area. There is also a par-three course on the grounds, but it's the big course people come for, with a hilly layout that is challenging at times but still playable for just about any golfer. Go for the views as much as the golf.

KLONDIKE GOLD RUSH NATIONAL HISTORICAL PARK

319 Second Ave. S., Seattle, 206-220-4240; www.klondikegoldrushwa.areaparks.com

The 1897 gold strike in the Canadian Yukon triggered an influx of tens of thousands of prospectors to Seattle and its commercial district, Pioneer Square. Motivated by dreams of riches, they arrived here to purchase food, equipment and pack animals in preparation for the arduous six-month trip into the frozen wilderness of the Klondike Gold Fields. While the gold rush provided an economic boost to the city, it was an economic failure for nearly all of the prospectors. Only a handful struck it rich. Most discovered no gold, and many lost their lives during the trek across the steep, snow-covered trail leading to the Klondike. The stampede of prospectors spurred commercial development in Pioneer Square, where the Klondike Gold Rush National Historical Park is located. The National Historical Park offers exhibits, audiovisuals and ranger programs that document the gold rush and its impact on Seattle. Daily 9 a.m.-5 p.m.

LAKE WASHINGTON CANAL

Seen from Seaview Avenue N.W. or N.W. 54th Street;
www.nws.usace.army.mil

Chittenden Locks raises and lowers boats to link saltwater and freshwater anchorages. More than 400,000 passengers and 6 million tons of freight pass through annually. Commodore Park and a salmon ladder with viewing windows are on the south side.

MUSEUM OF FLIGHT

9404 E. Marginal Way S., Seattle, 206-764-5720; www.museumofflight.org

As a major hub for plane-maker Boeing, Seattle is the ideal location for this impressive air and space museum. The facility is highlighted by the soaring Great Gallery, home of more than 50 vintage aircraft, many of which are suspended in formation six stories above the ground. On display here are the original presidential Air Force One and a replica of the Wright Brothers' biplane from Kitty Hawk, N.C., alongside mint-condition models of the first fighter jet (a 1914 Caproni Ca 20) and the first jumbo jet (a prototype Boeing 747). Many planes are open for visitors to sit in the cockpit or explore the hold. Located near Seattle-Tacoma International Airport in southern Seattle, the museum is also home to the restored Red Barn, where the Boeing Company was founded nearly a century ago, and several space-themed exhibits. Daily 10 a.m.-5 p.m., first Thursday of each month 10 a.m.-9 p.m., closed Thanksgiving Day and Christmas Day.

WASHINGTON

★
★
★
★
★

MUSEUM OF HISTORY AND INDUSTRY

2700 24th Ave. E., Seattle, McCurdy Park, 206-324-1126; www.seattlehistory.org

The showcase of the Seattle Historical Society, this excellent facility (popularly known as MOHAI) tracks the people and events that have shaped Seattle over its 150-year history. With a collection of more than a million photographs and historical artifacts, MOHAI gives visitors a comprehensive look into the social and economic roots of the Puget Sound area. The Great Seattle Fire is documented by an exhibit complete with a historic fire engine, murals and other relics of the disaster that razed the city in 1889; a mock-up of an 1880s street scene gives visitors a glimpse into the prefire Emerald City. Another highlight is the comprehensive collection of souvenirs from the 1962 World's Fair. Daily 10 a.m.-5 p.m., first Thursday of month to 8 p.m.

NORTHWEST OUTDOOR CENTER

2100 Westlake Ave. N., Seattle, 206-281-9694, 800-683-0637; www.nwoc.com

A 20-year-old Seattle institution on the docks of Lake Union, the Northwest Outdoor Center is a major hub for the Pacific Northwest's paddling community. At this combination school/store/guide service, over 100 kayaks are available for rental and a full slate of whitewater and sea kayaking classes, ranging from a 2 1/2-hour session to a six-day immersion, are offered. The center's guided tours include day trips spent sea kayaking in Puget Sound and multiday wildlife-watching adventures that take participants to the San Juan Islands and beyond. A bit off the beaten path, sunset and nighttime excursions explore Lake Union and the Lake Washington Ship Canal and the water elevator known as the Ballard Locks. The Northwest Outdoor Center is also the best source of paddling information and advice in the city.

★
★
★
★
★

PACIFIC SCIENCE CENTER

200 Second Ave. N., Seattle, 206-443-2001; www.pacsci.org

With subject matter that balances cutting-edge technology and natural history, the center features such permanent exhibits as an indoor butterfly house, a room-sized model of Puget Sound and "Dinosaurs: A Journey Through Time," complete with seven robotic dinosaurs; on the other side of the science spectrum is Tech Zone, where visitors can challenge a robot to a game of tic-tac-toe. Beyond the permanent and seasonal exhibits, movies are shown on a pair of giant-sized IMAX screens (one of which is coupled with a 3D projector) and there are astronomy demonstrations in the onsite planetarium and dazzling light displays with rock-and-roll soundtracks in the Adobe Laser Dome. Tuesday-Friday 10 a.m.-5 p.m.; Saturday-Sunday to 6 p.m.

PARAMOUNT THEATRE

911 Pine St., Seattle, 206-467-5510; www.theparamount.com

This 75-year-old theater brings a wide range of entertainment to Seattle: Broadway plays and musicals, ballet and modern dance performances, jazz and rock-and-roll concerts and comedy acts. It also shows silent films and hosts family-oriented entertainment. Checkout the Publix theater organ, one of only three remaining, which has been magnificently restored.

PIKE PLACE MARKET

First Avenue and Pike Street, 206-682-7453; www.pikeplacemarket.com

Farmers established the Pike Place Market in 1907 because they were tired of middle-men taking more than their fair share. Today, the indoor/outdoor market is a Seattle landmark and a cornucopia for the senses, with burly guys tossing fresh fish back and forth at the fish market, bin after bin of fresh, colorful fruits, vegetables and flowers, the sounds and sights of street performers and the wares of hundreds of artists on display. Pike Place Market also has dozens of restaurants and food stands, a day spa, barbershop, tattoo parlor and dating service onsite. Just two blocks east of the waterfront, the market is a quick walk from the center of downtown and surrounded by eateries and bars. Guided tours are available Wednesday-Sunday year-round. Monday-Saturday 10 a.m.-6 p.m., Sunday 11 a.m.-5 p.m.

PIONEER SQUARE

Bounded by First Avenue, James Street and Yesler Way (Community Association at 202 Yesler Way), Seattle, 206-667-0687; www.pioneersquare.org

Seattle's oldest neighborhood, the original Pioneer Square saw its beginnings in the early 1850s but soon met a blazing fate in the Great Seattle Fire of 1889. Today's Pioneer Square was built atop the scorched remains, resulting in a ghostlike underground beneath the city streets. (The Underground Tour allows visitors to explore this buried history.) The area boomed again after the lure of gold began attracting miners during the following decade, and a seedy underbelly (that remains to this day) followed in their wake. Now dominated by stately (and inflammable) Victorian and Romanesque red bricks above cobblestone squares, the neighborhood is a commercial and social hub: a melting pot of offices, stores, galleries, restaurants and nightclubs wedged between downtown and a pair of major stadiums, Safeco Field (baseball) and Qwest Field (football).

ROCK BOTTOM BREWERY

1333 Fifth Ave., Seattle, 206-623-3070; www.rockbottom.com

This brewpub in the heart of downtown Seattle is one of the flagships of the Rock Bottom chain, which consists of about 30 breweries in the United States. At any given time at least six beers are on tap, all of which are brewed onsite with Washington grown hops. The menu is varied, with burgers, pizzas, salads and steaks served inside in an upstairs dining room and a downstairs bar/poolroom or outside on a breezy patio.

SEATTLE AQUARIUM

1483 Alaskan Way, Seattle, 206-386-4300; www.seattleaquarium.org

A waterfront mainstay at Pier 59 since 1977, the Seattle Aquarium is an engrossing educational experience for curious minds of all ages. The top facility of its kind in the region, the aquarium is home to nearly 400 species of fish, birds, marine mammals and other sea life. The staff has celebrated several breakthroughs over the years, including the first live births of sea otters in North American captivity, which has happened six times here, and the rearing of a giant Pacific octopus to adulthood, another first. Another highlight is the underwater dome, which allows guests to immerse themselves in a transparent bubble on the bottom of a fish-filled, 400,000-gallon tank. An IMAX theater is adjacent, charging separate entry fees. Daily 9:30 a.m.-5 p.m.

WASHINGTON

SEATTLE ART MUSEUM

1300 First Ave., Seattle, 206-625-8900; www.seattleartmuseum.org

Its entrance guarded by an animated, 48-foot-tall sculpture named *Hammering Man*, the Seattle Art Museum (known locally as SAM) is the premiere facility of its kind in the Pacific Northwest. There is something for everybody here, from ancient Greek sculpture to modern Russian decorative art. Held in particularly high regard are the collections of contemporary art (with pieces by Andy Warhol, Jackson Pollock and Roy Lichtenstein) and northwest coast Native American art (comprised of nearly 200 masks, sculptures and household items). Temporary exhibitions are similarly diverse. A dynamic events calendar helps distinguish the museum, offering up a bevy of concerts, films, lectures, demonstrations, family programs and classes. Admission is waived on the first Thursday of every month, and a restaurant and two gift shops are onsite. Tuesday-Wednesday and Friday-Sunday 10 a.m.-5 p.m., Thursday 10 a.m.-9 p.m.

MARION OLIVER MCCAW HALL

305 Harrison St., Seattle, 206-684-7200; www.seattlecenter.org

The Opera House is home to the Seattle Opera Association, Pacific Northwest Ballet and Seattle Symphony. Bagley Wright Theatre is home to Seattle Repertory Theatre.

SPACE NEEDLE

400 Broad St., Seattle, 206-905-2180, 800-937-9582; www.spaceneedle.com

First a sketch on a placemat, then the centerpiece of the 1962 World's Fair and now Seattle's face to the world, the Space Needle is one of the most distinctive structures in the United States. Capping the 605-foot tower, the flying saucer-inspired dome is symbolic of both the Seattle Worlds Fair's theme—"Century 21"—and the coinciding national push into space. The dome houses an observation deck (with stunning city views) and SkyCity, a revolving restaurant that goes full circle every 48 minutes. There is also a banquet facility 100 feet above street level and a gift shop at the tower's base, where visitors board an elevator for the 43-second journey to the top. The Space Needle is the setting for one of the West Coast's premiere New Year's Eve celebrations every December 31.

SUR LA TABLE

84 Pine St., in Pike Place Market, Seattle, 206-448-2244;
www.surlatable.com

In the 1970s, Seattle spawned this clearinghouse for hard-to-find kitchen gear, and it soon became known as a source for cookware, small appliances, cutlery, kitchen tools, linens, tableware, gadgets and specialty foods. Sur La Table has since expanded to include cooking classes, chef demonstrations and cookbook author signings, as well as a catalog and online presence. Cooking connoisseurs discover such finds as cool oven mitts, zest graters, copper whisks, onion soup bowls and inspired TV dinner trays. Daily.

TEATRO ZINZANNI

222 Mercer St., Seattle, 206-802-0015; www.teatrozinzanni.org

An avant-garde dinner theater with a sister facility in San Francisco, Teatro ZinZanni offers entertainment like nothing else in town: a hyper-imaginative circus/nightclub act hybrid of music, comedy, trapeze, Kabuki and magic.

UNDERGROUND TOUR

608 First Ave., Seattle, 206-682-4646; www.undergroundtour.com

A fun and funny look at Seattle's colorful past, Bill Speidel's Underground Tour takes guests on a journey under the streets of Pioneer Square, where remnants of the frontier town that met its fiery end in 1889 still remain. The tour begins in a bar (Doc Maynard's Public House) and lasts about an hour and a half. Daily; closed holidays; advance reservations recommended.

BURKE MUSEUM OF NATURAL HISTORY AND CULTURE

17th Avenue N.E. and N.E. 45th Street, Seattle, 206-543-5590;
www.washington.edu/burkemuseum/

The Burke Museum is Washington State's official museum of natural and cultural history and a research hub for the entire Pacific Northwest. With its collections in anthropology, geology, zoology and botany, the museum is in possession of five-million specimens. The facility houses a pair of notable permanent exhibits (in addition to a number of rotating temporary displays each year): "The Life and Times of Washington State," a look at the last 500 million years of the state's geology and biology (with fossils and skeletons galore), and "Pacific Voices," which delves into the rich melting pot of cultures present in the Pacific Northwest. Also onsite is the Erna Gunther Ethnobotanical Garden, alive with hundreds of plants used by the region's natives, as well as a café and a gift shop. Daily 10 a.m.-5 p.m., first Thursday of the month 10 a.m.-8 p.m.

UNIVERSITY VILLAGE SHOPPING

45th Street N.E., Seattle, 206-523-0622; www.uvillage.com

Located near the University of Washington campus in northeast Seattle, University Village has a rare balance of national and local establishments.

VICTORIA CLIPPER CHARTERS

2701 Alaskan Way, Pier 69, Seattle, 206-448-5000, 800-888-2535,
250-382-8100 (Victoria, B.C.); www.victoriaclipper.com

This tour company operates a fleet of high-speed, passenger-only ferries on routes among Seattle, the San Juan Islands in Puget Sound, and Victoria, Canada. The trip to Victoria takes about two hours, and VCC offers many packages that integrate hotel stays, recreational excursions and other transportation. There are also narrated whale-watching cruises and the clippers have basic cafés and duty-free shops on board.

WEST SEATTLE GOLF COURSE

4470 35th Ave. Southwest, Seattle, 206-935-5187; www.seattlegolf.com

This public course, designed by course architect H. Chandler Eagan and opened in 1940, has drawn good reviews over the years. You can usually get on for less than $30, and early-bird specials make it even cheaper. It's a good course on which to learn, something the course staff realizes and is willing and able to help with.

WING LUKE ASIAN MUSEUM

407 Seventh Ave. South, Seattle, 206-623-5124; www.wingluke.org

An apt counterpart to the Seattle Asian Art Museum, the Wing Luke Asian Museum in Seattle's busy International District illuminates the Asian-American experience in

WASHINGTON

★
★
★
★
★

a historical and cultural light. A collection of diverse artifacts details the 200-year history of Asians in the Pacific Northwest. Another permanent exhibit, the Densho Project, allows visitors to access oral histories recorded by Japanese Americans who were detained in World War II-era internment camps. Tuesday-Friday 11 a.m.-4:30 p.m., Saturday-Sunday noon-4 p.m.; closed holidays.

WOODLAND PARK ZOO

5500 Phinney Ave. N., Seattle, 206-548-2500; www.zoo.org

One of the biggest and best zoos in the country sits in the park of the same name in north Seattle. The exhibits focus on ecosystems instead of single species: the Alaska enclosure is home to Kodiak bears that catch live trout out of a stream; Tropical Asia inhabitants include elephants, tapirs and orangutans; and the African Savannah features giraffes, hippos and zebras. There is also a Komodo dragon display, a petting zoo, Bug World (with such denizens as millipedes, scorpions and tarantulas), and an enclosed aviary housing hawks, falcons and owls. The special events calendar is dense and varied with breakfasts and overnighters for kids, as well as lectures, festivals and holiday happenings. Daily.

SPECIAL EVENTS
BUMBERSHOOT

Seattle Center, 206-281-7788; www.bumbershoot.com

This annual 4-day music fest is the largest of its kind on the West Coast. Legendary artists and rising stars alike perform in more than 30 different indoor and outdoor venues, stages and galleries. Bumbershoot also features poetry, dance, comedy and contemporary art exhibits. Labor Day weekend.

CHILLY HILLY BICYCLE CLASSIC

Bainbridge Island, Seattle, 206-522-3222; www.cascade.org

One of *Bicycle* magazine's top four recreational bike rides in the United States, this 33-mile course on Bainbridge Island attracts thousands of riders for a one-day organized ride in February. The course starts at the ferry dock and makes many gains and losses in elevation (with 2,700 feet of elevation change in all) before skidding to a stop at a finish line festival with a huge chili feast. Late February.

FREMONT OKTOBERFEST

Fremont District, 35th Avenue and Fremont Avenue N., Seattle;
www.fremontoktoberfest.org

The eccentric Fremont neighborhood puts its own stamp on the traditional Bavarian beer-drinking festival with a rambunctious chainsaw pumpkin-carving contest, a street dance, polka-dancing lessons and live bands that run the gamut from mainstream to bizarre. Held in the shadows of the Aurora Avenue Bridge, this street fair is considered one of the top Oktoberfest festivals outside of Germany, taking place over the course of the third weekend in September. The rowdy beer garden here is quite a sight, serving up a wide variety of beers (including root beer for kids) with an emphasis on local microbrews. The street fair is free and open to the public, but admission is charged to enter the beer garden; six beer tokens and a souvenir cup are included. Late September.

★
★
★
★
★

OPENING DAY REGATTA

1807 E. Hamlin St., Seattle, 206-325-1000; www.seattleyachtclub.org

A Seattle tradition since the 1910s, the opening day of yachting season takes place every year on the first Saturday in May with such featured events as a boat parade and a rowing regatta. Most of the action is centered on the Montlake Cut, which links Lake Washington and Lake Union, and there are a number of great viewpoints on and near the campus of the University of Washington. May.

SEATTLE INTERNATIONAL FILM FESTIVAL

321 Mercer St., at Seattle Center, Seattle, 206-324-9996; www.seattlefilm.com

Held annually from late May-mid-June, Seattle's top-notch film fest is one of the largest cinema showcases in the United States. While the content tends toward documentaries and international independent films, Hollywood is also well represented.

SEATTLE MARATHON

Downtown, Seattle, 206-729-3660; www.seattlemarathon.org

Held annually in late November, the Seattle Marathon is open to runners and walkers of all skill levels and registers more than 10,000 entrants each year. Much of the hilly, scenic route runs along the Lake Washington shoreline, taking entrants from the Seattle Center to Seward Park in southeast Seattle and back again. A kids' marathon, a half marathon and a marathon walk are also held. Late November.

SEATTLE REP

155 Mercer St., Seattle, 206-443-2222, 877-900-9285; www.seattlerep.org

Short for Seattle Repertory Theatre, the award-winning Seattle Rep is one of the top regional non profit theater companies in the United States. Two stages host six to 10 productions a year with the emphasis on presenting challenging dramatic works and time-tested classics injected with fresh perspectives. September-June.

SEATTLE TO PORTLAND BICYCLE CLASSIC

Seattle, 206-522-3222; www.cascade.org

This 200-mile road race draws up to 8,000 riders each year for a one- or two-day tour through Washington and Oregon's forests and farmlands starting at University of Washington. Early July.

HOTELS

★★★ALEXIS

1007 First Ave., Seattle, 206-624-4844, 866-356-8894; www.alexishotel.com

This luxury boutique hotel has been in operation since the turn of the 20th century, making it as much a Seattle landmark as the Space Needle. Warm tones and antiques fill the elegantly appointed rooms, which feature Aveda bath amenities, private bars, plush terrycloth bath robes and soft Egyptian cotton bed linens. A friendly staff offers services like evening turndown with chocolates, morning coffee, a complimentary evening wine reception and a concierge who assists guests with every aspect of their trip. The Library Bistro, a 1940s-style supper club, offers contemporary American cuisine in a cozy, bookstore-like setting, while the Bookstore Bar is the perfect spot

WASHINGTON

★
★
★
★
☆

to unwind with a cocktail at the end of the day. 109 rooms. Wireless Internet access. Restaurant, bar. Spa. **$$**

★★COURTYARD SEATTLE DOWNTOWN/LAKE UNION

925 Westlake Ave. North, Seattle, 206-213-0100, 888-236-2427;
www.courtyard.com
250 rooms. High-speed Internet access. Restaurant, bar. Fitness center. Indoor pool, whirlpool. **$$**

★★★★THE FAIRMONT OLYMPIC HOTEL

411 University St., Seattle, 206-621-1700, 800-257-7544; www.fairmont.com
The Fairmont Olympic Hotel brings grand tradition and pampering service to downtown Seattle. Carefully blending its 1920s Italian Renaissance heritage with 21st-century hospitality, The Fairmont is conveniently located in Rainier Square, only minutes from the city's top attractions. The guest rooms and suites are tasteful retreats with floral draperies, soft pastel colors and period furnishings, while fresh fruit and flowers make guests feel at home. The bounty of the Pacific Northwest is the focus at The Georgian, where pale yellow walls and crystal chandeliers set a refined tone. Shuckers is a popular oyster bar at which Seattle's famous microbrews are savored, and a selection of cocktails is available at The Terrace. Traditional high tea service is a treat worth making time for. 450 rooms. Pets accepted, some restrictions; fee. High-speed Internet access. Restaurant, bar. Fitness center. Spa. Indoor pool, whirlpool. **$$$**

★★GASLIGHT IN

1727 15th Ave., Seattle, 206-325-3654; www.gaslight-inn.com
Eight rooms. Children not allowed. Complimentary continental breakfast. Wireless Internet access. Outdoor pool. **$**

★★★GRAND HYATT SEATTLE

721 Pine St., Seattle, 206-774-1234, 888-591-1234; www.grandseattle.hyatt.com
The Grand Hyatt Seattle brings a contemporary dash to Seattle's bustling financial and business district. From the wired public spaces ideal for meetings and conferences to the fantastic in-room digital concierges, this hotel is a technology aficionado's paradise. Earth tones and Asian inspiration create a sanctuary-like ambience in the guest rooms and suites, where well-defined workspaces are a boon to business travelers. Large windows frame striking city or Puget Sound views, and guests can enjoy some quiet time soaking in the tub in oversized bathrooms. The Grand Hyatt offers a comprehensive fitness center and a variety of dining options, from Starbucks to Ruth's Chris Steakhouse. 425 rooms. Wireless Internet access. Restaurant, bar. Spa. Whirlpool. **$$$$**

★HAMPTON INN & SUITES DOWNTOWN

700 Fifth Ave. N., Seattle, 206-282-7700, 800-426-7866; www.hamptoninn.com
198 rooms. Complimentary continental breakfast. High-speed Internet access. Business Center. Fitness center. **$$**

★HOMEWOOD SUITES DOWNTOWN SEATTLE

206 Western Ave. W., Seattle, 206-281-9393, 800-225-5466;
www.homewoodsuites.com

161 rooms. Pets accepted, some restrictions; fee. Complimentary full breakfast. Business Center. Fitness center. **$$**

★★★HOTEL ÄNDRA

2000 Fourth Ave., Seattle, 206-448-8600, 877-448-8600; www.hotelandra.com

The Hotel Ändra combines northwest and Scandinavian design influences, creating a warm and inviting retreat in Seattle's vibrant Belltown neighborhood. Situated near art galleries, boutiques and restaurants, the hotel appeals to travelers who like to be out and about, getting a taste for the local scene. Guests are greeted by a dramatic lobby fireplace built from split-grain granite and bookended by a pair of golden maple bookcases. Above the fireplace, a plasma screen projects a collection of electronic fine art. Rooms include such luxuries as 300-thread-count cotton linens, goose down pillows and alpaca headboards. 119 rooms. Wireless Internet access. Restaurant, bar. Fitness center. Airport transportation available. Spa. **$$**

★★HOTEL DECA

4507 Brooklyn Ave. N.E., Seattle, 206-634-2000, 800-899-0251;
www.hoteldeca.com

158 rooms. Complimentary continental breakfast. Wireless Internet access. Restaurant, bar. **$$**

★★★HOTEL MAX

620 Stewart St., Seattle, 206-728-6299, 866-986-8087;
www.hotelmaxseattle.com

Sleek and chic, this boutique hotel caters to your every need with a spiritual menu, pillow menu, and Asian fusion menu in the Red Fin restaurant. Decorated with more than 350 original paintings and photos, the hotel's contemporary design features modern furniture including teak wood desks in the guest rooms. Pacific Northwesterners are caffeine addicts and aficionados for a reason. And the pillow-top mattresses, Aveda bath amenities, Torrefazione coffee and Tazo tea will energize your visit. 165 rooms. Wireless high-speed Internet access. Restaurant, bar. Fitness center. Business center. Pets accepted.

★★★HOTEL MONACO

1101 Fourth Ave., Seattle, 206-621-1770, 800-715-6513;
www.monaco-seattle.com

This hip hotel is centrally located near the waterfront, Pike Place Market, the Seattle Art Museum, convention centers and shops. Guests will enjoy the intimate setting: palettes of reds, yellows and blues; wrought iron chandeliers; and comfortable furnishings. The complimentary evening wine reception in the two-story lobby is the perfect place for guests to relax in front of the fireplace or mingle with others. Pets are accepted, and the hotel offers (upon request) a temporary pet goldfish for lonely pet owners. Both leisure and business travelers will enjoy the Southern-inspired restaurant, Sazerac. 189 rooms. Pets accepted, some restrictions. Wireless Internet access. Restaurant, bar. Spa. **$$$**

WASHINGTON

★
★
★
★

★★★HOTEL VINTAGE PARK

1100 Fifth Ave., Seattle, 206-624-8000, 800-853-3914; www.vintagepark.com

Built in 1922, this beautifully renovated hotel offers well-appointed and finely furnished (rich fabrics and cherry furniture) guest rooms, each named after a local winery or vineyard. Popular with business travelers, it is centrally located in the heart of the city just steps from shops, theaters and restaurants. Visitors will enjoy the comfortable lobby while sitting by the fireplace and tasting local wines and microbeers—a complimentary reception is held every night. After the reception, Tulio Ristorante, the in-house Italian cuisine restaurant and a local favorite, is the perfect place to grab a bite. 126 rooms. Pets accepted. Restaurant, bar. High-speed Internet access. Fitness center. $$

★★★THE INN AT EL GAUCHO

2505 First Ave., Seattle, 206-728-1337, 866-354-2824; www.elgaucho.com

Seattle's hip Belltown district is the setting for the ultra-swank Inn at El Gaucho. Guests will find rooms equipped with many luxurious amenities, including pillow-top beds with soft Egyptian cotton linens, rainfall showerheads, L'Occitane bath products, oversized Egyptian cotton towels, plasma TVs and CD players. The Inn understands that guests may find it hard to break away from the magnificent rooms, so in-room dining—with bedside preparation—is provided by the downstairs El Gaucho steakhouse. 18 rooms. Wireless Internet access. Restaurant, bar. Complimentary continental breakfast. $$

★★★INN AT HARBOR STEPS

1221 First Ave., Seattle, 206-748-0973, 888-728-8910; www.innatharborsteps.com

Guests of this inn on Seattle's waterfront will find themselves near all of the city's best attractions, including shops, galleries, cafés, Harbor Steps Park, Woodland Park Zoo and Pike Place Market. Rooms are elegant yet urban with floral-patterned bed spreads and furniture, fireplaces, garden views and sitting areas, as well as wet bars, refrigerators and high-speed Internet access. 28 rooms. Complimentary full breakfast. High-speed Internet access. Fitness center. Indoor pool, whirlpool. $$

★★★INN AT THE MARKET

86 Pine St., Seattle, 206-443-3600, 800-446-4484; www.innatthemarket.com

Seattle's renowned creative spirit is perhaps best felt at the delightful Inn at the Market. This boutique hotel enjoys a prime location at the vibrant Pike Place Market, overlooking the waters of Elliott Bay. Picturesque views and cultural attractions are just outside the door at this country-chic home-away-from-home. The spacious and stylish accommodations are the last word in comfort, with in-room massages and special Tempur-Pedic mattresses ensuring restful sleep. The rooftop garden provides the perfect place to daydream or keep watch on the goings-on at the market below. From guest privileges at the Seattle Club's state-of-the-art fitness facility (fee) to in-room dining provided by Café Campagne, guests reap the rewards of the inn's market location. 70 rooms. Pets accepted, some restrictions. Wireless Internet access. Restaurants, bar. $$$

★★★MARRIOTT SEATTLE AIRPORT

3201 S. 176th St., Seattle, 206-241-2000, 888-236-2427; www.marriott.com

The Marriott Seattle Airport offers a convenient location across from the airport. The indoor pool under an atrium is a nice touch with screening plants to give swimmers a sense of privacy. A nearby spa offers opportunities for pampering. Try the concierge level for services beyond the ordinary. 459 rooms. Wireless Internet access. Restaurant, bar. Indoor pool, whirlpool. Airport transportation available. $$

★★★MAYFLOWER PARK HOTEL

405 Olive Way, Seattle, 206-623-8700, 800-426-5100; www.mayflowerpark.com

The historic Mayflower Park Hotel offers a much-sought-after location in the heart of Seattle near the Monorail system, many eclectic shops and attractions like Pike Place Market and Seattle Center—but this beautiful hotel is still a destination on its own. First opened in 1927 as The Bergonian, the Mayflower has since been renovated to recapture the grandeur and classic style of days gone by. Guest rooms are luxuriously appointed with beautiful furnishings, rich fabrics, large-screen televisions, fluffy bath robes and Baudelaire bath amenities, while everyone from the Concierge to room service staff provides friendly and gracious service. The hotel's bar, Oliver's, consistently comes out on top in Seattle's annual Martini Classic Challenge. 171 rooms. Wireless Internet access. Restaurants, bar. $$

★★★PAN PACIFIC SEATTLE

2125 Terry Ave., Seattle, 206-264-8111; www.panpacific.com

Located in Seattle's South Lake Union neighborhood, this contemporary, upscale hotel is close to the city's best shopping. Rooms are of-the-moment with luxury linens, large plasma TVs, DVD players and free wireless Internet access. The hotel is connected to a shopping area that includes everything from a day spa to Starbucks, Whole Foods and several restaurants. 160 rooms. Wireless Internet access. Restaurant. Bar. $$$

★★THE PARAMOUNT

724 Pine St., Seattle, 206-292-9500, 800-716-6199; www.coasthotels.com

146 rooms. Restaurant, bar. Business Center. Fitness center. High-speed Internet access. $$

★★★RENAISSANCE SEATTLE HOTEL

515 Madison St., Seattle, 206-583-0300, 888-236-2427;
www.renaissancehotels.com

Located in the heart of Seattle, this hotel combines contemporary décor of marble and glass with earth-toned colors that convey a warm, rich ambience. Guests have magnificent city views from the 25th floor, where the indoor pool is located. Nearly everything that defines Seattle is less than a mile away: Pike Place Market and the waterfront, Pioneer Square, Safeco Field (home of the Mariners) and Qwest Field. 558 rooms. Pets accepted, some restrictions; fee. High-speed Internet access. Restaurant, bar. Indoor pool, whirlpool. $$

★★SALISBURY HOUSE BED & BREAKFAST

750 16th Ave. E., Seattle, 206-328-8682;
www.salisburyhouse.com

Five rooms. Complimentary full breakfast. Wireless Internet access. $

WASHINGTON

★
★
★
★
★

★★★W SEATTLE HOTEL

1112 Fourth Ave., Seattle, 206-264-6000, 888-625-5144;
www.whotels.com

The W Seattle Hotel combines cutting-edge style with top-notch comfort and cute and quirky touches like a candy necklace in the in-room munchies box. Young children may not be the best fit for the decidedly upscale atmosphere, but if you want your every business need catered to or are seeking a romantic getaway, look no further than the bright colors and cool leather of W Seattle. The lobby, adjacent bar and dining room are contenders in the "now" scene of Seattle. 426 rooms. Pets accepted, some restrictions; fee. High-speed Internet access. Restaurant, bar. $$$$

★★★SEATTLE MARRIOTT WATERFRONT

2100 Alaskan Way, Seattle, 206-443-5000, 800-455-8254; www.marriott.com

This waterfront hotel affords fantastic views of the city skyline, the Olympic Mountains, Mt. Rainier and Elliott Bay. Common areas feature modern touches like colorful blown-glass displays and eclectic mosaic tile floors, while guest rooms feature CD players, luxurious bedding with down comforters and pillows and complimentary Starbucks coffee service. The onsite restaurant, Fish Club, offers seafood-focused dishes with a Mediterranean influence along with a beautiful atmosphere, which includes floor-to-ceiling windows, chandeliers and floral arrangements. 358 rooms. Wireless Internet access. Restaurant, bar. Indoor pool, outdoor pool, whirlpool. Fitness center. $$$

★★★THE SHERATON SEATTLE HOTEL

1400 Sixth Ave., Seattle, 206-621-9000, 800-325-3535; www.sheraton.com/seattle

Located in the heart of Seattle's vibrant downtown area, The Sheraton Seattle Hotel offers a great location near many of the city's attractions, including Key Arena and Seattle Center, as well as close proximity to world-class shopping and fantastic dining. Guest rooms feature a host of amenities to make a stay here pleasant and comfortable, including Sheraton's signature "Sweet Sleeper Bed." 1,258 rooms. Pets accepted, some restrictions. Wireless Internet access. Restaurant, bar. Fitness center. Indoor pool. $$

★★★SORRENTO HOTEL

900 Madison St., Seattle, 206-622-6400, 800-426-1265; www.hotelsorrento.com

This historic Seattle hotel remains close to the attractions of downtown while maintaining an unparalleled intimacy. Jewel tones, stunning fabrics and rich mahogany furnishings set a regal ambience. Guest accommodations are the very definition of elegance, with brocade fabrics, marble baths, plush amenities and distinctive artwork. From knowledgeable concierges to shiatsu massage therapists, the hotel's seamless service makes it a perfect place for business and leisure travelers alike. Home to the Hunt Club, one of Seattle's revered landmarks, the Sorrento whets visitors' appetite with the cozy Fireside Room and the seasonal outdoor Café Palma. 76 rooms. Pets accepted, some restrictions; fee. Wireless Internet access. Restaurant, bar. Airport transportation available. $$$

SPECIALTY LODGINGS

ACE HOTEL

2434 First Ave., Seattle, 206-448-4721; www.acehotel.com

The ultra-hip Ace Hotel bills itself as the ultimate lodging for the urban nomad on a mission of experience. Modeled after European hotels, Ace presents a stylish décor with modern furnishings and clean white walls throughout. Rooms feature exposed brick walls, lofted ceilings and hardwood floors. Half of the hotel's accommodations have private bathrooms, while the other half utilize shared facilities. Each private bathroom is entered through a revolving door that's hidden in the wall. All rooms include a sink and vanity. 28 rooms. Pets accepted. Wireless Internet access. $$

CHAMBERED NAUTILUS BED & BREAKFAST

5005 22nd Ave. N.E., Seattle, 206-522-2536, 800-545-8459;
www.chamberednautilus.com

Built in 1912 by a professor at the University of Washington, this quaint Georgian colonial bed and breakfast offers cozy and distinctive rooms just a short walk from campus. Each antique-filled guest room offers a private bath and phone as well as its own resident teddy bear; there's also a library/sitting room with a fireplace and a sundeck. 10 rooms. Children over eight only. Complimentary full breakfast. Wireless Internet access. Pets accepted, fee. Business center. $

RESTAURANTS

★★★AL BOCCALINO

1 Yesler Way, Seattle, 206-622-7688; www.seattleslittleitaly.com

This intimate Italian restaurant in Pioneer Square features soft antique lighting and candlelit tables that set the stage for many marriage proposals or other special occasion celebrations. The owner, Carlos Tager, is a nightly fixture and warmly greets each guest. The menu features dishes from northern and southern Italy, but diners in the know come Sunday-Thursday to indulge in the five-course dinner-for-two offerings. Italian menu. Lunch, dinner. Closed Sunday; holidays. Business casual attire. Reservations recommended. Bar. $$

★★★ANDALUCA

407 Olive Way, Seattle, 206-382-6999; www.andaluca.com

With an intimate atmosphere and a James Beard Award-winning chef, Andaluca has had no problem maintaining its reputation as a favorite place to dine in Seattle. Mediterranean-influenced fare using local ingredients, such as chilled green gazpacho with Dungeness crab and grilled double-cut lamb chops with almond and current couscous keep both locals and tourists coming back time and time again. Mediterranean menu. Breakfast, lunch, dinner. Bar. Children's menu. Casual attire. Reservations recommended. Valet parking. $$

★★★ASSAGGIO RISTORANTE

2010 Fourth Ave., Seattle, 206-441-1399; www.assaggioseattle.com

Diners feel like family when they enter this Italian Belltown restaurant. The executive chef/owner Mauro Golmarvi meets and greets every person. The atmosphere is friendly, and the décor is Renaissance style with Michelangelo replica murals, wood booths, soft sconce lighting and intimate tables. The restaurant's authentic

Italian cuisine emphasizes the North Central Adriatic region of Italy, and Mauro takes numerous trips to Italy each year to replenish his wine offerings. Italian menu. Lunch, dinner. Closed Sunday. Casual attire. Reservations recommended. Valet parking. Outdoor seating. $$

★★ATLAS FOODS

2675 N.E. University Lane, Seattle, 206-522-6025; www.chowfoods.com
International, seafood menu. Breakfast, lunch, dinner, brunch. Bar. Children's menu. Business casual attire. Reservations recommended. $$

★BLUWATER BISTRO

1001 Fairview Ave. North, Seattle, 206-447-0769; www.bluwaterbistro.com
American, seafood menu. Lunch, dinner. Bar. Children's menu. Business casual attire. Reservations recommended. Valet parking. Outdoor seating. $$

★★★BRASA

2107 Third Ave., Seattle, 206-728-4220; www.brasa.com
Seattle's trendy residents gather at Brasa to indulge in chef Tamara Murphy's robust, Mediterranean-inspired fare. Two of the signature dishes show off the kitchen's culinary brilliance: the roast suckling pig and the mussels and clams served oven-steamed in a cataplana (a double-domed copper pot). All dishes are layered with the bold flavors of Spain, Portugal, France and Brazil. Brasa serves wonderful food that dazzles the palate and the eye and expertly balances the rustic and the sophisticated. Mediterranean menu. Dinner. Bar. Casual attire. Reservations recommended. Valet parking. $$$

★★★BRASSERIE MARGAUX

Fourth Avenue and Lenora Street, Seattle, 206-777-1990; www.margauxseattle.com
This French brasserie adjacent to the beautiful Warwick Seattle Hotel offers breathtaking views of the Seattle skyline, making it a great choice for special occasion meals. The intimate dining room is decorated with warm dark woods, upholstered chairs and candlelit tables. The menu specializes in northwest cuisine with French influences, and Brasserie Margaux is the only dining room in Seattle that carves prime rib tableside. For a special dining experience, try the wine pairing dinner—a delicious and educational choice. American, French menu. Breakfast, lunch, dinner, weekend brunch. Bar. Casual attire. Valet parking. $$$

★★CAFÉ CAMPAGNE

1600 Post Alley, Seattle, 206-728-2233; www.campagnerestaurant.com
French bistro menu. Breakfast, lunch, dinner, brunch. Bar. Casual attire. Reservations recommended. Outdoor seating. $$

★★★CAFÉ FLORA

2901 E. Madison St., Seattle, 206-325-9100; www.cafeflora.com
There are people who believe that the words *delicious* and *innovative* could never be used to describe vegetarian cuisine, but Café Flora proves them wrong. Since 1991,

this Seattle gem has been turning out perfect plates of fresh and nutritious fare that consistently receives raves from both vegetarians and carnivores alike. Herbs from the restaurant's own garden are used in seasonal dishes like mushroom asparagus risotto with artichoke bottoms, pine nuts, scallions, mascarpone and parsley oil. Vegetarian menu. Lunch, dinner, weekend brunch. Closed holidays. Children's menu. Reservations recommended. $$

★★CAFÉ LAGO

2305 24th Ave. East, Seattle, 206-329-8005; www.cafelago.com

Italian menu. Dinner. Closed holidays. Bar. Children's menu. Casual attire. $$$

★★★CAMPAGNE

86 Pine St., Seattle, 206-728-2800; www.campagnerestaurant.com

This charming French restaurant is located at Inn at the Market in the popular Pike Place Market. Its delicious menu focuses on regions of southern France and features entrées such as boneless rib eye steak with green peppercorn sauce; roasted leg of lamb on tomato, basil and marrow bean ragout with lamb jus and pan-roasted brined duck breast served on ratatouille. A majority of its ingredients are supplied from the local farmers market. French menu. Dinner. Bar. Casual attire. Reservations recommended. Outdoor seating. $$$

★★★CANLIS RESTAURANT

2576 Aurora Ave. N., Seattle, 206-283-3313; www.canlis.com

Guests come for the serene and spectacular views of Lake Union and the Cascade Mountains, but the ever-attentive service keeps them coming back. American, Pacific Northwest menu. Dinner. Closed Sunday; December; holidays. Bar. Jacket required. Reservations recommended. Valet parking. Casual attire. $$$$

★★CARMELITA

7314 Greenwood Ave. N., Seattle, 206-706-7703; www.carmelita.net

Vegan, vegetarian menu. Dinner. Closed Monday. Bar. Casual attire. Outdoor seating. Reservations recommended. $$

★★★CHEZ SHEA

94 Pike St., Seattle, 206-467-9990; www.chezshea.com

Tucked into Pike Place Market is Chez Shea, an old-world charmer featuring the finest ingredients of the northwest prepared with French technique and regional gusto. The intimate, candlelit dining room boasts picture-perfect views of the sun setting over the Puget Sound and is usually filled with couples well versed in the art of cross-table handholding. But locals in the know about cuisine dine here as much for the food as for the cozy ambience. The four-course prix fixe menu features hearty, home-style regional fare that makes use of local produce as the seasons dictate. The chocolate torte and the harvest apple cake are worth the splurge. An eight-course chef's tasting menu is also available. French bistro menu. Dinner, late-night. Closed Monday. Bar. Casual attire. Reservations recommended. Valet parking. $$$

★
★
★
★
★

★★★DAHLIA LOUNGE

2001 Fourth Avenue at Virginia Street, Seattle, 206-682-4142;
www.tomdouglas.com/dahlia

Chef/owner Tom Douglas (a James Beard Award winner) and his wife Jackie Cross (both also of Palace Kitchen and Etta's Seafood) oversee this fun, artsy eatery in the heart of downtown. Red walls, yellow pillars, glass sconces and chandeliers and upholstered booths create a colorful, playful backdrop for boldly flavored Pacific Northwest cuisine. The daily changing menu offers diners a variety of inventive beef, seafood and poultry dishes. Diners with a sweet tooth can visit the Dahlia Bakery next-door for take-home treats. American Pacific Northwest menu. Lunch, dinner. Bar. Casual attire. Reservations recommended. $$$

★★DULCES LATIN BISTRO

1430 34th Ave., Seattle, 206-322-5453; www.dulceslatinbistro.com

Latin American menu. Dinner. Closed Sunday-Monday. Bar. Reservations recommended. $$

★★★EARTH AND OCEAN

1112 Fourth Ave., Seattle, 206-264-6060; www.earthocean.net

A trendy, chic clientele matches the restaurant's New York-inspired scene with its ultrahip décor and fusion cuisine. Multicolored mosaic floors and candles decorate the room, and artfully prepared and creatively named dishes make up the tasting-style menu. Located in the W Seattle hotel, this downtown restaurant is also a great people-watching spot. American, Pacific Northwest menu. Breakfast, lunch, dinner, weekend brunch. Bar. Casual attire. Reservations recommended. Valet parking. $$

★★★EL GAUCHO

2505 First Ave., Seattle, 206-728-1337; www.elgaucho.com

Located just a few minutes from the center of downtown, this swanky, nostalgic restaurant—a former union hall for merchant seamen—is known mainly for its martinis and meat. Diners will also enjoy tableside preparations of Caesar salad, chateaubriand and bananas Foster. Nightly piano music sets the mood for an enjoyable meal, and the lively lounge area is the perfect place for a before- or after-dinner cocktail. Steak menu. Dinner, late-night. Closed holidays. Bar. Business casual attire. Reservations recommended. Valet parking. $$$

★★★ETTA'S SEAFOOD

2020 Western Ave., Seattle, 206-443-6000; www.tomdouglas.com

With an atmosphere as colorful as the food, Etta's brings in droves of hungry patrons both day and night. This casual seafood house is located just half a block from the popular Pikes Peak Market and is named after the owners' daughter, Loretta. Its large windows overlook the bustling farmers market, which supplies a majority of the fresh ingredients on the menu. There's something on the menu for everyone, from fish and chips to juicy crab cakes to Oregon country beef rib eye steak. Seafood menu. Lunch, dinner, weekend brunch. Bar. Children's menu. Casual attire. Reservations recommended. $$$

★
★
★
★
★

★★★FLYING FISH

2234 First Ave., Seattle, 206-728-8595; www.flyingfishseattle.com

At this hip Belltown seafood house, guests will find Asian-influenced fish dishes that are artfully presented in a fun and casual environment. The décor is eclectic with glass chandelier "tubes" hanging from a "popcorn" ceiling and various fish sculptures dotting the room. Chef/owner Christine Keff is committed to using fresh, organic ingredients. The fish served here comes directly from Puget Sound, and the organic produce is supplied by a farm in the Green River Valley, resulting in a wonderfully tasty dining experience. Seafood menu. Lunch, dinner, late-night. Closed holidays. Bar. Casual attire. Reservations recommended. Outdoor seating. $$

★★F.X. MCRORY'S STEAK CHOP & OYSTER HOUSE

419 Occidental Ave. South, Seattle, 206-623-4800; www.fxmcrorys.com

Steak menu. Lunch, dinner. Bar. Children's menu. Casual attire. Reservations recommended. Outdoor seating. $$$

★★★★THE GEORGIAN

411 University St., Seattle, 206-621-7889; www.fairmont.com/seattle

The Fairmont Olympic Hotel in Seattle houses this, the most acclaimed restaurant in the Pacific Northwest. The restaurant's elegant décor features crystal chandeliers, arched ceilings and potted palms. Executive chef Gavin Stephenson brought his culinary expertise to the restaurant after honing his skills first at the Savoy Hotel in London and then as personal chef to Saudi Prince Alwaleed Bin Talal Alsaud. While expressing a mastery of all dishes related to seafood, Gavin also excels on terra firma with such dishes as carpaccio of artichokes and spring asparagus, ashed goat cheese and tomato mousseline, filet of Kobe beef topped with shallot and oxtail braisage and double chocolate napoleon. American, French, Northwest menu. Breakfast, lunch, dinner. Bar. Children's menu. Business casual attire. Reservations recommended. Valet parking. $$$$

★★★HUNT CLUB

900 Madison St., Seattle, 206-343-6156; www.hotelsorrento.com

An elegant and intimate dining experience awaits guests here. The food is classic and American, and the use of fresh, seasonal ingredients makes each dish memorable. International menu. Breakfast, lunch, dinner, weekend brunch. Bar. Children's menu. Business casual attire. Reservations recommended. Valet parking. $$$

★★IL BISTRO

93A Pike St., Seattle, 206-682-3049; www.ilbistro.net

Italian menu. Dinner, late-night. Bar. Casual attire. Reservations recommended. Outdoor seating. $$$

★★★IL TERRAZZO CARMINE

411 First Ave. S., Seattle, 206-467-7797;
www.ilterrazzocarmine.com

High standards and a faithful clientele make this the darling of Italian restaurants in Seattle. While guests enjoy relaxing in the beautifully designed dining area, it's the fresh fare, well-selected wine list and impeccable service that are truly appreciated

WASHINGTON

here. Surprisingly, this classic Italian restaurant is located within an office building, but this is quickly forgotten as guests enter the dining room. Carmine's personal artwork graces the walls, the ceiling is accented with wood beams and the outdoor patio gives diners the option to enjoy their meal alfresco. Only the freshest ingredients are used in chef Smeraldo's distinctive pasta, veal, beef and chicken dishes. Italian menu. Lunch, dinner. Closed Sunday; holidays. Bar. Business casual attire. Reservations recommended. Valet parking. Outdoor seating. $$$

★★★★LAMPREIA RESTAURANT
2400 First Ave., Seattle, 206-443-3301; www.lampreiarestaurant.com
Not content with serving what many typically identify as Italian food, chef Scott Carsberg is intent on utilizing the highest-quality ingredients in preparations that continue to astound and challenge the palate. The Tomatoes Lampreia, a dish that showcases up to 10 different preparations of the humble fruit, is a signature. Numerous tableside presentations by the charming service staff add a sense of drama and flair to the dining room. International menu. Dinner. Closed Sunday-Monday. Business casual attire. Reservations recommended. Valet parking. $$$

★★★LOLA
2000 Fourth Ave., Seattle, 206-441-1430; www.tomdouglas.com
Located in Belltown and adjacent to the Hotel Andra, this Greek/Mediterranean restaurant is the most recent addition to Tom and Jackie Douglas's restaurant group (Dahlia Lounge is just across the street). The modern dining room is welcoming with warm brown colors, floor-to-ceiling windows, high-backed booths and hand-painted chandeliers. For dinner, the kabobs are a must, and the lamb and fish dishes are delicious. Breakfast offerings include favorites such as buttermilk pancakes with blueberries. Greek, Mediterranean menu. Breakfast, lunch, dinner, late-night, weekend brunch. Bar. Children's menu. Casual attire. Reservations recommended. Valet parking. Outdoor seating. $$

★★★MADISON PARK CAFÉ
1807 42nd Ave. East, Seattle, 206-324-2626; www.madisonparkcafe.ypguides.net
This intimate French bistro is located in a charming residential neighborhood across the street from a beautiful park—making guests feel as if they've been transported to Paris. The interior space has a warm, cozy feeling with its toasty fireplace, and works from local artists hang on the warm, sunny yellow walls. On nice summer nights, the outdoor patio is the perfect place to dine. The dinner menu offers French favorites such as onion soup, cassoulet and steak au poivre. There are no reservations taken for brunch, so come early. French menu. Dinner, weekend brunch. Closed Monday. Bar. Casual attire. Reservations recommended. Outdoor seating. $$

★★MARJORIE
2331 Second Ave., Seattle, 206-441-9842; www.trenchtownrocks.com
International/fusion menu. Dinner, late-night. Closed holidays; Sunday-Monday. Bar. Children's menu. Casual attire. Reservations recommended. Outdoor seating. $$

★
★
★
★
★

★★MAXIMILIEN FRENCH CAFÉ

81A Pike St., Seattle, 206-682-7270; www.maximilienrestaurant.com

French menu. Lunch, dinner. Sunday brunch. Bar. Children's menu. Business casual attire. Reservations recommended. $$$

★★★THE OCEANAIRE SEAFOOD ROOM

1700 Seventh Ave., Seattle, 206-267-2277; www.theoceanaire.com

The space offers a relaxed setting with stuffed fish on the walls, wine racks, blackboards with the daily specials and tables set with sea salt, oyster crackers, Old Bay seasoning, Tabasco and steel bowls with claw crackers. The menu changes daily since seafood, flown and trucked in daily, is the specialty. Diners can choose how they would like their fish prepared—grilled, broiled, sauteed, steamed or fried—any way is simply delicious. The restaurant also offers a nice lounge for pre- or post-dinner drinks and an impressive raw oyster bar. Seafood menu. Lunch, dinner. Bar. Casual attire. Reservations recommended. Valet parking. $$$

★★★PALACE KITCHEN

2030 Fifth Ave., Seattle, 206-448-2001; www.tomdouglas.com

Located under the monorail at Fifth and Lenora in Belltown, this theatrical restaurant/ saloon, owned and operated by Tom and Jackie Douglas, caters to a drinking crowd in search of imaginative rustic food. A horseshoe-shaped wood bar is the focal point of the space, just beating out the spectacular "Palace Feast" mural. Although the American cuisine menu changes daily, a delicious rotisserie dish (prepared over an applewood grill) is always available. And a slice of Douglas's legendary coconut-cream pie is the perfect ending to a great meal. American menu. Dinner, late-night. Bar. Casual attire. Reservations recommended. Valet parking.$$$

★★★PALISADE

Elliott Bay Marina, 2601 W. Marina Place, Seattle, 206-285-1000;
www.palisaderestaurant.com

Palisade is set on the Magnolia Marina with incredible waterfront views of the Seattle skyline and yachts galore. Guests cross a bridge over a large pond filled with fish. The appealing interior features unusual brown weave chairs and unique blown-glass artwork. Menu options include dishes such as passion fruit-glazed duck breast, rotisserie rack of lamb and wood oven-roasted prawns. Guests can also enjoy the views from the bar. American, seafood menu. Lunch, dinner. Sunday brunch. Late-night. Bar. Children's menu. Casual attire. Reservations recommended. Valet parking. Outdoor seating. $$$

★★★PALOMINO

1420 Fifth Ave., Seattle, 206-623-1300; www.palomino.com

This attractive restaurant is located on the third floor of the City Centre Mall—a great spot for people-watching. Tuscan colors, high ceilings, blown-glass chandeliers and sconces and an open kitchen add to cozy ambience. The menu features Italian-inspired American cuisine. Salads and pizzas are popular at lunch, as are the gorgonzola fries. American, Italian menu. Lunch, dinner. Bar. Children's menu. Casual attire. Reservations recommended. $$$

WASHINGTON

★
★
★
★

★★PIATTI RESTAURANT

2695 N.E. Village Lane, Seattle, 206-524-9088; www.piatti.com

Italian menu. Lunch, dinner. Bar. Children's menu. Casual attire. Reservations recommended. Outdoor seating. Free parking. $$

★★THE PINK DOOR

1919 Post Alley, Seattle, 206-443-3241; www.thepinkdoor.net

American, Italian menu. Lunch, dinner, late-night. Bar. Casual attire. Reservations recommended. Outdoor seating. $$

★★★PLACE PIGALLE

81 Pike St., Seattle, 206-624-1756; www.placepigalle-seattle.com

Crisp linens and a black-and-white parquet floor create a truly romantic setting alongside the bustling Puget Sound. Diners enjoy views of Elliott Bay and the San Juan Mountains while enjoying a delicious meal. American, Northwest regional menu. Lunch, dinner. Closed Sunday. Bar. Casual attire. Reservations recommended. Outdoor seating. $$$

★★★PONTI SEAFOOD GRILL

3014 Third Ave. North, Seattle, 206-284-3000; www.pontiseafoodgrill.com

A charming courtyard with a terra cotta lion fountain is located at the entrance of Ponti Seafood Grill. Guests can dine on the outside patio while taking in the views of Lake Union. Menu offerings include house-smoked Alaskan black cod, Ponti shellfish paella and Parmesan and spinach-stuffed chicken. Seafood menu. Lunch (December only), dinner. Bar. Children's menu. Casual attire. Reservations recommended. Valet parking. Outdoor seating. $$

★★QUEEN CITY GRILL

2201 First Ave., Seattle, 206-443-0975; www.queencitygrill.com

Seafood, steak menu. Dinner. Closed holidays. Bar. Casual attire. Reservations recommended. Outdoor seating. $$

★★★RAY'S BOATHOUSE

6049 Seaview Ave. N.W., Seattle, 206-789-3770; www.rays.com

Located in quaint Ballard, this upscale yet casual seafood house is a true Seattle landmark, approximately 20 minutes from downtown. Numerous old black-and-white photos line the walls. The deck is truly outstanding: Guests can sit on the benches (with warm blankets provided by Ray's) and watch the boats pass by as they come out of the Ballard Locks to Elliott Bay and the Pacific Ocean. American, seafood menu. Dinner. Bar. Children's menu. Casual attire. Reservations recommended. Valet parking. Outdoor seating. $$$

★★★★ROVER'S

2808 E. Madison St., Seattle, 206-325-7442; www.rovers-seattle.com

A small white clapboard cottage located in Madison Park houses Rover's, an intimate restaurant serving innovative and amazing contemporary cuisine. Thierry Rautureau, the chef and owner, stays true to the regional ingredients of the northwest while paying homage to impeccable French technique. Presented like precious little works of art, the portions are perfect in size, taste and appearance. The miraculous part of Rautureau's menu is that as soon as you finish the course in front of you, you are ready and salivating for the next. The restaurant offers five-course and eight-course tasting menus in addition to a five-course vegetarian menu; an á la carte menus also available. American, Northwest contemporary menu. Lunch (Friday only), dinner. Closed Sunday-Monday; holidays. Business casual attire. Reservations recommended. $$$$

★★★RUSTICA RISTORANTE ITALIANO

1106 Eighth Ave., Seattle, 206-624-2222; www.rusticaseattle.com

Owner/chef Sevala Kulovic creates her continental masterpieces using fresh northwest ingredients. With dishes such as jaeger schnitzel with mushrooms, bacon and onions; linguini with pan-seared sea scallops topped with roasted hazelnuts; and almond-crusted baked salmon, diners will have a difficult time choosing their meal. Continental, Northwest menu. Dinner. Closed Sunday-Monday. Bar. Business casual attire. Reservations recommended. Outdoor seating. $$$

★★★RUTH'S CHRIS STEAK HOUSE

727 Pine St., Seattle, 206-624-8524, 800-544-0808; www.ruthschris.com

Born from a single New Orleans restaurant that Ruth Fertel bought in 1965 for $22,000, the Ruth's Chris Steak House chain has made it to the top of every steak lover's list. Aged prime Midwestern beef is broiled to your liking and served on a heated plate, sizzling in butter; even healthier alternatives like chicken arrive at your table drenched in the savory substance. Sides like creamed spinach and fresh asparagus with hollandaise are not to be missed and are the perfect companion to any entrée. Choose from seven different preparations of spuds, from a one-pound baked potato with everything to au gratin potatoes with cream sauce and topped with cheese. Steak menu. Breakfast, lunch, dinner. Bar. Children's menu. Business casual attire. Reservations recommended. Valet parking. $$$

★
★
★
★

★★★SAZERAC

1101 Fourth Ave., Seattle, 206-624-7755; www.sazeracrestaurant.com

Sazerac serves reliably satisfying, southern-inspired food. The interior features a vibrant, eclectic décor, and the fun atmosphere makes it a hit with the happy-hour crowd. The restaurant is located adjacent to the Hotel Monaco. Guests can dine at the counter seating of the rotisserie grill and pizza oven or at tables or booths. American menu. Breakfast, lunch, dinner, late-night, weekend brunch. Bar. Children's menu. Casual attire. Reservations recommended. Valet parking. Outdoor seating. $$

★★SERAFINA

2043 Eastlake Ave. E., Seattle, 206-323-0807; www.serafinaseattle.com

Italian menu. Lunch, dinner, late-night, Sunday brunch. Bar. Children's menu. Casual attire. Reservations recommended. Outdoor seating. $$

★★SHIRO'S

2401 Second Ave., Seattle, 206-443-9844; www.shiros.com

Japanese, seafood menu. Dinner. Casual attire. Outdoor seating. $

★★★SHUCKERS

411 University St., Seattle, 206-621-1984; www.fairmont.com/seattle

When seeking an inviting and cozy seafood experience, **look** no further than Shuckers, located within the Fairmont Olympic Hotel. Enjoy dishes like applewood smoked salmon, garlic and rosemary roasted Dungeness crab with roasted potatoes. For dessert, black-and-white mud pie is a sure bet. Shuckers earned its name and favored reputation from its wide selection of oysters—13 at last count. They can be prepared a myriad of ways, including house-smoked, baked, Olympic, Rockefeller, Kilpatrick, Provençal, pan-fried, barbeque or half-shell. Seafood menu. Lunch, dinner. Bar. Children's menu. Casual attire. Reservations recommended. Valet parking. $$$

★★★SZMANIA'S MAGNOLIA

3321 W. McGraw, Seattle, 206-284-7305; www.szmanias.com

Guests at this favorite neighborhood hangout can always see the German chef at work in the open kitchen, which features counter seating. A unique, one-of-a-kind glass mural is located at the front of the restaurant, and vibrant paintings by a local artist hang throughout. The setting is intimate, eclectic and luxurious with cozy booths and fireplaces. German menu. Lunch (Friday only), dinner. Closed Monday; holidays. Bar. Children's menu. Casual attire. Reservations recommended. $$

★★★TAVOLÀTA

2323 Second Ave., Seattle, 206-838-8008; www.tavolata.com

Looking for a good handle on the community? This place is all about it. Soft lighting and a 30-foot long communal table made of reclaimed wood invite warm raves from chef/co-owner Ethan Stowell's devoted fans (won at his two other popular Seattle eateries, Union and How to Cook a Wolf). You'll find that you can't go wrong here, but there are a few must-tries. The buffalo mozzarella appetizer is as fresh as it gets; meat eaters' best bet is the T-bone, done to perfection and paired with a panzanella; and all of the desserts are diet-cheat-worthy. Italian menu. Dinner. Bar. No reservations accepted for parties under six. $26-$65

★★TRATTORIA MITCHELLI

84 Yesler Way, Seattle, 206-623-3883; www.mitchellis.com

Italian menu. Lunch, dinner, weekend brunch. Bar. Children's menu. Casual attire. Reservations recommended. Outdoor seating. $$

★★★TULIO RISTORANTE

1100 Fifth Ave., Seattle, 206-624-5500; www.tulio.com

The food, inventive yet unpretentious, is highlighted by ample tomatoes, cheeses and fresh pasta. A knowledgeable and gracious staff completes the inviting experience. Italian menu. Breakfast, lunch, dinner. Bar. Children's menu. Casual attire. Reservations recommended. Valet parking. Outdoor seating. $$$

★★★UNION BAY CAFÉ

3515 N.E. 45th St., Seattle, 206-527-8364; www.unionbaycafe.com

Eclectic artwork by a local artist adorns the yellow walls at Union Bay Café, a small, intimate restaurant located just 15 minutes from downtown. This long-standing bistro was "one of the first" to concentrate on local, organic ingredients. A well-known wine collection is featured here, and often there are special wine events. American menu. Dinner. Closed Monday. Bar. Casual attire. Reservations recommended. Outdoor seating. **$$**

★★★UNION SQUARE GRILL

621 Union St., Seattle, 206-24-4321; www.unionsquaregrill.com

Comfortable booth seating, a busy, vibrant, art deco-inspired design and quick service make this eatery, with an American bistro menu, a popular stop for business lunches and pretheater meals. American menu. Lunch, dinner. Bar. Casual attire. Reservations recommended. Valet parking. **$$$**

★★★WILD GINGER ASIAN RESTAURANT & SATAY BAR

1401 Third Ave., Seattle, 206-623-4450; www.wildginger.net

One of downtown Seattle's premier restaurants, Wild Ginger is a hot spot for celebrities, who sometimes come for Monday night jazz sessions. Pan-Asian menu. Lunch, dinner, late-night. Bar. Casual attire. Reservations recommended. **$$$**

SEDRO-WOOLLEY

A thick growth of cedar once cloaked the Skagit River Valley. It has been replaced with fertile farms for which Sedro-Woolley is the commercial center, but lumbering is still one of the main industries. The town represents the merger of the town of Sedro (Spanish for "cedar") and its onetime rival, Woolley, named for its founder. A Ranger District station of the Mount Baker-Snoqualmie National Forest is located here.

Information: Chamber of Commerce, 714-B Metcalf St., Sedro-Woolley, 360-855-1841, 888-225-8365; www.sedro-woolley.com

WHAT TO SEE AND DO
NORTH CASCADES NATIONAL PARK

810 Highway 20, Sedro-Woolley, 50 miles east on Highway 20, (portions of this road are closed in winter), 360-854-7200; www.nps.gov/noca

Authorized in 1968, this 504,781-acre area has beautiful alpine scenery, deep glaciated canyons, more than 300 active glaciers and hundreds of jagged peaks and mountain lakes. It is adjacent to the 576,865-acre Glacier Peak Wilderness dominated by 10,541-foot-high Glacier Peak and to Ross Lake and Lake Chelan National Recreation Areas.

SEQUIM

Sequim (pronounced SKWIM) is a Native American name meaning "quiet water."

Information: Sequim Dungeness Valley Chamber of Commerce, 1192 E. Washington St., Sequim, 360-683-6197, 800-737-8462; www.cityofsequim.com

SPECIAL EVENT
IRRIGATION FESTIVAL

360-683-6197; www.irrigationfestival.com

Irrigation may not sound like a very exciting reason to hold a festival, but the city of Sequim has been celebrating the gift of water for more than 100 years. The bringing of water to the parched Sequim Prarie enabled pioneer settlers to build a farming community here, and today's citizens remain thankful for the efforts that brought their

WASHINGTON

★
★★
★★
★
★

hometown into existence. Festival events include parades, carnivals, flower shows, contests and an arts and crafts street fair. First full week in May.

HOTEL

★ECONO LODGE

801 E. Washington St., Sequim, 360-683-7113, 877-424-6423; www.econolodge.com
43 rooms. Pets accepted; fee. Complimentary continental breakfast. Wireless Internet access. $

SPECIALITY LODGINGS

GREYWOLF INN

395 Keeler Road, Sequim, 360-683-5889, 800-914-9653; www.greywolfinn.com
This is a perfect inn for a romantic getaway. This bed and breakfast has a secluded location near Olympic National Park, the Pacific Ocean and great beaches. Five rooms. Children over 12 years only. Complimentary full breakfast. Wireless Internet access. Fitness center. $

GROVELAND COTTAGE BED AND BREAKFAST

4861 Sequim-Dungeness Way, Sequim, 360-683-3565, 800-879-8859;
www.grovelandcottage.com
Four rooms. Pets accepted, some restrictions; fee. Children over 12 years only. Complimentary full breakfast. High-speed Internet access. $

SPOKANE

Spokane is the booming center of the vast, rich "Inland Northwest," an area that includes eastern Washington, Northern Idaho, Northeastern Oregon, Western Montana and Southern British Columbia. A large rail center, the Spokane area also produces wheat, apples, hops, silver, gold, zinc and lead. Thanks to the surrounding mountain ranges, Spokane enjoys what it likes to term New Mexico's climate in the winter and Maine's in the summer. The city itself is in a saucerlike setting amid pine-green hills, with the Spokane River running through its 52 square miles. Located in a favorite Native American hunting and fishing ground, Spokane began as a sawmill, powered by Spokane Falls. This village, the name meaning "children of the sun," was the only point in a 400-mile-long north-south range of mountains where railroads could cross the Rockies and reach the Columbia Basin. Railroading sparked the city's early growth. The Coeur d'Alene gold fields in Idaho helped finance Spokane's continuing development and helped it survive an 1889 fire that nearly leveled the city. Farming, lumbering, mining and railroading aided Spokane's growth during the first decade of the 20th century. In 1974, the Havermale and Cannon islands in the Spokane River were the site of EXPO 74. The area has since been developed as Riverfront Park.

Information: Spokane Area Visitor Information Center, 801 W. Riverside Blvd., Spokane, 509-624-1341; 201 W. Main Ave. (downtown), Spokane, 509-747-3230, 888-776-5263; www.visitspokane.com

SPECIAL EVENT
SPOKANE INTERSTATE FAIR
Spokane County Fair and Expo Center, 404 N. Havana St., Spokane, 509-477-1766; www.spokanecounty.org/fair
The Spokane County Fair and Expo Center offers more than 140,000 square feet of exhibition space showcasing livestock, arts and crafts, food and a carnival. Nine days in mid-September.

HOTELS
★★COURTYARD BY MARRIOTT SPOKANE DOWNTOWN
N. 401 Riverpoint Blvd., Spokane, 509-456-7600, 888-236-2427; www.marriott.com
149 rooms. High-speed Internet access. Restaurant, bar. Fitness center. Indoor pool, whirlpool. $

★★★THE DAVENPORT HOTEL AND TOWER
10 S. Post St., Spokane, 509-455-8888, 800-899-1482; www.thedavenporthotel.com
Step back in time at this grand downtown hotel that opened in 1914 and has been restored it to its original grandeur. Once you step into the soaring two-story lobby, you'll see the attention to detail. Guest rooms feature hand-carved mahogany furniture, imported Irish linens (made by the same company that supplied the hotel when it first opened) and travertine marble bathrooms with spacious walk-in showers. Some suites and deluxe rooms have fireplaces, wet bars and jetted tubs. Exquisite ballrooms make the Davenport a popular site for weddings and other important celebrations. The upscale Palm Court Grill restaurant serves European cuisine with some Asian touches, while the Peacock Room serves cocktails and a light menu. The hotel also offers a candy shop, flower shop, art gallery and an impressive spa. 283 rooms. Pets accepted, some restrictions. Wireless Internet access. Restaurants, bar. Fitness center. Spa. Indoor pool, whirlpool. Airport transportation available. $$

★★DOUBLETREE HOTEL SPOKANE-CITY CENTER
322 N. Spokane Falls Court, Spokane, 509-455-9600, 800-222-8733; www.doubletree.com
375 rooms. Pets accepted; fee. Wireless Internet access. Restaurant, bar. Business Center. Fitness center. Outdoor pool, whirlpool. Airport transportation available. $

★★HAMPTON INN
2010 S. Assembly Road, Spokane, 509-747-1100, 800-426-7866; www.hamptoninn.com
129 rooms. Pets accepted. Complimentary full breakfast. High-speed Internet access. Business Center. Restaurant, bar. Fitness center. Indoor pool, whirlpool. Airport transportation available. $

★★★HOTEL LUSSO
1 N. Post St., Spokane, 509-747-9750; www.hotellusso.com
Lusso means "luxury" in Italian and that's exactly what you see when you stay here. This Italian Renaissance building is located in the business section of downtown Spokane. It's also conveniently located next to a skywalk, which provides access to shops, restaurants and entertainment. The interior is decorated with marble, hardwood and warm

WASHINGTON

★
★
★
★
★

Mediterranean colors. Guest rooms are comfortably appointed, and guests can enjoy a variety of leisure activities. The Cavallino Lounge is the perfect place for an after-dinner drink. 48 rooms. Complimentary continental breakfast. High-speed Internet access. Restaurant, bar. Airport transportation available. $$

★QUALITY INN VALLEY SUITES

8923 E. Mission Ave., Spokane, 509-928-5218, 800-777-7355;
www.spokanequalityinn.com
128 rooms, all suites. Pets accepted, some restrictions. Complimentary full breakfast. Wireless Internet access. Fitness center. Indoor pool, whirlpool. $

★★RED LION HOTEL AT THE PARK

303 W. North River Drive, Spokane, 509-326-8000,
800-733-5466; www.redlion.rdln.com
400 rooms. Pets accepted. Wireless Internet access. Restaurant, bar. Indoor pool, outdoor pool, whirlpool. Fitness center. Airport transportation available. $

★★RED LION RIVER INN

700 N. Division St., Spokane, 509-326-5577, 800-733-5466; www.redlion.rdln.com
245 rooms. Pets accepted; fee. Wireless Internet access. Restaurant, bar. Outdoor pool, whirlpool. Tennis. Airport transportation available. $

SPECIALTY LODGING

MARIANNA STOLTZ HOUSE BED AND BREAKFAST

427 E. Indiana Ave., Spokane, 509-483-4316, 800-978-6587;
www.mariannastoltzhouse.com
Each guest suite is unique and handsomely decorated, and the house is filled with antiques, dolls and wood toys. Guests awaken to scents from the kitchen, where puffy Dutch pancakes or peach Melba parfait are served. After breakfast, the wraparound porch is the perfect place to relax. The property is within walking distance of Gonzaga University and about two miles from downtown. Four rooms. No children allowed. Complimentary full breakfast. $

RESTAURANTS

★★FUGAZZI AT HOTEL LUSSO

1 N. Post St., Spokane, 509-747-9750; www.hotellusso.com
Euro-Asian menu. Lunch, dinner. Closed Sunday. Bar. Children's menu. Business casual attire. Reservations recommended. Valet parking. $$

★★★LUNA

5620 S. Perry St., Spokane, 509-448-2383;
www.lunaspokane.com
Located on Spokane's South Hill and a 10-minute drive from downtown, this Mediterranean/international restaurant is worth the drive. Locals come for breakfast lunch, dinner and brunch and are greeted in the foyer by a large Hungarian crystal chandelier, which sets the tone for the rest of the warm but eclectic interior. Diners enjoy the open kitchen, where they can watch their meal being made from scratch—everything here is, from the breads to the desserts. Mediterranean menu. Breakfast, lunch, dinner, brunch. Bar. Children's menu. Casual attire. Reservations recommended. Outdoor seating. $$$

★★★THE PALM COURT GRILL

10 S. Post St., Spokane, 509-789-6848, 800-899-1482;
www.thedavenporthotel.com

The signature dish here is crab Louis, named for the hotel's original owner, Louis Davenport. Meals can be capped off deliciously with homemade desserts. American menu. Breakfast, lunch, dinner, brunch. Bar. Children's menu. Business casual attire. Reservations recommended. Valet parking. $$

★★SPENCER'S

322 N. Spokane Falls Court, Spokane, 509-744-2372;
www.spencersforsteaksandchops.com

Steak menu. Lunch, dinner. Bar. Children's menu. Business casual attire. Reservations recommended. Valet parking. $$$

TACOMA

In its gemlike setting on Puget Sound, midway between Seattle and Olympia, Tacoma maintains its wood and paper industries and its shipping traditions. Its harbor is a port of call for merchant vessels plying the oceans of the world. Backed by timber, shipping facilities and low-cost water and power, more than 500 factories produce lumber, plywood, paper, millwork, furniture, foodstuffs, beverages, chemicals and clothing. Major railroad and shipbuilding yards are also located here. The health care industry is a major employer, and the high-tech industry continues to grow rapidly. The nearest metropolitan center to Mount Rainier National Park, Tacoma is a base for trips to Olympic National Park and Puget Sound. Mild weather keeps parks and gardens green throughout the year. In 1833, the Hudson's Bay Company built its second post (Fort Nisqually) on the north Pacific coast in the forest, 18 miles south of the present site of Tacoma. In 1841, Charles Wilkes, commander of a U.S. expedition, began a survey of Puget Sound from this point and named the bay around which Tacoma is built Commencement Bay. When the rails of the Northern Pacific reached tidewater here late in 1873, they sparked the industrial growth of the city.

Information: Tacoma-Pierce County Visitor & Convention Bureau, 15th street,
and Pacific Avenue, Tacoma, 509-624-1341; 201 W. Main Ave. (downtown),
Spokane, 253-627-2836, 800-272-2662; www.traveltacoma.compoint

DEFIANCE PARK

One of Tacoma's preeminent attractions, this 700-acre park, flanked by the waters of Puget Sound, contains a wealth of gardens, the city zoo and aquarium, and a number of recreational and historical sites. The park includes 14 miles of hiking trails, which wind through groves of old-growth forests and lead to sheltered beaches. The main paved road through the park is called Five Mile Drive; on Saturdays this scenic road remains closed to motor vehicles until 1 p.m., though it's open to cyclists, joggers and in-line skaters. Enter the park at Pearl Street and follow signs to the parking area at the Vashon Island Ferry. From here, watch as the ferries cross to and from Vashon Island, an agricultural island in the misty distance. Walk past the tennis courts and follow the path to the garden area.

Formal gardens are abundant at Point Defiance Park and are maintained cooperatively by members of local garden clubs, with help from Tacoma's Metropolitan Park District. Park gardens include the Japanese Garden with a torii gate and shinto shrine

★
★
★
★
★

received as gifts from Kitakyushu, Tacoma's sister city in Japan. Also found here are iris gardens, dahlia test gardens, herb gardens and a rhododendron garden that is ablaze with color in May. Just past the zoo entrance on Five Mile Drive is the civic Rose Garden, established in 1895, with more than an acre of bushes, many of heirloom varieties. The Northwest Native Garden, located near the Pearl Street entrance, presents a collection of indigenous plants ranging from trees to grasses. Just past the main garden area is the Point Defiance Zoo & Aquarium. Often considered one of the best in the United States, the Point Defiance Zoo is unusual in that it focuses primarily on species from the Pacific Rim, including polar bears, musk oxen and Arctic foxes. Peer at coastline mammals through the underwater windows at Rocky Shores. No fewer than 30 huge sharks swim among tropical fish and eels in the lagoon at Discovery Reef Aquarium. Elephants and apes and other zoo favorites are housed in the Southeast Asia complex.

From the zoo, follow trails north into the wild heart of the park. Point Defiance has been a public park for almost 125 years, and vast sections of it preserve old-growth forest and virgin meadowlands. Stop at Owens Beach to explore the shoreline or take in the sun along the sandy strand. Farther west, past a viewpoint onto Vashon Island, is Mountaineer Tree, a massive fir nearly 450 years old. The western edge of the park is at Gig Harbor Viewpoint, which overlooks the Tacoma Narrows, a constricted, surging strait between Point Defiance and the Kitsap Peninsula. Round the cap and walk south along the western flank of the park. From here, watch for vistas onto the Tacoma Narrows Bridge. At a mile in length, it is the fifth-longest span in North America. The present bridge replaced the infamous Galloping Gertie bridge that collapsed during a wind storm in 1940.

At the southwest corner of the park are a number of attractions. If you have kids in tow, they may enjoy Never Never Land, a 10-acre storyland theme park in an outdoor forest setting. Wooded paths lead to oversized sculpted figures of nursery-rhyme characters. On summer weekends, kids can meet living costumed characters. Adjacent is Fort Nisqually Historic Site. In 1833, the Hudson Bay Company trading post at Fort Nisqually was established 17 miles south of Tacoma, near DuPont. This restoration of the original fort includes the factor's house, granary, trade store, blacksmith shop, laborer's quarters and stockade, all furnished to reflect life on the frontier in the 1850s. Docents in period clothing demonstrate blacksmithing, spinning, beadwork and black powder.

Walk back toward the main park entrance, stopping by Camp six Logging Museum, an open-air logging museum and reconstruction of a pioneer logging camp. On spring and summer weekends, hitch a ride on a logging train with a steam locomotive. Back at the ferry terminal, refresh yourself with a stop at the Boathouse Grill, located above the marina with views over Vashon Island and the Olympic mountain peaks.

WHAT TO SEE AND DO
EMERALD QUEEN I-5 CASINO,
EMERALD QUEEN CASINO HOTEL
2024 E. 29th St., Tacoma (Casino), 5700 Pacific Highway E., Fife (Hotel/Casino),
253-594-7777, 888-831-7655; www.emeraldqueen.com
The Emerald Queen Casino is big and bright, brimming with antiques and Vegas-style tables (including blackjack, Caribbean stud poker, roulette, craps and others), as well as over 2,000 slots and video poker machines and live-action keno. The Hotel/Casino

★
★
★
★
★

in Fife also has hundreds of machines and keno. Both locations have smoke-free gaming areas. The stage regularly attracts national rock and country acts, some of them household names. In addition to the requisite casino buffet, the I-5 casino has a casual deli and an Asian eatery; the hotel has a full-service restaurant. Daily.

POINT DEFIANCE ZOO & AQUARIUM

5400 N. Pearl St., Tacoma, 253-591-5337; www.pdza.org

The zoo has a polar bear complex, a musk ox habitat, tundra waterfowl, elephants, beluga whales, walrus, seals and otters. The 38 perimeter display show off hundreds of Pacific Northwest marine specimens. The South Pacific Aquarium features coral reefs and sharks; the North Pacific Aquarium includes a hands-on Marine Discovery Center. January-March and October-December, daily 9:30 a.m.-4 p.m.; April-late May, daily 9:30 a.m.-5 p.m.; mid-May-early September, daily 9:30 a.m.-6 p.m.; early-late September, daily 9:30 a.m.-5 p.m.; closed July 16.

SEATTLE MUSEUM OF GLASS

1801 E. Dock St., Tacoma, 253-284-4750, 866-568-7386; www.museumofglass.org

The only museum in the United States focusing on contemporary glass art, the Museum of Glass first opened its doors at the waterfront in downtown Tacoma in 2001. The collection includes works by some of the best-known glass artists in the world, including Dale Chihuly, whose 500-foot Chihuly Bridge of Glass here is one of the largest outdoor glass installations in existence anywhere. Visitors can watch glass artists ply their trade at an on-site amphitheater. Tuesday-Saturday 10 a.m.-5 p.m., Sunday noon-5 p.m., third Tuesday of month 10 a.m.-8 p.m.; closed Monday, holidays.

UNION STATION

1717 Pacific Ave., Tacoma, 253-863-5173; www.unionstationrotunda.org

Built in 1911 by Northern Pacific Railroad, the station, with its 98-foot-high dome, has been restored. Now home to the federal courthouse, the rotunda houses the largest single exhibit of sculptured glass by Tacoma native Dale Chihuly. Monday-Friday; closed holidays.

HOTELS

★★★HOTEL MURANO

1320 Broadway Plaza, Tacoma, 253-238-8000, 877-986-8083;
www.hotelmuranotacoma.com

The restaurant level overlooks the three-story, skylit lobby, decorated with glass work by world-renowned local artist Dale Chihuly. At the top of the hotel is Altezzo, a rooftop restaurant where you can enjoy fine Italian cuisine and check out views of Mount Rainier and Commencement Bay. Guests may make use of the fitness facilities at the YMCA next door for a small fee. 319 rooms. Pets accepted, some restrictions; fee. High-speed Internet access. Restaurants, bar. Spa. Reservations recommended. $

★★KING OSCAR TACOMA INN

8726 S. Hosmer St., Tacoma, 253-558-2400, 888-254-5464; www.koscar.net

149 rooms. Pets accepted; fee. Complimentary continental breakfast. Restaurant, bar. Outdoor pool. $

WASHINGTON

★
★
★
★
★

★★LA QUINTA INN

1425 E. 27th St., Tacoma, 253-383-0146, 800-642-4271;
www.laquinta.com

161 rooms. Pets accepted. Complimentary continental breakfast. High-speed Internet access. Restaurant, bar. Indoor pool, whirlpool. Fitness center. **$**

★SHILO INN

7414 S. Hosmer, Tacoma, 253-475-4020, 800-222-2244; www.shiloinns.com

132 rooms. Pets accepted. Complimentary continental breakfast. Indoor pool, whirlpool. **$**

SPECIALTY LODGING

CHINABERRY HILL

302 Tacoma Ave. North, Tacoma, 253-272-1282; www.chinaberryhill.com

Nestled among century-old trees on a steep hill overlooking Puget Sound, this quaint 1889 Victorian mansion oozes old-world charm. Convenient to nearby shops, restaurants, theaters and galleries, as well as the university and the Tacoma Dome, this inn has lovely multiroom suites furnished with antiques and an inviting wraparound porch. In addition to five standard rooms, the two-story carriage house sleeps six to seven guests with two full baths and a private Jacuzzi. Six rooms. Complimentary full breakfast. **$**

RESTAURANTS

★★★BITE

1320 Broadway Plaza, Tacoma, 253-591-4151;
www.hotelmuranotacoma.com

This restaurant offers breathtaking panoramic views of Puget Sound, Commencement Bay and Mount Rainier. Italian menu. Breakfast, Lunch, Dinner. Bar. Business casual attire. Reservations recommended. Valet parking. **$$$**

★★★CLIFF HOUSE

6300 Marine View Drive, Tacoma, 253-927-0400, 800-961-0401;
www.cliffhouserestaurant.com

Visitors will find Northwest-influenced cuisine at this dusty rose and floral-accented dining room while enjoying views of Mt. Rainier and Puget Sound. Northwest menu. Lunch, dinner. Bar. Casual attire. Reservations recommended. **$$$**

★★HARBOR LIGHTS

2761 Ruston Way, Tacoma, 253-752-8600; www.anthonys.com

Seafood menu. Lunch, dinner, brunch. Closed holidays. Bar. Children's menu. Casual attire. Reservations recommended. **$$**

★★JOHNNY'S DOCK

1900 E. D St., Tacoma, 253-627-3186; www.johnnysdock.com

Seafood menu. Breakfast, lunch, dinner, brunch. Bar. Children's menu. Casual attire. Reservations recommended. Outdoor seating. **$**

★★★RUSTON WAY LOBSTER SHOP

4015 Ruston Way, Tacoma, 253-759-2165; www.lobstershop.com

This Commencement Bay restaurant has a bright look, boat moorage and outdoor dining (during spring and summer). The coastline location affords beautiful views. Seafood, steak menu. Lunch, dinner, Sunday brunch. Bar. Children's menu. Casual attire. Outdoor seating. $$$

VANCOUVER

Vancouver treasures a national historic site, Fort Vancouver, now completely encircled by the city. The fort served as a commercial bastion for the Hudson's Bay Company, whose vast enterprises stretched far to the north and across the sea to Hawaii, bringing furs from Utah and California and dominating coastal trade well up the shoreline to Alaska. Around the stockaded fort, the company's cultivated fields and pastures extended for miles; drying sheds, mills, forges and shops made it a pioneer metropolis. This community was a major stake in Britain's claim for all the territory north of the Columbia River, but by the treaty of 1846, Fort Vancouver became American. Settlers began to take over the Hudson's Bay Company lands, and an Army post established in 1849 continues to the present day. In 1860, all of Fort Vancouver was turned over to the U.S. Army.

The city is on the Columbia River, just north of Portland, Oregon. Vancouver has a diversified industrial climate, which includes electronics; paper products; fruit packing; malt production and the manufacture of textiles, furniture and machinery. The Port of Vancouver, one of the largest on the West Coast, is a deepwater seaport handling a wide range of commodities.

Information: Greater Vancouver Chamber of Commerce, 1101 Broadway, Vancouver, 360-694-2588; www.vancouverusa.com

WHAT TO SEE AND DO
FORT VANCOUVER NATIONAL HISTORIC SITE

612 E. Reserve St., Vancouver, 360-816-6230; www.nps.gov/fova

After extensive research and excavation, the fort has been partially reconstructed by the National Park Service. Now at the fort site are Chief Factor's house, a kitchen, wash house, stockade wall, gates, bastion, bake house, blacksmith shop and trade shop. The visitor center has a museum exhibiting artifacts, an information desk and video presentations. Tours, interpretive talks and living history programs are also offered. Daily, hours vary by season; closed holidays.

GIFFORD PINCHOT NATIONAL FOREST

10600 N.E. 51st Circle, Vancouver, 360-891-5000; www.fs.fed.us/gpnf

The forest's 1,379,000 acres include the 12,326-foot-tall Mount Adams, the 8,400-foot-tall Mount St. Helens and 180,600 acres distributed among seven wilderness areas.

HOTELS
★COMFORT SUITES

4714 N.E. 94th Ave., Vancouver, 360-253-3100, 877-874-5474; www.comfortsuites.com

67 rooms. Complimentary continental breakfast. Indoor pool, whirlpool. Wireless Internet access. $

WASHINGTON

★
★
★
★
★

★★★THE HEATHMAN LODGE
7801 N.E. Greenwood Drive, Vancouver, 360-254-3100, 888-475-3100;
www.heathmanlodge.com
For travelers who like a little sophistication when retreating to the woods, the Heathman Lodge is just the place. This restful resort is just 15 minutes from downtown Vancouver and only a short distance from Portland, Ore., yet it maintains a peaceful, mountain-retreat ambience. Part woodsy, part elegant, guest rooms and suites have an inimitable charm with Pendleton blankets and leather lampshades. Hudson's elevates simple comfort food to a new level with its delightful riffs on favorite dishes, and the casual setting perfectly complements the laid-back attitude of this resort. 146 rooms. Restaurant, bar. Spa. Fitness center. Indoor pool, whirlpool. Wireless Internet access. **$**

★RAMADA VANCOUVER
9107 N.E. Vancouver Mall Drive, Vancouver, 360-253-5000, 800-272-6232;
www.ramada.com
56 rooms. Complimentary continental breakfast. Indoor pool, whirlpool. **$**

WALLA WALLA
Walla Walla Valley was first the site of a Native American trail and then an avenue for white exploration and settlement of the west. Lewis and Clark passed through the area in 1805. Fur traders followed, and Fort Walla Walla was established in 1818 as a trading post where the Walla Walla and Columbia rivers meet. One of the key figures in the area's history was Dr. Marcus Whitman, a medical missionary, who in 1836 founded the first settler's home in the northwest, a mission seven miles west of present-day Walla Walla. The Whitmans were killed by Native Americans in 1847. No long-lasting settlement was made until after the Indian Wars of 1855-1858.

In 1859, the city became the seat of Walla Walla County, which then included half of present-day Washington, all of Idaho and a quarter of Montana. It also had the first railroad in the northwest, the first bank in the state, the first meat market and packing plant and the first institution of higher learning.

Walla Walla means "many waters," but local enthusiasts will tell you that this is "the city they liked so much they named it twice." Agriculture is the major industry, with wheat the most important crop and green peas the second. Industries concentrate chiefly on food processing. The Walla Walla onion is known for its sweetness; a festival is held each July to honor the important crop. A Ranger District office of the Umatilla National Forest is located here.
Information: Walla Walla Valley Chamber of Commerce, 29 E. Sumach St.,
Walla Walla, 509-525-0850, 877-998-4748; www.wwvchamber.com

WHAT TO SEE AND DO
WHITMAN MISSION NATIONAL HISTORIC SITE
328 Whitman Mission Road, Walla Walla, 509-529-2761, 509-522-6360;
www.nps.gov/whmi
The memorial shaft, erected in 1897, overlooks the site of the mission established by Dr. Marcus and Narcissa Whitman in 1836. A self-guided trail with audio stations leads to the mission grounds, Old Oregon Trail, memorial shaft and grave. The visitor center has a 10-minute slide presentation and a museum. In summer, there are cultural demonstrations.

HOTEL

★BEST WESTERN WALLA WALLA INN & SUITES

7 E. Oak St., Walla Walla, 509-525-4700, 800-780-7234; www.bestwestern.com

78 Rooms. Pets accepted, some restrictions; fee. Indoor pool, whirlpool. High-speed Internet access. **$**

SPECIALTY LODGING

GREEN GABLES INN

922 Bonsella St., Walla Walla, 509-525-5501, 888-525-5501; www.greengablesinn.com

Five rooms. Children over 11 years only. Complimentary full breakfast. High-speed Internet access. **$**

WENATCHEE

Nestled among towering mountains are fertile irrigated valleys where residents care for apple orchards. Cherries, pears, peaches and apricots are also grown here. With the establishment in 1952 of a huge aluminum smelter and casting plant, Wenatchee's economy is no longer based only on agriculture. The headquarters of the Wenatchee National Forest is located here.

Information: Wenatchee Valley Chamber of Commerce, 300 S. Columbia, Wenatchee, 509-662-2116; www.wenatchee.org

WHAT TO SEE AND DO

SQUILCHUCK STATE PARK

Nine miles southwest on Squilchuck Road, 509-664-6373; www.parks.wa.gov

This 288-acre park at an elevation of 4,000 feet offers day use and group camping, 10 miles of hiking and biking trails and ample opportunities for winter sports like skiing and snowshoeing. May-late September, 6:30 a.m.-dusk.

WENATCHEE VALLEY MUSEUM & CULTURAL CENTER

127 S. Mission St., Wenatchee, 509-888-6240;
www.wenatcheevalleymuseum.com

This regional history museum includes a restored, operational 1919 Wurlitzer pipe organ, a Great Northern Railway model, a fine art gallery, an apple industry exhibit, an exhibit on the first trans-Pacific flight (Japan to Wenatchee) and archaeological and Native American exhibits. Tuesday-Saturday 10 a.m.-4 p.m.

SPECIAL EVENT

APPLE BLOSSOM FESTIVAL

2 S. Chelan Ave., Wenatchee, 509-662-3616; www.appleblossom.org

The Apple Blossom Festival celebrates the area's apple production and is the oldest festival in the state. Late April-early May.

HOTELS

★★BEST WESTERN CHIEFTAIN INN

1017 N. Wenatchee Ave., Wenatchee, 509-665-8585; www.bestwestern.com

77 rooms. Complimentary continental breakfast. Restaurant, bar. Outdoor pool. High-speed Internet access. **$**

★
★
★
★
☆

★★RED LION
1225 N. Wenatchee Ave., Wenatchee, 509-663-0711, 800-733-5466;
www.redlion.com
149 rooms. Pets accepted. High-speed Internet access. Restaurant, bar. Fitness center. Outdoor pool, whirlpool. Airport transportation available. **$**

SPECIALTY LODGING
APPLE COUNTRY BED & BREAKFAST
524 Okanagon Ave., Wenatchee, 509-664-0400; www.applecountryinn.com
Five rooms. **$**

WESTPORT
Near the tip of a sandy strip of land separating Grays Harbor from the Pacific, Westport is home to probably the largest sports fishing fleet in the northwest. Pleasure and charter boats take novice and experienced anglers alike across Grays Harbor Bay into the Pacific for salmon fishing in the summer and deep-sea fishing nearly all year. In the winter, commercial fleets set their pots for crab and have their catch processed at one of Westport's large canneries. Whale-watching excursions operate from March-May.
Information: Westport-Grayland Chamber of Commerce, 2985 S. Montesano St., Westport, 360-268-9422, 800-345-6223; www.westportgrayland-chamber.org

WHAT TO SEE AND DO
WESTPORT MARITIME MUSEUM
2201 Westhaven Drive, Westport, 360-268-0078;
www.westportwa.com/museum
This museum complex features exhibits on the Coast Guard, shipwrecks and rescue operations, whales and the area's cranberry and logging industries. The Children's Room has educational games and displays designed for elementary students. Also on the grounds are two Whale Houses, which exhibit sea mammal skeletons and other items, and the Lens Building, which contains a 100-year-old, 18-foot-tall rotating lens with 1,176 glass prisms. Memorial Day-Labor Day, Daily 10 a.m.-4 p.m.; October-May, Thursday-Monday noon-4 p.m.

WINTHROP
Redesigning the entire town on an Old West theme has transformed it into the "Old Western town of Winthrop," complete with annual events in the same vein.

Fifty-five miles west on the North Cascades Highway (Highway 20) is North Cascades National Park. A Ranger District office of the Okanogan National Forest is located here.
Information: Chamber of Commerce, Information Office, 202 Highway 20, Winthrop, 509-996-2125, 888-463-8469; www.winthropwashington.com

WHAT TO SEE AND DO
SHAFER MUSEUM
285 Castle Ave., Winthrop, 509-996-2712;
www.ghosttownsusa.com
This log house built in 1897 by the town's founder, Guy Waring, has been redecorated as a turn-of-the-century pioneer home and includes early farming and mining implements

★
★
★
★
☆

from the nearby gold and silver mines. Also onsite are a schoolhouse, stagecoach and early print shop. Memorial Day-Labor Day, Thursday-Monday 10 a.m.-5 p.m.

HOTELS

★AMERICA'S BEST VALUE-CASCADE INN

1006 Highway 20, Winthrop, 509-996-3100, 800-468-6754;
www.winthropwa.com

30 rooms. Pets accepted, some restrictions; fee. Outdoor pool, whirlpool. High-speed Internet access. $

★★★SUN MOUNTAIN LODGE

604 Patterson Lake Road, Winthrop, 509-996-2211, 800-572-0493;
www.sunmountainlodge.com

Whether carpeted in wildflowers or blanketed in snow, Sun Mountain Lodge is a perfect destination. Active families take advantage of the endless opportunities for recreation on the resort's 3,000 acres located east of Seattle. During the summer months, hiking, biking and fly-fishing are popular pursuits while winter months draw cross-country skiers, ice-skaters and sleigh riders. Firmly rooted in mountain traditions yet forward-thinking, Sun Mountain Lodge is far from backwoods, offering impressive dining complete with a 5,000-bottle wine cellar and a full-service spa. 102 rooms. Breakfast, lunch, dinner. Restaurant, bar. Two outdoor pools, whirlpool. Spa. $$

RESTAURANT

★★★THE DINING ROOM

604 Patterson Lake Road, Winthrop, 509-996-2211, 800-572-0493;
www.sunmountainlodge.com

A casual, rustic setting overlooking towering snow-capped mountains is the backdrop for a hearty meal of fresh regional cuisine. The kitchen skillfully combines fish, seafood and meat with a local blend of herbs and vegetables that accentuate the natural flavors. American menu. Breakfast, lunch, dinner, brunch. Bar. Children's menu. $$$

WOODINVILLE

Woodinville sits at the northern end of the Sammamish River Valley, a short drive northeast of Seattle on either Highway 522 or Interstate 405. Its main artery, northeast 175th Avenue, cuts through a downtown area occupied by shops and restaurants, as well as small offices. South of downtown, in the Tourist District, highlights include two wineries, a brewery and romantic accommodations and lodging at the Willows Lodge and its two restaurants, The Herbfarm and Barking Frog. Once a community of loggers, the city retains much of its Pacific Northwest woodland charm, though today its residents are much more likely to work at the nearby Microsoft headquarters than at a sawmill.

Information: Woodinville Chamber of Commerce, 14421 Woodinville-Redmond
Road N.E., Woodinville, 425-481-8300; www.woodinvillechamber.org

WHAT TO SEE AND DO
CHATEAU STE. MICHELLE
14111 N.E. 145th St., Woodinville, 425-488-1133, 800-267-6793;
www.ste-michelle.com

Washington state's oldest winery offers free tours and tasting at its 87-acre estate. The grapes are grown east of the Cascade Mountains in the sunny and dry Columbia Valley. During the busy summer season, arrive early to avoid the post lunch throng of wine aficionados. The winery welcomes 250,000 visitors annually. Premium tastings are available for a nominal fee. Daily 10 a.m.-5 p.m.; closed holidays.

COLUMBIA WINERY
14030 N.E. 145th St., Woodinville, 425-482-7490, 800-488-2347;
www.columbiawinery.com

Columbia Winery's humble beginnings can be traced back to a garage in the Seattle neighborhood of Laurelhurst. In that garage in 1962, the first bottles were vinted. Founded by 10 friends, the operation has grown steadily over the years, helping to launch Washington's wine industry, which now ranks only behind California's in premium wine production. On weekends, tours and tasting are available at the winery's Victorian-style manor in Woodinville. Group tours on weekdays are available by appointment. Retail shop: daily 10 a.m.-7 p.m.

MOLBAK'S
13625 N.E. 175th St., Woodinville, 425-483-5000, 866-466-5225;
www.molbaks.com

Each year more than one million green thumbs pay a visit to Molbak's, a garden shop located 20 miles northeast of Seattle. Egon and Laina Molbak emigrated from Denmark to Woodinville in 1956, purchasing a small greenhouse and becoming a wholesaler of cut flowers. Ten years later, the Molbaks expanded their business by opening a 700-square-foot retail shop. Their business has flourished ever since, and today Molbaks employs 200 people to oversee garden, gift and floral shops, as well as a store selling Christmas items and patio furniture. Sunday-Friday 10 a.m.-6 p.m., Saturday 9 a.m.-9 p.m.

REDHOOK ALE BREWERY
14300 N.E. 145th St., Woodinville, 425-483-3232; www.redhook.com

In the early 1980s, Paul Shipman and Gordon Bowker identified that import beers were becoming increasingly popular and that the Pacific Northwest held the nation's highest per-capita draft beer consumption. The pair responded by founding Redhook Brewing Company, producing their ale at a brewery in the Ballard area of Seattle. They sold their first pint in 1982. Sales took off with the 1984 release of Ballard Bitter, and Redhook grew to become one of the most successful microbreweries in the United States. To keep pace with demand, a brewery was built in Woodinville in 1994. For a mere $1, visitors can tour the brewery, sample several of Redhooks eight ales, receive a free tasting glass and learn about the company's history. After the tour, sidle up to the bar in the Forecasters Public House and partake of pub-style food and, of course, fresh Redhook ale. Daily.

★
★
★
★
☆

HOTEL

★★★WILLOWS LODGE

14580 N.E. 145th St., Woodinville, 425-424-3900, 877-424-3930;
www.willowslodge.com

Bordering the Sammamish River in Washington's western wine country, Willows Lodge is an exceptional getaway. Industrial chic meets Native American sensibilities at this former hunting lodge. Stained concrete, slate and sleek lines reveal a modern slant in the accommodations, while dynamic artwork crafted by northwest coast Native Americans showcases local pride. Luxuries are not lost on this country escape, where Frette linens and 300-thread-count bedding pamper guests. Lush, landscaped gardens complete with hidden courtyards create a veritable Eden, and the herb and edible plant gardens inspire the excellent menus at The Herbfarm and Barking Frog restaurants. The resort's sanctuary-like atmosphere is enhanced by a full-service spa that offers a host of soothing and beautifying treatments. 86 rooms. Pets accepted, some restrictions. Complimentary continental breakfast. Restaurant, bar. Spa. Whirlpool. Reservations recommended. **$$$**

RESTAURANTS

★★★BARKING FROG

14580 N.E. 145th St., Woodinville, 425-424-2999; www.willowslodge.com

After a busy day touring nearby wineries, take a seat and relax at this cozy, lodgelike bistro. A quaint and casual atmosphere of warm earth tones and exposed wood complements the rustic regional northwest menu, which changes seasonally and features choices like organic chicken breast, Grand Marnier prawns and grilled New York strip. American menu. Breakfast, lunch, dinner, brunch. Bar. Children's menu. Casual attire. Reservations recommended. Outdoor seating. **$$$**

★★★★THE HERBFARM

14590 N.E. 145th St., Woodinville, 425-485-5300;
www.theherbfarm.com, www.willowslodge.com

A four-hour meal of nine courses and five perfectly paired wines. A flamenco guitarist strumming in the half-light of flickering candles in an antique-filled dining room. The sun setting over a gracious, fragrant garden lying just outside your window. If this were real life in the rural world, America's cities would be empty. Here, chef (and gentleman gardener) Jerry Traunfeld creates seasonal, themed meals based on the bounty of the restaurant's own gardens and farm, plus produce, meats and artesian cheeses sourced from local growers, producers, ranchers and fishermen. American menu. Dinner. Closed Monday-Wednesday. Business casual attire. Reservations recommended. **$$$$**

YAKIMA

Yakima (YAK-e-ma) County ranks first in the United States in production of apples, hops, sweet cherries and winter pears. Irrigation was started as early as 1875, when early settlers dug crude canals. Orchards and farms replaced sagebrush and desert. The city takes its name from the Yakama Nation, whose reservation lies to the south. There are about 300 days of sunshine annually, with an average yearly rainfall of just eight inches.

Information: Greater Yakima Chamber of Commerce, 10 N. Ninth St., Yakima,
509-248-2021; www.yakima.org

WASHINGTON

★
★
★
★
★

WHAT TO SEE AND DO
YAKIMA VALLEY TROLLEYS
307 W. Pine St., Yakima, 509-249-5962;
www.yakimavalleytrolleys.org
Trolley cars make trips around the city and the surrounding countryside on a historic railroad line. Board the trolley at the car barns at Third Avenue and West Pine Street. Mid-May-mid-October, weekends at 10 a.m., noon and 2 p.m.

YAKIMA VALLEY WINE TOURS
5808A Summitview, Yakima, 800-258-7270;
www.yakimavalleywine.com
The river-carved Yakima Valley, about 100 miles southeast of Seattle, has a climate that is nearly ideal for grape growing. The abundance of great wine is reminiscent of Northern California's Napa Valley, as is the requisite armada of bread and breakfasts, but Yakima Valley is not nearly as exclusive or expensive. Almost all of the wineries here offer free tours and tasting, and the area draws big crowds for such annual traditions as the Red Wine and Chocolate Festival over Presidents Day weekend and Merlotfest in May.

SPECIAL EVENT
SPRING BARREL TASTING
800-258-7270; www.yakimavalleywine.com
Area wineries open their doors to visitors eager for a taste of the latest vintages. Last full weekend in April.

HOTELS
★★CLARION HOTEL
1507 N. First St., Yakima, 509-453-8981, 877-424-6423; www.choicehotels.com
208 rooms. Pets accepted; fee. Restaurant, bar. Fitness center. Two outdoor pools, whirlpool. High-speed Internet access. $

★OXFORD INN YAKIMA
1603 E. Yakima Ave., Yakima, 509-457-4444, 800-521-3050;
www.oxfordinnyakima.com
96 rooms. Complimentary continental breakfast. Bar. Outdoor pool, whirlpool. High-speed Internet access. $

★★RED LION
607 E. Yakima Ave., Yakima, 509-248-5900, 800-733-5466; www.redlion.com
153 rooms. Pets accepted; fee. Restaurant, bar. Two outdoor pools. Airport transportation available. Business Center. High-speed Internet access. $

WASHINGTON

★
★
★
★
★

WYOMING

FROM THE HIGH WESTERN PLATEAUS OF THE GREAT PLAINS, THE STATE OF WYOMING
stretches across the Continental Divide and into the Rocky Mountains. This is a land
of scenic beauty and geographic diversity; mountain ranges, grasslands and desert
can all be found within Wyoming's borders.

The first Europeans to explore this region were French; brothers Louis and Francois Verendrye trapped here in 1743. The first American to enter what is now Yellowstone National Park was John Colter, a member of the Lewis and Clark expedition,
during the winter of 1807-1808. The 1820s saw a number of trappers and fur traders
become established in the area. The territory became the site of important stops along
the pioneer trails to the West Coast in the 1840s-1860s.

Trails across Wyoming allowed pioneers to cross the rugged spine of the Rocky
Mountains on an easy grade, following grass and water over the Continental Divide.
Of the approximately 350,000 individuals who made their way along the various
westward trails, some 21,000 died en route, claimed by disease, accidents and mountain snow. After 1847, thousands of Mormons came along the Mormon Trail to join
Brigham Young's settlement at Salt Lake. The situation improved dramatically for the
westward bound when the Union Pacific Railroad pushed across Wyoming during
1867-1869. The "iron horse" made the journey considerably safer and easier, not to
mention faster. Permanent settlement of the West then began in earnest.

The hard existence wrought from a sometimes inhospitable land bred a tough, practi-
cal people who recognized merit when they saw it. While still a territory, Wyoming in
1869 became the first area in the United States to grant women the right to vote. Subse-
quently, Wyomingites were the first in the nation to appoint a woman justice of the peace;
the first to select women jurors; and the first to elect a woman, Nellie Tayloe Ross, governor in 1924. This reputation has earned Wyoming the nickname "the Equality State."

The civic-mindedness of its citizens spread beyond the political arena with equal
vigor. Wyoming introduced the nation's first county library system and instituted a
public education system that today ranks among the finest in the United States.

Cattle and sheep outnumber people by more than five to one in Wyoming, which
is the least populated state in the country. It is, therefore, easy to see how the cowboy
has become such a prominent symbol here. The bucking horse insignia has appeared
on Wyoming license plates since 1936. It also appears in various versions on road
signs, storefronts and newspapers.

Mineral extraction is the principal industry in Wyoming, which has the largest coal
resources in the country. Tourism and recreation ranks second, with approximately
four million visitors per year entering the state. Generally, they come to visit the
numerous national parks, forests and monuments. But Wyoming offers a wide range
of attractions, from abundant camping to rustic guest ranching, all set among some of
the finest natural beauty to be found in the nation.

The country's first national park (Yellowstone), first national monument (Devils
Tower) and first national forest (Shoshone) are all located in Wyoming.

275

WYOMING

★
★
★
★
★

DRIVING THE OLD OREGON TRAIL

Between 1843 and 1860, an estimated 53,000 pioneers trekked across the North American continent on the Oregon Trail. This resolute group journeyed up the North Platte River and across Wyoming's Great Divide Basin before crossing the Continental Divide at South Pass, from whence they followed the Snake and Columbia rivers to Oregon. Modern highways parallel the Oregon Trail across much of the state, and many of the same landmarks greet today's travelers.

Begin the tour on Highway 26 near Torrington. Fort Laramie was constructed at the confluence of the North Platte and Laramie rivers, first as a fur-trading post and then as a military fort to protect the influx of white settlers from the local Native Americans. Today, the many buildings of the original fort complex have been reconstructed by the National Park Service and serve as a fascinating reminder of frontier life. Thirteen buildings stand around a central parade ground, many filled with period artifacts. The Fort Laramie Museum and Visitor Center houses artifacts, uniforms and weapons from the fort's heyday.

Just west of Fort Laramie on Highway 26 is Guernsey, where the Register Cliff State Historic Site preserves a sandstone bluff on which migrating pioneers left initials, dates and other messages carved in stone. The pioneer graveyard near the site is testimony to the hardships of this epic trek. Continue west on Interstate 25 (I-25) through Douglas, with a town center dominated by a statue of a jackalope, and then on to Glenrock.

Casper, Wyoming's largest city, didn't exist during Oregon Trail days, but the ford on the North Platte River made it a hub for the many trails that brought pioneers to the West. The Oregon, Mormon, Pony Express, California and Pioneer trails all converged here. Fort Casper was established in 1855 by the army to protect migrating settlers from hostile Indians and over the years served as a military fort, Pony Express station, trading post and stage stop. The fort was reconstructed during the 1930s by the Civilian Conservation Corps according to the original floor plans. Today, the fort buildings serve as museums of the frontier West, complete with living history activities that demonstrate daily life in the 19th century. Also near Casper is the National Historic Trails Interpretive Center, a Bureau of Land Management facility that commemorates the pioneer trails that intersect at Casper.

From Casper, follow Highway 220 west. Independence Rock was named by pioneer William Sublette, camped here on July 4, 1830. Independence Rock became a landmark for Oregon Trail pioneers, who knew that if they reached Independence Rock by July 4, they would get across the mountains to Oregon before snowfall. The pioneers also chiseled names and dates into the rock; among the names carved here are Jesuit missionary Father De Smet and Mormon leader Brigham Young.

A few miles west of Independence Rock is another landmark of the Oregon Trail. Here the Sweetwater River carves a narrow chasm through a high rock outcrop.

At Muddy Gap, follow Highway 287 west across a desolate desert basin. Roadside markers tell the harrowing story of Oregon Trail pioneers as they passed though this high-elevation wasteland. Follow Highway 28 south as it climbs steadily toward South Pass. Unlike many Rocky Mountain passes, South Pass is not a high mountain divide. Rather, it's a high desert plateau covered by sagebrush and short prairie grasses ideal for Oregon Trail pioneers and their wagon trains.

As the road climbs to the pass, it passes two historic Gold Rush towns from the 1870s. Atlantic City, a near-ghost town, still boasts the Mercantile, a steakhouse and

★
★
★
★
★

saloon that's been serving locals for more than a century. South Pass City preserves 39 acres of abandoned buildings from the days when Gold Rush fever brought thousands of residents to this lofty corner of Wyoming. *Approximately 340 miles.*

THE BIG HORN MOUNTAIN SCENIC LOOP

This loop tour departs from Cody, a Wild West town if there ever was one, and travels east across the arid plains to the Big Horn Mountains. This fault-block range rises precipitously to tower 13,000 feet above the neighboring rangeland. The route passes geological curiosities and sacred Native American sites before dropping back down to traverse the dramatic Big Horn Canyon on its return to Cody.

Cody is named for Buffalo Bill Cody, the showman famous for his traveling Wild West Show. The town was established in 1895, and though he didn't help found it, Cody was brought in shortly thereafter to promote the town. As befits a showman's adoptive home, the town of Cody overnight became a Wild West tourist destination.

Be sure to visit the complex of downtown museums and galleries that make up the Buffalo Bill Historical Center, particularly the Whitney Gallery of Western Art, which contains one of the world's foremost collections of 19th-century western art. As you leave Cody's too-perfect Wild West town center, consider a detour to Old Trail Town, west of town off Highway 20. This open-air museum preserves a collection of 26 historic frontier structures in their authentic state. Included are the actual cabins lived in by the likes of Butch Cassidy, plus the saloons, schoolhouses and ranch houses that represented everyday life for frontier pioneers.

Travel east of Cody on Highway 14, leaving behind the Yellowstone foothills to cross the increasingly barren ranchland of the Big Horn Basin. The gray, sparsely vegetated buttes and badlands that increasingly dominate the landscape are remnants of volcanic ash deposits from Yellowstone's ancient volcanoes. Dunes of ash built up here over millions of years; these are now mined for bentonite, a source material of cement.

Two things characterize this arid prairie: oil, made evident by the rise and fall of rigs scattered to the horizon, and dinosaurs. To get an idea of the plant and reptile Eden that once existed here, stop in Greybull (pronounced Grable) to visit the Greybull Museum. For a small regional museum, this institution houses an impressive number of significant fossils, including a five-foot-diameter ammonite and the remnants of a cycad tree forest from 120 million years ago.

Eight miles east of Greybull, on the Red Gulch-Alkali National Back Country Byway, is another important paleontological destination. The Red Gulch Dinosaur Tracksite preserves hundreds of dinosaur tracks left in oozy ocean shoreline mud about 167 million years ago. These tracks were only discovered in 1997 and are, worldwide, some of the only known tracks from the Middle Jurassic Era.

East of the town of Shell, Highway 14 begins to climb up through a wonderland of red hoodoos, the result of iron-rich ash deposits, to the near-vertical face of the Big Horn Mountains. This unusual mountain range was formed by uplifts along vertical fault lines: One side of the fault line has been pushed up over two miles into the sky, whereas the other dropped into the Big Horn Basin. The road climbs steeply up the red cliffs, eventually passing through dense forests and, even in midsummer, snowfields. Stop at the Shell Falls Viewpoint to gawk at Shell Creek as it tumbles into an extremely narrow canyon cut through limestone and granite.

WYOMING

★
★
★
★
★

The top of the Big Horns is a series of rolling mountain peaks flanked by vast alpine meadows, which in summer are spangled with wildflowers and tiny ponds of snowmelt. Watch for beaver dams in the coursing streambeds. Moose and elk are frequently seen in these high-country marshes.

At Burgess Junction, turn west onto Highway 14A. The road begins to drop back down the western face of the Big Horn range. Midway down the mountainside is a side road leading to the Medicine Wheel National Historic Landmark, a fascinating ritual site built by ancient Paleo-Indians. Perhaps dating back 10,000 years, this large ring of rocks with 28 radiating spokes aligned around a central hub is thought to be a Native American Stonehenge. Scientists believe the Medicine Wheel was used to make astronomical calculations and predictions. The Medicine Wheel is a one-mile hike from the parking area.

Continue the descent of the Big Horns and again you'll reach arid basin land. The road traverses the now dammed Big Horn River in its awe-inspiring canyon. Turn north on Highway 37 to catch glimpses of the canyon, more than 1,000 feet deep in places, threaded by the blue waters of the lake. To the north rise the Pryor Mountains, home to one of the West's last free-ranging herds of wild horses.

From Big Horn Canyon, return east along Highway 14A through Lovell and Powell to Cody. *Approximately 200 miles.*

BUFFALO

Buffalo began as a trading center at the edge of Fort McKinney, one of the last of the old military posts. In 1892, trouble erupted here between big cattlemen and small ranchers with their allies, the nesters, in the Johnson County Cattle War. Several people were killed before federal troops ended the conflict.

Located at the foot of the Big Horn Mountains, Buffalo attracts many tourists, hunters and anglers; the economy is dependent on tourism, as well as lumber, minerals and cattle. A Ranger District office of the Bighorn National Forest is located in Buffalo.

Information: Chamber of Commerce, 55 N. Main St., Buffalo,
307-684-5544, 800-227-5122; www.buffalowyo.com

HOTEL
★COMFORT INN
65 Highway 16 E, Buffalo, 307-684-9564, 877-424-6423; www.choicehotels.com
62 rooms. Wireless Internet access. Complimentary continental breakfast. Whirlpool, pool. Pets accepted. **$**

SPECIALTY LODGING
PARADISE GUEST RANCH
282 Hunter Creek Road, Buffalo, 307-684-7876;
www.paradiseranch.com
This magnificent dude ranch, the inspiration for *The Virginian,* is the West at its best. The beautiful log cabins have outdoor porches. At the French Creek Saloon, there are talent shows and square dancing. 18 rooms. Closed October-May. Complimentary full breakfast. Bar. Airport transportation available. Outdoor pool, whirlpool. No credit cards accepted. **$$$$**

★
★★
★★★
★★★★
★★★★★

CASPER

Before oil was discovered, Casper was a railroad terminus in the cattle-rich Wyoming hinterlands, where Native Americans and migrants on the Oregon Trail had passed before. Casper was known as an oil town after the first strike in 1890 in the Salt Creek Field, site of the Teapot Dome naval oil reserve that caused a top-level government scandal in the 1920s. World War I brought a real boom and exciting prosperity. A half-million dollars in oil stocks were traded in hotel lobbies every day; land prices skyrocketed and rents inflated while oil flowed through some of the world's biggest refineries. The crash of 1929 ended the speculation, but oil continued to flow through feeder lines to Casper. Oil continues to contribute to the area's economy; also important are tourism, agriculture, light manufacturing, coal, bentonite and uranium mining.

Information: Chamber of Commerce Visitor Center, 500 N. Center St.,
307-234-5311, 866-234-5311; www.casperwyoming.org

WHAT TO SEE AND DO

FORT CASPAR MUSEUM AND HISTORIC SITE

4001 Fort Caspar Road, Casper, 307-235-8462; www.fortcasparwyoming.com

A U.S. Army post in the 1860s, Fort Caspar served as a base for soldiers who first sought to protect pioneers, telegraph linemen and mail carriers and later fought Lakota warriors in a series of increasingly violent battles. Abandoned in 1867 after the railroad became the focal point of cross-country travel, Fort Caspar now features a number of replica buildings built in 1936 to depict the fort as it was in 1865. Also on site is a museum stocked with artifacts of regional historic importance. May and September, Monday-Sunday 8 a.m.-5 p.m.; June-August, Monday-Sunday 8 a.m.-7 p.m.; October-April, Tuesday-Saturday 8 a.m.-5 p.m.

NATIONAL HISTORIC TRAILS INTERPRETIVE CENTER

1501 N. Poplar St., Casper, 307-261-7700; www.wy.blm.gov/nhtic

Casper sits on numerous historic trails, including the Oregon, California, Mormon, Pioneer and Pony Express trails, all prime westerly routes of the mid-19th century. To commemorate the region's rich trail legacy, the Bureau of Land Management opened the National Historic Trails Interpretive Center in 2002, with exhibits covering everything from packing for a cross-country journey in a covered wagon to negotiating such a wagon across a raging river. The historic trail route is now marked and runs directly through the center's property. April-late October, daily 8 a.m.-7 p.m.; November-late March, Tuesday-Saturday 9 a.m.-4:30 p.m.; closed holidays.

HOTELS

★COMFORT INN

480 Lathrop Road, Evansville, 307-235-3038, 877-424-6423; www.comfortinn.com

56 rooms. Complimentary continental breakfast. Indoor pool, whirlpool. Pets accepted, some restrictions. $

★HAMPTON INN

400 W. F St., Casper, 307-235-6668, 800-426-7866; www.hamptoninn.com

121 rooms. Complimentary continental breakfast. High-speed Internet access. Airport transportation available. Fitness center. Indoor pool, whirlpool. $

★
★
★
★
★

★SHILO INN
739 Luker Lane, Casper, 307-237-1335, 800-222-2244; www.shiloinns.com
101 rooms. Complimentary continental breakfast. Spa, sauna, steam room. Business Center. Indoor pool, whirlpool. Pets accepted. **$**

RESTAURANT
★★SILVER FOX RESTAURANT AND LOUNGE
3422 S. Energy Lane, Casper, 307-235-3000
American menu. Lunch, dinner. Closed Sunday; holidays. Bar. Children's menu. Casual attire. **$$**

CHEYENNE
Cheyenne was named for an Algonquian tribe that roamed this area. When the Union Pacific Railroad reached what is now the capital and largest city of Wyoming on November 13, 1867, there was already a town. Between July of that year and the day the tracks were actually laid, 4,000 people had set up living quarters, and land values soared. Professional gunmen, soldiers, promoters, trainmen, gamblers and confidence men enjoying quick money and cheap liquor gave the town the reputation of being "hell on wheels." Two railways and three transcontinental highways made it a wholesale and commodity jobbing point, the retail and banking center of a vast region. Cheyenne is the seat of state and county government. Agriculture, light manufacturing, retail trade and tourism support the economy of the area.
Information: Cheyenne Convention & Visitors Bureau, 1 Depot Square
(121 W. 15th St.), Cheyenne, 800-426-5009; www.cheyenne.org

CHEYENNE FRONTIER DAYS
The rodeo equivalent of the Super Bowl, Cheyenne Frontier Days is not just a sporting event; it's also a rollicking street party, a family-friendly country fair and an annual celebration of the Wyoming capitol city's cowboy heritage. Nicknamed The Daddy of 'Em All, the "'em all" referring to the rest of the country's rodeos, the event lives up to its name.

Frontier Days began in 1897 at the behest of an agent from the Union Pacific Railroad. In an effort to increase leisure traffic, the company encouraged the cities on its lines to organize annual festivals and fairs. Cheyenne's entry took off quickly: The second Frontier Days (1898) saw a performance by Buffalo Bill Cody's Wild West Show. In 1903, President Teddy Roosevelt paid a visit, putting Frontier Days on the national stage.

By and large a volunteer effort, Frontier Days grew and grew (and got rowdier and rowdier, until the city buckled down on drinking and roughhousing), becoming one of the best-attended annual events in the west. Today, it attracts about 400,000 people every year, especially impressive in relation to Cheyenne's population of 50,000.

Held over the course of 10 days in late July and early August, Frontier Days kicks off with a Grand Parade through historic downtown Cheyenne that features innumerable horses, even more cowboys and a small faction of rodeo clowns. Most of the ensuing events take place at Frontier Park's Cheyenne Frontier Days Rodeo Arena, but all of Cheyenne bustles with activity for the duration.

The meat of the schedule is made up of nine rodeos, which run Saturday through the next weekend's Sunday, all of them sanctioned by the Professional Rodeo Cowboys

A GOOD OL' FRONTIER TOWN

Cheyenne grew up with the arrival of the railroad in 1867, going from a population of zero to 3,000 in five months. By 1880, 10,000 people made their home here. This rapid growth produced an unusual unity of architectural design. Cheyenne has one of the best-preserved frontier town centers in Wyoming.

Begin at the Wyoming Transportation Museum, 15th Street and Capitol Avenue. Formerly the depot for the Union Pacific Railway, this massive structure of stone and brick surmounted by a bell tower was built in 1886. The building now serves as a railway museum.

Walk north to 16th Street, the city's main street during the frontier era. Many of the handsome red-brick storefronts from the 1880s are still in use. Stop by the Old Town Square, a pedestrian-friendly, two-block area with boutique shopping and re-enactments of Old West activities, including a nightly shoot-out with gunslingers in period garb.

At the corner of 16th Street and Central Avenue is the **Historic Plains Hotel** *(1600 Central Ave.)*. Built in 1910, this grand old hotel has a wonderfully atmospheric lobby and one of the oldest restaurants and bars in the state. The Plains is a favorite watering hole for Wyoming's political movers and shakers.

Walk up Capitol Avenue, past opulent, late-Victorian state office buildings and storefronts with the state capitol building looming in the distance. Turn right on 17th Street and walk east to **Lexie's Café** *(216 E. 17th St.)*, a Cheyenne dining institution. This period restaurant is located in the city's oldest structure, the luxurious 1880s home of Erasmus Nagle. In summer, there's alfresco dining against the backdrop of the town's historic district.

Continue north along House Street, past more historic homes, to the **Historic Governors' Mansion** *(200 E. 21st St.)*. Built in 1904, this beautifully preserved sandstone structure was the home of Wyoming's governors until 1977. Today, free tours of the building focus on period furnishings and artifacts.

Head west on 23rd Avenue. **The Wyoming State Museum** *(2301 Central Ave.)* is the state's foremost history museum, telling Wyoming's story from the era of the dinosaurs to the present with especially good exhibits on the state's Native American and early settlement history. The museum also houses the state's art collection, rich in late 19th-century western art.

Continue one block west to Capitol Avenue and turn north. The **Wyoming Arts Council Gallery** *(2320 Capitol Ave.)* is housed in an 1880s carriage house and is dedicated to mounting the works of contemporary Wyoming artists.

With its gleaming 24-karat gold leaf dome and French Renaissance architectural sensibility, the Wyoming State Capitol Building at 24th and Capitol Avenue has dominated Cheyenne's skyline since 1888. The interior is equally grandiose with marble floors, mahogany woodwork and banks of stained glass. Free tours lead through the legislative chambers or visitors can explore the building's art, historical displays and huge stuffed buffalo (the state's symbol) on their own.

From there, continue south along Capitol Avenue, turning west at 18th Street. The **Nelson Museum of the West** *(1714 Carey Ave.)* offers 11,000 square feet of exhibits focusing on Native America and the Old West. One block farther south, at Carey and 16th Street, is Cheyenne's farmers market, where local growers sell produce on Saturday mornings.

WYOMING

★
★
★
★
★

Association. Top cowboys compete in staple events such as bull riding, calf roping, barrel racing and steer wrestling at the CFD Rodeo Arena.

The Frontier Days' pancake breakfasts, held three times over the course of the event, are also legendary. About 30,000 attendees gobble up 100,000 free flapjacks, which are poured on the griddle and flipped by the local Kiwanis club. (Legend has it that the batter is mixed up in a cement truck.) Chuck wagon cook-offs, also free, are another culinary highlight.

Beyond sport and food, music is another big source of entertainment at Frontier Days. Nightly concerts feature big Nashville names such as George Strait and Kenny Chesney, as well as rockers like ZZ Top. Concert tickets are sold separately from those for the rodeo events. There are also free performances almost every day at Frontier Park.

Organizers invited members of Wyoming's native Shoshone tribe to perform at the second Frontier Days in 1898; the tradition continues to this day. Native American dancers, storytellers and musicians perform regularly at the Indian Village, and vendors from various area tribes sell jewelry, food and crafts.

A carnival midway, aerial show and re-created Old West town are among the other diversions.

Tickets for the rodeos and concerts are available by calling 800-227-6336 or visiting www.cfdrodeo.com. Reserve early and be prepared to pay a premium for accommodations during the event—most Cheyenne hotels charge 50 to 100 percent more for a double room during Frontier Days. The same goes for commercial campgrounds and RV parks.

WHAT TO SEE AND DO
HISTORIC GOVERNORS' MANSION
300 E. 21st St., Cheyenne, 307-777-7878; www.wyoparks.state.wy.us
The residence of Wyoming's governors from 1905 to 1976, this was the first governor's mansion in the nation to be occupied by a woman, Nellie Tayloe Ross (1925-1927). September-May, Tuesday-Saturday 9 a.m.-5 p.m., closed Sunday, Monday, holidays; June-August, Monday-Saturday 9 a.m.-5 p.m., Sunday 1-5 p.m.

STATE CAPITOL
24th Street and Capitol Avenue, Cheyenne,
307-777-7220; www.ai.state.wy.us/
Art and architecture fans will be impressed by the Beaux Arts building, with murals in the senate and house chambers by Allen T. True and stained glass ceilings. Guided tours: Monday-Friday 9 a.m.-3:30 p.m.; closed weekends, holidays.

HOTELS
★COMFORT INN
2245 Etchepare Drive, Cheyenne, 307-638-7202, 877-424-6423; www.comfortinn.com
77 rooms. Wireless Internet access. Complimentary continental breakfast. Fitness center. Outdoor pool. Pets accepted. $

★FAIRFIELD INN
1415 Stillwater Ave., Cheyenne, 307-637-4070, 888-236-2427; www.fairfieldinn.com
62 rooms. Wireless Internet access. Complimentary continental breakfast. Fitness center. Indoor pool, whirlpool. Spa. Business Center. $

★★HITCHING POST INN RESORT & CONFERENCE CENTER

1700 W. Lincolnway, Cheyenne, 307-638-3301, 800-272-6232; www.ramada.com
166 rooms. Wireless Internet access. Restaurant, bar. Airport transportation available.
Fitness center. Indoor pool, outdoor pool, whirlpool. Business Center. Pets accepted. **$**

★★LITTLE AMERICA HOTEL - CHEYENNE

2800 W. Lincolnway, Cheyenne, 307-775-8400, 800-445-6945; www.littleamerica.com
188 rooms. High-speed Internet access. Restaurant, bar. Airport transportation available. Fitness center. Outdoor pool. Pets accepted. **$**

RESTAURANT
★POOR RICHARD'S RESTAURANT

2233 E. Lincolnway, Cheyenne, 307-635-5114; www.poorrichardscheyenne.com
American menu. Lunch, dinner. Closed Sunday. Bar. Children's menu. Casual attire. **$$**

CODY

Buffalo Bill Cody founded this town, gave it his name, and devoted time and money to its development. He built a hotel and named it after his daughter Irma, arranged for a railroad spur from Montana and, with the help of his friend Theodore Roosevelt, had what was then the world's tallest dam constructed just west of town.

Cody is located 52 miles east of Yellowstone National Park; everyone entering Yellowstone from the east must pass through here, making tourism an important industry. A Ranger District office of the Shoshone National Forest is located here.
Information: Cody Country Chamber of Commerce,
836 Sheridan Ave., Cody, 307-587-2777; www.codychamber.org

WHAT TO SEE AND DO
BUFFALO BILL DAM AND VISITOR CENTER

4808 North Fork Highway, east end of reservoir, Cody, 307-527-6076; www.bbdvc.org
Originally called the Shoshone Dam, the 350-foot dam's name was changed in 1946 to honor Buffalo Bill, who helped raise money for its construction. The visitor center has a natural history museum, dam overlook and gift shop. May and September, Monday-Saturday 8 a.m.-6 p.m., Sunday 10 a.m.-6 p.m.; June-August, Monday-Friday 8 a.m.-8 p.m., Saturday 8 a.m.-6 p.m., Sunday 10 a.m.-6 p.m.; closed, October-April.

BUFFALO BILL MUSEUM

720 Sheridan Ave., Cody, 307-857-4771; www.bbhc.org
Browse personal and historical memorabilia of the great showman and scout including guns, saddles, clothing, trophies, gifts and posters.

SHOSHONE NATIONAL FOREST

808 Meadow Lane, Cody, 307-527-6241; www.fs.fed.us/r2/shoshone/
This nearly 2.5 million-acre area is one of the largest in the national forest system. It includes a magnificent approach route (Buffalo Bill Cody's Scenic Byway) to the east gate of Yellowstone National Park along the north fork of the Shoshone River. The Fitzpatrick, Popo Agie, North Absaroka, Washakie and a portion of the Absaroka-Beartooth wilderness areas all lie within its boundaries. It includes outstanding lakes, streams, big-game herds, mountains and some of the largest glaciers in the continental United States.

WYOMING

★
★
★
★
★

WHITNEY GALLERY OF WESTERN ART

720 Sheridan Ave., Cody, 307-857-4771; www.bbhc.org

A major collection and comprehensive display of Western art by artists from the early 1800s through today, the gallery mostly features painting and sculpture.

SPECIAL EVENTS
CODY NITE RODEO

Stampede Park, 519 W. Yellowstone Ave., Cody,
307-587-5155, 800-207-0744; www.codystampederodeo.com

Cody is known as the Rodeo Capital of the World and for good reason. Since the 1940s, the city has been the site of the Cody Nite Rodeo, the only nightly rodeo in the country. All summer long, patrons are treated to staple events such as calf roping, steer wrestling, barrel racing and—the big event—bull riding. Upstart competitors hail from all over the globe, making Cody Nite Rodeo something of a minor league for the pro rodeo circuit. Geared toward families, the event also features a number of kid-oriented sidelights, most notably the audience participation in the Calf Scramble, when kids in attendance race to snatch a ribbon off an unsuspecting calf. The rodeo clowns are the unofficial hosts, serving up comedy skits when they're not doing their real duty: keeping angry bulls from stomping dispatched riders. Daily June-last Saturday in August.

YELLOWSTONE JAZZ FESTIVAL

Cody and Powell; www.yellowstonejazz.com

Each year the Yellowstone Jazz Festival attracts top jazz performers and musicians to the Yellowstone National Park area to participate in numerous jazz concerts. Mid-July.

HOTELS
★COMFORT INN

1601 Sheridan Ave., Cody, 307-587-5556, 877-424-6423;
www.blairhotels.com

75 rooms. Wireless Internet access. Complimentary continental breakfast. Restaurant. Airport transportation available. $$

★★HOLIDAY INN

1701 Sheridan Ave., Cody, 307-587-5555, 800-315-2621; www.holidayinn.com

189 rooms. Wireless Internet access. Restaurant, bar. Airport transportation available. Fitness center. Outdoor pool. $

SPECIALTY LODGINGS
MAYOR'S INN BREAD AND BREAKFAST

1413 Rumsey Ave., Cody, 307-587-0887, 888-217-3001; www.mayorsinn.com

Five rooms. Complimentary full breakfast. $$

RIMROCK RANCH

2728 North Fork Highway, Cody, 307-587-3970; www.rimrockranch.com

Nine rooms. Closed October-April. Complimentary full breakfast. Airport transportation available. Outdoor pool, whirlpool. $$$$

DEVILS TOWER NATIONAL MONUMENT

The nation's first national monument, Devils Tower was set aside for the American people by President Theodore Roosevelt in 1906. Located on 1,347 acres approximately five miles west of the Black Hills National Forest, this gigantic landmark rises from the prairie like a giant tree stump. Sixty million years ago, volcanic activity pushed molten rock toward the earth's surface. As it cooled, Devils Tower was formed. Towering 1,267 feet above the prairie floor and Ponderosa pine forest, the flat-topped formation appears to change hue with the hour of the day and glows during sunsets and in moonlight.

The visitor center at the base of the tower offers information about the area, a museum and a bookstore (April-October, daily). A self-guided trail winds around the tower for nature and scenery lovers. There are picnicking and camping facilities with tables, fireplaces, water and restrooms (April-October).
Information: 307-467-5283; www.nps.gov/deto/

SEVEN D RANCH
774 Sunlight Road, Cody, 307-587-9885, 888-587-9885;
www.7dranch.com
11 rooms. Closed mid-September-mid-June. Complimentary full breakfast. Restaurant. Airport transportation available. **$$$$**

UXU RANCH
1710 Yellowstone Highway, Wapiti, 307-587-2143, 800-373-9027;
www.uxuranch.com
10 rooms. Closed October-May. Restaurant, bar. Whirlpool. **$$$$**

DOUGLAS

Cattlemen were attracted here by plentiful water and good grass. Homesteaders gradually took over, and agriculture became dominant. The town was named for Stephen Douglas, Lincoln's celebrated debating opponent. A Ranger District office for the Medicine Bow National Forest is located in Douglas.
Information: Douglas Area Chamber of Commerce,
121 Brownfield Road, 307-358-2950, 877-937-4996;
www.jackalope.org

WHAT TO SEE AND DO
FORT FETTERMAN STATE HISTORIC SITE
752 Highway 93, Douglas, 307-684-7629;
www.wyoparks.state.wy.us
Established in 1867 on a plateau above the North Platte River, Fort Fetterman served as a supply base for U.S. wars against native tribes for 15 years. Now mostly in ruins, the fort offers a snapshot into the Douglas area's history, with a pair of restored buildings showcasing historic displays. The facilities include campsites, picnic areas and an interpretive trail. Daily sunrise-sunset; closed winter; museum: Memorial Day-Labor Day, daily 9 a.m.-5 p.m.

HOTEL
★★BEST WESTERN DOUGLAS INN AND CONFERENCE CENTER
1450 Riverbend Drive, Douglas, 307-358-9790, 800-780-7234;
www.bestwestern.com
117 rooms. Wireless Internet access. Complimentary continental breakfast. Restaurant, bar. Fitness center. Indoor pool, whirlpool. Pets accepted. $

DUBOIS
On the Wind River, 56 miles from Grand Teton National Park, Dubois is surrounded on three sides by the Shoshone National Forest. The Wind River Reservation (Shoshone and Arapahoe) is a few miles east of town. Dubois, in ranching and dude ranching country, is a good vacation headquarters. There are plentiful rock hounding resources, and a large herd of Bighorn sheep roam within five miles of town. A Ranger District office of the Shoshone National Forest is located here.
Information: Chamber of Commerce, 616 W. Ramshorn St.,
307-455-2556; www.duboiswyoming.org

HOTEL
★SUPER 8
1412 Warm Springs Drive, Dubois, 307-455-3694, 800-800-8000; www.super8.com
34 rooms. Complimentary continental breakfast. High-speed Internet access. Fitness center. Whirlpool. Pets accepted, some restrictions. $

SPECIALTY LODGING
BROOKS LAKE LODGE
458 Brooks Lake Road, Dubois, 307-455-2121; www.brookslake.com
Built as an inn for Yellowstone travelers in 1922, this historic property offers guests accommodations in the spirit of the early west in beautiful surroundings. 14 rooms. Closed mid-April-mid-June and mid-September-early October. Complimentary full breakfast. Restaurant, bar. Airport transportation available. Fitness center. Spa. Whirlpool. $$$

EVANSTON
Coal from the mines at Almy, six miles north of Evanston, supplied trains of the Union Pacific Railroad, which operated a roundhouse and machine shop in Evanston beginning in 1871. By 1872, the mines employed 600 men.

While cattle and sheep ranching remain important industries, the discovery of gas and oil has triggered a new "frontier" era for the town. Evanston is also a trading center and tourist stopping point.
Information: City of Evanston, 1200 Main St., Evanston,
866-783-6300; www.evanstonwy.org

HOTEL
★★BEST WESTERN DUNMAR INN
1601 Harrison Drive, Evanston, 307-789-3770, 800-870-7234; www.bestwestern.com
165 rooms. Wireless Internet access. Restaurant, bar. Fitness center. Outdoor pool, whirlpool. $

GILLETTE

The city calls itself the "Energy Capital of the Nation" due its location near the development of coal, oil and methane gas. Its newspaper, *The News Record*, began in 1904 and is now the oldest business in Campbell County.

Information: Campbell County Chamber of Commerce,

314 S. Gillette Ave., 307-686-0040, 800-544-6136; www.gillettechamber.com

WHAT TO SEE AND DO

KEYHOLE STATE PARK

22 Marina Road, Moorcroft, 307-756-3596; www.wyoparks.state.wy.us

Within sight of Devils Tower, the mountains in Keyhole State Park form the western boundary of the Black Hills. Antelope, deer and wild turkeys are common to this area and the reservoir is excellent for water sports including swimming, fishing and boating. Picnicking, lodging, camping and tent and trailer sites are available.

HOTEL

★★CLARION HOTEL

2009 S. Douglas Highway, Gillette,

307-686-3000, 800-686-3068; www.westernplaza.com

159 rooms. Wireless Internet access. Complimentary continental breakfast. Restaurant, bar. Airport transportation available. Fitness center. Indoor pool, whirlpool. $

RESTAURANT

★★PAISLEY SHAWL

416 W. Birch St., Glenrock, 307-436-9212; www.higginshotel.com

American menu. Lunch, dinner. Closed Sunday-Monday; holidays. Bar. Children's menu. Outdoor seating. $$

GRAND TETON NATIONAL PARK

These rugged, block-faulted mountains began to rise about nine million years ago, making them some of the youngest on the continent. Geologic and glacial forces combined to buckle and sculpt the landscape into a dramatic setting of canyons, cirques and craggy peaks, which cast their reflections across numerous clear alpine lakes.

287

WYOMING

★
★
★
★
★

The Snake River winds gracefully through Jackson Hole ("hole" being the old fur trapper's term for a high-altitude valley surrounded by mountains).

John Colter passed through the area from 1807 to 1808. French-Canadian trappers in the region thought the peaks resembled breasts and applied the French word *teton* to them.

Entering from the north, from Yellowstone National Park, Highway 89-191-287 skirts the eastern shore of Jackson Lake to Colter Bay, continuing to Jackson Lake Junction, where it turns eastward to the entrance at Moran Junction (at Highway 26). The Teton Park Road begins at Jackson Lake Junction and borders the mountains to Jenny Lake, then continues to park headquarters at Moose. Highway 89-191-26 parallels Teton Park Road on the east side of the Snake River to the south entrance from Moran Junction. All highways have a continuous view of the Teton Range, which runs from north to south. Highway 26-89-191 is open year-round from Jackson to Flagg Ranch, two miles south of Yellowstone National Park's South Gate, as is Highway 26-287 to Dubois. Secondary roads and Teton Park Road are open May-October.

The park is open year-round (limited in winter), with food and lodging available in the park from mid-May through September and in Jackson. There are three visitor centers with interpretive displays: Moose Visitor Center (daily; closed December 25), Colter Bay Visitor Center & Indian Arts Museum (mid-May-late September, daily), and Jenny Lake Visitor Center (June-Labor Day). Ranger-led hikes are available (mid-June-mid-September, daily; inquire for schedule), and self-guided trails are marked. A 24-hour recorded message gives information about weather: 307-739-3611.

The park can be explored by various means. There is hiking on more than 200 miles of trails. Corrals at Jackson Lake Lodge and Colter Bay have strings of horses accustomed to rocky trails; pack trips can be arranged. Boaters and anglers can enjoy placid lakes or wild streams; the Colter Bay, Signal Mountain and Leek's marinas have ramps, guides, facilities and rentals. Climbers can tackle summits via routes of varying difficulty; the more ambitious may take advantage of Exum School of Mountaineering and Jackson Hole Mountain Guides classes that range from a beginner's course to an attempt at conquering the 13,770-foot Grand Teton, considered a major North American climbing peak.

Horses, boats and other equipment can be rented. Bus tours, an airport, auto rentals, general stores and guide services are available. Five National Park Service campgrounds are maintained: Colter Bay, Signal Mountain, Jenny Lake, Lizard Creek and Gros Ventre. Slide-illustrated talks on the park and its features are held each night (mid-June-Labor Day) at the amphitheaters at Colter Bay, Signal Mountain and Gros Ventre.

Many river and lake trips are offered, and visitors can choose an adventure to suit their individual tastes. Five-, 10- and 20-mile trips on rubber rafts navigate the Snake River. A self-guided trail tells the story of Menor's Ferry and the Maude Noble Cabin. Jenny Lake has boat trips and boat rentals. Jackson Lake cruises are available, some reaching island hideaways for breakfast cookouts. Boat rentals also are available at Jackson Lake. The Grand Teton Lodge Company offers a full-day guided bus and boat trip covering major points of interest in the park (June-mid-September). Call 307-543-2811.

A tram with a vertical lift of 4,600 feet operates at Teton Village, rising from the valley floor to the top of Rendezvous Peak, just outside the park's southern boundary.

The Chapel of the Transfiguration, located in Moose, is a log chapel with a large picture window over the altar framing the mountains (daily; services held late May-September).

★
★ ★
★ ★
★

The park is home to abundant wildlife, including pronghorn antelopes, bighorn sheep, mule deer, elk, moose, grizzly and black bears, coyotes, beavers, marmots, bald eagles and trumpeter swans. Never approach or feed any wild animal. Do not pick wildflowers.

A park boat permit is required for boating. A Wyoming fishing license is required for any fishing and may be obtained at several locations in the park. Camping permits are required for backcountry camping.

Grand Teton and Yellowstone national parks admission is $20 per car.

Information: Moose, 307-739-3300; www.nps.gov/grte/

HOTELS

★★★JACKSON LAKE LODGE

North Highways 89 and 1191, Moran,
307-543-3100, 800-628-9988; www.gtlc.com

This lodge is a full-service property located in Grand Teton National Park. It offers a view across Jackson Lake and views of Mount Moran and the Grand Tetons. The grand lobby has two fireplaces and a 60-foot picture window. 385 rooms. Closed early October-mid-May. Restaurant, bar. Airport transportation available. Outdoor pool. $$

★★TOGWOTEE MOUNTAIN LODGE

Highway 26/287, Moran, 307-543-2847, 800-543-2847; www.cowboyvillage.com
89 rooms. Restaurant, bar. $

GREEN RIVER

Green River, seat of Sweetwater County, is known as the trona (sodium sesquicarbonate) capital of the world. As early as 1852, Jim Bridger guided Captain Howard Stansbury on a Native American trail through the area. By 1862, the settlement here consisted mainly of an overland stage station located on the east bank of the Green River. In 1868, Major John Wesley Powell started from here on his expedition on the Green and Colorado rivers. This point of departure is now known as Expedition Island. The Green River, one of Wyoming's largest, is the northern gateway to the Flaming Gorge National Recreation Area.

Information: Chamber of Commerce, 1155 W. Flaming Gorge Way,
307-875-5711, 800-354-6743; www.grchamber.com

HOTEL

★★LITTLE AMERICA HOTEL

I-80 exit 68, Little America, 307-875-2400, 888-652-9042; www.littleamerica.com
140 rooms. Restaurant, bar. High-speed Internet access. Fitness center. Outdoor pool. Pets accepted. $

JACKSON

Jackson, uninhibitedly western, is the key town for the mountain-rimmed, 600-square-mile valley of Jackson Hole, which is surrounded by mountain scenery, dude ranches, national parks, big game and other vacation attractions. Jackson Hole Mountain Resort is one of the most famous ski resort areas in the country, known for its spectacular views and abundant ski slopes. It has three Alpine ski areas, five Nordic ski areas and miles of groomed snowmobile trails. Annual snowfall usually exceeds

38 feet, and winter temperatures average around 21 F. Teton Village, or "the Village," surrounds the base of Jackson Hole Mountain Resort and is 12 miles northwest of Jackson Hole.

The Jackson Hole area, which includes Grand Teton National Park, the town of Jackson and much of the Bridger-Teton National Forest, has all the facilities and luxuries necessary to accommodate both the winter and summer visitor. Jackson Hole offers winter sports, boating, chuck wagon dinner shows, live theater productions, symphony concerts, art galleries, rodeos, horseback riding, mountain climbing, fishing and several whitewater and scenic float trips. Two Ranger District offices of the Bridger-Teton National Forest are located in Jackson.

Information: Jackson Hole Area Chamber of Commerce,
990 W. Broadway, Jackson Hole, 307-733-3316; www.jacksonholechamber.com

WHAT TO SEE AND DO
AERIAL TRAMWAY
Jackson, 307-733-2292; www.tram-foundation.com
The tram makes a 2 1/2-mile ride to top of Rendezvous Mountain for spectacular views. Late May-early October.

BRIDGER-TETON NATIONAL FOREST
Jackson, 307-739-5500; www.fs.fed.us/btnf
With more than 3.3 million acres, the forest literally surrounds the town of Jackson. Bridger-Teton was the site of one of the largest earth slides in U.S. history, the Gros Ventre Slide in 1925, which dammed the Gros Ventre River (to a height of 225 feet and a width of nearly a half mile), forming Slide Lake, which is approximately three miles long. There are scenic drives along the Hoback River Canyon, the Snake River Canyon and in Star Valley. Unspoiled backcountry includes parts of Gros Ventre, Teton and Wind River ranges along the Continental Divide and the Wyoming Range. Teton Wilderness (557,311 acres) and Gros Wilderness (247,000 acres) are accessible on foot or horseback. There are also places for swimming, fishing, rafting, hiking, mountain biking, winter sports and camping. Also in the forest is Bridger Wilderness.

NATIONAL MUSEUM OF WILDLIFE ART
2820 Rungius Road, Jackson, 307-733-5771, 800-313-9553; www.wildlifeart.org
Nearly blending into the hillside across from the National Elk Refuge, this organic-looking structure (made of red sandstone from Arizona) houses an impressive collection of wildlife art: nearly 4,000 works dating from 2000 B.C., the 21st century and just about every artistic era in between. The museum is the largest arts facility committed to the theme of wildlife and includes galleries dedicated to the American bison and legendary wildlife impressionist Carl Rungius. Among the other artists represented here are bird specialist John James Audubon, Dutch master Rembrandt and cowboy artist Charles M. Russell. The kids program is excellent, with many interactive exhibits and a strong educational component. There is a restaurant and a gift shop on site. In winter, sleigh tours of the National Elk Refuge originate here, and combination admission-sleigh tour packages are available. Mid-May-mid-October, daily 9 a.m.-5 p.m.; mid-October-mid May, Monday-Saturday 9 a.m.-5 p.m., Sunday 1-5 p.m.; closed holidays.

★
★★
★★★
★★
★

SOLITUDE FLOAT TRIPS

110 E. Karns Ave., Jackson, 307-733-2871,
888-704-2800; www.grand-teton-scenic-floats.com

Take a five- or 10-mile scenic trip within Grand Teton National Park. Reservations suggested.

TRIANGLE X FLOAT TRIPS

Two Triangle X Ranch Road, Moose, on the Snake River in Grand
Teton National Park, 307-733-2183; www.trianglex.com

Trips include 10-mile floats, sunrise and evening wildlife floats and cookout supper floats. Most trips originate at Triangle X Ranch. May-October.

SPECIAL EVENTS

GRAND TETON MUSIC FESTIVAL

4015 W. Lake Creek Drive, Wilson, 307-733-3050; www.gtmf.org

Symphony and chamber music concerts include a virtuoso orchestra of top professional musicians from around the world. Early July-late August.

JACKSON HOLE FALL ARTS FESTIVAL

Jackson, 307-733-3316; www.jacksonholewy.com

A three-week celebration of the arts, the Jackson Hole Fall Arts Festival features special exhibits in more than 30 galleries, demonstrations, dance, theater, a mountain film festival, Native American arts and culinary arts. Mid-September-early October.

HOTELS

★BEST WESTERN THE LODGE AT JACKSON HOLE

80 Scott Lane, Jackson, 307-739-9703, 800-458-3866; www.lodgeatjh.com

153 rooms. Complimentary continental breakfast. Wireless Internet access. Indoor, outdoor pool, whirlpool. Complimentary ski shuttle (winter). Fitness center. $$

★QUALITY INN 49'ER INNS & SUITES

330 W. Pearl Ave., Jackson, 307-733-7550,
800-451-2980, 800-483-8667; www.townsquareinns.com

142 rooms. Complimentary continental breakfast. Wireless Internet access. Fitness center. Whirlpool. Pets accepted, some restrictions. $

★★★RUSTY PARROT LODGE

175 N. Jackson St., Jackson, 307-733-2000, 888-739-1749; www.rustyparrot.com

Just minutes from Grand Teton and Yellowstone national parks and Jackson Hole, the lodge is also just three blocks from Town Square. Rustic rooms are filled with mountain-style touches: antler chandeliers, hand-made furniture and goose-down comforters. A hearty breakfast is included in the rates. To rejuvenate the body and the spirit after a day on the slopes, try one of the many treatments available at the Body Sage, the onsite day spa. 31 rooms. Complimentary full breakfast. Restaurant, bar. Spa. Whirlpool. $$$

WYOMING

★
★
★
★
★

★★★SPRING CREEK RANCH
1800 Spirit Dance Road, Jackson, 307-733-8833,
800-443-6139; www.springcreekranch.com
Offering a view of the Teton Mountain Range and surrounded by two national parks
and tons of wildlife, this resort features great accommodations and ways to prepare
you for or unwind after a day of hiking or skiing including yoga classes and personal
training at the spa. After you've stretched, relax in front of the wood burning fireplace
in each room. 122 rooms. Wireless Internet access. Restaurant, bar. Airport transpor-
tation available. Fitness center. Spa. Outdoor pool, two whirlpools. Tennis. $$$

★★★THE WORT HOTEL
50 N. Glenwood St., Jackson, 307-733-2190, 800-322-2727; www.worthotel.com
Reflecting the history and culture of Jackson Hole, this popular country inn is deco-
rated with fabrics and furnishings of the Old West. 59 rooms. Restaurant, bar. Airport
transportation available. Fitness center. Whirlpool. $$$

★WYOMING INN
930 W. Broadway, Jackson, 307-734-0035, 800-844-0035; www.wyoming-inn.com
73 rooms. Wireless Internet access. Complimentary continental breakfast. Airport
transportation available. Business Center. $$

SPECIALTY LODGINGS
THE ALPINE HOUSE COUNTRY INN & SPA
285 N. Glenwood St., Jackson, 307-739-1570, 800-753-1421;
www.alpinehouse.com
22 rooms. Closed April and November. $$

GRAND VICTORIAN LODGE
85 Perry Ave., Jackson, 307-739-2294, 800-584-0532; www.grandvictorianlodge.com
11 rooms. Complimentary full breakfast. Wireless Internet access. Whirlpool. $$

INN ON THE CREEK
295 N. Millward, Jackson, 800-669-9534; www.innonthecreek.com
Nine rooms. Closed three weeks in April. Complimentary full breakfast. Wireless
Internet access. $$

PARKWAY INN
125 N. Jackson St., Jackson, 307-733-3143, 800-247-8390; www.parkwayinn.com
49 rooms. Complimentary continental breakfast. Fitness center. Indoor pool, whirl-
pool. No credit cards accepted. $$

THE WILDFLOWER INN
3725 N. Teton Village Road, Jackson, 307-733-4710; www.jacksonholewildflower.com
Five rooms. Complimentary full breakfast. Wireless Internet access. Whirlpool. $$$

RESTAURANTS

★★★BLUE LION
160 N. Millward St., Jackson, 307-733-3912; www.bluelionrestaurant.com

Housed in a charming old home, this restaurant offers creative preparations of many dishes. American menu. Dinner. Bar. Children's menu. Casual attire. Reservations recommended. Outdoor seating. $$$

★★★CADILLAC GRILLE
55 N. Cache Drive, Jackson, 307-733-3279; www.cadillac-grille.com

Aglow with neon lights, this energetic restaurant on the town square's west side has been open since 1983. The creative dishes are served in a fun, casual atmosphere. American menu. Lunch, dinner. Closed November. Bar. Casual attire. Reservations recommended. Outdoor seating. $$$

★★CALICO
2650 Teton Village Road, Jackson, 307-733-2460; www.calicorestaurant.com

Italian menu. Dinner. Bar. Children's menu. Casual attire. Outdoor seating. $$

★★MILLION DOLLAR COWBOY STEAK HOUSE
25 N. Cache St., Jackson, 307-733-2207; www.milliondollarcowboybar.com

Steak menu. Dinner. Closed April and early November-early December. Bar. Children's menu. Casual attire. Reservations recommended. $$$

★★★SNAKE RIVER GRILL
84 E. Broadway, Jackson, 307-733-0557; www.snakerivergrill.com

A cozy stone fireplace is set in the center of this rustic restaurant where you'll find novel dishes like sake-steamed black cod and wood-fired steak tartar pizza. American menu. Dinner. Closed April and November. Bar. Casual attire. Reservations recommended. Outdoor seating. $$$

TETON VILLAGE

Easily Wyoming's highest-profile ski resort, Jackson Hole Mountain Resort is set on the eastern flank of the Teton Range, south of Grand Teton National Park and northwest of Jackson itself. Spread across two mountains (Apres Vous and Rendezvous), the resort's ski terrain features the longest continuous rise in the United States—4,139 feet and 2,500 acres geared toward the skilled skier (10% beginner, 40% intermediate and 50% expert). There is also a super pipe and a terrain park for the snowboarders, as well as a Nordic Center for cross-country skiers. Among the 11 lifts are an aerial tram (which also runs in summer) and an eight-person gondola. The booming base village is buzzing with activity with a number of new hotels and time-share complexes, as well as restaurants, stores and a ski school. While not as well known for warm-weather recreation, the resort also is a good base for hiking, golf and horseback riding. December to mid-April, daily.

Information: Jackson Hole Mountain Resort, 3395 McCollister Drive, Teton Village, 307-733-2292; www.jacksonhole.com

WYOMING

★
★
★
★
★

HOTELS

★★ALPENHOF LODGE

3255 W. Village Drive, Teton Village, 307-733-3242,
800-732-3244; www.alpenhoflodge.com

42 rooms. Closed November. High-speed Internet access. Complimentary continental breakfast. Restaurant, bar. Outdoor pool, whirlpool. Spa. **$$**

★★★★★FOUR SEASONS RESORT JACKSON HOLE

7680 Granite Loop Road, Teton Village,
307-732-5000; www.fourseasons.com/jacksonhole

Laidback western style is paired with big-city attention to detail in this full-service resort set amid the natural beauty of the Teton Mountains. Rooms are warm and welcoming, with gas fireplaces and décor that hints at the area's Native American heritage. Besides ski-in/ski-out access to the area's famous trails, the resort boasts a ski concierge, who handles lift tickets, advises skiers on trails and assists with equipment selections. Guests can reward themselves after a day of skiing or fly-fishing with a meal at the cozy Westbank Grill, where local specialties such as mustard- and tarragon-crusted Colorado lamb fill the menu. 124 rooms. Wireless Internet access. Restaurant, bar. Airport transportation available. Fitness center. Spa. Outdoor pool, whirlpool. Pets accepted; some restrictions.

★★THE INN AT JACKSON HOLE

3345 W. Village Drive, Teton Village, 307-733-2311, 800-842-7666;
www.innatjh.com

83 rooms. Restaurant, bar. Outdoor pool, whirlpool. High-speed Internet access. Spa. **$$**

★★★SNAKE RIVER LODGE & SPA

7710 Granite Loop Road, Teton Village,
307-732-6000; www.snakeriverlodge.rockresorts.com

Get away from it all and let The Snake River Lodge take care of the rest. From the 7,000 square-foot spa to the beautiful indoor/outdoor pool with waterfalls, warmed walkways and a hot tub inside a steamy cave, to the five-spiced duck breast in the restaurant, Gamefish, they've taken your every whim into consideration. Work out in the state-of-the-art gym and book the Sportsman's Relief massage at the spa for when you ski back in. 93 rooms, 58 condominiums. Wireless Internet access. Restrictions on children. Complimentary (continental, buffet, made-to-order) breakfast. Restaurant, bar. Fitness center. Pool. Spa. Business center.

★★★TETON MOUNTAIN LODGE

3385 Cody Lane, Teton Village, 307-734-7111, 800-631-6271;
www.tetonlodge.com

Just steps away from the sites of Grand Teton National Park, skiers will enjoy the in-room boot dryers and overnight ski storage and tuning. After hitting the slopes indulge with an aromatherapy or hot stone massage at Solitude Spa or warm up near the fire place over a plate of potato and goat cheese ravioli at Cascade Grill House & Spirits. 129 rooms. High-speed Internet access. Restaurant, bar. Fitness center. Indoor pool, outdoor pool, children's pool, whirlpool. Spa. **$$$**

SPA
★★★★THE SPA AT FOUR SEASONS RESORT JACKSON HOLE
7680 Granite Loop Road, Teton Village,
307-732-5200; www.fourseasons.com/jacksonhole

The Four Seasons Resort Jackson Hole marries the rugged style of the west with international elegance, service and style. Therapies, like the mountain clay body wrap, reflect the resort's alpine location and draw from local ingredients. The massage menu is well rounded, offering everything from aromatherapy and deep tissue treatments to moonlight massages and native stone therapies. Hair and nail care is available in the adjacent salon, while the fitness center and pool complete the well-rounded experience here.

RESTAURANTS
★★★THE ALPENROSE IN THE ALPENHOF LODGE
3255 W. Village Drive, Teton Village, 307-733-3242,
800-732-3244; www.alpenhoflodge.com

At the base of the Jackson Hole ski area, the restaurant at this Bavarian-style lodge is the best regarded dining room in the area. Here the emphasis is on hearty dishes of western-influenced continental cuisine. Variations on classic themes include the tableside preparation of caribou steak Diane and a great bananas Foster. The property's upstairs bistro offers more casual fare. American menu. Dinner. Closed Sunday-Monday, November. Bar. Casual attire. **$$$**

★★★THE WESTBANK GRILL AT THE FOUR SEASONS RESORT
7680 Granite Loop Road, Teton Village,
307-732-5000; www.fourseasons.com/jacksonhole

The Westbank Grill is the finest example of sophisticated western flavors. It also offers diners awe-inspiring views of the Teton Mountains. The restaurant is divided into an indoor dining room and outdoor terrace. The dining room boasts a large stone fireplace, tile floors, exposed wood beams vaulted ceilings and, of course, plenty of windows. The outdoor terrace (with outdoor fireplace) is heated. The menu focuses on Jackson Hole's proximity to wild game, fish and beef. Choices range from buffalo jerky-wrapped Hudson Valley foie gras to pan-seared wild king salmon to smoked salt-roasted pheasant to mesquite-smoked and pepper-crusted buffalo tenderloin. Be sure to try the signature entre, espresso-rubbed antelope loin. American menu. Breakfast, lunch, dinner. Bar. Children's menu. Business casual attire. Reservations recommended. Outdoor seating. **$$$**

WYOMING

★
★
★
★
★

JACKSON HOLE
Jackson Hole is the valley formed by the Teton Range on the western side and the Gros Ventre range on the eastern side and is roughly 48 miles long. It was named for David Edward Jackson, a fur trapper, but was first recorded in the diary of John Colter, who was part of the Lewis and Clark expedition and the first American to see the valley. While Jackson, the town that is situated here, is often mistaken as Jackson Hole, the valley is home to several communities as well as the Teton Range, the Great Teton National Park and the Snake River, which runs through it.

HOTELS

★★★★AMANGANI

1535 N.E. Butte Road, Jackson Hole, 307-734-7333,
877-734-7333; www.amanresorts.com

Perched on the edge of a butte outside one of the country's most popular ski resorts, this American outpost of the acclaimed Aman resort group is a welcoming blend of Eastern minimalism and Western style. With only 40 rooms, the atmosphere is one of relaxation and renewal. Rooms are streamlined and contemporary with fireplaces and deep soaking tubs, while the resort's public spaces take advantage of the impressive mountain views. The culinary staff at The Grill keeps the focus on fresh organic ingredients, and the staff at the onsite health center accommodates every whim, from private yoga sessions to soothing spa treatments. 40 rooms. Wireless Internet access. Restaurant, bar. Fitness center. Spa. Outdoor pool, whirlpool. Airport transportation available.

★★JACKSON HOLE LODGE

420 W. Broadway, Jackson Hole, 307-733-2992,
800-604-9404; www.jacksonholelodge.com

59 rooms. Wireless Internet access. Indoor pool. $

SPECIALTY LODGINGS

BENTWOOD INN BED AND BREAKFAST

4250 Raven Haven Road, Jackson Hole, 307-739-1411; www.bentwoodinn.com

Five rooms. Complimentary full breakfast. Pets accepted. $$$

THE SASSY MOOSE INN

3859 W. Miles Road, Jackson Hole, 307-413-2995,
800-356-1277; www.sassymoose.com

Five rooms. Complimentary full breakfast. Spa. Wireless Internet access. Pets accepted. $

LANDER

Lander was once called the place where the rails end and the trails begin. Wind River Range, surrounding the town, offers hunting and fishing, mountain climbing and rock hunting. The annual One-Shot Antelope Hunt opens the antelope season and draws celebrities and sports enthusiasts from all over the country. Sacajawea Cemetery (burial place of Lewis and Clark's Shoshone guide) is located in Fort Washakie, 15 miles northwest on Highway 287. A Ranger District office of the Shoshone National Forest is located in Lander.

Information: Chamber of Commerce, 160 N. First St., Lander,
307-332-3892, 800-433-0662; www.landerchamber.org

WHAT TO SEE AND DO

SINKS CANYON STATE PARK

3079 Sinks Canyon Road, Lander, 307-332-6333;
wyoparks.state.wy.us

In a spectacular canyon amid unspoiled Rocky Mountain beauty lies the middle fork of the Popo Agie River, which disappears into a cavern and rises again several hundred yards below in a crystal clear, trout-filled spring pool. The park features abundant wildlife in certain seasons, a visitor center, observation points, fishing (except in the Rise of the Sinks), hiking and nature trails with groomed cross-country ski and snowmobile trails nearby. Campers will find limited tent and trailer sites though other sites are nearby. Spring-fall, 9 a.m.-6 p.m.; winter, 1-4 p.m. Grounds: sunrise to sunset.

SOUTH PASS CITY
125 S. Pass Main, South Pass City, 307-332-3684; www.southpasscity.com
An example of a once-flourishing gold mining town, 1,200 people lived in South Pass City during the gold rush of 1868-1872. Women were first given equal suffrage by a territorial act introduced from South Pass City and passed in Cheyenne on December 10, 1869. The town is currently being restored and has more than 20 historic buildings on display. May 15th-September 30th, Daily 9 a.m.-6 p.m.

HOTEL
★★BUDGET HOST INN
150 E. Main St., Lander, 307-332-3940, 800-424-6423;
www.pronghornlodge.com
56 rooms. Pets accepted; fee. Restaurant. Complimentary continental breakfast. Fitness center. Whirlpool. Wireless Internet access. $

LARAMIE
Laramie had a rugged beginning as a lawless leftover of the westward-rushing Union Pacific. The early settlement was populated by hunters, saloonkeepers and brawlers. When the tracks pushed on, Laramie stabilized somewhat, but for six months, vigilantes were the only law enforcement available against desperate characters that operated from town. Reasonable folk finally prevailed; schools and businesses sprang up, and improved cattle breeds brought prosperity. A Ranger District office of the Medicine Bow National Forest is located here.
Information: Albany County Tourism Board, 210 E. Custer St., Laramie,
307-745-4195, 800-445-5303; www.laramie-tourism.org

WHAT TO SEE AND DO
MEDICINE BOW NATIONAL FOREST
Laramie, west on Highway 130, southwest on Highway 230, east on I-80 or north via Highway 30, Highway 34 or Interstate 25, 307-745-2300; www.fs.fed.us/r2/mbr/
The more than 1 million acres of this forest include the Snowy Range Scenic Byway. One 30-mile stretch on Highway 130, west from Centennial, is particularly scenic with elevations as high as 10,800 feet at Snowy Range Pass.

UNIVERSITY OF WYOMING
1000 E. University Ave., Laramie, between Ninth and 30th streets,
307-766-1121; www.uwyo.edu
The state's only four-year university has the highest elevation of any campus in the United States. The UW Visitor Information Center (1408 Ivinson Ave.) has displays, and community and campus literature.

EXPLORING LARAMIE

Laramie has an oddly bifurcated nature: Born of the railroad boom that followed the nation's first transcontinental railway, the town preserves the rough-around-the-edges feel of an Old West frontier town. Since 1887, however, Laramie has also been the home of the University of Wyoming, for many years the state's only college, which gives the town a patina of sophistication lacking in other Wyoming towns of this size. Laramie's well-preserved Victorian architecture and a comparative wealth of art and museums make it an excellent town to explore on foot.

Start a walking tour of Laramie on the steps of the town's **city hall** (*406 Ivinson St.*). Just to the north is **St. Matthews Cathedral** *(104 S. Fourth St.),* an imposing neo-Gothic Episcopal church with an attached English-style garden. The church was constructed with funds donated by Edward Ivinson, one of the town's original settlers, who made his fortune on real estate and banking. Two of the church's impressive stained-glass windows memorialize the lives of Mr. and Mrs. Ivinson.

The Ivinsons' 1892 home is also among the town's landmarks. Now operated as the **Laramie Plains Museum** *(603 Ivinson St.),* this Queen Anne Victorian home was slated to be demolished (and the land used for a parking lot) before citizens raised money to turn it into a museum. The Ivinson mansion houses a valuable collection of household items from Laramie's pioneer days. Also on the spacious landscaped grounds are a carriage house and a one-room log schoolhouse.

Continue east on Ivinson Street to the campus of the University of Wyoming, beginning at Ninth Street. This oasis of well-tended lawns and huge spruce trees contains a number of worthwhile museums and handsome university buildings, many constructed of the local yellow sandstone. At the corner of Ivinson and 10th Street is Old Main, the university's original structure from 1887. An imposing building fronted by columns and capped by a bell tower, Old Main is now office to the university president.

Head north on 10th Street past classroom buildings to the university's Geology Museum near 10th and Clark streets. The museum has a major collection of Wyoming rocks and minerals, as well as some impressive fossils. Highlights include a mounted *Apatosaurus (Brontosaurus)* skeleton (one of only five in the world) and Big Al, the most complete *Allosaurus* fossil ever found. A life-sized, copper-clad statue of *Tyrannosaurus rex* marks the museum's entrance.

Walk a block east to Prexy's Pasture, the heart of the University of Wyoming campus. This large, grassy area was originally a pasture where the university's first president kept his personal herd of cattle. Today, it's the place to hang out in the sun and toss Frisbees. Continue southeast on the campus to the Anthropology Museum. The museum has excellent exhibits on the history and prehistory of Wyoming's Native Americans.

Walk north one block to University Street, where across a meadow of manicured lawn, the school's sororities and fraternities face each other. Head east past the Fine Arts Center, then go north to the Centennial

★
★★★★
★★★
★★
★

Complex. This imposing structure, fashioned to resemble a six-story teepee, houses both the American Heritage Center, one of the finest museums in the state, and the University Art Museum. Unlike many large collections of art in the American West, this museum focuses on 20th-century and contemporary art.

HOTEL

★★RAMADA CENTER HOTEL

2313 Soldier Springs Road, Laramie, 307-742-6611, 800-272-6232; www.ramada.com

100 rooms. Pets accepted; fee. Restaurant, bar. Fitness center. Indoor pool, whirlpool. Airport transportation available. Complimentary continental breakfast. Business Center. Wireless Internet access. **$**

LOVELL

A Ranger District office of the Bighorn National Forest is located here.

Information: Chamber of Commerce, 307-548-7552; www.lovellchamber.com

WHAT TO SEE AND DO

BIGHORN CANYON NATIONAL RECREATION AREA

Lovell, south entrance two miles east on Highway 14A, then eight miles north on Highway 37, 406-666-2412, 307-548-2251; www.nps.gov/bica/

The focus of the area is 71-mile-long Bighorn Lake, created by the Yellowtail Dam in Fort Smith, Montana. Boats may travel through Bighorn Canyon, which cuts across the northern end of the Bighorn Mountains in north-central Wyoming and south-central Montana. The solar-powered Bighorn Canyon Visitor Center is in Lovell on Highway 14A (open daily). The Fort Smith Visitor Contact Station is in Fort Smith, Montana (open daily). Both centers are closed New Year's Day, Thanksgiving and Christmas Day. Recreational and interpretive activities are available at both ends of the area, as are fishing, boating, picnicking and camping.

LUSK

Raising livestock has always been important in Lusk; fine herds of Simmental and Angus cattle and sheep are the local pride. Hunting is excellent for deer and antelope.

Information: Chamber of Commerce, Lusk, 307-334-2950, 800-223-5875; www.luskwyoming.com

★BEST VALUE INN COVERED WAGON MOTEL

730 S. Main St., Lusk, 307-334-2836, 888-338-2836; www.coveredwagonmotel.com

51 rooms. Complimentary continental breakfast. Wireless Internet access. Fitness center. Indoor pool, sauna. **$**

MOOSE

Located in the Grand Teton National Park, which is part of the Jackson Hole valley, Moose is a neighbor to the resort town of Jackson Hole.

Information: www.moosewyoming.com

HOTEL

★★★JENNY LAKE LODGE

Inner Loop Road, Moose, 307-733-4647, 800-628-9988; www.gtlc.com

Nestled at the base of the Tetons in Grand Teton National Park, this rustic, all-inclusive retreat is actually a cluster of western-style cabins outfitted with down comforters and handmade quilts. The pine-shaded property welcomes visitors from June-October for elegantly rustic accommodations and back-to-nature recreation, including the Jackson Hole Golf & Tennis Club, numerous hiking trails and three lakes. 37 rooms. Closed early October-late May. Complimentary full breakfast. Restaurant. $$$$

SPECIALTY LODGINGS

GROS VENTRE RIVER RANCH

18 Gros Ventre Road, Moose, 307-733-4138; www.grosventreriverranch.com

Guests stay in a log cabin or lodge, each with a magnificent view of the Teton Mountains. Eight rooms. Closed October-mid-May. Complimentary full breakfast. High-speed Internet access. Restaurant. Fitness center. Airport transportation available. No credit cards accepted. $$$$

LOST CREEK RANCH

Old Ranch Road, Moose, 307-733-3435; www.lostcreek.com

It is difficult to imagine a place more awe inspiring than Lost Creek Ranch, where snow-capped mountain peaks tower over wilderness. This guest ranch occupies a spectacular location, bordered by Grand Teton National Park and Bridger Teton National Forest and just 20 miles south of Jackson Hole. One- and two-bedroom log cabins provide comfortable accommodations, and recreational activities include horseback riding, tennis, hiking, auto tours to nearby Yellowstone National Park and float trips down the Snake River. The spa presents a more sybaritic experience with mineral wraps, sea salt body scrubs and Dead Sea Fango mud massages. Enjoy family-style meals and traditional cookouts, and in the evenings revisit the Old West with swing dancing, cowboy poetry and serenades. 30 rooms. Closed October-late May. Complimentary full breakfast. Wireless Internet access. Restaurant, bar. Fitness center. Spa. Outdoor pool, whirlpool. Tennis. Airport transportation available. $$$$

RESTAURANTS

★DORNAN'S CHUCK WAGON

10 Moose St., Moose, 307-733-2415; www.dornans.com

American menu. Breakfast, lunch, dinner. Closed mid-September-mid-June. Bar. Outdoor seating. $

★★★JENNY LAKE LODGE DINING ROOM

Inner Loop Road, Moose, 307-733-4647; www.gtlc.com

Located in a restored log cabin, Jenny Lake Lodge Dining Room offers à la carte lunch and five-course prix fixe dinners along with an extensive wine list. American menu. Breakfast, dinner. Closed early October-May. Jacket required. Reservations recommended. $$$$

PINEDALE

Pinedale is a place where genuine cowboys and cattle drives are still found. Mountains, conifer and aspen forests and lakes and rivers combine to make this a beautiful vacation area. There are fossil beds in the area, and rock hounding is popular. Cattle and sheep are raised on nearby ranches. A Ranger District office of the Bridger-Teton National Forest is located in Pinedale.

Information: Sublette County Chamber of Commerce, 26 Tyler,
Pinedale, 307-367-2242; www.sublettechamber.com

HOTEL

★BEST WESTERN PINEDALE INN

850 W. Pine St., Pinedale, 307-367-6869, 800-780-7234; www.bestwestern.com
84 rooms. Pets accepted, some restrictions. Complimentary continental breakfast. Indoor pool, whirlpool. High-speed Internet access. $

RAWLINS

Rawlins, a division point of the Union Pacific Railroad, is located 20 miles east of the Continental Divide. In 1867, General John A. Rawlins, chief of staff of the U.S. Army, wished for a drink of cool, clear water. Upon finding the spring near the base of the hills and tasting it, he said, "If anything is ever named after me, I hope it will be a spring of water." The little oasis was named Rawlins Springs, as was the community that grew up beside it. The city name was later shortened to Rawlins.

Information: Rawlins-Carbon County Chamber of Commerce, 519 W. Cedar,
Rawlins, 307-324-4111, 800-228-3547; www.wyomingcarboncounty.com

HOTEL

★★DAYS INN

2222 E. Cedar St., Rawlins, 307-324-6615, 800-329-7466; www.daysinn.com
118 rooms. Pets accepted. Complimentary continental breakfast. Restaurant, bar. Outdoor pool. High-speed Internet access. $

WYOMING

RIVERTON

Riverton is the largest city in Fremont County. Resources extracted from the region include natural gas, oil, iron ore, timber and phosphate. Irrigation from the Wind River Range has placed 130,000 acres under cultivation on which barley, alfalfa hay, beans, sunflowers and grain are grown. The town is surrounded by the Wind River Reservation, where Arapaho and Shoshone live.

Information: Chamber of Commerce, 213 W. Main St.,
Riverton, 307-856-4801; www.rivertonchamber.org

★
★★
★★
★★
★

HOTEL

★★HOLIDAY INN

900 E. Sunset Drive, Riverton, 307-856-8100, 800-315-2621; www.holiday-inn.com
122 rooms. Pets accepted; fee. Restaurant, bar. Fitness center. Indoor pool. Airport transportation available. High-speed Internet access. $

ROCK SPRINGS

Rock Springs traces its roots to a spring that offered an ideal camping site along a Native American trail and, later, served as a welcome station on the Overland Stage route. Later still, Rock Springs became a supply station that provided millions of tons of coal to the Union Pacific Railroad. Noted for its multiethnic heritage, the town's first inhabitants were primarily Welsh and English immigrants brought in by the railroad and coal companies. West of town are large deposits of trona, used in the manufacture of glass, phosphates, silicates, soaps and baking soda.

Information: Rock Springs Chamber of Commerce, 1897 Dewar Drive, Rock Springs, 307-362-3771; www.rockspringswyoming.net

HOTEL

★★HOLIDAY INN

1675 Sunset Drive, Rock Springs, 307-382-9200, 800-315-2621; www.holiday-inn.com
171 rooms. Pets accepted; fee. Restaurant, Bar. Fitness center. Indoor pool, whirlpool. Airport transportation available. High-speed Internet access. **$**

SHERIDAN

Sheridan, named for General Philip Sheridan, was not settled until after a series of wars with the Cheyenne, Sioux and Crow. While the land, rich with grass, was ideal for grazing livestock, ranchers only moved in their herds after the tribes were driven onto reservations. For years, the town had a reputation for trouble because of rustling and boundary disputes. Nevertheless, the first dude ranch in history was established near Sheridan in 1904.

Today, the town is a tourist center with dude ranches, hotels and motels and sporting facilities. The nearby Big Horn Range, once a favored hunting ground of Native Americans, is rich in big game and fishing. A Ranger District office of the Bighorn National Forest is located in Sheridan.

Information: Convention and Visitors Bureau, Sheridan, 307-673-7120, 888-596-6787; www.sheridanwyoming.org

WHAT TO SEE AND DO

BIGHORN NATIONAL FOREST

2013 Eastside Second St., Sheridan, 307-674-2600; www.fs.fed.us/r2/bighorn/
The Big Horn Mountains rise abruptly from the arid basins below to elevations of more than 13,000 feet. Fallen City, a jumble of huge rock blocks, can be viewed from Highway 14, as can Sibley Lake and Shell Canyon and Falls. From Burgess Junction, Highway 14A passes by Medicine Mountain, the site of the "medicine wheel," an ancient circular structure. Highway 16 features Meadowlark Lake and panoramic views of Tensleep Canyon and the 189,000-acre Cloud Peak Wilderness. The forest has resorts and campgrounds, backpacking and horseback trails and skiing at Antelope Butte Ski Area (60 miles west on Highway 14) and High Park Ski Area (40 miles east of Worland). Memorial Day-mid September, daily 8 a.m.-5:30 p.m.

BRADFORD BRINTON MEMORIAL

239 Brinton Road, Sheridan, 307-672-3173; www.bradfordbrintonmemorial.com
A historic ranch house, the building was built in 1892, purchased in 1923 by Bradford Brinton and enlarged to its present 20 rooms. It now contains collections and

★
★
★
★
★

furnishings that make this a memorial to the art and history of the West with more than 600 oils, watercolors and sketches by American artists include Russell and Remington. You'll also find bronzes, prints, rare books, ranch equipment, saddles and Native American artifacts. Mid-May-Labor Day and early December-December 24, daily 9.30 a.m.-5 p.m.

SHERIDAN INN

856 Broadway St., Sheridan, 307-674-5440; www.sheridaninn.com

The Sheridan Inn opened in 1893 with a bang: William Buffalo Bill Cody led a Wild West parade right into the dining room! (He later watched over auditions for his traveling show from the front porch.) The three-story hotel was immediately marketed as the finest hotel between Chicago and San Francisco, and it is now on the National Register of Historic Places. Nearly demolished in the 1960s, the hotel was lovingly restored in the 1990s to house a restaurant and a museum.

TRAIL END HISTORIC CENTER

400 Clarendon Ave., Sheridan, 307-674-4589; www.trailend.org

Once home of John B. Kendrick, governor of Wyoming (1915-1917) and later U.S. Senator (1917-1933), the building now houses historical and family memorabilia. The mansion showcases Flemish-Revival architecture with beautifully carved and burnished woodwork and landscaped grounds. March 1-May 31 and September 1-December 14, daily 1-4 p.m.; June 1-August 31, daily 9 a.m.-6 p.m. Closed December 15-February 28, Veterans' Day, Thanksgiving.

HOTELS

★DAYS INN

1104 E. Brundage Lane, Sheridan, 307-672-2888, 800-329-7466; www.daysinn.com

47 rooms. Complimentary continental breakfast. Indoor pool, whirlpool. High-speed Internet access. Pets accepted. $

★★HOLIDAY INN

1809 Sugarland Drive, Sheridan, 307-672-8931, 800-315-2621;
www.holidayinn.com

219 rooms. Pets accepted, some restrictions. Wireless Internet access. Restaurant, bar. Fitness center. Indoor pool, whirlpool. Airport transportation available. $

THERMOPOLIS

The world's largest mineral hot spring is at Thermopolis, which lies in a beautiful section of Big Horn Basin where canyons, tunnels and buttes abound. The town is surrounded by rich irrigated farm and grazing land.

Information: Chamber of Commerce, 107 N. Fifth St., Thermopolis,
307-864-3192; www.thermopolis.com

WHAT TO SEE AND DO

HOT SPRINGS STATE PARK

538 N. Park St., Thermopolis, 307-864-2176; wyoparks.state.wy.us/

The second-most-visited tourist attraction in Wyoming after Yellowstone National Park, Hot Springs State Park in Thermopolis is the result of one of the largest mineral hot springs in the world. The springs created the magnificent Mineral Terrace—a colorful formation that is the result of eons of mineral deposits—and provide water for three facilities: the free State Bath House and a pair of commercial facilities with pools and water slides. There is also a free-ranging herd of bison, a pair of hotels and a number of flower gardens, which bloom brightly each summer. The Bighorn River runs right through the park, and a boat ramp allows floaters and anglers access to its waters. About 30 miles outside of Thermopolis is the Legend Rock Petroglyph Site, a sandstone cliff wall engraved with art that dates back 2,000 years; access must be arranged through an attendant at the State Bath House. Bath house: Monday-Saturday 8 a.m.-5:30 p.m., Sunday noon-5:30 p.m. Closed October 1-April 30.

WYOMING DINOSAUR CENTER
110 Carter Ranch Road, Thermopolis,
307-864-2997, 800-455-3466; www.wyodino.org
The Center exhibits mounted dinosaurs, dioramas and fossils and offers guided tours of excavation sites. Summer, daily 8 a.m.-6 p.m.; winter, daily 10 a.m.-5 p.m. Closed Thanksgiving Day, Christmas Day and New Year's Day.

HOTELS
★COMFORT INN
100 N. Road, 11, Worland, 307-347-9898, 877-424-6423; www.comfortinn.com
50 rooms. Complimentary continental breakfast. Fitness center. Indoor pool, whirlpool. Airport transportation available. High-speed Internet access. **$**

★SUPER 8
166 Highway 20 South, Thermopolis, 307-864-5515, 800-800-8000; www.super8.com
52 rooms. Pets accepted; fee. Complimentary full breakfast. Wireless Internet access. Indoor pool, whirlpool. **$**

WHEATLAND
The southern edge of Medicine Bow National Forest is 20 miles west.
Information: Platte County Chamber of Commerce, 65 16th St.,
Wheatland, 307-322-2322; www.wheatlandwy.com

WHAT TO SEE AND DO
GLENDO STATE PARK
397 Glendo Park Road, 307-735-4433; wyoparks.state.wy.us
Rising out of Glendo Reservoir's east side at Sandy Beach are a series of sand dunes, some reaching from the Great Divide Basin to the sand hills in Nebraska. Chips, scrapers and arrowheads dating back 8,000 years are sometimes found. The park includes abundant wildlife swimming, waterskiing, fishing, boating, hunting, picnicking, a restaurant and grocery, lodging, tent and trailer sites. Park grounds open 24 hours.

HOTEL
★BEST WESTERN TORCHLITE MOTOR INN
1809 N. 16th St., Wheatland, 307-322-4070, 800-780-7234; www.bestwestern.com
50 rooms. Pets accepted; fee. High-speed Internet access. Outdoor pool. **$**

YELLOWSTONE NATIONAL PARK

SNOWMOBILING IN AND AROUND YELLOWSTONE

Once synonymous with winter in Yellowstone, snowmobiling in the park has recently become the focal point of evolving environmental policies. For years, use of the machines has been a controversial, divisive issue in the park and the gateway communities.

A study in the late 1990s concluded that the pollution from the snowmobiles both in terms of carbon monoxide and noise was negatively impacting the park's wildlife. As a result, there has been much back and forth among politicians, snowmobile manufacturers, rental operations in the town of West Yellowstone and others about the implementation of a phase-out of snowmobiles in Yellowstone and Grand Teton national parks. Currently, a judge has issued an order so that a compromise can be negotiated that would be fair to all parties.

Regardless of the park's snowmobile policy, Yellowstone is a fantastic, frigid wonderland in the wintertime. As most roads, hotels and campgrounds are closed, traffic is lighter, and cold and snow drive wildlife to lower elevations, making it easier to spot. The steaming thermal features are especially impressive in this icy landscape. And snowcoach tours and ski outings are attractive alternatives to straddling a noisy snowmobile.

The only roads that are open to cars during winter run from Gardiner, Montana, south to Mammoth Hot Springs and east to Cooke City, Montana; lodging is only available in Mammoth and Old Faithful. However, all paved roads are open to over-snow vehicles, snowmobiles (for now) and snowcoaches from mid-December into March.

The current guidelines call for a daily quota of snowmobiles at each entrance and a licensed guide to lead all snowmobile expeditions. A list of licensed guides, as well as cross-country ski and snowcoach operations, is available at the Yellowstone Web site (www.nps.gov/yell).

While snowmobiles are likely on their way out in Yellowstone, the surrounding forests are an attractive alternative. In particular, the Gallatin National Forest (406-522-2520) is crisscrossed by miles of snowmobile trails, and it will likely become the area's prime snowmobiling destination in the event of an outright ban in the park. West Yellowstone, Montana, has the highest concentration of rental operations and excellent access to trails into both Yellowstone and the Gallatin National Forest.

To the south, in and around Grand Teton National Park, the groomed Continental Divide Snowmobile Trail connects the Togwotee Pass area with Yellowstone, but the trail's in-park stretch could well be closed to snowmobiles in coming winters. However, since the trail starts to the southeast of the park, the area will undoubtedly remain a snowmobiling destination. There are hundreds of miles of trails in the Bridger-Teton National Forest and especially near the towns of Lander, Pinedale and Dubois.

YELLOWSTONE ASSOCIATION INSTITUTE

With its steaming geysers, vast forests and abundant wildlife, the country's first national park begs for a bit of interpretation. In response, the Yellowstone Association Institute presents a predominately adult-oriented curriculum that runs the gamut from wolf watching to fly-fishing, educating more than 1,000 students annually. Courses are held in both winter and summer with a heavy emphasis on the Leave No Trace philosophy.

★
★
★
★
★

The annual course catalog includes more than 400 classes, including courses on wildlife biology, geology, history, arts and recreation. A few of them are one-day classes, but serious adventurers can embark with instructors on multiday back-country adventures that delve into the ecology of wolves or bears. The Web site, www.yellowstoneassociation.org, features an online catalog.

While Yellowstone's 2.4 million acres serve as an amazing extension, the Institute's main campus, nicknamed The Serengeti of North America for its diversity of wildlife, is at the Lamar Buffalo Ranch in the Lamar Valley. After bullets and exotic diseases deci-mated the iconic beasts in the 19th century, the National Park Service domesticated 28 of the parks few remaining bison at the ranch in 1907. Yellowstone's buffalo prospered under the sponsorship of *Homo sapiens*. The original 28 boomed into a self-sustaining population by the time the ranch hands left the picture in 1952. Today, about 4,000 bison roam the park, a living legacy of the old ranch.

In 1979, the nonprofit Yellowstone Association adopted the ranch as a campus for its field studies program, now known as the Yellowstone Association Institute. The cynical image of a modern Yellowstone vacation includes animal-induced traffic jams, throngs of tourists at Old Faithful and mad dashes from overlook to overlook, but the old Lamar ranch is a hubbub-free zone and a window into the park consider-ably clearer than a bug-splattered windshield.

The Institute's tuition fees are very democratic: about $70 per day. A cot in a cabin runs about $25 a night, and students and staff share a well-equipped kitchen in the bunk-house. There are 16 basic guest cabins at the ranch with three cots to a cabin. The bunk-house houses two classrooms, a common kitchen and three bathrooms with showers.

There is a definite sense of community at the old buffalo ranch, and the kitchen is its social hub. Meals are serve yourself; guests supply their own food, which they can store in the fridge (one bin and one shelf per guest).

The Lamar ranch is also a study in sustainable living. It has its own well and septic system. A system comprised of two banks of solar panels and a pair of propane gen-erators provides electricity.

Several institute courses are done in conjunction with Xanterra, Yellowstone's pri-mary concessionaire. Guests spend nights at the park's historic lodges and hotels while taking an instructor-led class during the days. Custom outings are also available.

Information: Yellowstone Association Institute, Yellowstone National Park,
307-344-2293; www.yellowstoneassociation.org

WHAT TO SEE AND DO
YELLOWSTONE NATIONAL PARK

Northeast Entrance Road and Grand Loop Road, 307-344-7381; www.nps.gov/yell

In 1872, the U.S. Congress set aside more than 3,000 square miles of wilderness in the Wyoming Territory, establishing the world's first national park. More than a century later, Yellowstone boasts a marvelous list of sights, attractions and facilities: a large freshwater lake, the highest in the nation (7,733 feet); a waterfall almost twice as high as Niagara; a dramatic, 1,200-foot-deep river canyon and the world's most famous geyser, Old Faithful.

Most of the park has been left in its natural state, preserving the area's beauty and delicate ecological balance. Yellowstone is one of the world's most successful wild-life sanctuaries. Within its boundaries live a variety of species, including grizzly and black bears, elk, deer, pronghorn and bison. Although it is not unusual to encounter animals along park roads, they are more commonly seen along backcountry trails and in more remote areas. Never approach, feed or otherwise disturb any wild animal. Stay in your car with the windows up if you're approached by wildlife. Animals may look friendly but are unpredictable.

The **Grand Loop Road**, a main access way within the park, winds approximately 140 miles past many major points of interest. Five miles south of the North Entrance is **Mammoth Hot Springs**, the park headquarters and museum (open year-round). The visitor center provides a general overview of the history of the park. Naturalist-guided walks are conducted on boardwalks over the terraces (summer).

The **Norris Geyser Basin** is 21 miles south of Mammoth Hot Springs. The hottest thermal basin in the world provides a multitude of displays; springs, geysers, mud pots and steam vents hiss, bubble and erupt in a showcase of thermal forces at work. The visitor center has self-explanatory exhibits and dioramas and is open daily June-Labor Day. A self-guided trail (2 1/2 miles) offers views of the Porcelain and Back basins from boardwalks. The Museum of the National Park Ranger is also nearby.

At **Madison**, 14 miles southwest of Norris, the **West Entrance Road** *(Highway 20-91 outside the park)* joins the Grand Loop Road. Heading south of Madison, it is a 16-mile trip to **Old Faithful**. Along the route are four thermal spring areas; numerous geysers, mud pots and pools provide an appropriate prologue to the spectacle ahead. Old Faithful has not missed a performance in the more than 100 years since eruptions were first recorded. Eruptions occur on the average of every 75 minutes, although intervals have varied from 30-120 minutes. A nearby visitor center provides information, exhibits and a film and slide program. May-October and mid-December-mid-March, daily.

From Old Faithful, it is 17 miles east to **West Thumb**. **Yellowstone Lake**, the highest natural freshwater lake in the United States, is here. Early explorers thought that the shape of the lake resembled a hand, with the westernmost bay forming its thumb. A variety of rare species of waterfowl make their home along its 110 miles of shoreline. The 22-mile road from the South Entrance on the **John D. Rockefeller, Jr. Memorial Parkway** *(Highway 29-287 outside the park)* meets the Grand Loop Road here.

Northeast of West Thumb, about 19 miles up the western shore of Yellowstone Lake, the road leads to **Lake Village** and then to **Fishing Bridge**. Although fishing is not permitted at Fishing Bridge (extending one mile downstream, to the north, and a quarter mile upstream, to the south of Fishing Bridge), the numerous lakes and rivers in the park make Yellowstone an angler's paradise. At Fishing Bridge the road splits; 27 miles east is the East Entrance from Highway 14/16/20 and 16 miles north is **Canyon Village**. Canyon Village is near Upper Falls (a 109-foot drop) and the spectacular Lower Falls (a 308-foot drop). The colorful and awesome **Grand Canyon** of the Yellowstone River can be viewed from several points; there are self-guided trails along the rim and naturalist-led walks during summer. Groomed cross-country ski trails are open in winter. Museum: Mid-May-late September, daily.

Sixteen miles north of Canyon Village is **Tower**. Just south of Tower Junction is the 132-foot Tower Fall, which can best be observed from a platform at the end of the path leading from the parking lot. The Northeast Entrance on Highway 212 is 29 miles east of Tower; Mammoth Hot Springs is 18 miles west.

The rest of the park is wilderness with more than 1,100 miles of marked foot trails. Some areas may be closed for resource management purposes; inquire at one of the visitor centers in the area before hiking in backcountry. Guided tours of the wilderness can

WYOMING

★
★
★
★
★

be made on horseback; horse rentals are available at Mammoth Hot Springs, Roosevelt and Canyon Village.

HELPFUL HINTS

Do not pick wildflowers or collect any natural objects. Read all regulations established by the National Park Service and comply with them, as they are for the protection of all visitors as well as for the protection of park resources.

Recreational vehicle campsites are available by reservation at Fishing Bridge RV Park (contact TW Recreational Services, Inc, at 307-344-7901 for general information or 307-344-7311 for reservations). During July and August demand often exceeds supply, and many sites are occupied by midmorning. Overnight vehicle camping or stopping outside designated campgrounds is not permitted. Reservations are required for Bridge Bay, Canyon, Madison and Grant Village as well as Fishing Bridge RV Park. There are seven additional National Park Service campgrounds at Yellowstone; these are operated on a first-come, first-served basis, so arrive early to secure the site of your choice. Campfires are prohibited except in designated areas or by special permit obtained at ranger stations. Backcountry camping is available by permit only, no more than 48 hours in advance, in person, at ranger stations. Backcountry sites can be reserved for a $15 fee.

Fishing in Yellowstone National Park requires a permit. Anglers 16 years and older require a $10 10-day or $20 season permit. Rowboats, powerboats and tackle may be rented at Bridge Bay Marina. Permits are also required for all vessels (seven-day permit: motorized, $10; non motorized, $5) and must be obtained in person at one of the following locations: South Entrance, Bridge Bay Marina, Mammoth Visitor Center, Grant Village Visitor Center, Lake Ranger Station or Lewis Lake Campground. Information centers near Yellowstone Lake are located at Fishing Bridge and Grant Village (both Memorial Day-Labor Day, daily).

At several locations, there are visitor centers, general stores for provisions, photo shops, service stations, tent and trailer sites, hotels and lodges. Bus tours run through the park from mid-June-Labor Day (contact Xanterra Parks and Resorts at 307-344-7311). Cars can be rented in some of the gateway communities.

The official park season is May 1-October 31. However, Highway 212 from Red Lodge, Montana, to Cooke City, Montana (outside the northeast entrance), is not open to automobiles until about May 30 and closes about October 1. In winter, roads from Gardiner to Mammoth Hot Springs and to Cooke City, Montana, are kept open, but the road from Red Lodge is closed; travelers must return to Gardiner to leave the park. The west, east and south entrances are closed to automobiles from November one to about May one but are open to over snow vehicles from mid-December-mid-March. Dates are subject to change. For current road conditions and other information, contact park headquarters at 307-344-7381. The entrance permit, $20 per vehicle per visit, is good for seven days to Yellowstone and Grand Teton.

Weather conditions or conservation measures may dictate the closing of certain roads and recreational facilities. In winter, inquire before attempting to enter the park.

TOURS

Self-guided car audio tours are produced in cooperation with the National Park Service. Visitors rent a self-contained player (about the size of a paperback book) that

★
★ ★
★ ★ ★
★ ★
★

plugs into a car's cigarette lighter and broadcasts an FM signal to its radio. A screen on the unit displays menus of chapters and topics, which may be played in any order for an individualized narrated auto tour (total running time approximately five hours). Rent a player by contacting Xanterra Parks and Resorts at 301-344-7311.

HOTELS

★★GRANT VILLAGE
307-344-7311, 866-439-7375; www.travelyellowstone.com
300 rooms. Restaurant, Bar. Open mid-May-late September. **$**

★★LAKE YELLOWSTONE HOTEL
Yellowstone National Park, 307-344-7311, 866-439-7375; www.travelyellowstone.com
158 rooms. Closed mid-October-late May. Restaurant, bar. **$$**

★★OLD FAITHFUL INN
307-344-7311, 866-439-7375; www.travelyellowstone.com
325 rooms. Closed mid-October-early May. Restaurant, bar. **$$**

★★OLD FAITHFUL SNOW LODGE
307-344-7311, 866-439-7375; www.travelyellowstone.com
95 rooms. Closed mid-October-mid-December and mid-March-early May. Restaurant, bar. **$$**

RESTAURANT

★★LAKE YELLOWSTONE DINING ROOM
Highway 89, Yellowstone National Park, 307-344-7311,
866-439-7375; www.travelyellowstone.com
American, seafood menu. Breakfast, lunch, dinner. Reservations recommended for dinner. Closed October-May. Bar. Children's menu. **$$**

WYOMING

★
★★
★★★
★★★★
★★★★★

INDEX

★
★
★
★
★

313

INDEX

★
★
★
★

315

INDEX

★
★
★
★
★

317

INDEX

★
★
★
★
☆

318

INDEX

★
★
★
★
★

319

INDEX

★
★
★
★
★

320

INDEX

★
★
★
★
★

321

INDEX

★
★
★
★
★

★
★
★
★
★

324

INDEX

★
★
★
★
★

325

INDEX

★
★
★
★
★

★
★
★
★
★

INDEX

★
★
★
★
★

330

INDEX

★
★
★
★
★

NOTES

NOTES

INDEX

★
★
★
★
★

NOTES

NOTES

334

★
★
★
★
★

NOTES

NOTES

INDEX